Eurasian Perspectives

Eurasian Perspectives

In Search of Alternatives

Edited by
Anita Sengupta
Suchandana Chatterjee

Maulana Abul Kalam Azad Institute of Asian Studies, Kolkata

SHIPRA

ISBN: 978-81-7541-558-4

First Published in India in 2010

Eurasian Perspectives: In Search of Alternatives

Published by:
SHIPRA PUBLICATIONS
H.O.: LG 18-19, Pankaj Central Market, I.P. Ext., Patparganj,
Delhi-110092, Tel: 91-11-22235152, 22236152
Br.Off.115, Munish Plaza, 20, Ansari Road, Darya Ganj,
New Delhi-110002, Tel: 65946453
E-mail: info@shiprapublications.com
www.shiprapublications.com

Preface

Problems associated with resuscitation of the Eurasian paradigm have resulted in renewed debates and discussions about a space that though imagined as a 'heartland' tends to be represented as a periphery. In recent times, changes in the global map have led to new interpretations of realities. Stereotypical images have been reexamined and new discourses are in the offing. There have been reappraisals about culture and identity that relate not only to the present but also re-contextualizes the past. The future is also being re-envisioned through alliances and partnerships among regional and international players. The spirit of 'go global but give space to the local' has assumed primacy and critical social issues have been addressed more emphatically by various sections of society. There is also increasing recognition of the need for new methodological terminologies that take note of these alternative perspectives in the present context. The aim of the book is to indicate scholarly engagement with these re-assesments. The emphasis is on the need to historicize connections and contemplate issues that are intrinsic to the Eurasian region.

The book poses the central question- why does an understanding of Eurasia assume significance beyond the exploration of either the exotic or the repressive. Why does an understanding of the ways in which history is being re-written or forms of representation debated within the Eurasian space become at all important either for the academic or more importantly for the policy maker? A simplistic explanation can be offered in terms of a globalized and therefore interconnected world where at least in economic terms the discussion assumes importance. This is also very close to the way in which the significance of the region is emphasized from a global perspective. As distinguished from this discourse is one that focuses on the 'representational' understanding of realities. Here stereotypical images are reexamined and new discourses offered as viable alternatives. Similarly, a new mapping of space, people and resources of Eurasia is underway where various state and non-state actors are introducing their respective perceptions, priorities and policies within the region.

This 'new' salience of the Eurasian region must therefore be approached and understood in imaginative ways where competing representations continue to be tested by complex and dynamic realities. Neither the discourse of 'block' centric geo-economics nor the geographical imagination of a greater Middle East/New Heartland/ Eurasian Balkans, captures the multi-dimensional, multi-level complexities involved. However, as the essays indicate they remain significant since they influence and are in turn influenced by the mental maps of policy makers. An alternative would be to look beyond clashing imaginations towards a convergence that reflects the interconnectedness of regions. The book is therefore also a search for new perspectives from within the region. It presents an opportunity not only for reflecting and reviewing existing ideas but also reformulating and conjoining them in ways that better reflect the reality of the region and allow newer practices and institutions to emerge in the future. The book hopes to underline the fact that the Eurasian region requires visions that are not prone to self-fulfilling hypotheses about conflict as the persistent interpretations of the new Great Game or the thesis on the 'clash of civilizations'.

Four essays in the book highlight the reflections on the alternatives, and contemplates Eurasianism, the concept of the "heartland" and debates that have emerged within that framework. Vladimir Boyko argues that the rhetoric of a Eurasian "heartland" is lopsided because it revolves around the internal geopolitics of the Central Asian region while regions like the Altai hardly receive attention. Farkhod Tolipov is of the opinion that bilateral relationships are almost non-existent in the Central Asia region and indicates the necessity to concentrate on regional integration projects that are multidimensional. Roy Allison deals with the pros and cons of "virtual regionalism" which, according to him, signifies functional cooperation as far as the Central Asian states and Russia are concerned, but hardly any substantive commitment on their part in terms of regional integration. The disinclination towards integration emanates from a series of internal constraints as well as suspicion about regional policy-making of their neighbours. Sattar Mazhitov discusses the Eurasianists' world community approach, which tries to integrate the Asian and non-Asian parts of a historical-cultural space. Speaking of the reverberations of Eurasianism in Kazakhstan, he highlights the

Kazakh authorities' inclination towards the Eurasianists' principles of moral judgment and pragmatic behaviour.

A series of essays represent ideas about history and culture in the Eurasian region. Uyama Tomohiko presents a post-Soviet profile of "autonomy" in several regions, indicating how "small areas," for instance of the Bokey Horde, are marginalized in the mega-narratives of the Golden Horde, and how cross-cultural elements in the Horde structures are seldom dealt with in Russian imperial historiography or the nationalist historiography of the Kazakhs. Recent trends in history writing in Aktobe and Uralsk have filled this gap to a certain extent. Uyama has also considered regions of the former Soviet space, such as the Gorno-Badakhshan Autonomous region, where the Pamiris, despite their prominence as an intellectual community were swept away by the tide of factionalism in Tajikistan during the 1990s. It is only very recently that Gorno-Badakhshan has been able to reassert itself as a development-oriented region, due to the initiatives of the Aga Khan Foundation. This is also true, Uyama suggests, for Abkhazia, a Caucasian stronghold that maintained its autonomous stance throughout the 19th and 20th centuries; in current reappraisals of Caucasian history the group identity of the Abkhazians has been a prominent focus of analysis. Naganawa Norihiro explores interregional contacts as he profiles *hajjis* as a source of contact between the Ottoman Empire, India, and Central Asia since the 19th century. Norihiro unravels the components of *hajji* activity, reflecting on their travel, the places they visited and their diplomatic contacts in the region under review. Norihiro's broader research agenda is to locate the new development of the *hajj* in contemporary Russia. Marina Baldano reflects on Geser epic tradition in Buryatia, describing how this tradition became the marker of national identity and national culture. The epic has a Tibetan Mongolian version and has over the years been widely circulated throughout Buddhist-populated realms to the north of India. Jeta Sankritayana gives an account of the writings of his father, Rahula Sankrityayana, the Indian scholar-traveler who also traveled in the region in the 1940s where Buddhism once enjoyed predominance. Both Baldano and Jeta Sankrityayana focus on the multicultural linkages that existed between South and Central Asia for centuries, something that this Buddhist link reflects. There is today a renewed desire to search for these links between cultural traditions. Cultural representations are also pivotal in Judith Beyer's article that profiles the changing character of law and authority in Talas,

Kyrgyzstan. Beyer's paper explores social interaction between elders and the general population, indicating biased approaches about chaotic change on the one hand and the 'order' of legacy or tradition on the other, both of which seem to dominate post-Soviet writings about transition in Central Asia.

The book indicates positive and negative reflections about linguistic transformations. Maria Gritsko focuses on the problem of linguistic security and notes that despite its role as a communicator, the Russian language faces a lot of problems in the autonomous territories of the RSFSR, especially in the North Caucasus, Bashkiria, Tatarstan, and Yakutia. Saltanat Meiramova and Anna Yessengalieva tend to imply that language is considered to be a source of mobilization and a major aspect of social interaction in Kazakhstan. The internal and external dynamics of Eurasia have been explored by two case studies on migration and demography. Muzaffar Olimov projects Tajikistan's new interest in China, while keeping its military partnership with Russia, cultural contacts with Iran, and institutional commitments with the West intact. Sharad Soni deals with the character of the Kazakh diaspora in Mongolia, tracing their origins to the border movements across Xinjiang and the Russian Altai region into Mongolia and back.

The search for viable alternatives for economic integration is the central argument of the essays by P.L. Dash and Sreemati Ganguly. The former highlights Yuri Krupnov's vision of the 'New Middle East' that attempts integration of Russia's North with South Asia and West Asia, especially India and Iran, via a North-South Corridor bypass link. The latter considers energy security as an important guideline for alliance building in Eurasia. Discussing strategic perspectives, Sanjay Chaturvedi focuses on climate change in Northern Eurasia that has affected the Arctic ecosystem and its marginalized communities. Spatial geography, Chaturvedi argues, needs to be reassessed through new agendas that are related to environmental justice making human security and climate matters crucial. Abdomajid Eskandari has studied the new contours of strategic defence, pinpointing the axis of alliances centering on Iran. Eskandari examines the option of building an energy transfer structure via Iran. The Caspian energy shelf is, according to Eskandari, the new West Asian alternative for sustainable development of Eurasia. Ajay Patnaik also looks into the energy profile in the Caspian sector, one of the prime areas of American engagement that Iran has been trying to thwart. Mirzoid Rakhimov and Oybek Makhmudov engage in discussions about the challenges and complexities of regional organizations, skeptically reviewing interim measures (CACO, EurAsEC, PfP, SCO) that have hardly augured well for the Central Asian republics. Rakhimov speculates that there are regional options, pointing to the new priorities of the Central Asian regimes. According to him, the present primary concern is with economic stability that was not seriously addressed by the regional organizations in the past. In their search for regional stability, the Central Asian states have become more and more receptive to the trans-continental transport and communication projects that promote connectivity among neighbouring countries such as Iran, Turkey, Pakistan and China. Makhmudov also tries to address the new priorities from a security perspective. In his opinion, there should be an attempt to understand the compulsions that the authorities are facing and there should be more awareness of the options that the present situation offers. One has to take into account the entire range of traditional and non-traditional security threats that are jeopardizing the prospect of Central Asian regional integration. Makhmudov is enthusiastic about a Central Asian regional security agenda that needs to be addressed more specifically.

The book, based on presentations at the international conference *Eurasian Perspectives: In Search of Alternatives* organized by the Maulana Abul Kalam Azad Institute of Asian Studies in Kolkata on February 4-6, 2009, addresses a wide gamut of questions focusing on the engagements of the present and experiences of the past. Case-based analyses of continuities and discontinuities, symptomatic of the challenges and opportunities within, reflect manifold perspectives about the region. The central argument is that the word 'transition' has become questionable in many ways. Perceptions about Eurasian alternatives, especially in the case of Siberia and the Caucasus, the infrastructural reorientation in these regions, the emergence of a regional direction indicating migration patterns and development have seldom been addressed. Fresh possibilities and initiatives outside the dominant rhetoric of regional integration have often been overlooked. Speaking about a West Asia or a South Asia reach, the essays point to new directions of research.

Contents

1

Endangered Heartland: Russian Central Asia between Domestic and External Geopolitics

Vladimir Boyko

Any analysis of 'Eurasian perspectives' requires macro-regional approach, which means to take into consideration the complicated and dynamic geopolitical profile of the vast area conventionally called *Eurasia.* The generally accepted notion of Eurasia as spatial and cultural phenomenon with mixed identity and civilizational substance should be reconsidered and specified in the light of recent geopolitical changes (USSR's breakdown and the emergence of new independent states, unprecedented China's economic growth, the establishment of new regional networks such as SCO, Iran's ambitious stand for technological and geopolitical breakthrough, India's new role as emerging regional superpower, etc.). All these changes have resulted in large-scale re-configuration of the supra-state, state and non-state actors and their roles in domestic and international politics. It's especially relevant for Russia which maintains a significant portion of former Soviet Union's territory and power, but is coming through new experiences in governance, economic development, security, etc. This paper aims to analyze new Russia's stand in Eurasia from regional point of view that focusing on certain border areas, such as Altai and adjacent territories of RF, which constitute by now its southern belt and are destined by their location and other features to be the gates (*gateways*) to outer Asia.

Russian Asiatic Borderlands in New Landscapes of Central Eurasia: Theoretical Framework

To deal with this subject, some spatial dimensions should be analysed with reference to traditional and new concepts of regional studies. The most appropriate framework is classical *Greater Central Asia* concept, developed by Harvard professor Richard Frye, the doyen of world orientalist studies. "Greater Central Asia, in my opinion, does possess a cultural unity since similar geographic features combined with common historical problems have given a cohesion to the land and peoples extending from Hungary to North China and from Siberian tundra to the Indian Ocean.... The historical divisions of the Central Asian cultural areas: eastern Persia, Khwarazm, Sogdiana, Bactria, the Hindukush, Chinese Turkestan, and the Altai will be examined showing the important differences between them, yet all being "frontier" cultures between the major settled areas of China, India, the Semitic Near East and woodlands of Eastern Europe".[1] This approach is followed by approaches of scholars belonging to different research traditions.[2] One more task is not only spatial but to put the area of interest into the most appropriate macro-regional context. Thus, Alexei Voskressenski, a prominent Russian orientalist with a strong methodological focus, frames the vast Eurasian space as consisted of several mega zones, which in turn are constituted by regions, etc. According to him, the specific countries can be divided into different regions within two or even three different regional clusters on various parameters, forming a "Eurasian Far East and Siberian Meso-Area".[3] The former macro-toponym seems doubtful as Siberia is by now some archaic term reflecting only historical-geographic phenomenon with occasional references to current socio-cultural and economic developments.[4]

The innovative thematic of regional identities and meso-mega area dynamics is developed by school of regional studies at Slavic Research Centre (Hokkaido, Japan).[5] Besides *geographical* macro-regions – Asia, Africa, etc., this point of view distinguishes the meso-regions: Central, Northern, South America, Northeast, Southeast, Southern, Western and Central Asia from the subregions.[6] It also allocates *historical-cultural regions*, featured by historical-cultural parameters. The value of this concept is that it stresses the possibility of civilizational amalgamation and a compromise along border lines. Its proponents are appealing for positive rethinking of the mutual history of different countries that constitute modern Eurasia.[7]

Russian Central Asia: Opportunities and impediments for sustainable development and trans-Eurasian cooperation

Regional Identity and Ethnicity Factor

While conceptualizing the generalized identity of certain Russian Asian borderlands as not only neighbouring, but also substantially Central Asian, one ought to take into account the complicated socio-historical phenomenon. First of all, the so-called Siberian region is an Asian domain in ethno-cultural and other terms. Since the middle of the first millennium Siberia at the whole was populated by Turkic peoples, who came here a century before Slavs settled in the upper Dnepr valley and established their state in Kiev. The state of Muscovy and the Siberian khanate both were the products of the disintegration of the Mongol-Turkic Golden Horde. Russians reached Siberia in the sixteenth and seventeenth centuries and peacefully merged with indigenous patterns of local life. Far more complicated were the ethno-cultural processes and interrelations over the landmass of Asiatic Russia. Russian ethnologist L. Sherstova on the basis of comprehensive archival and fieldwork research came to the conclusion that over time russified groups of Turko-Siberian origin had developed a new Asiatic regional self-consciousness, whereas a new Russian sub-ethnos was formed by diverse migrants.[8] When the Russian state shifted eastwards and southwards in 16th-18th century, it brought not only territorial expansion, but also ethnical interactions and mixings with aboriginal folk, Tatars, Bukharans, etc. Thus, western Siberia, being earlier a peripheral part of the Turkic world, evolved into the main base of Russian influence and presence in Asia, a kind of bridge for the transfer of Russian goods to the nomadic Kazakhs, Mongols and other peoples of the western Chinese steppe. Conversively, Siberia processed of steppe production, whereas Siberian towns became centers for the purchase (V.P. Zinoviev).

The 19th century witnessed Russian expansion and colonization of the vast territories to the south, producing a cohesive yet socio-politically and ethno-culturally diverse system that endured in various forms for a century and a half. With the passage of time Siberia's ethnical structure had been changed under impact of plenty of historical, geographic and geopolitical factors – massive labour (peasant) migration in late 19th and early 20th resulted in a Russianized landscape and it was forcefully reconfigured by Stalinist ethnic cleansing of the late 1930s. In the 20th and 21st centuries, there has been a high level of tolerance and peaceful co-existence among the aborigines (like Turkic Altaians), Slavic and others, Germans (different patterns and waves of migration), colonizers and the rest of migrants, either internal or external, with growing number of ethnic Asians.

The new feature of Asiatic Russia's population at the eve of Soviet breakdown and after is the formation of diasporic groups – in Altai these are represented by ethnic Central Asians (although returning Russians represent by now specific cultural-ethnographic group, distinctive from local Slavonic groups), and migrants incoming from distant Asia – Afghans, Vietnamese, Koreans, and Chinese. The largest among them are Kazakhs, Uzbeks and other Turkic groups – each numbered in main Siberian cities between 10 to 20 thousands. This growing diversity of Russian Asian borderlands is going to be a long-run trend due shortage of human resources in Russia herself and pressing economic difficulties in former soviet states. Kazakhstan is representing some exclusion, primarily because of demographic crisis at home, and Kazakh migration is unchallenging by number and patterns. However, there is a Kazakh community, which caused some problems for local authorities – for instance, in Altai province the leaders of Kazakhs established regional cultural autonomy – the deal tolerantly accepted when it was done by Tatars, and irritated regional government officials in Kazakh case. The reason is that Kazakhs are suspected to claim for unification with border [Eastern] Kazakhstan province and bureaucrats concerns to deal on daily basis with complicated social, cultural and somehow geopolitical problems.

The Far East has a good composition of Koreans – they are an assimilated community. According to well-known legends, the ancestors of Koreans were migrants from Manchuria and Siberia who moved to the peninsula about 4,000 years ago. Some historical evidence prove this phenomenon, but it was certainly broken during Middle Ages and modern times – Koreans developed sophisticated forms of state and governance, whereas Siberian aborigines were remained tribally organized herdsmen. Korean migrants came to Russia and specifically to Altai in late 19th century, their number had grown since Japanese occupation of Korean peninsula in 1910. Koreans learnt Russian, converted to Russian Orthodoxy and adopted Russian/Soviet citizenship, but they heavily suffered from ethnic cleanses of 1930s. However, at the moment there are these several thousands of Koreans who may be considered as one more reminiscence of Asiatic Russia's ethno-cultural diversity – the argument for interested Koreans abroad (tourists, businessmen, etc.) and Russian image-makers as well all developing international cooperation and exploiting every attractive brand, either ethnical or natural, visual etc. The idea to restore several Korean settlements of 1920s-30s was recently considered in local government and business circles.

The next example of multiple ethnicity in Asiatic Russia (with particular focus on Altai border area) is the formation and existence of Afghan community – the output of geopolitical events of 1980s-90s. This small group had easily accommodated to local conditions even in hard post-soviet times, it mirrors country of origin's ethnical composition. Surprisingly, being isolated physically from motherland, many Afghans maintained their political and other attributes irrespective of the changing political situation in Russia (some even were Taliban followers, although changed their mind when visiting country under Taliban, but re-considering again their position under current conditions). Anyway, there are Afghans, who are tolerant of local Altai folk and outside migrants who are ethnically and culturally different. Sometimes the impression is that they originated from certain Altai districts.

Final, but not the last point on migration is the story on Chinese – in this case the analysis is surprisingly brief and prospects appear uncertain. The reason is probably unique and not relevant to the rest of Russian Asian borderlands (e.g., Far East, Eastern Siberia, etc.) – Russian Altai is the only area of this country that borders primarily with Muslim-populated Xinjiang. This mere fact protects much Russian Altai from undesirable Chinese migration, which is real or imagined threat for many Chinese neighbours – the Chinese authorities themselves are concerned by closeness of this part of state border, either for own migrants or any external influences. This situation may be retained until there are significant changes in ethnic composition of Xinjiang or Chinese attitude. Ethnic disturbances occurred in Xinjiang in early July 2009 may have resulted in installing more strict order and rules about external migration.

This brief and case-focused survey of ethnic composition and dynamics of Asiatic Russia's areas is done not only for a selective portrayal of contemporary Eurasia – reflecting ongoing trends of migration, external flows from Central Asia etc. – it also forms a basis for concluding that Asianization of Russia's southern borderlands seems to be unavoidable which may be managed in different ways – inclusive or exclusive. Thus, inclusive approach suggests the programmes of accommodation, learning, social assistance, the preservation of migrant heritage and its promotion among local population, especially cadres in government, business, academia. Exclusive approach has very few prospects bearing in mind the border politics and, not the least, the state of border infrastructure, in post-soviet space, especially friendly relations between Russia and Kazakhstan – Kazakhstan is the main route for the majority of Central Asian migrants, going to Russia.

Eurasian Regionalism and the "Greater Altai" Project

The proposal to establish a "Greater Altai partnership" in the field of trade and transport offers an illuminating case study of both opportunities and impediments for regional interaction in this larger zone of Asia. The Russian Altai region, consisting of the Altai province and Altai Republic, lies in the strategically important borderland of the Russian Federation and Kazakhstan. The Russian Altai, together with Novosibirsk and Tomsk provinces, constitutes one of the main elements of the current Russian *heartland.* Altai's political situation is relatively stable, its economy remains stagnant. Recent regional government decisions on cutting social programmes resulted in public (primarily elderly) protests and disputes in local parliament between opposition fractions and "United Russia" dominating group.

The Altai business community and many politicians consider China as the most promising international trade partner. Whether the region advances economically well depends on whether or not proposed highways and gas pipelines to China are actually constructed. However, serious environmental arguments against these projects may in the long run undermine their viability. Meanwhile, ties between the Russian and Mongolian Altai zones are weak and even decreasing, in spite of mutual demands for economic and cultural cooperation. At the same time, the delineation of the Russian-Kazakhstan state border is proving a challenging process, the outcome of which will also affect trade and security. Against this background, it is surprising that Tajikistan, northern Afghanistan, and even Pakistan and India present tremendous opportunities for the Russian Altai, thanks to the mutually complementary nature of their economies and forefront location of Altai southwards in comparison with other border territories of RF.

The Russian Altai belongs historically, culturally and economically to Central and Inner Asia and is in turn part of a larger Altai region that is sometimes called "*Greater Altai*", which comprises also the East Kazakhstan province of Kazakhsntan, the Xinjiang-Uyghur Autonomous Region of China, and the Bayan-Ulgy and Khovd aymak*s* of Mongolia. This term was introduced long ago but is now gaining currency, thanks to the new spirit of regionalism that is developing there. This unique Eurasian regionalism manifests some features of European integration, but is more reminiscent of the "soft" interrelationships that have developed in South-East and South Asia. Strictly speaking, Greater Altai had existed in the past, as a changeable political-geographic entity in terms of borders and cohesiveness (archaic quasi-states of 17th-18th centuries, economically cooperative territories of soviet republics and in a lesser degree – border areas of USSR, Mongolia, and PRC). But new – ongoing and future – realities are demonstrating the relevance of Greater Altai as constructive term, framing new and growing type of border cooperation. At least, it seems more meaningful, than large-scale "codes" like Greater Central Asia, Greater Middle East, etc.

The history of sub-regional cooperation among adjacent territories of Russia, Kazakhstan, China, and Mongolia is short, but encouraging. There were Chinese who in 1996 raised the idea of forming an East Central Asia economic zone, connecting more cohesively East Kazakhstan, Russia's Altai Republic and Altai province, Bayan-Ulgy and Kobdo *aymaks* of Mongolia, and China's Xinjiang region. This idea was furthered in 2000, when representatives of these six regions signed in Urumchi a Declaration on International Cooperation in the Altai Mountain Region. Since 1998 the Chinese-Russian initiative to build a transport corridor via Kanas pass (the so-called "Eurasian continental bridge") has been under discussion. This project is complemented by the Mongolian initiative of 2000 to create a "Eurasian continental bridge". Whereas proponents of Altai economic development have merely suggested certain ideas on international transport, environmentalists have already implemented some integrative ecological projects, among them the "Long-Term Protection of Bio-Diversity of the Altai-Sayan Ecoregion" (1997), and UNDP's "Development and Implementation of Local Strategies of Sustainable Development in the Altai Republic"(2001). At the moment researchers and government agencies from Mongolia, China, Kazakhstan, and Russia, with support from the German government and UNESCO are developing the concept of a trans-border bio-sphere territory for sustainable development in Altai. The authors of this project suggest that it might eventually mesh with such economic projects such as the "Eurasian trans-continental bridge".

In September, 2002, Russia, Kazakstan, and Mongolia, and China established a joint committee, called "Altai: Our Common Home", to develop the resources of the Alta mountain range and link them with the broader world. The signatories agreed to focus on trade, transport, tourism, environmental protection, and education. The goal is to develop the entire region as an eco-tourism destination with world-class agriculture and a base for new technologies. This quadripartite project of regional cooperation has now become an institutionalized network involving the academic communities and legislators, with the support of the business communities and governments. By now thee are governors of the regions concerned who are assigned to be the vehicles of trans-regional cooperation – the thing which sounds bureaucratic, but, probably, unavoidable in area with primarily post-socialist heritage.

The projects like "Greater Altai/Altai – our common home" are aimed to increase the level of cooperation between border territories of Eurasia, up to the establishment of organizationally and legally moduled inter-state Euro-region-like unities, or, more precisely, Eurasia-regions. But this scenario of integration is constrained by norms of national and international law, disparities of partners involved, the differences of socio-demographic, cultural, etc. nature, and some other limits. Accordingly, there is the necessity to expand international cooperation geographically and thematically – the most prospective and natural direction for Asiatic Russia, including her Central Asian belt, would be outer, or distant, Asia.[9]

The Altai-Altai Project for Roads and Gas Pipelines

One of the most controversial aspects of the development of the Altai region is the proposed construction of a highway from Barnaul, the administrative center of Altai province, to Urumqi, the capital of the Xinjiang Uyghur Autonomous Region of China. The project to build a road connecting Russia and China through the Altai was developed by Russia and China and is supported by Western development organizations. However, it has foundered on the massive opposition mobilized by local Russian environmentalists and nationalists. The length of this new trans-national transport line will be 260 km., of which 140 km. is already constructed. The Xinjiang government is ready to allocate funds to build the remaining 120 km. There is still no checkpoint on the 55 km., western border sector between China and Russia, and all cargos are going instead through Kazakhstan, leading to increased costs. The proposed highway connecting China and Russia will go via the Ukok plateau and will cross the border at the Kanas pass. Opponents point out that the Ukok plateau is included among UNESCO's World Heritage Sites because of its many archaeological sites. For example, it is here that the archaeologist N. Polosmak found the famed "Altai princess" mummy. Many ethnic Altaians consider the region to be holy and explain the earthquake of 2003 as being the consequence of the "princess's" spirit having been disturbed. Altai Republic authorities are also opposed to the idea of road construction and are offering to build a link to China via Mongolia, using the alternative route Tashanta-Ulgiy (Mongolia)-Kobdo (Mongolia)-Taikishken in China.

The highway is not the sole project of possible economic linkages. In March, 2006, than President Putin announced Russia's plans to construct two pipelines from Siberia to China. Russia hopes to export to China 60-80 billion cubic meters of gas annually by this route. The Chairman of Gazprom, Aleksei Miller, stated that the cost of this new gas pipeline could reach $10 billion and that it might be completed by 2011. Greens again strongly oppose this project. Altai's Governor Alexander Karlin told the media that the project will definitely go forward with direct financing and will cross 450 km. of Altai territory, but recent developments – shortage of investments as well the implementation of alternative projects via Eastern Siberia – make gas pipeline "Altai" highly doubtful expenditure even in a middle run.

Socio-economical and Geopolitical Challenges

The argument of this paper is that Russian Central Asia (the historical part of Greater Central Asia) is experiencing today, together with opportunities for trans-Eurasian cooperation, many challenges of economic, migration, and security nature – all threatening social, political and even military stability of the whole area. Central (Moscow) state authorities are ignoring the problems of this border region, which was for a long time subsided from federal sources. The efforts to develop sustainable strategies such a transit multimodal "bridge" Asia-Europe project by construction of road/gas-pipeline to

China or introduction of large tourist-recreational zones with substantial external (including foreign) investments are ill-accepted by local population and regional elite. The prevailing consciousness of local population with remaining public (kolkhoz-like) habits of work is still an obstacle for the development of family-based and individual services that are related to the business of tourism. One more serious obstacle for implementing tourism is of financial nature – while federal and local authorities are ready to support the projects in this field, foreign investors are very careful as they are questioning the prospects of infrastructure (roads, international airports, etc.). One of the promising projects of current Altai regional administration – "unique agrarian territory" Altai Ob [river] basin scheme, which goal is to develop original and ecologically clean agricultural products for local and external consumers and markets. It was proposed recently by Altai province governor A. Karlin at Baikal Economic Forum, then approved at Russian government level and may be promising instrument of economic income or even a kind of breakthrough.

The lack of modern-trained cadres is another shortcoming of local social infrastructure – many of its sectors are still managed by former communist party of komsomol bosses, which follow strictly corporate or even clan/family patterns of work. Many cadres of new wave are often their junior family members promoted due these linkages or via ruling party structures (cadres reserve of "United Russia"). One of undesirable social consequences is the formation of looking-to-the past estate/class society with lack of social dynamics and formation of multiple clan groups. This problem is weighted by long-time comparative weakness of scholarly and educational network, which was determined by interplay of central authorities' line and local socio-economic conditions. Despite early efforts to establish in Russian Altai university-like institutions (the first one of such kind was opened in 1935, whereas "classical" university inaugurated only in 1973), local academic community still exists in embryonic state – partially due many field (ministerial, institutional, field, etc.) divisions and in a more extent because of lack of real academic organizations, which were and are concentrated in neighbour areas (Novosibirsk, Tomsk, etc.). This disadvantage weakens not only scholarship and teaching, but also the expert basis of decision-making activities by government and other agencies, either local or even federal (branches). Very few exceptions (the Institute of Water and Ecological Problems, Altai branch of Russian cancer center – both of Russian Academy of

Sciences) prove the truth of this argument. By now new scheme of university education and scholarly training is under consideration by government and legislative (federal, research, regional universities network with the rest of baccalaureate colleges) – it seems ill-promising for already marginalized Russian Central Asia under current competitive situation and shortage of sources. Altai goes to be a looser region with the lack of central lobby and strong competition from established players around. The lack of opportunities for horizontal/vertical promotion of cadres adds the problems for local intellectual class and accordingly the whole socio-economic body. Possible solution might be the establishment of branches of powerful central/macro-regional institutions and intra-/trans-Eurasian cooperation, including partnership with distant, but prospective universities, particularly these located in border areas – University of Kashmir (Srinagar, India), University of Peshawar (Peshawar, Pakistan), etc. – above-mentioned have, among all, similar interrelated scholarly/expert fields such as Central Asian studies programme and units (centres, majors, etc.).

This problem is weighted by growing competition between neighbouring regions for resources, roles and quotas in federal programmes. This new relationship causes new tensions, including "domestic geopolitics" that is the competition of certain regions, first of all border areas, for external markets, projects of international cooperation, access to transport routes, etc. Altai is one of most marginalized within Siberian federal district in terms of infrastructure, education, academic and applied sciences – all these factors are determining the migration of youth and experienced cadres. Not minor challenge is "external geopolitics" is geopolitics itself, that is proper international context of local developments, either economic or security-shaped. Altai is the main target of illegal migration (not external labour, but just temporal haven of migration flows), drugs as it's the main gate from outer Central Asia due existed railway network. This marginalized situation is influenced not only by discriminative politics of federal center, but also international institutions which consider the area under analysis as standard Russian territory, without any regards to its historical and current status as a part of Central Asian world. Meantime, current trends of ethno-social dynamic (slowly and ill-managed Asiatization and social marginalization of local population) and stagnant economic development of Russian Central Asia may considerably increase security challenges not only for this very area, but also for Russia as a whole. In turn, this may have negative impact for the security of new Eurasia.

Conclusions

Since the breakup of the Communist system in the early 1990s Russia has become a dynamically developing state and society, where democratic norms and patterns of economic and political life are steadily gaining strength. Due to historical factors and to its geographic location, Russia is a Eurasian power, with a substantial part of its territory located socially and economically in Asia, and with certain southern border-belt regions falling within Central Asia proper. Russia's Asianness (or Central Asianness) while shifting over time, has always been a factor in its domestic and external politics. This fact, as well as geo-political and geoeconomic factors, assures the permanence of Russia's interest in Asia and her cooperation with its Asian neighbours, whether it is China, Kazakhstan, India, or Japan. Integrative projects in the strategic and economic sphere are important for Russia. Of particular importance are the states of Central Eurasia – the vast landmass that includes certain Russia's own territories, former Soviet republics and other states with similar ethno-cultural roots including China's Xinjiang region, the Turco-Tajik north of Afghanistan, the Turkic north of Iran, and India and Pakistan, with their Central Asian territories of Kashmir.

Any partnership framework for Greater Central Asia and more broadly Central Eurasia should involve Russia fully and give it one of key roles, including an appropriate role of Russian regions especially those comprising its border belt. This includes the exploitation of North-and Western Siberian energy resources and related pipelines between Siberia, Central Asia, and South Asia (including possible facilitation of the *Siberian-Indian* corridor). Russia, while burdened by her own domestic problems, including those caused by "internal geopolitics", has not yet begun to play its full role in the region, which constituted the borderlands of both the Russian imperial and post-imperial states. In the future Russia will surely play a bigger role in reframing the broader geo-political and geo-economic space than it has for the past about twenty years and will demonstrate its capacity for cooperation with its neighbours and distant partners, among which India would be much-respective and highly desired as a growing regional power with unlimited human resources and opportunities of peaceful cooperation. This India's new role would be the best sign of significant changes in Eurasian geopolitical and geo-economical landscape – the formation of really multi-polar world. To be *heartland* or at least its constituent part today means not to gain any upper roles as it was in old imperial times, but to contribute in one or another way either on [Altai] sub-regional or [India] major power level to security and development of the globe in 21st century.

NOTES AND REFERENCES

1. Frye, Richard N. The Meaning of Central Asia, in: Conference on the Study of Central Asia", March 10–11, 1983, Woodrow Wilson International Center for Scholars, Washington, 1983, pp. 11-13; Pre-Islamic and early Islamic cultures in Central Asia//Turko-Persia in historical perspective. Ed. By Robert L. Canfield. Columbia University 1991. pp. 35–52; *see also* the transcript of his presentation "Pre-Islamic and Early Islamic Cultures in Greater Central Asia" at seminar "Central Asia as a Cultural Area", Papers of Richard Frye, Harvard University Archives, box 12933.
2. See, for instance: Canfield, R.L. The Collision of Evolutionary Process and Islamic Ideology in Greater Central Asia//Afghanistan and soviet Union. Collision and Transformation. Ed. By Milan Hauner and Robert L. Canfield. Westview Press, Boulder, 1989. pp. 13–35; Canfield, Robert L., "Restructuring in Greater Central Asia: Changing Political Configuration", *Asian Survey*, vol. 32 no. 10, October 1992, pp. 875–887; Belokrenitsky V.Y., "Russia and Greater Central Asia", *Asian Survey*, vol. 33 no. 12, December 1993, pp. 1093-1108; Naumkin V.V. (ed.), *Tsentral'no-Aziatskii makroregion i Rossiia,* Moscow, 1993.
3. Voskressenski, Alexei D., "Regional Studies in "Russia and Current Methodological Approaches for the Social/Historical/Ideological Reconstruction of International Relations and Regional Interaction in Eastern Eurasia", *Reconstruction and Interaction of Slavic Eurasia and Its Neighboring Worlds*., Ieda. Osamu and Uyama, Tomohiko, Slavic Research Center, 2006. http://srch.slav.hokudai.ac.jp/coe21/publish/no10_ses/contents.html.
4. The existed all-Russia's administrative structure with vast Siberian district reflects rather the Putin's programme/system of multiple centralization (the main modules of territorial governance and control),

then the cohesive political-economic unit, not saying about its territorial integrity.

5. Ieda Osamu, 'Regional Identities and Meso-Mega Area Dynamics in Slavic Eurasia: Focused on Eastern Europe', in Matsuzato Kimitaka (ed.), *Emerging Meso-Areas in the Former Socialist Countries: Histories Revived or Improvised?* (Sapporo, 2005), pp. 19–41.
6. The emergence of the Meso-Mega area dynamics approach was related to the fact that the mega area of Eurasia, the former Soviet Union and the East Europea, has changed its face dramatically since the collapse of the communist regimes. As a result, new regions/sub-regions came into existence in the mega area, such as post-soviet Central Asia, Caucasia, South Eastern Europe, Central Eastern Europe, the Russian Far East, Eastern and Western Siberia. The task is to analyse these regions in broad Eurasian context, focusing on regional integration and 'interaction in borderlands'.
7 Some scholars are tending to stress the value and long roots of geo-cultural identity in Central Asia, which sometimes proves ill-assessable linkages (such as between Altaic peoples, etc.). Han-Woo Choi. Geo-Cultural Identity of the Western Turkestan, *International Journal of Central Asian Studies*, 2003, v. 8
8. Sherstova, L.I., Turki i russkie v Yuzhnoi Sibiri: etnicheskie protsessy i etno-culturnaia dinamika v XVII-nachale XX vv, Novosibirsk, 2005
9. More detailed account of opportunities to cooperate Altai with outer Asia in V. Boyko, 'Mezhdunarodniye svyazi Altayskogo kraya: aziatskiy vector', *Rossiya, Sibir I Tsentralnaya Aziya: vzaimodeystviye narodov I kultur* Vip. 4, Barnaul, 2005.

2

Towards a New Paradigm of International Relations: The Implications of Central Asian Geopolitics

Farkhod F. Tolipov

International scholarship in the field of Central Asian studies collected a massive set of works since this geographical name began to designate the so called Newly Independent States (NIS). To my mind this scholarship today reveals ontological and conceptualization problems. Post-independence studies of the region lack adequate and strong scientific approaches. The spectrum of incorrect views of Central Asia stretches from the assertions about the Uzbekistan's expansionism and hegemonist aspiration in the region and prognosis of "Balkanization" of Central Asia, to rejection of the applicability of the regional integration concept with regard to the five countries of the region. The new studies of Central Asian political processes are dominated with consideration of the overall relations among Kazakhstan, Kyrgyzstan, Tajikistan, Turkmenistan and Uzbekistan, as well as their foreign policy strategy, through the prism of the balance of power and the identification of the relations as conflictual.

Meanwhile a new geopolitics arises in this part of the world: geopolitical transformation of Central Asia that has been taking place since the collapse of the Soviet Union 11 September just accelerated this process. Many scholarly works on Central Asia suffer from the lack of theory: we often observe the passage from old stereotypes and prejudices to new ones. Different wide spread analytical speculations, official statements, public suspicions and allegations about newly established American military-political presence in Central Asia can prove this thesis.

Central Asia today faces a twofold geopolitical problematique which has recently been scientifically actualized and politically articulated: (1) new, post-Soviet Central Asian geopolitics of great powers and the overall geopolitical transformation of the region after 11 September 2001; one of the manifestations of this process is the US coming in the region of Central Asia – the Heartland of Eurasia – that inevitably changes the status-quo in this part of the world. (2) The Central Asia's response to the (1). I believe that the Central Asian scholarship can be further developed more effectively on the base of Central Asian Methodology Reversed, Central Asian Geopolitics Revised, and Central Asian Integration Revisited.

Central Asian Methodology Reversed

A number of methodological approaches to the study of Central Asia appeared to be incorrect or narrow, simplistic and superficial. The real Central Asia has always been exposed to a set of different factors that make it very uneasy to foresee the future scenarios of development of the region. Indeed, when we study geopolitical scenarios (plus new world order scenarios) *versus* religious scenarios *versus* civilizational scenarios *versus* security scenarios we notice that each sphere taken separately develops according to its own laws, and when we juxtapose all scenarios we will see a very complicated picture of Central Asian reality.

New World Order... for Central Asia

One basic international concept as applied to Central Asian region and three basic intraregional methodological approaches towards each Central Asian country should be revised. The former is that of new world order (NWO) and geopolitics of zero-sum game that failed to yield any victory or defeat of any superpower in the region. After the dissolution of one "pole" of the "bipolar world" a number of new concepts were advanced as to features of the new order the world lives in: from the unipolar world to the multipolar one with different variations in between and visible adherence of majority of analysts to the latter concept.

Although multipolarism seems more democratic and, in this sense, more fair, vis-à-vis unipolarism, it has its own serious deficiencies. We can briefly consider the dichotomy: multipolarism vs multilateralism. The former is more static and the latter is more dynamic; the former means what can be called "*vague presence*" the latter means "*clear participation*". Multipolarism reflects the fact that there are 'poles' that is, certain *exclusive 'club' of privileged actors* who, in fact, will obviously demonstrate different and competitive vision of the world order. Multilateralism reflects the fact that there are 'laterals' that is, *inclusive 'club' of interested* actors who, because they are involved, will demonstrate, though different, cooperative vision of the world order (which is a positive posture).

So, 'multipolar world' is rather status-designating conception than 'multilateral world', which is action-oriented one. As we see, 'multipolarism vs multilateralism' dichotomy is all about 'exclusive vs inclusive' approach, in other words, 'aristocratic vs democratic' approach to the world order. As Alvaro de Vasconcelos, Director of the EU Institute for Security Studies, rightly argues, multipolarity implies balance of power game whereas the multilateral order implies a system governed by rules and norms[1].

In the age of globalization and multiplication of international actors the very idea of balancing one power by another power is losing its relevance. This is especially noticeable in Central Asia. It is hardly possible to draw the "magic formula" of balance of power in terms of whose power should be balanced and by which means. In our case, we have at least three main groups of actors: great powers, international organizations, and Central Asians themselves. When it comes to the equation with multiple unknowns, the international situation, especially geopolitical situation becomes much more sophisticated than that described by the balance of power model. Indeed, when the same Central Asian state is a member of the allegedly anti-Western (or at least non-Western) alliance – the Shanghai Cooperation Organization, the SCO, – and participates in the NATO Partnership for Peace Programme or demonstrates its eagerness to establish strategic relationships with the US, then the balance of power will hardly work. Or, when the Central Asian states use the SCO or CIS formats as being non-democratic states and, at the same time, take responsibilities within the OSCE, then the balance becomes really a senseless concept. So, the world as a whole and Central Asia, in particular, is rather multilateral than multipolar.

Nationalization and Geopolitization of the Idea of Democracy

The above mentioned two basic methodological approaches towards each Central Asian country that should be revised are: (1)

Easternization/Asianization/Nationalization of the issue of democracy which distorted the very concept of democracy and only yielded self-legitimization of authoritarianism and discreditation of the democratic idea in the countries concerned; (2) the theory of distinctive national evolution which appeared to be very narrow and superficial in describing and understanding the phenomenon of national evolution and national history; (3) the simplistic interpretation of secularism that can yield ideological friction and overlooking of the political awakening of Islam in this part of the world.

Let's briefly consider the first one. The phenomenon of the NIS revealed a new paradox: the global tendency of internationalization of the idea of democracy cannot but contradict, so to speak, the renationalization of democracy in the NIS-space. This paradox was especially reinforced in the wake of the so-called 'colour revolutions' in some post-Soviet countries. The Western policy of democracy promotion was met by the post-Soviet states, primarily Russia, with deep anxiety as a plot directed to overthrow the current regimes and to establish pro-Western governments. The NIS, especially Central Asians, is headed towards a new deadlock caused by the unproductive and false search for the mythic national model of democracy and rejection of the universality of democracy. In most of Central Asia the state takes it for granted that the only right way is a step-by-step democratization, since it is believed that the people is not ready for the radical democratic changes. However, no proof of the correctness of this choice is provided. As a result, we witness the phenomenon that the people will be unready for democracy to the extent that its primary democratic nature will be neglected and atrophied[2].

Let's consider briefly the second issue. Nationalism and Supranationalism

It has to be noted that the nationalist background, nationalist outlook and nationalist political programme prevail in most of political debates, strategic and geopolitical calculations in every Central Asian state. Even the history of the region is "privatized" and common destiny ignored in many political discourses. Quite painful discussions between Tajik and Uzbek historians throughout the year 2006 about history of the area currently occupied by Tajikistan and Uzbekistan can be a proof of our thesis of "privatization" of history. At the same time, the study of transformation processes, which take place in Kazakhstan, Kyrgyzstan, Tajikistan, Turkmenistan and Uzbekistan, reveals in their content, direction and peculiarities, so to speak, a national-regional dualism. Therefore, the overall geopolitical transformation of the region might be characterized as a real revitalization and reinforcement of regionalism in Central Asia. However, the regional unity of 5 countries concerned that was restored right after the liquidation of the Soviet Union was recently sacrificed.

The matter is the Central Asian region has constantly since independence suffered from strong external geopolitical pressure. This pressure reveals itself in a wide spread stereotype that Central Asians cannot accomplish post-Soviet reintegration on their own, as was announced in 1991. On the summit of the Central Asian Cooperation Organization (CACO) held in Saint-Petersburg on October 6, 2005, the member-states – Kazakhstan, Kyrgyzstan, Tajikistan, Uzbekistan and Russia – announced that the CACO merged with the Eurasian Economic Community (EAEC). As a response to such a visible and invisible pressure the regional activists, elites, scientists, arts and culture representatives should, to my mind, recall the Jadidist movement which existed in the first two decades of the XXI century. Jadids actually established a Turkistan-wide unification movement by means of enlightening, opening new schools, public actions and so on with an ultimate goal of creating Turkistan Autonomy.

Let's consider briefly the third issue. Identities, Religion and Ideological Friction

The collapse of the Soviet Union caused not merely an independence of 5 countries concerned but also revealed a confusion of identities in public consciousness. Nationalism versus regionalism, democracy versus autocracy, Islam versus secularism are just a few dichotomies that fill up the minds of those who seriously think about the future development and prospects of the region. Islam itself creates a very sophisticated background on which the socio-political process is unfolding nowadays in Central Asia. Rapidly increasing significance of Islamic way of life for citizens produces what I call an ideological friction. Meanwhile, in the wake of increasing challenge of Islamism to Central Asian peoples, states and societies some analysts, rightly point out the threat of Islamic extremism to the regional security. But I think that in a larger perspective there is a possibility of one of the following scenarios of self-activation of Islam in a social and political development of the region:

- Algerian scenario – Islamists win elections but are denied the power by the military and the civil war occurs;

- Palestinian scenario – terrorist/extremist organization wins elections and comes to power;
- Iranian scenario – Islamic revolution breaks out and theocracy is established;
- Pakistani scenario – geopolitical involvement of Islamism and clash between democratic secular political system and Islamists forces;
- Afghanistan scenario – talibanization;
- Tajikistani scenario – legalization of the Islamic Party which merges with criminal elements and is involved in the inter-clan power struggle in the country; the civil war occurs which is resolved by means of incorporation of Islamists in state structures;
- Turkish-Malaysian scenario – some form of incorporation of Islam in a democratic political process.

One can draw some other possible scenarios, but one thing should be clear, namely: all the period since independence has been the first period of the Renaissance of Islam as culture. I anticipate the coming of the period of Prosperity of Islam as a way of life and the third period of Rise of Islam as part of political process.

Security Challenges and Security Policies

Finally, there is one more element of the old paradigm of Central Asian studies – it is about security, regional *versus* national. The old paradigm says that the countries of the region are not self-sufficient in the field of security and therefore they need security assistance. Given the "security impotence" of the countries concerned, the so-called "market of security services" appeared in the region[3]. Different "security umbrellas", in turn, are bringing with them inevitable geopolitical dimension. The only establishment and implications of strategic partnership between the US and the Republic of Uzbekistan (RUz) in the wake of the counter-terrorist campaign in Afghanistan caused so much anxieties on the part of Russia and China that these two great powers were compelled to take steps through the mechanism of the SCO to remove the growing, albeit mythic, American threat.

On the other hand, on the part of Central Asian regimes, the security of the nation has been conceived of as the security of the regime. The concept of security is manipulated and exploited by ruling elites of Central Asia, especially Uzbekistan and Turkmenistan, for their own, rather than national, interests. As a side-effect of this policy we can observe securitization of ideology and ideologization of security, especially in Uzbekistan.

Central Asian Geopolitics Revised

Since its discovery the Heartland remained not only geographically far away from the oceans due to its location deeply in the continent, but also strategically locked by the dominant power of the Heartland, the status ascribed initially to Tsarist Russia and later the Soviet Union. So, Russia has been, so to speak, a Heartland-keeper or Master of the Heartland. Although struggle over Heartland, according to the geopolitical theory, constituted the permanent factor of international relations, this area, and Central Asia inside it, have been triple isolated from the world political affairs and world trade – isolated by geography, isolated by superpower, and, since 1991, self-isolated due to misconduct of regional integration project. The "great game" was the term that was used to describe the permanent geopolitical struggle between great powers for gaining control of the region. This term has served as the connotation of the dominant paradigm of power politics in this part of the world.

Nowadays, Central Asian geopolitics needs to be revised. Any attempt at analyzing great power geopolitics and Central Asian geopolitics, in particular, should take into account the fact that the very complicated process of geopolitical transformation in the region has coincided with the emergence of a new world order and a revision of much that was previously accepted by the old geopolitical theory. Nowadays, a new current, a so-called critical geopolitics, is coming into being.[4] For us, several new factors of today's world politics that are emerging in connection with the NWO stipulate the necessity to reconsider the classical geopolitical theory especially regarding its Central Asian "chapters".

Gearoid O Tuathail suggests reading Geopolitics as Structure and as Culture. He points out that "rather than being an objective recording of the realities of world power, geopolitics is an interpretative cultural practice. Further, this practice is not a narrow one confined to formal experts but a broad one shared by populations (popular geopolitics) and governments (practical geopolitics)".[5]

O Tuathail and John Agnew argue that geopolitics "should be critically re-conceptualized as a discursive practice by which intellectuals of statecraft 'spatialize' international politics in such a way as to represent it as a 'world' characterized by particular types of places, peoples and dramas".[6]

I call the new trend of geopolitical thought 'democratic geopolitics', whereas the old practices I call imperial geopolitics (see the table). The new one is 'democratic' because it implies and requires public opinion, demos attitude to and reflection of geography, and, what is interesting, necessity for political elites and state leadership to use geopolitical reasoning and rhetoric for self-legitimization as well as explaining and promotion of one or other political decision. In the frameworks of critical geopolitics Benedict Anderson's "imagined community" turns into an "imagined geography". Nick Megoran quotes J. Sharp and points out that whilst it is "through the construction of an imagined geography of national identity that a sense of belonging is achieved"[7], the relationship between space, identity, ideology and power still largely awaits investigation in the Central Asian context[8].

The sharp illustration of such a relationship is reflected in the phenomenon of 'de-bordering' and 're-bordering'[9] in Central Asia. Megoran, having studied border issue between Uzbekistan and Kyrgyzstan, assumed that "the impact of these border disputes and closures on local populations was traumatic. At the same time, the 'border question' facilitated entrenchment of the authoritarian regime in Uzbekistan, and provided a platform for anti-minority propaganda in Kyrgyzstan. That geographical arguments were at the heart of these debates entails a moral imperative to expose and challenge the operation of geography in exclusionary practices of state violence, an imperative that is at the heart of the project of critical geopolitics".[10]

By the way, the Heartland concept can no longer apply as a foundation of the geopolitical theory because, among other reasons, there are today a number of Heartland-like places in other parts of the world which attract great power aspirations and become the epicenters of most significant international political events and unalienable elements of the emerging NWO. Central Asia is only one of such places.

From this point of view and given our adherence to the 'multilateral world order' concept which we described above, we can assert that democratic geopolitics should substitute the imperial geopolitics in Central Asia.

Imperial Geopolitics	*Democratic Geopolitics*
Geopolitics of hostility	Geopolitics of recognition
Geopolitics of alienation	Geopolitics détente
Geopolitics of distrust	Geopolitics of confidence building
Geopolitics of exclusion	Geopolitics of participation
Geopolitics of balance of power	Geopolitics of opportunities
Geopolitics of hard power	Geopolitics of soft power
Geopolitics of containment	Geopolitics of engagement
Geopolitics of seizure of resources	Geopolitics of distribution of resources
Geopolitics of dominance	Geopolitics of cooperation
Geopolitics of spheres of influence	Geopolitics of globalization
Multipolarity	Multilateralism
Sovereignty absolute	Sovereignty shared

As a rule, geopolitics is understood as an embodiment of a broader international theory of *Realpolitik*, that's why the left column of the table typically is read as describing the essence of geopolitics. Therefore, being more the reflection of political idealism, the right column looks less pertinent to what geopolitics is. Here, I would like to make clear my view of democratic geopolitics. It is indeed still *geopolitics* but it is not so much about the seizure of control over population and resources of a particular territory as about the proper political accommodation of the population and resources of that territory. It is not political geography, so long as it is about international relations, and even power politics, with respect to particular geographical territory. So, the main difference between imperial geopolitics and democratic geopolitics lies in the nature of the NWO. In democratic geopolitics the importance of the Heartland remains and even increases, but the theoretical emphasis and research attention is shifted from the great power rivalry over the closed Heartland to the components of the open Heartland. These components simply NEED democratic geopolitics because, as NIS, they do not want to fall again into dependence and victims of that rivalry. Thus, they are supposed and expected to behave accordingly.

In a more concise way, the difference between the two schools of geopolitics can be formulated as follows: imperial geopolitics is based on the premise that war is possible, while democratic geopolitics is founded on the conviction that peace is inevitable. Classically geopolitics *a priory* is read as geopolitics of great powers. But geopolitics of today goes with non-great powers, small states, failed states, interstate and non-state actors. Moreover, unlocked after 1991

Heartland is no longer mastered by one superpower; it is no longer isolated, on the contrary it is involved in world politics. In this sense the old Central Asian geopolitics was *about* and *over* Central Asia. But new geopolitics is expected to be also that *of* and *by* Central Asia. Meanwhile, the current geopolitics in CA carries an *ad-hoc* feature.

Indeed, by-and-large, the contemporary studies of Central Asian geopolitics of great powers are made on the base of perception of either rivalry or cooperation between them. Three following analytical positions are quite illustrative in this sense. Lasha Tchantouridze argues that "the United States keeps on pushing toward more openness in Eurasia, as it did with the United Kingdom and France in the 1950s and the 1960s, and the Soviet Union from 1940s to 1980s, while Russia insists on having Eurasia closed for outside actors".[11] Ekaterina Borisova argues that contemporary geopolitics reveals a new phase of westernization. She asserts that this process can be successful pnly where the archetype of the Sea acts. However, the westernization is not accepted inside the continental zone.[12] Anita Sengupta pays attention to the controversial character of what can be perceived of as a new struggle over the Heartland. She point out to coexistence of geopolitical rivalry and strategic partnership between the United States and the Russian Federation.[13]

At the same time, one can also observe some sort of by-product of '*macro-geopolitics*' of great powers in the region which can be illustrated as '*micro-geopolitics*' of Central Asians themselves *vis-à-vis* each other. In other words, the well known Big Game is accompanied by a less known Small Game that is being played by local states. Therefore, the basic rule of macro-geopolitics, that is 'balance-of-power', was imposed on micro-geopolitics. Here, the Hans Morgenthau's axiom deserves mentioning: "The more intimately a local balance of power is connected with the dominant one, the less opportunity it has to operate autonomously and the more it tends to become merely a localized manifestation of the dominant balance of power".[14] As a result, we can assume, nationalism became a geopolitical phenomenon, democracy became a geopolitical phenomenon, security a geopolitical phenomenon, integration a geopolitical phenomenon, and so on.

So, the new methodological question arises: will the old (imperial) geopolitics persist or will the new (democratic) geopolitics prevail in the XXI century? Meanwhile, some analytical motion toward the revised approach to the region is already underway. When it comes to Russian geopolitics, one has to take into account that the foreign policy of the Russian Federation is a product of uneasy convergence of different political forces ranging from neo-communists and neo-imperialists to democrats and Eurocentric liberals. As Russian analyst Dmitri Trenin rightly pointed out, "In the early twenty-first century, Russia looks ahead to a long and painful period of post-imperial disengagement from the former provinces *and* simultaneous re-engagement with its new neighbours on a new set of principles."[15] He suggests an integrated "southern strategy" which includes, among other things, the following policy recommendation:[16]

– Do not attempt to become the sole security guarantor for Central Asia; that is beyond Russia's capacity.
– Recognize that, in Central Asia, the fundamental interests of Russia and the United States coincide. Cease regarding the American presence in the region as inherently anti-Russian.

The American analysts Eugene Rumer, in turn, while recommending a new Central Asia strategy of the United States, argues that any new US strategy must have a substantial component that will address various Russian and Chinese perspectives on developments there[17].

Central Asian Integration Revisited

The following expression can characterize the current state of affairs in the overall relationships among Central Asians: united in culture but divided in politics, united in traditions and heritage but divided by circumstances. The prevailing scholarly perception of the overall regionalism phenomenon which arose here after gaining independence in 1991is that this region is fragmented and doomed to disintegrate further. Typically, scholars contemplating of perspectives of regional developments, point out to different economic systems, different degrees of socio-economic development, Turko-Persian division, and some mistrust between leaders of Central Asian states. However, they often overlook or neglect the significance of existing assets of integration of 5 countries, assets existed from ancient times and gained after independence. They are common ethnic origin, common religion, common history, quite successful, albeit modest, institutionalization process since 1991.

As a result, the lack of integrationist strategy of Central Asian states undermined overall attempt at creating the collective security system in the region and became a reason for their geopolitical vulnerability. By-and-large, analogously with the European history of integration, the same process in Central Asia is accompanied with two attitudes which can be called Central Asian optimism and Central Asian pessimism.

I think all 5 countries of Central Asia must take full responsibility for the regional affairs and restore the CACO, and move further towards political unification. But this will depend on what extent they will be able to overcome the pressure of macro-geopolitics and hurdles of micro-geopolitics, and on the extent to which great powers will be able to pass from imperial geopolitics to democratic geopolitics.

There is another explanation of the failure of regional integration in Central Asia: the elites and leadership of all 5 states have been, since independence, preoccupied with the nation and statehood ideology. Therefore, the "regionalization of Central Asia" should be the paradigm of relations between and among 5 countries concerned for the next generation of leaders.

Conclusion

Simon Dalby argues that "geopolitics is certainly about the rivalry between states, but it is also about other matters that flow across the state boundaries and require policy options of international co-operation and co-ordination rather than confrontation".[18] This is especially true when it comes to Central Asia. I suggest a new – integrationist – paradigm of international relations for Central Asia. It is based on several premises:

1. democratic geopolitics;
2. neo-Jadidist ethics of enlightenment;
3. non-privatization of history of the region and recognition of common destiny;
4. understanding and recognition of the common security challenges, and common responses to those challenges;
5. the federalist model of unification.

I would like to finish this short analysis with the words that American analyst Ariel Cohen said in one conference: Central Asia is a large field of cooperation if we focus on cooperation, and it is a large field of confrontation if we focus on confrontation[19].

NOTES AND REFERENCES

1. Alvaro de Vasconcelos. 'Multilateralising' multipolarity, in "Partnership for effective multilateralism. EU relations with Brazil, China, India and Russia", edited by Giovanni Grevi and Alvaro de Vasconcelos (Paris: EUISS, May 2008). p. 24.
2. The analysis of this issue the author of this paper presented in the article "Central Asia: universal democracy, national democracy, or enlightened authoritarianism?" in *Central Asia and Caucasus*, No. 2, 2007. See also: Tolipov, F. The Gap Between de-jure and de-facto Democratization in Uzbekistan. Nine Problems of Proto-democracy, in Irina Morozova edited, "Towards Social Stability and Democratic Governance in Central Eurasia: challenges to regional security", by IOS Press, Amsterdam, within the NATO Science Series 2005.
3. Tolipov, F. "Multilateralism, Bilateralism and Unilateralism in Fighting Terrorism in the SCO Area", in *The China and Eurasia Forum Quarterly*, Vol. 4, No. 2, May 2006.
4. On the subject of the critical geopolitics, see, for example: *Geopolitics: Global Problems and Regional Concerns*. Edited by Lasha Tchantouridze. (Winnipeg, Manitoba: Center for Defence and Security Studies, 2004. See also: Amineh, M.P., *Globalization, Geopolitics and Energy Security in Central Eurasia and the Caspian Region*. (The Hague: Clingendael International Energy Programme, 2003).
5. Gearoid O Tuathail, "Geopolitical Structures and Cultures: Towards Conceptual Clarity in the Critical Study of Geopolitics", in *Geopolitics: Global Problems and Regional Concerns*. Edited by Lasha Tchantouridze. (Winnipeg, Manitoba: Center for Defence and Security Studies, 2004, pp. 75–102.
6. Gearoid O Tuathail and John Agnew, "Geopolitics and Discourse: Practical Geopolitical Reasoning and American Foreign Policy", *Political Geography*, (11) 1992, pp. 190–204.
7. Sharp, J., "Remasculinising geo-politics? comments on Gearoid O'Tuathail's critical geopolitics." *Political Geography*, (19) 2000, 361–364. p. xi.
8. Megoran, N., "The Critical Geopolitics of the Uzbekistan-Kyrgyzstan Fergana Valley Boundary Dispute, 1999-2000," in *Political Geography*, (23) 2004, p. 29.

9. Berg, E., and van Houtum, H., "Prologue: a border is not a border. Writing and reading borders in space." In E. Berg, and H. van Houtum (Eds.), *Routing borders between territories, discourses and practices. Critical Security Studies*. Aldershot: Ashgate, 2003.
10. Megoran, N., "The Critical Geopolitics of the Uzbekistan-Kyrgyzstan Fergana Valley Boundary Dispute, 1999–2000", in *Political Geography*, 23 (2004), p. 30.
11. Tchantouridze, L. "Eurasia, Geopolitics, and American Foreign Policy," in *Central Asia and Caucasus*, No. 5, 2008.
12. Borisova, E., "The Evaluation of Mackinder's Ideas in Today's Realities," in *Central Asia and Caucasus*, No. 4, 2005.
13. Sengupta, A., "11 September 2001 and Central Asia (in light of discussion on the theory of the heartland)," in *Central Asia and Caucasus*, No. 4, 2005.
14. Morgenthau, H.J., *Politics Among Nations. The Struggle for Power and Peace* (NY: Alfred-A-Knopf, 1985), p. 219.
15. Trenin, D., "Russia and Central Asia. Interests, Policies, and Prospects", In Eugene Rumer, Dmitri Trenin, and Huasheng Zhao, eds., *Central Asia: Views from Washington, Moscow, and Beijing* (N.Y.: M.E. Sharpe, 2007), p. 80.
16. *Ibid.*, p. 130.
17. Rumer, E., "United States and Central Asia". In Eugene Rumer, Dmitri Trenin, and Huasheng Zhao, eds., *Central Asia: Views from Washington, Moscow, and Beijing* (N.Y.: M.E.Sharpe, 2007), p. 68.
18. Simon, Dalby, *Geopolitics after the Cold War: Rethinking the Theme of Empire*, p. 109.
19. "Problems of Security in Central Asia". Materials of the international conference held on 21–22 October, 2005 in Tashkent (Tashkent: "Turon-Iqbol" Press, 2006), p. 26.

3

Virtual Regionalism and Protective Integration in Central Asia

Roy Allison

The purpose of this paper is to examine how a form of regionalism in Central Asia which generally lacks deep, substantive commitments has come to play a growing *political* function both for Central Asian states and for Russia. The regionalism examined is that expressed in two large macro-regional groupings: the Collective Security Treaty Organisation (CSTO) and the Shanghai Cooperation Organisation (SCO). The cooperative projects of these organisations are mostly only partially and inconsistently implemented by Central Asian or Russia leaders. The multilateral output of these bodies has not added significantly to the complex of agreements which Central Asian states have reached on a bilateral basis with Russia, China or each other. The research question then is to determine why Central Asian leaders and Russia continue quite vocally to proclaim their interest in this kind of shallow regionalism.*

One explanation could be that Central Asian countries still have rather weak state capacities to fulfil well-intentioned international agreements. However, it is argued here that the gap between the formal objectives and limited output of these regional structures and the absence in practice of any deeper regionalist impulse behind them may be explained to a significant extent by the dominant political function they have for Central Asian states and Russia alike. This function is the consolidation of *regime security and legitimacy* and it has priority over other security, economic or trade goals. This kind

---

* This paper draws from and extends my previous analysis 'Virtual regionalism, regional structures and regime security in Central Asia', *Central Asian Survey*, Vol. 27, No. 2, June 2008, pp. 185–202.

of politically instrumental approach to regionalism means that it continues to be viewed positively by the Eurasian leaders concerned, even if the phenomenon represents 'virtual' rather than substantive regionalism.

The core argument developed in this article is that in greater or lesser degree the CSTO and SCO offer the role of '*protective integration*' – a form of collective political solidarity with Russia (as well as with China in the case of the SCO) against international political processes or agendas that since the 'coloured revolutions' during 2003-05 in Georgia, Ukraine and Kyrgyzstan have been interpreted explicitly as challenging incumbent regimes and their leaders. Yet Central Asian states still feel wary of excessive Russian influence.

Political bandwagoning on the international stage though the CSTO and SCO is consistent with an emphasis in domestic politics on the statist principle of 'constitutional order' and a strong emphasis on national sovereignty. Indeed the Central Asian states remain beset by rivalries that reflect their efforts to forge national identities and substantiate their sovereignty. The virtual regionalism that results reflects a contradiction between the interest of Central Asian leaders and Russia in regional collusion for purposes of political solidarity and the continuation of competitive dynamics between the local states.

'Protective Integration' and Virtual Regionalism

Commitment to the virtual regionalism of the CSTO and SCO, especially since the 'colour revolutions' of 2003–05 (in Georgia, Ukraine and Kyrgyzstan) reflects the function of protective integration.[1] Regional coordination, frequently cast in the grandiose language of regional integration creates a basis for political solidarity between state leaders and for their protection against or resistance to a perceived interventionist agenda of democracy-promotion by Western states, international organisations and donor agencies.

Protective integration is directed not just against rising political demands that could trigger off another colour revolution in Central Asia. Central Asian leaders and elites seek to rally in particular against part of the neo-liberal reform agenda, good governance – establishing institutions, ensuring accountability, transparency and democratic participation – which could undermine their dominance of the domestic political scene. In at least Kazakhstan and Kyrgyzstan the elites are prepared simultaneously to take advantage of the economic promise and financial benefits of market reforms. The priority here is that of regime consolidation and security – the secure control and maintenance in power of incumbent rulers and their political entourage.

Good governance is perceived as a challenge to the existing political order in Central Asia even if local leaders do not reject democratic principles per se. To greater or lesser extent they all retain the nominal existence of democratic institutions, including constitutions, human rights ombudsmen, government affiliated NGOs, as well as political parties and election. But in reality is these institutions exert little influence on major political decisions, especially foreign policy, which is kept under firm presidential control. These institutions of a 'virtual politics' crucially do not enable a transfer of power from incumbent rulers to opposition politicians. Nor do they assist the mediation of serious political conflict, as demonstrated by the chaotic overthrow President Askar Akayev in March 2005 after demonstrations over the results of Kyrgyzstan's parliamentary elections.

The focus of Central Asian rulers on regime security has stimulated political bandwagoning by their states (except Turkmenistan) in pan-regional structures with an increasingly authoritarian Russia during and beyond President Putin's second presidential term and with China. This political solidarity is not directly expressed in the official discourse as resistance to democratic principles or good governance; the rallying cry instead is resistance to the imposition or export into the region of 'external' or alien values. A putative struggle around values is the preferred battlefield by Central Asian regimes and this spectre of alien values forms part of an ideology of national sovereignty for popular consumption. It is accompanied in Central Asia by a call for Eurasian exceptionalism.

In brief, the CSTO and SCO, in an expression of protective integration, have rounded on efforts by others to impose external values on their member states. They have tended to use language that tends to assert the relativity rather than universality of human rights. Tellingly they also supported Uzbekistan's use of force in Andijan in 2005.

Since at least 2003 the mutual support system of these regional structures and the associated effort to bypass Western definitions of political legitimacy has relied increasingly on heavyweight Russian political backing. The entrenchment of authoritarian practices in Russia has reinforced political bonds with like-minded Central Asian rulers.[2] The Russian leadership has become transparent in accepting the full legitimacy of incumbent rulers in Central Asia and in presenting itself as a bulwark of regional regime security. Putin's eager display of three separate congratulations messages to Karimov for his re-election as president of Uzbekistan in December 2007 left no doubt about this.[3] Russia's former Chief of General Staff, Colonel-General Yuri Baluevsky went so far as to describe American efforts to promote its 'own version of democracy' within Central Asia as a security threat in itself.[4]

Russia has come to occupy a central position in a broad strategy of what can be termed 'authoritarian resistance' to democratization and to Western policies that encourage democratic tendencies, though of course Moscow does not cast it in these terms. This approach finds a ready reception in Central Asian capitals.[5] One element of this Russian strategy has been to encourage regional organisations to advance agendas which are effectively aimed to counter the diffusion of democracy or, as Moscow and Central Asian leaders in essence tend to view it, to counter externally-promoted efforts aimed at the subversion of constitutional order in sovereign states.[6] The Russian Foreign Ministry in its foreign policy review of 2007 called for the potential of the CSTO and SCO in Central Asia to be activated so that 'our neighbours should associate with Russia their future, the possibility of an evolutionary transformation without upheavals, and the prospects for stabilising their social and economic position'.[7]

The CSTO and SCO to be sure have real and reasonable security responsibilities within their mandates. But for some if not all member states these shade into expectations of general support for regime security and an attempt to bolster the international legitimacy of their governments and they have scant regard for the notion of human security favoured by UN agencies. The scope of cooperation in combating new transnational threats and extremism agreed at CSTO or SCO meetings of security services can easily be broadened to cover 'unconstitutional' activities by opposition groups, or these groups can be defined as linked to proscribed Islamist movements or just as terrorist-inspired. This can then be used domestically and internationally to justify rigorous centralized political control.

Central Asia and the Collective Security Treaty Organisation

The CSTO was launched in 2003 with the initial membership of Russia, Belarus, Armenia, Kazakhstan, Kyrgyzstan and Tajikistan. A political cooperation directorate of the CSTO was given the task of encouraging common foreign policy positions and coordinating the international activities of member states. But these bodies were not very active. It took until March 2007 for a draft resolution to be issued by the CSTO Foreign Minister's Council on improving foreign policy coordination.

The difficulty in developing common 'CSTO foreign policy thinking' reflected the wariness of the Central Asian member states of any Russian efforts to reign in their sovereignty. They could all agree on the desirability of some cooperation in the CSTO over counter-terrorism, but they probably harboured doubts about Moscow's capacity for effective and impartial counter-terrorist military intervention in Central Asia. It was also not clear if the benefit of CSTO membership of the supply of cheap Russian arms, amounted to much.[8] The core Central Asian state of Uzbekistan scorned the CSTO during 2003–05 and by remaining outside it left the organisation hollowed out in Central Asia.

The function of the CSTO for the Central Asian presidents appeared to change as the spectre of 'coloured revolutions' began to loom over Central Asian political elites. The CSTO began to be viewed as an instrument for enlisting Russian support for regime security. This provided Moscow with new political leverage. Russia has been well-positioned to develop discreet contacts with different secular political groupings in Central Asia. Knowledge of this could be part of bargaining between Moscow and Central Asian leaders, who have become interested in political support from their powerful northern neighbour in the event of power struggles in their states.

This also has, however, an explicit military dimension. Russian forces locally deployed in Central Asia, under the guise of CSTO mutual support and reinforced by bilateral agreements, could offer limited military assistance to shore up beleaguered local regimes. After President Akayev was ousted in 2005 the Russian Defence Minister Sergei Ivanov admitted that Russia had been prepared during the uprising unilaterally to airlift troops to Bishkek, supposedly to protect Russian citizens.[9] Russian and CSTO 'military assistance' could be blurred, especially during unrest in Russia's important new-found ally, Uzbekistan.

The forces at Russia's air base in Kant, Kyrgyzstan (which Moscow describes as a component of a CSTO rapid reaction force), could possibly be called upon in the event of a serious power struggle in Tashkent (or of course during further unrest in Bishkek). This could of course seriously backfire. But the treaty basis for a Russian military deployment to Uzbekistan, with Tashkent's approval, in the event of a national crisis, is also laid out in a far-reaching Russian-Uzbek bilateral treaty of November 2005, which was agreed after Russia's support for Karimov's military action in Andijan. The CSTO as a whole pointedly refrained from any criticism of Uzbekistan over Andijan and in mid-August 2006 Uzbekistan was admitted to the organisation. Tashkent has been cautious, however, to avoid the further step of consenting to even a small permanent Russian military presence on its territory under a supposed CSTO aegis.

The Russian leadership has to be aware from its previous military deployments (in Tajikistan, for example) of the risks of military intervention in various forms of political turmoil in Central Asian states, but Moscow seems to be pondering its options for future scenarios. CSTO Secretary-General Nikolai Bordyuzha emphasised in 2006 that the option of using military force in internal conflicts has not even been discussed in the CSTO at any level. Yet he specified that in this context 'the potential of the CSTO can be used only for the prevention of armed conflict, bloodshed and mass unrest on the part of warring political groups striving for power in this or that country' and that this is a 'political potential of the presidents heading CSTO countries'. This offers a justification for using the CSTO for sustaining Central Asian presidents when faced by political unrest of various kinds.[10]

In 2007 Bordyuzha reaffirmed that the CSTO 'was not established to deal with member states' domestic affairs or political processes', that 'we have never practiced operations to save this or that regime within the framework of the CSTO'. But it all depends here on the definition of *external* interference or aggression (a threat which the CSTO is charged to repel) since, Bordyuzha continued, 'if any external forces are reckless enough to try destabilizing the situation, then the CSTO should react to any such attempt'.[11] Of course a Russian-led CSTO military response in such a scenario is far from inevitable. Bordyuzha does not formally represent the Russian government and he may be trying to talk up the role and responsibilities of the organisation he heads to attract greater attention and resources to it.

We should also keep in mind that Central Asian leaders' interest in Russian support for regime security is double-edged. They would probably only welcome such Russian-led military intervention, as opposed to political or intelligence support, as a last resort, if their regime is in serious jeopardy, since they must be aware of the long-term effects of Russian military interventions in conflict situations in other CIS states – Tajikistan, Georgia and Moldova – including the lasting deployment of Russian troops. It may also be unrealistic for Central Asian leaders to expect that Moscow will actually and necessarily take their side in major political crises in their states, rather than balance more strategically between favoured local political candidates.

However, the option of CSTO 'mandated' Russian assistance during internal political challenges in Central Asia applies only to situations of crisis. In more normal conditions the CSTO has offered another important function, as we have suggested previously: the Central Asian presidents became ready to use it as a vehicle to bandwagon with Russia in developing a kind of Eurasian political club that only selectively promotes and applies Euro-Atlantic political principles and values (or openly resists them) in what is sometimes termed the 'zone of CSTO responsibilities'. This function of 'protective integration' is intended to bolster presidential political legitimacy on the international stage (when the OSCE, the EU and Western dominated international organisations raise questions about such legitimacy) and is an important explanation of the CSTO's attraction in Central Asia.[12]

This role of the CSTO does not mean that the organisation's military security functions are completely bogus. First, the various counter-terrorist exercises between CSTO member states offer some practical experience of joint operations against possible transnational terrorist acts. But in this context counter-terrorism is a fungible concept. A new CSTO Counter-Terrorism Committee is planned to counter not only terrorism *per se* but also 'fringe challenges and threats to national, regional and international security'.[13] It is likely that such challenges could encompass various forms of opposition and resistance that local leaders seek to control, as well as less politically controversial non-traditional security threats.

Secondly, the CSTO's function of collective security against external military incursions has gained some more credibility as the Taliban's reach in Afghanistan has extended since 2006. A CSTO Working Group on Afghanistan, which visited Kabul in March 2007, proposed regular contacts with Afghanistan's military, security and law-enforcement agencies and offered various forms of assistance.[14]

Practical tasks related to Afghanistan, including counter-narcotics, are likely to continue to coexist with the more political functions of the CSTO analyzed above.

Central Asia and the Shanghai Cooperation Organisation

It has been difficult for the Central Asian states to sway the proceedings of the SCO and they risk being caught up in wider geopolitical (primarily Russian) or geo-economic (Chinese) plans. China and Russia have sought to instrumentalize the SCO for their own purposes and to 'guide' Central Asian states, one Kazakh scholar has concluded.[15] Even so, the Central Asian states recognise the need for some kind of consultations forum with China. They seek certain practical benefits from the SCO in non-security fields, such as assistance with regional infrastructure projects that involve China, or in the case of Kazakhstan energy cooperation that allows access to the Chinese market.

The security policy profile of the SCO is in flux. Since 2001 in practice the Central Asian states have received much more practical assistance for countering regional security threats from bilateral security programmes, particularly from the US, than from the SCO.[16] Well-publicized SCO multilateral exercises for supposed anti-terrorist scenarios, such as the Peace Mission 2007 SCO exercise held in China and Russia, have provided spectacles, but have left little behind for the Central Asian states. SCO defence ministers met for the first time only in April 2006.

For Central Asian rulers this leaves a significant political function for the SCO, like the CSTO, of protective integration. The solidarity it offers provides symbolic political legitimacy and equality to Central Asian regimes that struggle to assert this on the broader international stage. Central Asian leaders have accepted the development of SCO principles which are effectively norms that differ to those currently promoted globally by the US and like-minded powers and in this sense the SCO acts to reinforce illiberal political tendencies in the region.

These SCO principles are rooted in the organisation's dedication already in 2001 to combat the 'three evils' of 'terrorism, separatism and extremism'. These 'evils' provide blanket coverage of undesirable challenges. They are left undefined in SCO documents, so SCO members essentially have been 'able to make their own decisions regarding which domestic crises should be attributed to which of the three evils', although some common understanding is developing over prohibited organisations on the territory of SCO members.[17] National discretion over the 'three evils' and the absence of any reference in the SCO Charter to democracy as a goal in domestic politics or to the self-determination of peoples encourages a permissive environment for SCO states to act as they wish against general forms of domestic political opposition and dissent to sustain regime security.[18]

Action against the political dimension of the 'three evils' is viewed mostly as a responsibility of national governments. But the SCO offers some help through its proposal 'to strengthen international information security' among SCO member states'[19] and through coordination forums under the SCO Council of the Heads of Government (including meetings of Heads of Law Enforcement Agencies, of General Public Prosecutors, of Minsters of Emergency Measures), as well as the well-publicized SCO Regional Anti-Terrorist Structure based in Tashkent.

This kind of active multilateralism by the SCO in Central Asia is limited by differing understandings by Central Asian states of religious extremism and how to respond to it, for example by Uzbekistan and Tajikistan. Yet the SCO carefully avoided any criticism of the Karimov government in 2005 in the aftermath of the Uzbek security crackdown in Andijan and emphasis was placed instead on future multilateral cooperation to enable the SCO to counteract terrorism and political extremism.[20] This expressed well the protective integration role of the SCO for Central Asian regimes and their forms of centralised political control.

The protective integration function of the SCO has been expressed in solidarity in resisting externally 'imposed' norms. The SCO summit in June 2006 affirmed that 'differences in cultural traditions, political and social systems, values and models of development...should not be taken as pretexts to interfere in other countries' internal affairs'.[21] This was a diplomatically phrased endorsement of President Karimov's blunt assertion at the summit that 'we have a common aim to counter resolutely external attempts to impose Western methods of democratisation and public development on our countries'.[22] At root, the SCO summit formulations are 'clearly designed to provide a basis for asserting the relativity rather than universality of standards for political, civic and individual human rights'.[23]

To the extent that the norms and values of the SCO are based on preserving the non-democratic status quo in the region, the organisation could be viewed as part of a 'strategy of authoritarian resistance to regional and global democratic trends'. One analyst of this phenomenon describes it as 'an attempt to socialise the states of Central Asia into an authoritarian "Shanghai Spirit".[24] It is notable also in this context that the proceedings of the SCO, like those of the CSTO, 'take place in an exclusively state-to-state mode, with minimal transparency and no significant means of democratic control'.

The Impact of the Russia-Georgia War on Virtual Regionalism in Central Asia

The politics of virtual regionalism, analyzed above, progressively developed during 2003-08. However, this phenomenon may now be challenged by the Russia-Georgia war in September 2008 and Russian recognition of South Ossetia and Abkhazia as separate states, which pose political challenges for all Eurasian states.

First, the Russian attack on Georgia was the first case of an interstate war between former Soviet states since the dissolution of the USSR and it suggested that the threshold for large-scale Russian military intervention in a CIS neighbour state had been lowered and the political inhibitions against such action had been removed. For Central Asian states this raised serious questions whether overly close relations with Russia posed new challenges to their sovereignty and whether the option of Russian intervention or assistance in domestic crises through regional structures, as analyzed previously, could take unwanted forms. At the same time Russian operations in Georgia could be viewed as a warning to all CIS states against seeking too close relations with NATO or bilaterally with the US at the expense of Russia-dominated structures like the CSTO and this raised the pressure for political conformity with Moscow among the Central Asian members of this organisation.

Secondly, Eurasian states have to come to terms with a basic challenge to the prevailing international order and concept of statehood in the post-Soviet region. The structure that symbolized the common heritage of the post-Soviet states, the Commonwealth of Independent States, was based on recognition of borders – of the former Union republics' borders as state borders. By recognising Abkhazia and South Ossetia Moscow overturned a basic international norm, that the only territories that merited recognition would be those corresponding to first-level administrative subdivisions of the old

Soviet state – the Union republics. These became the new post-Soviet states, whereas South Ossetia and Abkhazia formed lower-level subdivisions. All Central Asian states have been challenged by such redrawing of post-Soviet international borders, especially since the dominant regional power, Russia, has been driving the process and perhaps even expecting to acquire new territory as a result (as least South Ossetia, which may unite with North Ossetia).

Thirdly, in the aftermath of the Russian-Georgian war Central Asian leaders witnessed not only the ethno-territorial division of a CIS state, but the empowerment of separatism in Georgia. For many years the ethnically diverse Central Asian states have viewed separatism as a particular sub-state threat. They have routinely condemned separatism in their foreign policy statements, as well as in regional bodies including the CSTO and, alongside China, in the SCO. In varying degrees they all have their local secessionist concerns (China – Xinjiang and Tibet; Kazakhstan – ethnic Russians in the country's northern regions; Kyrgyzstan – the Uzbek community in the southern Ferghana Valley regions; Uzbekistan – the northern province of Karakalpakstan; Tajikistan – the southeast region of Badakhshan). The leaders of these states regard recognition of the separatist regions of South Ossetia and Abkhazia is as having direct implications for the ethno-territorial cohesion of their own states. Their refusal to recognise Kosovo reflected the same concern and they have argued that their position on South Ossetia and Abkhazia should be consistent with that decision on Kosovo.

A central issue is whether the political solidarity underlying the protective integration function of the macro-regional structures in Eurasia can be sustained after Russia's campaign in Georgia. The question is whether the common front in resisting ostensibly non-Eurasian 'external' values and agendas can be sustained if Moscow can not attract solidarity with its position on the highly divisive Russian-Georgian conflict, especially since Moscow has tried to force a binary choice on the issue – almost along the lines of the American response to the 9/11 attacks of 'you are with us or against us'.

The first test came with the SCO summit at the end of August 2008. In its final declaration this summit took a neutral stand over Moscow's military action in Georgia and urged 'the sides to solve existing problems peacefully, through dialogue, and to make efforts facilitating reconciliation and talks'. The presidents actually reaffirmed their commitment to 'efforts aimed at preserving the unity of a state and its territorial integrity' in a statement that could be applied to Georgia's struggle with its breakaways regions. It seems that China played a key role in blocking Russian efforts to gain an endorsement of its actions in Georgia in the SCO communiqué, for which President Medvedev explicitly appealed (he anticipated in his speech at the summit that 'the SCO member states' position will evoke the international reaction it deserves').[25]

The joint SCO declaration, however, still contained familiar code language that reflected the values agenda of protective integration, about 'the need to respect each country's and each nation's historical and cultural traditions' and mutual interaction 'in the fight against terrorism, separatism and extremism'. Kazakhstan's president went further than other Central Asian leaders in offering his personal support for Russian actions in Georgia, on the margins of the SCO summit (although his previous position on the issue had been equivocal and he also suggested that Kazakhstan could serve as a mediator in multilateral talks on settling the conflict).[26] In varying degrees during autumn 2008 the other Central Asian leaders also offered placatory forms of verbal support for Russia's military drive in Georgia after bilateral meetings with Russian leaders.

Yet this left the SCO as a body as unwilling to endorse Russia's position on the most significant political conflict between Russia and Western states since the end of the USSR, let alone to recognise Abkhazia and South Ossetia. Inevitably this weakens the international political cohesion of the SCO and sense of common purpose in foreign policy. It also seems to eliminate even the theoretical option of the SCO sponsoring some form of intervention to maintain the political status quo in a crisis in a CIS Central Asian state. After Russia's violent campaign to 'coerce Georgia to peace', in support of a secessionist region and in open violation of the sovereignty of a post-Soviet state, both China and Central Asian states are necessarily more wary about Russian objectives in conflict management in Eurasia.

Given this SCO response it has been all the more important for Russia to garner political support over the Georgia crisis from the CSTO, where Chinese influence is not available to offset Russian lobbying of and pressure on smaller Central Asian states. A meeting of CSTO foreign ministers in September 2008 did indeed condemn the Georgian government's 'aggression' and approved Russia's 'peacekeeping efforts' in the campaign in Georgia. But significantly it failed to mention recognition of the independence of Georgia's secessionist territories.[27] Russian Foreign Minister Lavrov put the best face on it and praised the extent of political solidarity offered, noting that the CSTO ministers had agreed 'in a coordinated way on the basis of this declaration to act in international organisations where this theme [of Georgian action against South Ossetia] may one way or another be touched upon'. He also emphasised that a plan of consultations on foreign policy, security and defence issues had been endorsed by the CSTO ministers.[28] This shows that Moscow hopes that the CSTO can act as the locus of foreign policy solidarity with Central Asian partners.

The rhetorical endorsement Russian received from the CSTO, however, only papered over the striking fact that the CSTO had played no role at all in the active phase of the Georgia crisis. The CSTO was neither used for consultations nor even engaged as some kind of cover for Russian operations in Georgia even though previous CSTO documents refer loosely to the 'CSTO zone of responsibility', had defined the Caucasus as a CSTO 'collective security region', and had undertaken to establish CSTO peacekeepers. It was only after the conflict with Georgia that an offer was made for 'CSTO representatives' to join a mission of OSCE military observers to monitor the conflict zone in Georgia.[29]

All this may not be surprising, since the other CSTO member states would be far from willing to take part in a significant military intervention in another CIS state (and outside their region, for Central Asian states) just at Russia's behest and Russia would not risk any constraint on its military plans from CSTO partners. Nevertheless, the extremity and scale of Russia's intervention in Georgia must now also raise serious questions for Central Asian states about any ideas for engaging Russian assistance via the CSTO in the event of domestic political challenges or local insurgencies.[30] Since the Russia-Georgia war Russia has proposed that its Interior Ministry's special-purpose units become part of the planned CSTO rapid reaction forces. The force of some 150 Russian officers on offer would be drawn from anti-riot police units. This indicates that the operational planning for CSTO forces could extend to subduing political demonstrations.[31] But one question for other CSTO states is whether such Russian involvement could act as the tripwire for a wider, more open-ended intervention.

Even in the event of being subjected to a more traditional direct attack or the threat of such attack, the protocol on military assistance to member states of the CSTO carefully defines the assistance to 'free or preferential deliveries of military products for the combat ability of CSTO member states' and does not presume any other automatic Russian combat support.[32] This reflects the Central Asian leaders' fixation on sovereignty.

For Central Asian states the benefits of political solidarity with Russia through regional structures to shore up domestic regime security now need to be weighed against the risks of overly close association with an interventionist-minded Russian leadership that even proclaimed in September 2008 that 'there are regions in which Russia has privileged interests', regions that 'are home to countries with which we share special historical relations'.[33] This arrogation of special interests in post-Soviet Eurasian states is similar to pronouncements by Russian leaders earlier in the 1990s, but by 2008 would be roundly rejected not only by unambiguously Western-leaning states such as Ukraine, but also by also by Central Asian states that strongly defend their sovereign decision-making authority, such as Uzbekistan.

Indeed in December 2008 the CSTO secretary-general felt the need to repudiate rumours that Uzbekistan would withdraw from the CSTO and denied claims that Tashkent had scaled down its activities in this regional structure.[34] Nonetheless, following Uzbekistan's withdrawal from the Eurasian Economic Community (EAEC) (see below) this could well be the next step and would seriously weaken the CSTO. Meanwhile, Russia is defensively seeking to shore up fractures in the CSTO and allay doubts over its protective integration function, through the decision to set up a new Terrorism and Extremism Resistance Coordination Centre under the CSTO,[35] through promoting a meeting for the first time of ministers of the interior and heads of police agencies of the CSTO member states,[36] and through convening a meeting of foreign ministers in February 2009 specially to 'boost solidarity within the CSTO'.[37]

This effort to pull the ranks in line politically under the CSTO, however, came after the news in November 2008 that Uzbekistan had 'suspended' – in effect withdrawn – its membership of the EAEC (the EAEC charter specifies provisions for withdrawal but not for suspension). Karimov claimed that the EAEC does not take into account vital interests of each member state.[38] His decision came shortly after the European Union withdrew sanctions that had previously been imposed on Uzbekistan after the Andijan events. It also happened against the background of rumours that the US might regain access to military facilities in Uzbekistan. This suggests that,

Uzbekistan's interest in the benefits of protective integration, if this means rallying behind high intensity Russian military interventions, is waning and that it may be positioning itself again to manoeuvre bilaterally between Russia and Western states. In this scenario Tashkent would not wish to be constrained by the CSTO to the extent that it can not explore the possible restoration of ties with NATO.[39]

Given Chinese determination that the SCO should not take sides over the 2008 Georgia crisis this indicates that serious fractures have opened in the common political front that has supported the system of virtual regionalism in Central Asia. The Russian-Georgian war and Russian recognition of secessionist regions has alarmed other Eurasian states and overshadowed their receding concerns about the challenges of coloured revolutions or the Western promoted agenda of governance. Russia has received rhetorical support for its claims of Georgian 'aggression' in bilateral discussions with Central Asian states. But this is essentially the lip service that is the price for maintaining cordial relations with Moscow. It will now be more difficult for Russia to instrumentalize multilateral regional structures to build political coalitions against the spread of Western policies or norms. At the same time the Central Asian states' own fixation on sovereignty is likely once again to lead them to develop strategies – balancing as well as traditional bandwagoning – to offset the proximity and unpredictability of Russian power.

Conclusion

The leaders of Central Asian states (except Turkmenistan) have stressed the importance and relevance of the macro-regional structures of the CSTO and SCO, despite their modest security or economic policy results (and their tendency to repackage previous bilateral agreements), since these organisations have played a significant political role for Central Asian regimes. This role of 'protective integration' is short on real integration. It provides some regional coordination, but crucially it has offered the benefits of political solidarity, especially in the aftermath of the 2003-05 'colour revolutions', and a vicarious legitimacy to Central Asian political leaders who find difficulty in establishing this on the wider international stage. They seek to deflect appeals for good governance and substantive democracy in their domestic arrangements through a common front against the diffusion of 'external' values in Central Asia.

For Central Asian rulers the core objective of such coordination through the CSTO and SCO has been to reinforce regime security. For this it has been perceived as essential to participate alongside Russia, which conveniently for Central Asia leaders has presented itself since 2004 increasingly as a bastion of defence against the 'export' of values or political principles by outsiders into the CIS 'space'. China also supports this position in the SCO. Such close engagement with Russia has also potentially facilitated the containment of tensions within Central Asia between the local states, as well as the management of their relations with China.

However, this political landscape has been shaken by the Russian-Georgian conflict in 2008 and Russia's open support for sub-state secessionism in Georgia at the expense of Georgian territorial integrity. Russian collusion with and instigation of the break-up of a CIS state and apparent interest for a time in September 2008 in overthrowing the incumbent Georgian president projects Russia in an altogether different light to its Central Asian partners and is also unsettling for China.

After Russian action in Georgia it will be difficult for Russia and Central Asian states to coalesce politically around the SCO as before 2008. They may continue to share a determination to resist 'external' agendas on governance or the democratic process, but Central Asian leaders are now more wary about Russia's commitment to territorial integrity, will look askance at Russian promises to protect its citizens abroad and will feel more defensive about Russian great power 'responsibilities' in Eurasia. This is also likely to undermine the sense of common political and foreign policy purpose in the CSTO, even if member states (with the possible exception of Uzbekistan) will retain their formal involvement with this structure as a means to bandwagon with and placate Moscow. Overall, virtual regionalism will remain a phenomenon in Eurasia, but its political purpose will be more diffuse and the substance of foreign policy in the region will continue to be determined by the evolution of bilateral relationships.

NOTES AND REFERENCES

1. A term proposed by Alexander Libman, *see* 'Regionalisation and Regionalism in the Post-Soviet Space: Current Status and Implications

for Institutional Development', *Europe-Asia Studies*, 58, 3 (May 2007), 401–415.

2. There is a growing literature on the extent and nature of this new Russian authoritarianism. For a succinct interpretation of the Russian system as one of 'patrimonial authoritarianism', *see* Celeste A. Wallander, 'Russian Transimperialism and its Implications', *The Washington Quarterly*, 30, 2 (Spring 2007), 115–117.
3. BBC Summary of World Broadcasts. Former Soviet Union, available from http://www.bbc.monitoringonline.com (henceforth BBC), Mon CAU 190108 nu/oh.
4. Jamestown Foundation, *Eurasia Daily Monitor*, available from http://www.eurasia.org, 3 October 2007, Vol. 4, Issue 183.
5. This claim is well analyzed in Thomas Ambrosio, 'Insulating Russia from a Colour Revolution: how the Kremlin Resists Regional Democratic Trends', *Democratization*, 14, 2 (April 2007), 232–252.
6. Ambrosio, *ibid.* p. 249, in his conclusion, encourages research on the question 'whether Russia has sought to influence regional and global organisations to advance its anti-democratic agenda' – an issue not covered in his article.
7. *Survey of Russian Federation Foreign Policy*, Russian Foreign Ministry, p. 27, available from http://www.mid.ru/brp_4.nsf/e78a48070fl28a7b43256999005bcbb3/89a30b3a6b65b4.
8. Russia offers weapons and military hardware to the armed forces and special services of CSTO member states at 'domestic' prices – the prices they are purchased by the Russian Ministry of Defence from the Russian Defence Export monopoly Rosoboronexport. But this subsidy may not amount to much of benefit since there is evidence that 'domestic' and export prices are similar; Jamestown Foundation, *Eurasia Daily Monitor*, Vol. 4, Issue 187, 10 October 2007.
9. Interview in *Profil*, 22 June 2005, 13–19.
10. Interview of Bordyuzha in *Nezavisimaya Gazeta*, 13 January 2006, p. 9. It has also been claimed that at the time of the Astana SCO in July 2005 summit Russia aired a proposal to prevent regime change in Central Asian countries through some 'mechanism of mutual assistance', legitimised by the SCO, that would provide Moscow with permission to carry out special operations in Central Asian states, as 'requested' by their regimes. Sergei Strokan, *Kommersant*, 5 July 2005, p. 9.
11. Interview in *Novie Izvestiya*, 11 September 2007, p. 4.
12. This process of political bonding is a probable function, for example, of the CSTO Parliamentary Assembly, which had its inaugural session in St Petersburg in March 2007. More specific measures are likely to be considered at the six monthly meetings of the Committee of Secretaries

of the Security Councils of the CSTO. A meeting of the latter in September 2007 discussed 'development trends in the military and political situation in the area of CSTO operations and measures on countering emerging challenges and threats'; Kyrgyz Television 1, Bishkek, 21 September 2007, BBC Mon CAU 220907 ad/nj.

13. Vyacheslav Volokh, Chief of the Directorate of Threats and Challenges of the Secretariat of the CSTO, in *Nezavisimoe Voennoe Obozrenie*, 31, 14-20 September 2007, p. 1.
14. Jamestown Foundation, *Eurasia Daily Monitor*, 16 March 2007.
15. Murat Laumulin, 'The Shanghai Cooperation Organization as 'geopolitical bluff?'. A view from Astana', in Thomas Gomart and Tatiana Kastueva-Jean, eds, *Russsie.Nei.Visions 2007*, IFRI, Paris, 2007, pp. 166–174, 178–180.
16. Kyrgyzstan, which has Russian (Kant) and American (Manas) air bases on its territory has suggested that a SCO logistics centre should be established in Kyrgyzstan's south for the use of SCO emergency ministries. This can be interpreted as a way to engage China in a low profile way, without duplicating security assistance programmes from other quarters. Kyrgyz Television 1, 20 September 2007, BBC Mon CAU 210907 ad/nj.
17. As noted by the Russian commentator Sergei Strokan in assessing the 2005 Astana SCO summit, *Kommersant*, 5 July 2005, p. 9. Efforts have been made in the SCO Regional Anti-Terrorist Structure since 2006 to agree on a list of organisations prohibited on the territory of SCO member states. An incomplete list exists of 'international religious extremist organizations banned in SCO states'; Meeting of SCO member states in Bishkek, AKIpress news agency website, Bishkek, 24 July 2007, BBC Mon CAU 240707 ta/atd.
18. The argument that the SCO is mainly an internally focused framework aimed at addressing non-traditional security challenges and built on the concept of regime security is developed in Stephen Aris, 'Tackling the "three evils": Shanghai Cooperation Organisation (SCO) – A Regional Response to Non-traditional Transnational Security Challenges in Central Asia', *Europe-Asia Studies*, forthcoming.
19. Communique of the 2007 Bishkek SCO summit; 24.kg website, Bishkek, 16 August 2007, BBC Mon CAU AS1 AsPol sa/mk/atd.
20. 'Shanghai group considers post-Andijan security in Central Asia', Jamestown Foundation, *Eurasia Daily Monitor*, Vol. 2, Issue 110, 7 June 2005.
21. Unpublished communiqué of the 2006 Shanghai SCO Summit, 15 June 2006; and *Nezavisimaya Gazeta*, 16 June 2006, pp. 1, 6.

22. Jamestown Foundation, *Eurasia Daily Monitor*, Vol. 3, Issue 118, 19 June 2006.
23. Alyson Bailes, Pal Dunay, Pan Guang and Mikhail Troitskiy, *The Shanghai Cooperation Organisation*, SIPRI Policy Paper No. 17, Stockholm International Peace Research Institute, May 2007, pp. 6–8.
24. Thomas Ambrosio, 'Catching the "Shanghai Spirit": how the Shanghai Cooperation Organization Promotes Authoritarian Norms in Central Asia', *Europe-Asia Studies*, 60, No. 8 (October 2008), 1341. Ambrosio shows here how the SCO as a regional organisation supports the trend of authoritarian resistance to democratic norms that he analyzed in Ambrosio, 'Insulating Russia from a Colour Revolution', 2007 (note 5).
25. Text of joint SCO declaration, Tajik president's website, Dushanbe, 28 August 2008, BBC Mon CAU 280808 nu/fm/abm/mk. Medvedev's speech at SCO summit, 28 August 2008, http://www.mid.ru.
26. Report by RIA news agency, Moscow, 28 August 2008, BBC Mon Alert CAU 280808 abm/akh. See Interfax news agency, 3 September 2008, BBC Mon Alert CAU 030908 sa/sg for the offer of Kazakhstan's good offices.
27. Statement of CSTO foreign ministers, 4 September 2008, available from http://www.mid.ru.
28. Russian Foreign Minister Sergive Lavrov at press conference, 4 September 2008, http://www.mid.ru.
29. Interfax-AVN news agency website, Moscow, 27 August 2008, BBC Mon FS1 FsuPol iu.
30. The example of Russian 'peacekeeping' in Georgia also places in doubt plans to develop CSTO Collective Peacekeeping Forces, although Russian CSTO officials have anticipated that such forces could be used in peacekeeping operations from the second half of 2010. *See* CSTO Deputy Secretary-General Valeriy Semerikov, *Krasnaya zvezda*, 20 November 2008.
31. Jamestown Foundation, *Eurasia Daily Monitor*, Vol. 6, Issue 76, 21 April 2009.
32. As specified by the Kazakh law that ratified this protocol in December 2008. *See* Interfax-AVN military news agency, Moscow, 15 December 2008, BBC Mon CAU 151208 mi.
33. See speech to and meeting with members of the Valdai Club, 12 September 2008, available from http://kremlin.ru/eng/text/speeches/2008/09/12/1644, interview for TV Channel One, Rossia, NTV, 31 August 2008, available from http://www.kremlin.ru/eng/text/speeches/2008/0831/1150, statement on 8 August 2008, http://www.mid.ru.
34. See report in Interfax-Kazakhstan news agency, Almaty, 17 December 2008, BBC Mon Alert CAU 171208 nu/dia; Itar-Tass news agency, Moscow, 18 December 2008, BBC Mon Alert CAU 181208 sa/dia.

35. Decision at December 2009 meeting of Security Council secretaries of CSTO member states. See Arminfo, Yerevan, 10 December 2009, BBC Mon TCU 101208 ra/ah.
36. Meeting in Yerevan on 15 April 2009, Armenian news agency Arminfo, in Russian, 15 April 2008, BBC Mon TCU 150409 ca.ah.
37. Statement by CSTO Secretary-General Nikolay Bordyuzha, Interfax news agency, Moscow, 18 December 2008, BBC Mon FS1 MCU 181208 hb/ym.
38. Kazakhstan Today news agency website, Almaty, 14 November 2008, BBC mon CAU 141108 bma/ad. For an interpretation of this decision by a former senior Russian foreign ministry specialist on Central Asia see Sergei Rasov, 'Islam Karimov's demarche', Politkom.ru website, Moscow, 13 November 2008, BBC Mon CAU 151108 nu/osc.
39. For a discussion of this topic, based on interviews in Tashkent, see Roy Allison, *Security Cooperation between Western States and Russia over Central Asia/Afghanistan: The Changing Role of Uzbekistan*, Programme Paper, Chatham House, 24 November 2008, available from www.chathamhouse.org.uk/files/12767_241108_rep_allison.pdf.

4

Eurasian Doctrine of Kazakhstan: Historical, Social and Political Parametres

Sattar F. Mazhitov

Globalization is one of the leading tendencies of development of world community and influences not only economic and political processes but also interrelations in the cultural sphere. The objectives of the states were oriented towards something new, to the globalization process and relations even as tried to preserve their specific traditional valuable orientations.

It is known that Eurasianists were the first who engaged in the realistic study of those interlinks that existed between geographical conditions of people and nations and their cultures. "Eurasianism in distinction to western European and mostly Russian historians was oriented towards re-interpretation of natural historical regularities of life of people and states and it is necessary to point out that it has achieved impressive success in this direction. (It is necessary to mention, for example, the conception of specific geographical myths of P.N. Savitsky). From here takes the roots the idea of existing Russia – Eurasia as specific historical-cultural region, equally dissimilar to Western Europe, Near East or China. That is why, the idea Russian – Eurasia gives fully authentic moral coordination – the idea of brotherhood and natural historical closeness among all different Eurasian nations".[1]

The establishment of the Republic of Kazakhstan as sovereign state and formation of its foreign policy coincided with cardinal changes of the world geopolitical situation: the collapse of the USSR and emergence of new states in the post Soviet space, affected by economic collapse, social problems, political instability; end of bipolar world order, birth of "unipolar moment" and US aspiration to establish unipolarity as the ground for forming new world order in the absence of serious competition.

The absence of any practical experience of creating independent states, economic downfall, unclear foreign policy directions, ready availability of nuclear weapons were the objective reasons for the doubt that was created among Great Powers regarding the future of our state. At the same time, western experts considered Central Asia as a region of conflicts that might affect Eurasia's geopolitical space.

President Nursultan Nazarbayev characterized the situation of the first days of independence in the following words: "History has shaped in such way that Kazakhstan became the epicenter of world policy during the collapse of the bipolar world. Supra states were replaced by new states and there was lot of interest in our country. By twist of fate this attention was connected to a large part of the nuclear potential of the former USSR which was located on the territory of our country. Ignorance of our reality formed a negative image of Kazakhstan as if it was an Islamic state having nuclear weapons and threatened the world community. This negative image disturbs not only us but our future partners".[2]

In this situation it was extremely important to demonstrate our principal commitment to the world community, to show Kazakhstan as the state aspiring to establish its relations with other states on the basic of equality, pragmatic constructivism and observance of all standards of the international law by practical actions.

On the territory where Europe meets Asia and further east, the people are influenced by modern ideas for almost three centuries of the past millennium. The objectives may have been serious but the fate of the population often determined the survival of the ethnos. When energy and inner resources ran out, there began a period of so-called prosperity of the nation, which in actual fact meant depression and economic stagnation. When the time came to realize that, destructive results were already taking place and a new generation of leaders thinkers started thinking about the next stage of mobilization. Another irritant was the western model of transition. Such are the paradoxes of historical cycles in Eurasia.

The sources of Eurasianism, according to "the special world perception" of N. Trubetskoy, lie in the steppe subcontinental zone from Hungarian Valley up to the Manchurian Plateau in China. The uniqueness of its location was determined by the nomadic character of the Great Mongolian uluses – empires which united the representatives of Finno-Ugric, Slavonic, Turkic, Mongolian, Iranian, Caucasian and other nations. Moreover the tolerance ensured pure pragmatic interest of preservation of political control and stability as well as loyalty to the khanates.

Asian spaces, especially nomadic zones represented a certain arbitrariness in life style, changed borders of habitation and even attempts to introduce new religions. The replacement of technological equipment of the traditional society and their neutralization as active historical-cultural phenomena was carried out intentionally. Moreover it was carried out by clumsy methods and sincere men of faith often imparted their lessons of education through crude methods like punishment of their disciples or exiling them through military tribunals. In Kazakh history it can be followed from the initially ecstatic perception of the Russian presence ("Russian science, culture is the key to the world treasure", according to Abai) including the folk legend-mournings during the period of forced collectivization. On the other hand, subcontinental space was intrinsic to Eurasianist debates – to simplify this, one can say that there was a game between two local civilian groups: one professing that Europeans must become a little more like Asians while Asians must acquire European gloss and on this basis there should be some analysis of the new world perception. After the First World War which proved that the ideals of Christianity haven't prevailed in Europe and instead there have been common egoistic interests, such formulation of a problem hardly could cause more than pure conceptual interest.

Philosophers like N.S. Trubetskoy, P.P. Suvchinskiy, G.V. Florovskiy and P.N. Savitskiy presented abstract theories in Sofia in 1921 in the midst of Bolshevik action. The Eastern Question was dealt with by the Russian intelligentsia and was followed by a call for revision of homeland history. At the same time "the right of the nation for self-determination, including separation" was proposed as the priority of the national policy of the new regime. The Turkic-Islamic extremity of Eurasia, from Bosporus up to China, due to this Eastern challenge, received impetus and the alternative paradigm Usul-i-Dzhadid obtained legitimacy and initiated competitiveness among colonial nations that aspired to respond to the new situation. What was being addressed was the very important question of getting power for itself, and considering the Turkic-Moslem nationalism was a derivative of European bourgeois values and Asian specificity. The influence of socialist doctrine and the ideals of national-communism were considered. In the same way, there was an isolationistic doctrine of totalitarianism, which more purposefully moved towards independent statehood without any desire to dominate over the world.

As is well known, the power that won was not stable enough. Artificially supported, the Soviet empire had enemies within and outside. Modernization was forcibly imposed and left its indelible mark on the national perceptions. During the Soviet period, the main thrust was on ethnic majorities and the ideal of Messianism had unequal results. For the eastern republics this period coincided with active stage of national consolidation, accompanied with elimination of traditional life style, nomadic education of bearers of ethnic culture and revolutionary reforms in the national economy. As a result, the soviet man was an amorphous creature with powerful gravitation to state paternalism with a remote understanding about Eurasianism that represents the synthesis of Western and Eastern philosophies.

A new type of Eurasianism emerged in the 21st century that opposed the polycentric world of Messianism of Empires and ideologies of the selected few. The President of Kazakhstan N. Nazarbayev said: "Recognition of the formed institutions of different states" gives the right to irreversible decision of questions of reintegration on the principally new basis of mutual coexistence. In space-time dimension it is widely correlated not with Mongolian ulus, but with land routes of the countries-satellites of the Great Silk Route, not with chronology and cartography of military campaigns, but with cross-cultural mutual enrichment and cultivation of common world civil values. However, geo-economic situation of the subcontinent are dictating its own conditions through networks of information, communication and hydrocarbon pipelines that leads to the globalization of economic styles, ethnic affiliations as the ground for the variety of peace, inevitably preserving its competitive functions of social control, cultural self-expression, mode of life and use of resources. In the given context the ways to end discrimination between advanced and developing nations must be searched for, taking into consideration the values of technical progress and nationalism.

For Kazakhstan and Russia located at the mid point of this Eurasian landmass, the task will be difficult due to the historically formed polyethnic structure of the society. Russia because of its wide space was the homeland of many European people with diverse identities.

Kazakhstan also a Eurasian nation, gravitated towards eastern parts of Eurasia and comprised of multiethnic groups. However, in comparison to Russia and China, ethnic groups here lived peacefully preserving the collective right to develop their vernacular language, traditional values and styles of life. Moreover, in the Soviet period the Kazakh homeland became "the laboratory of friendship of people" and was the polygon not only for nuclear and chemical weapons of mass destruction but also for experiments about the ideal Soviet man. The result of this was that autochthons lost their nomadic traits of controlling their economy and their pastures. They were the sole survivors of a Turkic nomadic culture. Thus, Kazakhstan was always represented as the most "soviet" in comparison to all other Soviet republics and the last generation of communist leaders was extremely surprised to see the Kazakhs in the line of defence vis-à-vis the great powers as early as the mid 80's when the fashionable national fronts were yet to emerge. The Central Committee Resolution of the CPSU made cryptic remarks about Kazakh nationalism and emphasized the growing importance of the ethnic issue indicating the insignificance of the concept of the most favoured titular nationality which was nothing but fiction.

In the Eurasian space, for the population that experienced a totalitarian regime, this inculcation of pluralism and democracy has the chance of success if there is synchronization between tolerance and respect of others' interests. In the recent past, ethnicities of large and small nations have faced uncertainty due to the imbalance in ideological and political determination and natural identity that is based on culture, history and statehood. Transformation processes are often accompanied by xenophobic mood that can be controlled only by powerful state policy of the independent countries and the interaction across ethnic borders inculcating the ideal of economic freedom of the population and also encouraging identification at a multidimensional level.

Abai introduced the Kazakh philosophical concept "tolyk adam" that means a morally perfect person. He envisaged not the cult of race power, but the need for self-criticism as the basis for development. The given postulate had the same meaning as the oldest Persian legend about Emperor Dzhamshid who was exhausted by flattery and tall praises and obtained realistic information about his actions and affairs of neighbours. Common sense always seeks variants of decision in history and biography of the previous generations. Drawing the contours of a new Eurasianism as the high demand of the time, we must also pay attention to the past and prevent ourselves from unconditional optimism, as well as from radical prognoses.

By the dictates of fortune Kazakhstan is located between Europe and Asia, not geographically but more demographically and culturally. Thus, it is the European country, a part of European civilization by its status. It is necessary to mark here that there is a border between the largest world religions – Islam and Christianity on the Eurasian space, which represents religious beliefs of two super ethnoses: Turanic and Slavonic. At first sight it can be seen that the natural way of development of the contemporary Kazakhstan may be its entry into Turkic-Islamic world, which is connected by several hundred years of community of national roots, languages, traditions and customs. However, in distinction to our eastern neighbours, pure Islamic culture is hardly dominant in Kazakhstan. In ancient times in the steppes of Kazakhstan were professed and peacefully coexisted various religions among which were the ancient Christianity, Buddhism, Zoroastrianism, Manicheism and tengrism side by side with Islam. At that time there was always a dialogue of religions and faiths. Today favourable conditions for regulating a dialogue for achieving national and civil consolidation, maintaining a stable and dynamic economic development, advancement of ideals of democracy and civil society, stability, security and independence of the young states are promoted in the context of world development. Such are the historical, social-political parameters of the Eurasian doctrine of Kazakhstan. The important regulations are positive process of interconfessional dialogue, spiritual harmony in the Republic of Kazakhstan, constituting a new public consciousness about Eurasianism.

The idea of Eurasianism, combines the ideas of the West and the East and at the same time doesn't contradict them. On the contrary, it allows synthesis of the two ideas that aim at achieving national unity. It is implied that there has to be an interactive process. In other words, for full scale reform of the nation there has to be individual spiritual and moral development and one should not isolate oneself from the world but make real actions that would transform life.

NOTES AND REFERENCES

1. Eredzhen Hara Dawan, *Chinghiz-khan as the commander in chief and his legacy*, Alma-Ata, 1992, pp. 7–8.
2. N.A. Nazarbayev, *On the eve of the XXI century*, Almaty, 1996, p. 205.

5

Central Asia, Siberia and Asian Russia: Theoretical Approaches and Methodological Reappraisals of Connotations and Terminology

Evgeny Vodichev

For a long time, studies about historical development of the Russian Empire and the Soviet Union has been connected with the growing role of Asia in Russian state policy. The country was looking for new lands in Asia, on the east, firstly on the Urals, and then in Siberia and Far East, as well as on the south – by those territories which in the post Soviet period are represented by independent Central Asian republics. According to the conceptual approach widespread in Russian historiography, "a contribution of Asian Russia to the development of the Russian state has been enormous and multi-dimensional, as enormous and diverse were risks connected with penetration of Russia into Asia, into its new, not fully colonized geopolitical and civilization dimension. Even counting of gains and losses, achievements and prices paid for these achievements makes considering Asian Russia not as "a fragment" or "random appendage" of the Russian state but as an important basis and reserve for its development"[1].

Territorial expansion into Asia was the result of objective factors explained by the strategy of creating a continental empire. However, this created a historical paradox. In many cases, though the Russian state was attempting to position itself as a European power, the economic and geopolitical justification for its place on the world political stage came from the east, from Asia. It was due to the fact that, for all its peculiar characteristics, since the beginning of the 18th century the Russian Empire was attempting to use, albeit in "prepared" form, European scenarios of the social and economic modernization[2]. Of course, the territorial growth of the Empire was driven by a complex combination of different factors and not just by the economy alone. However, the modernization of the country which involved increasingly rapid industrial growth, the urbanization and bureaucratisation of society, required a constantly expanding resource base. The country possessed such resources on a seemingly unlimited scale on the east, and partially on the south. Moreover, due to the specifics of colonization of the new territories, the Asian regions were burdened by the traditional forms of Russian economy, which hindered the processes of modernization in Central Russia.

According to the prevalent concept, relations between European and Asian parts of the country were defined as "the home country – colony" relations. It should be mentioned, however, that there is no unanimity of views about the "colonial" character of economic and political development of Siberia. The question of "What is colony?" in its Siberian context is still disputed. The "colonial" character of Siberia's development was popular in the past and is getting popularity again among Siberian intellectuals, although it always provoked furious reaction among state administrators. The ideas of the Siberian regionalists ("oblastniki") indicate such a reaction since the major book of the key Siberian regional leaders, N.M. Yadrintsev, under the symbolic title "Siberia as a Colony" has recently been re-published by the academic Institute of History in Novosibirsk.[3] The obvious reason for such a reaction is seemingly an assumption that once colonies should separate from their home countries, it means a perspective of separatism connected with Siberia.

Obviously, practical implementation of the "colonial" strategies caused many systematic problems in the country as a whole, as well as in its Asian regions in particular. These territories initially aroused a lot of interest as they possessed enormous resources and had immense geopolitical potential. The resources were developed selectively, depending on the military and strategic factors and their economic relevance to the development of the state.

In its basic components, this strategy was largely passed on to the Soviet period in Russian history. As in the previous centuries, a shift in the development of industry from the centre of Russia to the eastern regions was dictated by modernization. Both for Russia as heart of the Russian Empire, and for Russia as the major component of the Soviet Union the 20th century was a period of search for the optimal model of modernization. Russia achieved clear successes on the way to the capitalist modernisation by the end of the 19th – beginning of 20th centuries, which, however remained far from complete. As a result, after the Bolshevik revolution the new regime faced similar challenges of economic and social transformation into an industrial society.

Methods and mechanisms were tried to promote modernization in the Asian regions of Russia. In the Soviet period, the country maintained the 19th century model of modernisation, and adopted the "colonial" approach in its relations with the Asian regions. However, after the end of World War II Russia faced the challenges of the post-industrial era. In principle, it raised the issue of development priorities in the regional and centralized sectors of development. Within the new paradigm the centralized state relevance without regional relevance could not have remained the dominant factor of the state development.

In practice no serious changes were made, and the opportunity to replace the semicolonial vector of development for the eastern regions with a policy of balanced and comprehensive growth was lost. During the second half of the 20th century up to the collapse of the USSR in 1991, economic development was subject to geopolitical aims and the plans to shift industrial production to the east was entirely subservient to the concept of the "region for the country". The decision to compensate a shortage of resources for the industrial enterprises located in the western part of the Soviet Union by the resources from the east became a practical option. The external challenges such as strategic competition with China that finally resulted in serious complication of the political situation in the east should also be taken into consideration. As a result, in spite of substantial quantitative changes in the economic, demographic and technological sectors, there was not too much impact on the socio-economic and cultural sectors in the eastern regions of the USSR and the country in large. Although some modifications took place, the situation remained the same until the collapse of the USSR in 1991.

These are some basic features about development in the east of Russia. Formally regarded as a modernization programme in its Marxist version which is the basis of historical studies on the eastern regions of Russia. It has been so in the Soviet period, and the format has not been substantially revised Russian historiography till now. This approach can be interpreted as the "state approach" based on the economic determinism model which is adopted while analyzing and assessing the historical processes and their outcomes. It also rationalizes the centre – periphery model whereby the "centre" (state and the upper levels of administration) is considered as initiator and major driver of the development process, while regions are just mediators of strategies designed by the "centre" and they are to implement them. The economic rationale of the centre is considered a basis for such strategies, as well as the key criterion for assessing their effectiveness. The "region for the country as a whole" and not a "region for itself" approach has always been considered as a correct and justified one, as the regional option was seen as provoking separatism.

Such a concept is the dominant feature of the majority of scholarly works that are devoted to the history of Asian Russia or history of Siberia and neighbouring territories that were published during the Soviet period. What really changed since that time is the development processes and their consequences in pre-Soviet and Soviet periods. While rationale and effectiveness of the policies directed to the development of peripheral territories of Russia in the pre-Soviet period was debated, the Soviet experience of such development was mostly justified. However, irrespective of positive or negative conclusions, the economic imperative expressed in the state policies was the key factor for such interpretations, and this consideration levelled the two approaches which otherwise seemed contradictory.

Despite varying interpretations, the modernization theory remains the key methodological instrument for assessing historical processes in Asian Russia till today. In many respects this theory may be considered as appropriate. However, recent developments indicate that such approaches are limited. Firstly, one might see limited application of the economic determinism method while assessing the history of Asian Russia. Considering economic imperatives, there has to be a comprehensive representation of the development factors. This is equally applicable to the "centre-periphery" model. The inability of the traditional schemes to explain the historical process in Siberia raises the issue of expanding methodology of historical research through economic-geographical, geopolitical, socio-cultural, ethno-cultural and other approaches.

Secondly, an equally important aspect is the necessity to reconsider traditional connotations connected with Asian Russia as the object of historical research, and with conceptualization of the Asian territories of the Russian Empire and the USSR in different, wider perspective and the "system of coordinates". Under such approach the problem of connotation is not seen as an exclusively terminology problem, for it receives a methodological meaning.

This conclusion is to be addressed to such categories as Asian Russia, Siberia and Central Asia. Central Asia is seen today as one of the most dynamic regions which attract attention of all the key geopolitical actors. The high interest in Central Asia is explained by its strategic potential, growing economic meaning and priorities of international security and stability. However, the connotation of Central Asia as a mega-region remains disputed, multi-dimensional and, in some ways, vague.

Up to 1990s, Russian historians, geographers and economists rarely used this category as applied to the territories belonging to the Russian Empire and later to the Soviet Union. By the beginning of the 20th century all these territories were often addressed as Siberia, together with "genuine" Siberian territories, the lands stretching between the Ural Mountains, and territories beyond Lake Baikal. In the Soviet period and specifically since 1930s the southern republics of the USSR with the exception of Caucasus were attributed as Middle Asia and Kazakhstan that contradicted to the world-wide use of such category as Middle Asia. There were two reasons for this. From one hand, there was an intention in the official historiography to draw a dividing line between the Soviet republics belonging to the USSR and those Central Asian territories which were not incorporated into the Soviet Union, such as, for example, Mongolia. Thus, this explanation was reasoned mostly by ideology and politics.

On the other hand, a new approach to economic and geographical division of the country was elaborated and accepted in social science. Central Asian part of the USSR was divided into two big regions – Middle Asian Economic rayon and Kazakhstan as separate economic rayon. Simultaneously, the Urals Economic rayon, West-Siberian Economic rayon, East-Siberian Economic rayon and Far-Eastern Economic rayon were identified in Asian Russia. Evidently, only two of these rayons were formally attributed as belonging to Siberia.

After the collapse of the USSR in 1991, the concept of "Middle Asia and Kazakhstan" rapidly disappeared from scholarly use and was substituted by the category "Central Asia". This omission and inclusion of categories occurred in the 1930s for political reasons. On one hand, the new independent states were eager to demonstrate their break with the Soviet past. On the other hand, these nations were looking for new arguments and models for positioning themselves in the modified system of international relations and setting up regional alliances. To a certain extent, the category signified a return to a long-lasting tradition in world science. Similar connotations were utilised yet in the last decades of the 20th century. For example, in 1970s UNESCO initiated a huge cultural project referring to Asia. The term Central Asia proposed within the framework of this project in geographical terms connotes territories of Mongolia, Xingjiang and Tibet in China, north-east of Iran, Afghanistan, Pakistan, some northern states of India, as well Soviet (at this time) republics of Central Asia, Kazakhstan and southern part of the eastern regions of Russia[4].

After 1991 the issue of borders of Central Asia as a mega-region received specific meaning in connection with recent changes on the political map of the world. Such factors as the weigh of some countries in the system of international relations, and the struggle for influence over specific countries from the side of the leading world and regional powers started to play decisive role when impacting both connotations and territorial borders of Central Asia. In other words, the term "Central Asia" received clear geopolitical meaning. In American political science, there was a category called "Greater Central Asia".[5] Simultaneously, a new push was received for continuing historical, political and philosophical discourse referring to the sense and borders of Central Asia as a scholarly connotation.

Immediately after that two variants of translation for this term have appeared in the Russian language – as "Great Central Asia" with the emphasis on the potential of the region and its role in the world policy, and as "Big Central Asia", as a mega-region in geographical and cultural respects. In the latter sense Central Asia included the north of Iran, Afghanistan, Xinjiang, Mongolia, all five Asian former Soviet and now independent states, including Kazakhstan, as well as the south of Siberia and Volga region in the Russian Federation.[6] However, a narrower connotation of Central Asia has also remained in the Russian historiography which geographically includes Kazakhstan, Kyrgyzstan, Uzbekistan, Tajikistan, Turkmenistan and Afghanistan.

As a rule, the choice of connotation of Central Asia as the term determines historical approaches to the assessment of ongoing processes in the region. According to the first approach, a classical triangle of Russia – China – Mongolia impact is used as a background for analysis of different civilization platforms which influence interactions in Central Asia. According to the alternative option, the starting point for analysis lays in the fact of former belonging (or not belonging) the territories referred to "Minor" Central Asia to the Russian Empire and then – to the USSR, and most of the processes there are interpreted through the prism of Russian (until 1917) and Soviet (up to 1991) impact.[7]

As for the connotation of the term "Siberia", it also has diverse and variable meanings. The connotation of Siberia as a region and as a cultural space has already been addressed in this paper. In contemporary historiography Siberia is a significant issue in the global discourse on European and Asiatic components of Russia's entity.[8] The border between European and Asian Russia was more or less clearly defined in the beginning of the 18th century. Before that there were several proposals regarding the borders of Asiatic Russia and Siberia. The Ural mountains was identified as the natural dividing line between Europe and Asia – and this was advocated by Vasily Tatishchev. Other two variants proposed as dividing lines such rivers as Volga or Yenisey. If they were accepted, there would have been different configuration of Siberia and Eurasia.

In economic and geographical respects Siberia is currently seen as a part of Asian Russia which does not include the Urals and Russian Far East. There is also subdivision of this territory into Eastern and Western Siberia. It firstly appeared in the second half of the 18th century in connection with setting up of Tobolsk and Irkutsk provinces, and Western Siberian and Eastern Siberian governor generalates in the beginning of the 19th century. However, from the historical point of view all territories from the Urals to the Pacific Ocean inclusively are often attributed as Siberian. The Russian Far East as a separate and specific region firstly appeared on the maps in the 18th-19th centuries only.

Towards the end of the 19th century for some time in official documents and in historiography the term "Siberia" was substituted by the term "Asian Russia". To a certain extent it envisaged separatist notions that were connected with Siberian regionalists' ideology. As has been already noted, at this time the connotation of Siberia was extended to all Asian territories of Russia including contemporary Kazakhstan and now independent Central Asian republics.

In addition to historical ones, there have been recent interpretations about Siberia. In 2000 Russia was divided into several macro-regions or the so-called federal districts. Three of them – Ural Federal District, Siberian Federal District and Far Eastern Federal District were set up on the territory of Asian Russia. In the meantime, some traditional Siberian territories like Tumen and Kurgan oblasts on the west, and the Republic of Sakha (Yakutia) on east-north were not included into Siberian Federal District. The new gradation in the administrative division of Russia stimulated attempts to limit the territory of Siberia with the borders of the existing federal district. However, such an "administrative" approach is not seen relevant from historical, as well as from geographical and economic points of view and is not accepted by most experts.

In this connection the opposite opinion should also be considered. There is currently a resurgent opinion about treating Siberia as an entity that includes which leads to efforts to treat all Russian territories from the Urals to the Pacific Ocean as Siberian. This trend is popular now not just among historians but in the geographers' and economists' circles as well and is being addressed by the Historical Encyclopedia of Siberia which is the major work that is being prepared by the Institute of History in Novosibirsk.[9] The same approach is utilized in another recent Siberian publication – "The Atlas of Asian Russia".[10]

What is worth to underline is that, despite variety of approaches, modern connotations do not draw an unbreakable line between Siberia and Central Asia. They are based on understanding of common entity on these mega-regions as integrated within a multi-dimensional and multi-sided economic and geographical socio-cultural thesaurus. For such an understanding it is necessary to analyse processes which took place in the past and are ongoing on the huge territory of Central Asia. Such interpretations of Siberia represent Siberia not only as a part of the Russian state but also as a segment of the integrated Central Asian economic, geopolitical and socio-cultural space.

NOTES AND REFERENCES

1. V.V. Alexeev, A.V. Alexeeva, K.I. Zubkov, I.V. Poberezhnikov, *Aziatskaia Rossiia v Geopoliticheskoi I Tsivilizatsionnoi Dinamike. 16-20 veka*, Moscow: Izdatelstvo Nauka, 2004. p. 586.
2. V.V. Alexeev, ed. *Opyt Rossiyskikh Modernizatsii 16-20 veka*, Moscow: Izdatelstvo Nauka, 2000, p. 15.
3. N.M. Yadrintsev, *Sibir kak Koloniia v Geograficheskom,*

Etnograficheskom I Istoricheskom Otnoshenii, Novosibirsk: Sibirskii Khronograf, 2003. (First published in St. Petersburg in 1882).

4. A.A. Ulunian, "Geoprostranstvennyi Kontsept "Bolshoi Tsentralnoi Azii". Funktsionalizatsiia Protiv Ideologizatsii", *Istoricheskoe Prostranstvo. Problemy Istorii Stran SNG*, 2, 2007, p. 173.
5. A.A. Ulunian, "Geoprostranstvennyi Kontsept "Bolshoi Tsentralnoi Azii". Funktsionalizatsiia Protiv Ideologizatsii", *Istoricheskoe Prostranstvo. Problemy Istorii Stran SNG*, 2, 2007, pp. 174–175.
6. V.S. Boyko, 'Rossiiskii Altai v Geopolitike Tsentralnoi I Vnutrennei Azii v 1990-Nachale 2000 godov', In V.A. Moiseev edited Tsentralnaia Aziia Sibir (in italics please) Barnaul: Izdatelstvo AzBuka, 2003, p. 221.
7. S.G. Luzianin, 'Rossiia – Kitai – Tsentralnaia Aziia: Problemy Regionalnoi Bezopasnosti', In *Bezopasnost v "Kontaktnykh Zonakh" Aziatskoi Rossii I Tsentralnoi Azii: Opyt I Praktika Regulirovaniia Etnopoliticheskikh Napriazhenii.* Barnaul: Izdatelstvo Altaiiskogo Gosudarstvennogo Universiteta, 2002, p. 23.
8. Mark Bassin, 'Rossiia Mezhdu Evropoi I Aziei: Ideologicheskoe Konstruirovanie Geograficheskogo Prostranstva', In *Rossiiskaia Imperiia v Zarubezhnoi Istoriografii. Raboty Poslednikh Let.* Moscow: 2005.
9. www.history.nsc.ru
10. *Atlas Aziatskoi Rossii*, Novosibirsk – Moscow: Izadatelstvo Feoriia, 2007.

6

The Roles of Small Regions in Intercultural Relations and Conflicts: The Bökey Horde, Gorno-Badakhshan and Abkhazia[1]

Uyama Tomohiko

Small regions tend to be neglected in analyses of world politics. This tendency was clearly manifested in the 2008 crisis in Georgia, when most analysts concentrated their attention on the US-Russia rivalry, without due reference to the situation in South Ossetia and Abkhazia, the regions directly involved in the conflicts. Are small regional political entities merely pawns in great power politics, or do they have their own roles in intercultural relations and conflicts? We will examine this question by taking the examples of three small regions of diverse places and times: the Kazakh Bökey Horde in the Russian Empire, Gorno-Badakhshan in Soviet and post-Soviet Tajikistan, and Abkhazia in the post-Soviet Caucasus.

Bökey Horde[2]

The Bökey Horde was a khanate inside the Russian Empire, formed by the Kazakhs who moved to the area between the Ural and the Volga rivers. In 1801, in order to escape from internal conflict, a part of the Kazakhs of the Junior Juz[3] led by Bökey Sultan received permission of the Russian Tsar to move to the area between the Ural and the Volga rivers that had been almost abandoned by the Kalmyks who fled to Jungaria in 1771. In 1812, the Tsar approved Bökey as a khan. Bökey was the son of Nŭralï Khan (r. 1748-1786) of the Junior Juz and the grandson of Äbílqayïr (Abulkhayr) Khan (r. 1710-1748), the first Kazakh khan who took an oath of allegiance to the Russian empress in 1731.

The Bökey Horde was the sole Kazakh khanate that kept its official status recognized by the Russian government after the abolition of the title of khan in the Junior Juz proper (east to the Ural river) in 1824. The situation in the Horde was relatively stable, as the power was concentrated in the hands of Bökey's family under Russian protection and there were less conflict among sultans than in other Kazakh territories; and the Horde did not border on Uzbek khanates (Khiva, Bukhara and Kokand), which often intervened in Kazakh politics or helped Kazakh rebels. However, reformative and at the same time oppressive policy of Jängír Khan (r. 1824-1845), the son of Bökey Khan, occasionally aroused discontent of the masses, which was epitomized by the revolt of Isatay Taymanov (1836-1837).

The Horde became an object of keen interest of Russian scholars and administrators when Jängír Khan actively promoted education and culture. We can find a number of cross-cultural phenomena in the Bökey Horde through the materials left by these scholars. Its capital, Khanskaia Stavka (Khan Ordasï), and Jängír himself, were symbols of the symbiosis of Kazakh, Russian and Tatar cultures, and also of nomadic and sedentary cultures. Jängír, brought up at the home of the Astrakhan governor, was loyal to Russia and at the same time devoted to Islam. He knew Russian, Arabic, Persian, and other languages. He sponsored Prof. Mirza Aleksandr Kazem-Bek's research on Islamic jurisprudence, and bought valuable Persian, Arabic and Turkic manuscripts from Bukhara for Kazan University. Appreciating this, the university appointed him as an honourary member in 1844.[4]

Jängír was married to the daughter of the Tatar mufti of the Orenburg Muslim Spiritual Assembly, and as she experienced difficulties in wintering in nomadic tents, he decided to build a permanent residence and a capital town.[5] The town of Khanskaia Stavka had a semi-sedentary character: in spring and fall, when seasonal fairs were opened, a large number of merchants came to the town from various parts of Russia, but in summer, not only merchants were gone, but also local people went out to summer pastures.[6] Tatars, Kazakhs, Russians, and Armenians lived in Khanskaia Stavka and later also in the towns of Novaia Kazanka and Talovka, which were Cossack outposts until 1871.[7] The composition of the Kazakh population was also heterogeneous: there were from 500 to 2,000 households of Noghay-Qazaqs,[8] and about 200 Qojas who were believed to be descendants of the first four caliphs.[9]

The administrative, economic, and educational system of the Bökey Horde was specific and cross-cultural. Bökey Khan and Jängír Khan introduced zakāt (Islamic tax). Although zakāt in the Bökey Horde was deprived of the original function to distribute wealth to the poor and was spent for the needs of the khan's court, this was the most systematic taxation in the history of the Kazakh khanates.[10] Semi-sedentarization and land privatization, phenomena that were either absent or slow-paced in other parts of the Kazakh steppe, were better developed here, partly under Russian influence.[11]

Semi-sedentarization, together with Jängír Khan's devotion to Islam, created a favourable condition for building mosques and Islamic schools. Mullahs were recruited from among both the Volga Tatars and the Kazakhs,[12] and Kazakhs went to study at various *madrasa*s of the Volga-Ural region and Bukhara. Even the criminal world was transboundary: some Kazakhs in the Bökey Horde, together with Kalmyks, Bashkirs and others, formed a network of horse thieves that covered a vast area from the Urals to the Caucasus and Central Russia. These thieves quickly drove stolen horses from one to another distant place and sold them.[13]

The Horde was not devoid of interethnic and inter-religious tension. In its early years, some Kalmyks still remained between the Volga and the Ural, and the regulation of conflicts and trade among the Kazakhs, Kalmyks, and Kundrovsky Tatars was a matter of concern for the Russian government.[14] Land disputes between the Kazakhs and the Ural Cossacks remained hot for a long time.[15] Kazakhs feared the possibility of forced Christianization, and although Jängír did not oppose construction of a church in Khanskaia Stavka, he declined to financially help it because he was afraid of evoking distrust of the masses.[16] In their turn, the Russian authorities did not always welcome close interethnic contacts, and reinforced the ban (originally introduced in 1747) on intermarriage between the Kazakhs on one hand and the Tatars and Bashkirs on the other hand in 1831. The Orenburg Border Commission rejected Jängír's request to lift the ban, arguing that Tatars would evade conscription by escaping to their relatives in the Kazakh steppe.[17]

Overall, however, devotion to Islam and loyalty to Russia harmonized with each other in the Bökey Horde. Jängír established not only Islamic schools but also the first European-style Kazakh school in 1841, where they taught Russian, Tatar, Arabic, arithmetic, geography, and Russian history.[18] The history of the Bökey Horde thus presents an example of coexistence of Muslim and Christian cultures, as well as nomadic and sedentary cultures.

Jängír Khan died in 1845. Unexpectedly for his family, his death brought the end to the khanate itself. The Russian government did not approve his son, Saqïpkerey (Sahib-Girey), as the new khan, and although the government was ready to make him the Horde's ruler after his coming of age, Saqïpkerey died in 1849 at the age of about 18.[19] In the early 1850s, Russian high officials criticized late Jängír Khan for abuse of his power and cultivation of "fanatic" Islam, and removed his family from the administration of the Inner Horde (former Bökey Horde).[20]

However, the administrative system of the Inner Horde, with the "Provisional Council for Administration" as its head, remained distinct from that of the other parts of the Kazakh steppe until the fall of the Russian Empire. Moreover, even after the Kazakhs of the Steppe provinces were removed from the jurisdiction of the Orenburg Muslim Spiritual Assembly in 1868 to prevent the growth of influence of Islam and the Tatars, the Inner Horde remained under its jurisdiction because of its geographical location in the "inner" part of Russia, and Islamic culture continued to flourish. Socio-economic situation seemed stable, and the population grew from around 23,000 at the moment of Bökey Sultan's migration in 1801 to 214,796 in 1897.[21]

Up until the early Soviet years, the Inner Horde maintained a prominent position in the cultural development of the Kazakh steppe. It produced prominent intellectuals and politicians such as Baqtïgerey Qŭlmanov (deputy of the First and Second Russian State Duma), Ghŭmar Qarashev (poet and Islamic scholar elected as one of the qādīs of the Orenburg Muslim Spiritual Assembly in 1917), and Seyítqali Mengdeshev (the first Chairman of the Central Executive Committee of the Kazakh ASSR). In the Soviet and the post-Soviet periods, however, the central government has paid little attention to the territory of the former Inner Horde, which remains an underdeveloped countryside today.

Gorno-Badakhshan

Gorno-Badakhshan is a mountainous region that comprises 45 percent of the territory of Tajikistan but only 3 percent (206,000 in 2000) of the country's population. It is populated by Pamiri ethnic groups and a small group of Kyrgyz. The Pamiri people is officially regarded as a part of the Tajiks, but while other Tajiks are Sunnis, most Pamiris adhere to Ismailism, a branch of Shiism introduced into this region by Nāsir-i Khusraw in the eleventh century. Their Pamiri languages are also different from Tajik, although the majority in Darvaz (the westernmost part) are Sunni Tajiks, and people in Vanj were Tajikified in the nineteenth century.

It is believed that Gorno-Badakhshan, in most cases, was ruled by Sunnis before the advent of Russians,[22] but Ismailis largely preserved their own religion. There were two strategies for preservation. One was to hide their own belief and pretend to be Sunnis or Twelver Shiites.[23] The second was to enhance the authority of Ismaili religious leaders, such as Sayyid Farrūkh Shāh, who was enormously influential in the late nineteenth century. Pamiris also preserved their unwritten languages and at the same time mastered the written Persian (Tajik), even creating their own school of Persian poems.[24]

Princes in Gorno-Badakhshan (Shughnan, Rushan, Vanj, Darvaz, Ishkashim, etc.) were often nominally subordinate to the rulers of Badakhshan proper (which is now in Afghanistan with its center in Faizabad), but maintained relations also with Kunduz, Hunza, Eastern Turkistan and other regions. For example, Yūsuf ʻAlī Khān of Shughnan got allied with Yaʻqūb Beg, a Kokandi warlord who built an independent state in Eastern Turkistan, by marrying his sister to him.[25]

In the late nineteenth century, the Pamirs became a scene of Anglo-Russian rivalry, but intricate games among the local rulers were no less important to the political change in this region. Russia and the Great Britain agreed to make the Panj river the northern frontier of Afghanistan in the Pamirs in 1873, but in the same year, Afghanistan imposed tribute on Shughnan, which was situated on the both sides of the Panj.[26] The Afghan army invaded Shughnan in 1883, when Sayyid Farrūkh Shāh asked the Afghan amir to remove Yūsuf ʻAlī Khān.[27] Russia protested, and at its request, the Great Britain half-heartedly demanded Afghanistan to withdraw from the right bank of the Panj, but the Afghan amir did not implement this demand, and the two imperial governments did not take further measures.[28] The Afghan occupation proved disastrous to the Shughnan people including Sayyid Farrūkh Shāh, and only after their repeated rebellions against the Afghans and their application for becoming Russian subjects did Russia send troops.

Russia and the Great Britain more precisely demarcated the Afghan border in 1895, and the Afghans withdrew from the right bank of the Panj at last. But Russia gave Shughnan and Rushan to the Bukharan Emirate in 1896 in compensation for the latter's relinquishment of the part of Darvaz on the left bank of the Panj. People in Shughnan and Rushan strongly resisted Bukharan rule, and *de facto* accepted Russian rule in 1905.

The resistance to Bukhara was led by Sayyid Yūsuf 'Alī Shāh, the son of Sayyid Farrūkh Shāh. He had followers not only in Shughnan, but also in Darvaz, Yarkand and Osh. In 1922, he was arrested on the suspicion of anti-Soviet activities. Even after that, Ismailis in Gorno-Badakhshan continued their contacts with coreligionists outside the Soviet Union, and sent zakāt to Aga Khan in Bombay. By the mid-1930s, however, many of the religious leaders were killed, and others emigrated.[29] Their families were harassed and compelled to work as simple workers.[30]

After losing religious freedom, the Pamiris concentrated their strength on education, and competed with other regional groups in Tajikistan in cultural and political spheres. A number of people from Gorno-Badakhshan, which received the status of an autonomous province in 1925, became prominent in the Tajik academic circles that were originally dominated by people from Samarkand and Khujand. They also occupied key positions in the KGB and the Ministry of Internal Affairs. Pamiri officials' role in the crackdown on illegal economic activities in the Kulab province was one of the factors that led to future confrontation between the Kulabis and the Pamiris.[31]

While far from being separatists, the Pamiris became politically active during the *perestroika* and established an autonomous movement called La'l-i Badakhshan (Ruby of Badakhshan). Dawlat Khudoinazarov, a Pamiri filmmaker, was the candidate of the opposition coalition in the presidential election in November 1991. Although defeated in the election by Rahmon Nabiev, a former first secretary of the Communist Party, he gained 30 percent of votes, a significant number for an opposition candidate in Central Asian republics.

The start of the Tajik civil war (1992-1997) was also closely related to the Pamiris: the conflict between the governing elite and the opposition extremely intensified when the Presidium of the Supreme Soviet demanded the resignation of the Interior Minister

Mamadayoz Nawjuvonov (a Pamiri), and the Chairman of the Supreme Soviet Safarali Kenjaev insulted the Pamiris. The supporters of La'l-i Badakhshan began a protest rally in front of the Presidential Administration on March 26, although Islamists soon took the lead in the rally that gathered a hundred thousand people at its peak. However, the fact that Pamiri Ismailis along with democrats and nationalists cooperated with Sunni radicals, despite their totally different attitudes to religion,[32] indicates the diversity and flexibility of the Tajik opposition.

Once the civil war began, people in Gorno-Badakhshan tried to minimize the warfare in their region. In July 1992, Kharugh (Khorog, the capital of Gorno-Badakhshan) hosted a meeting of conflicting parties of the civil war, which declared a ceasefire, although it was soon violated. In Dushanbe, Akbarsho Iskandarov from Darvaz, who worked as the acting President and led a government consisted of both Communists and oppositionists in the most difficult time (autumn of 1992), tried to stop the escalation of the conflict but had little success. He ceded the power to Emomali Rahmonov, a Kulabi who was elected as the chairman of the Supreme Soviet in November. The Communist government retook Dushanbe next month, and Pamiris living there suffered from the hatred of Kulabis.

Refugees and opposition fighters flooded into Gorno-Badakhshan, while economically it was almost cut off from the other regions of Tajikistan. In this critical situation, local Communists and oppositionists cooperated with each other for the region's survival. The Communist chairman of the provincial Soviet, Garibsho Shahbozov, requested Rahmonov not to send governmental armed forces here. Oppositionists formed a Political Council and Self-Defense Forces of Badakhshan in March 1993, and defended its borders with Afghanistan and other regions of Tajikistan. In July, radical field commanders returning from Afghanistan planned to occupy Kharugh and set up a provisional government, but the Political Council and the provincial Soviet thwarted this plan. Former Communists and oppositionists agreed to share the posts in local governmental bodies fifty-fifty, thus creating a precedent for reconciliation, which was to be implemented on the national level four years later.

However, the central government, alarmed by the conflicts on the Afghan border that had already cost lives of Russian soldiers, did not seem to welcome this conciliatory move. On 1 August 1993, the governmental forces entered the territory of Gorno-Badakhshan and fought with the Self-Defense Forces. The latter destroyed the road between Tavildara and Darvaz, and stopped further invasion. There were troubles inside the opposition as well: for example, the Sunni Islamic group of Vanj split with the Political Council. Gradually, however, the relations with the central government normalized, and in March 1994, Rahmonov attended the ceremony to celebrate the completion of the first part of the Pamir-1 hydroelectric power plant, whose construction had been proceeding despite the wartime conditions.[33]

The Self-Defense Forces of Badakhshan were largely independent from the central leadership of the United Tajik Opposition led by the Islamic Renaissance Movement, and began to cooperate with the border guards in 1995. Conciliatory attitudes of both the governmental and opposition activists in Gorno-Badakhshan can be regarded as one of the factors that softened the confrontation in the whole country and eventually ended the civil war in June 1997. It is worth noting that in other regions as well, local people considered the defense of their own district from outside forces to be the most important task, and officials and opposition field commanders often negotiated and cooperated with each other.[34] Thus, field commanders held a meeting with representatives of the army and police in Gharm in September 1996 without notifying the leadership of the UTO beforehand, an event that urged the UTO to accelerate the peace negotiation with the government.

Nowadays, Gorno-Badakhshan still suffers from poverty and problems with narcotraffic, but seeks development through cooperation with international NGOs, especially the Aga Khan Foundation and its related institutions.[35] The Aga Khan Foundation is active throughout Tajikistan, but its interest in this country is closely connected with the presence of Ismailis in Gorno-Badakhshan. Thus the cultural identity of the Pamiris helps their economic survival, although some people complain that Aga Khan's teachings do not always harmonize with local customs.

Abkhazia

The Abkhazians live in the South Caucasus, but they are very close to the Adyges and the Circassians in the North Caucasus in linguistic and cultural terms. In 1810, the Russian Empire annexed Abkhazia with the Russian marines storming Sukhum-Kale,[36] but Abkhazia kept its status of an autonomous principality inside the empire. After the principality was abolished in 1864, the Abkhazians rose in revolt in 1866, and many of them emigrated to the Ottoman Empire together with the Circassians. Thus, in contrast to today's Russo-Georgian confrontation with Abkhazia on the Russian side, in the nineteenth century it was the Abkhazians who fiercely resisted Russian rule, while the Georgians entered the Russian Empire largely with their own will. The exodus to the Ottoman Empire is one of the reasons why the Abkhazian population in Abkhazia today is so small (94,606 in 2003[37]).

Abkhazia was declared a Soviet Socialist Republic in 1921 but soon concluded a treaty with the Georgian SSR and yielded diplomatic and other competences to it. Abkhazia's ambiguous status was finally clarified by becoming an autonomous republic inside Georgia in 1931, an event that caused repeated protests later. Nestor Lakoba, the Chairman of the Central Executive Committee of Abkhazia and a friend of Iosif Stalin, defended Abkhazia's interests as far as he could. However, after his death in 1936 (he is thought to have been poisoned by Lavrenti Beria), Georgia carried out a Georgianization policy: Abkhazian schools were closed from 1944 to 1953, and the Georgian population, which had already been a majority in Abkhazia, sharply rose because of intense immigration.

After Stalin's death, the Central Committee of the Georgian Communist Party admitted that it had pursued erroneous policies toward minorities, but tensions persisted between Abkhazians who demanded the secession from the Georgian SSR, and Georgians who alleged that the Abkhazians had come from the North Caucasus as late as the seventeenth century and had no right as Abkhazia's indigenous population.[38] In any case, the Georgianization policy failed: the Abkhazians preferred Russian to Georgian as a lingua franca in their multiethnic autonomous republic, and many of them went to Russia, rather than to Tbilisi, to receive higher education.[39]

During perestroika, Georgian and Abkhazian nationalism provoked each other. The Abkhazians' demand to upgrade their region's status to a union republic antagonized the Georgians, and triggered a demonstration in Tbilisi in April 1989 that was violently suppressed by Soviet troops, an event that proved to be an early symptom of the demise of the Soviet Union.

Georgia declared its independence in 1991, but Abkhazia did not recognize itself as a part of independent Georgia. The Georgian leader Edvard Shevardnadze ordered the army to attack Abkhazia in 1992, but it was repelled by Abkhazians and volunteers from the North Caucasus. Shevardnadze's speech at the General Assembly of the United Nations about "Pygmies revolting against the human race" and "Lilliputs enmeshing Gulliver" showed his disdain for the Abkhazians, but was at the same time a frank recognition that the Georgians could not defeat them in spite of the numerical superiority.[40]

Although independently minded, Abkhazia recognized its historically close relations with Georgia, and left a room for negotiation about its political status until it officially declared independence as late as 1999. Moreover, despite its common image as Russia's puppet state, Abkhazia's relations with Russia have not always been smooth. It was blockaded by Russia in the second half of the 1990s because of the Abkhazians' perceived pro-Chechen attitude and the relatively warm relations between Yeltsin and Shevardnadze during that period. In January 1996, at the Russian initiative, the CIS Council of the Heads of States condemned the "destructive position" of the Abkhazian side in the conflict resolution, and decided not to make economic contacts with Abkhazia.[41] Later, in 2004, Sergei Bagapsh defeated Raul Khajimba in the Abkhazian presidential election, although the Kremlin supported Khajimba and the Russian media unfoundedly blamed Bagapsh for being pro-Georgian.

Abkhazia is a geopolitically important region (its Black Sea shore is two times longer than that of Georgia proper), and its stubborn aspiration for the recognition of their independence has seriously hurt sentiments of Georgian nationalists, and eventually became an important factor of the Russo-Georgian confrontation in 2008. Although South Ossetia served as the ignition of the military confrontation, Abkhazia had been the most serious concern for the Georgian leadership. However, it is not appropriate to regard Abkhazia as a purely nationalistic entity. It is a multiethnic region where Abkhazians, Georgians, Armenians, Russians and other nationalities live, and while most Georgians fled Abkhazia during the war in 1992-1993, many of them (mostly Megrelians) have returned to the southeast Gali district and have coexisted with Abkhazians, preserving their own culture.

It is also noteworthy that the Georgian-Abkhazian conflict is largely devoid of religious elements, because most Abkhazians today share the faith in Orthodox Christianity with the Georgians. True, Abkhazians' devotion to Christianity is apparently weaker than Georgians, and there are a number of Muslims and followers of Paganism as well. The organizational aspects of the church in Abkhazia are also complicated: the Sukhum-Abkhazian Eparchy has got *de facto* independent from the Georgian Orthodox Church and has close contacts with the Russian Orthodox Church, but the latter, reluctant to change the canonical status of local church organizations (it does not recognize independence of the Ukrainian Orthodox Church), continues to regard the Sukhum-Abkhazian Eparchy officially as a part of the Georgian Orthodox Church even after the Russian government recognized Abkhazia's independence.

Thus, we have examined three types of small regions. The Bökey Horde originally had no significant difference with other parts of Kazakh society, but enjoyed relative stability and cultural development thanks to its location in the inner part of Russia, and embodied a symbiosis of Kazakh, Russian, and Islamic cultures. Gorno-Badakhshan is an integral part of Tajikistan but is culturally and religiously a specific place, and played both a radicalizing and a harmonizing roles in the civil war. Abkhazia is not only culturally distinct from Georgia but has refused to be subjugated by the Georgian government, and has sought independence despite the common practice of the former Soviet space, according to which only the former union republics are to be accorded independence. The historical and political roles of these three regions vary, but their history cannot be reduced to a mere part of the national history of Kazakhstan, Tajikistan and Georgia. They represent examples of active exchanges and coexistence of different cultures, and play significant roles in intensifying or resolving conflicts. By the now popular word "empire", we often assume a situation where major powers dictate to small countries and regions. In reality, however, they often display their negotiation ability and bargaining power in relation with the central government or bigger powers, and have undeniable influence on domestic and international politics.

NOTES AND REFERENCES

1. This work has been funded by the projects "Local History of Modern Central Asia: Regional Identities and Interactions" (Grant-in-Aid for

Scientific Research, Japan Society for the Promotion of Science) and "Comparative Research on Major Regional Powers in Eurasia" (Grant-in-Aid for Scientific Research on Innovative Areas, Japanese Ministry of Education, Culture, Sports, Science and Technology).

2. In this section I repeat some parts of my previous paper, but in a different context and using additional materials: Uyama Tomohiko, "Historiography of Local and Regional Studies in Western Kazakhstan: An Alternative to National History?" *Central Eurasian Studies Review* 7, no. 2 (2008), pp. 16–22.
3. The Junior (Kíshí) Juz is one of the three large tribal confederations of the Kazakhs. The other two are the Middle (Orta) Juz and the Senior (Ŭlï) Juz.
4. B.T. Zhanaev *et al.*, eds., *Istoriia Bukeevskogo khanstva, 1801–1852 gg.: Sbornik dokumentov i materialov* (Almaty: Daik-Press, 2002), pp. 413–417, 431–437. The famous Orientalist Kazem-Bek was the son of the Shaykh al-Islām in Derbent but converted to Presbyterianism.
5. M. Ia. Kittary, "Stavka khana Vnutrennei kirgizskoi ordy", *Zhurnal ministerstva vnutrennikh del* 28 (1849), pp. 107–111.
6. *Ibid.*, pp. 175–176.
7. I.S. Ivanov, "Vnutrenniaia kirgizskaia orda: Kratkii statisticheskii ocherk", in *Bukeevskoi Orde 200 let*, vol. 2 (Almaty: Ölke, 2001; orig. pub. Astrakhan, 1895), pp. 152–155.
8. V.M. Viktorin, "'Nugai-kazaki' Zhanybekskogo raiona Zapadno-Kazakhstanskoi oblasti: problemy mezhtiurko-kypchakskogo vzaimodeistviia", *Voprosy istorii i arkheologii Zapadnogo Kazakhstana* 1–2 (2006), pp. 80–84. Noghay-Qazaqs are descendants of Nogays assimilated into the Kazakhs.
9. Allen J. Frank, *Muslim Religious Institutions in Imperial Russia: The Islamic World of Novouzensk District and the Kazakh Inner Horde, 1780–1910* (Leiden: Brill, 2001), p. 279. Qojas migrated from the Middle Syr-Daria to Western Kazakhstan and were sometimes not considered to be Kazakhs.
10. A. Evreinov, "Vnutrenniaia ili Bukeevskaia kirgiz-kazach'ia orda", *Sovremennik* 29, otd. 2 (1851), pp. 78–80; M. Ivanin, "Vnutrenniaia ili Bukeevskaia kirgizskaia orda", *Epokha* 1864, no. 12, p. 10.
11. S.Z. Zimanov, *Rossiia i Bukeevskoe khanstvo* (Alma-Ata: Nauka KazSSR, 1982), pp. 43–66.
12. As of 1845, the akhun (the highest-ranking theologian in the Horde) and two mullahs of the central mosque were Tatars. According to a list compiled in 1850, there were 113 mullahs who served Kazakh tribes, and judging from their names, a significant part of these mullahs were Kazakhs. Zhanaev *et al.*, *Istoriia Bukeevskogo khanstva*, pp. 721, 776–779.

13. Ivanin "Vnutrenniaia ili Bukeevskaia", pp. 43–44.
14. Zhanaev *et al.*, *Istoriia Bukeevskogo khanstva*, pp. 33–37, 44–47, 59–84, 104–109, 129–130, 133, 184.
15. Mukhammed-Salikh Babadzhanov, "Spor ural'skikh kazakov s kirgizami Vnutrennei ordy", in his *Sochineniia* (Almaty: Sanat, 1996; orig. pub. 1868), pp. 98–109.
16. Zhanaev *et al.*, *Istoriia Bukeevskogo khanstva*, pp. 408, 418.
17. Zhanaev *et al.*, *Istoriia Bukeevskogo khanstva*, pp. 400–401, 407.
18. Zimanov, *Rossiia i Bukeevskoe khanstvo*, pp. 141–145.
19. Zhanaev *et al.*, *Istoriia Bukeevskogo khanstva*, pp. 770–773.
20. Zhanaev *et al.*, *Istoriia Bukeevskogo khanstva*, pp. 808–824; Robert D. Crews, *For Prophet and Tsar: Islam and Empire in Russia and Central Asia* (Cambridge, MA: Harvard University Press, 2006), p. 210.
21. N.A. Troinitskii, ed., *Pervaia vseobshchaaia perepis' naseleniia Rossiiskoi imperii 1897 g.*, vol. 2, *Astrakhanskaia guberniia* (St. Petersburg, 1904), pp. 42–43.
22. Information about the religious denomination of the rulers of Shughnan, who were also related to the rulers of other neighboring principalities, is confused. A single dynasty is thought to have ruled Shughnan from 1581 to 1883, and according to legends, its founders came from Persia to propagate Ismailism. It seems, however, that many of their descendants, including the last ruler of the dynasty, Yūsuf 'Alī Khān, were Sunnis. B.I. Iskandarov, Sotsial'no-ekonomicheskie i politicheskie aspekty istorii pamirskikh kniazhestv (Dushanbe: Donish, 1983), pp. 57-60; Istoriia Gorno-Badakhshanskoi avtonomnoi oblasti, vol. 1 (Dushanbe: Paivand, 2005), p. 307; Istoriia Shugnana (Tarikh-i Shugnan), trans. A.A. Semenov (Tashkent, 1916) <http://www.vostlit.info/Texts/rus12/Sugnan/text.phtml?id=1467> (accessed 5 July 2009).
23. A.A. Bobrinskii, *Sekta Ismail'ia v russkikh i bukharskikh predelakh Srednei Azii: geograficheskoe rasprostranenie i organizatsiia* (Moscow, 1902), pp. 1–2.
24. *Istoriia Gorno-Badakhshanskoi avtonomnoi oblasti*, vol. 1, pp. 402–404.
25. A.V. Postnikov, *Skhvatka na "Kryshe Mira": politiki, razvedchiki i geografy v bor'be za Pamir v XIX veke* (Moscow: Pamiatniki istoricheskoi mysli, 2001), p. 201.
26. Postnikov, *Skhvatka na "Kryshe Mira"*, p. 183.
27. *Istoriia Gorno-Badakhshanskoi avtonomnoi oblasti*, vol. 1, p. 332.
28. Postnikov, *Skhvatka na "Kryshe Mira"*, pp. 183–188.
29. L.N. Khariukov, *Anglo-russkoe sopernichestvo v Tsentral'noi Azii i ismailism* (Moscow: MGU, 1995), pp. 110–146.

30. My interview with Shāh-i Kalān (b. 1920), a grandson of Sayyid Farrūkh Shāh and Ismaili spiritual leader (Porshinew, 6 September 2006).
31. Stéphane A. Dudoignon, *Communal Solidarity and Social Conflicts in Late 20th Century Central Asia: The Case of the Tajik Civil War* (Tokyo: Islamic Area Studies Working Paper Series, no. 7, 1998), pp. 3–6.
32. Pamiri Ismailis seem to have been more secularized than Tajik Sunnis, although their dwellings preserve religious symbolism. For example, the ceiling of a Pamiri house consists of four layers of timber that symbolize earth, water, fire and air. Frank Bliss, *Social and Economic Change in the Pamirs (Gorno-Badakhshan, Tajikistan)* (London: Routledge, 2006), pp. 170–171.
33. Dzhamshed Kadyrov, "Voina i mir na kryshe mira", Fakty i kommentarii, 28 June 2008 <http://blogs.mail.ru/bk/lezvie00/>; Kurbon Alamshoev, "Garibsho Shakhbozov: na strazhe mira i poriadka", ASIA-Plus, 6 September 2007 <http://www.toptj.com/ShowNews.aspx?news_id =F35910E2-13C6-4CFD-8AB8-C1A4E356AD05> (accessed 5 July 2009).
34. My interviews with former officials and field commanders in various parts of Karategin and Gorno-Badakhshan, August and September 2006.
35. Bliss, *Social and Economic Change*, pp. 297–329.
36. For an Abkhazian historian's account on the complicated roles of Abkhazian and Megrelian rulers in Russia's annexation of Abkhazia, see Stanislav Lakoba, Abkhazia posle dvukh imperii, XIX-XXI vv. (Sapporo: Slavic Research Center, 2004), ch. 1 <http://src-h.slav.hokudai.ac.jp/coe21/publish/no5_ses/contents.html>.
37. "Naselenie Abkhazii" <http://www.ethno-kavkaz.narod.ru/rnabkhazia.html> (accessed 5 July 2009). The total population of Abkhazia in 2003 was 215,972, out of which 45,953 were Georgians (including Megrelians) and 44,870 were Armenians.
38. Bruno Coppieters, "In Defence of the Homeland: Intellectuals and the Georgian-Abkhazian Conflict", in Bruno Coppieters and Michel Huysseune, *Secession, History and the Social Sciences* (Brussels: VUB Brussels University Press, 2002), pp. 89–116, esp. pp. 91–97.
39. See biographies of Abkhazian elites in Lakoba, *Abkhazia posle dvukh imperii*, pp. 146–200.
40. Stanislav Lakoba, *Abkhaziia-de-fakto ili Gruziia de-iure? O politike Rossii v Abkhazii v postsovetskii period, 1991-2000 gg.* (Sapporo: Slavic Research Center, 2001).
41. "Reshenie o merakh po uregulirovaniiu konflikta v Abkhazii, Gruziia" <http://lawrussia.ru/texts/legal_105/doc105a825x652.htm>.

7

Authority as Accomplishment: Intergenerational Dynamics in Talas, Northern Kyrgyzstan[1]

Judith Beyer

"One has to respect the elders" – this is one of the most fundamental principles of intergenerational interaction in the province of Talas in Northern Kyrgyzstan[2]. A village historian once explained this utterance to me which orders the relations between the old and the young in the following way:

> One of the laws (*myizam*)[3] since ancient times concerns the relation between elders and young people. The oldest one is an *aksakal*, and the youth should listen to him. The oldest one rules, governs, and advises young people, teaches all kinds of handicraft such as smithing and how to train a bird and a dog; how to play an instrument, how to recite Manas, how to tell the genealogy. A young man learns everything from the elders. And elders teach everything. Young people listen to him and serve him: if he wants to ride, the younger one prepares a horse for him, if he asks to call somebody from a field, then the young man calls, if he asks the young man to slaughter a sheep, the latter slaughters, if he asks to sweep the road, the young sweeps it; an *aksakal* commands and the young man implements everything. And an elder is obliged to teach everything (20051103).

In this statement the historian does not talk about actual persons or real situations. Instead, he lists a number of activities an unspecified young man has to perform for an unspecified *aksakal*. We also learn that while having to implement what the old man says, the young man benefits in that he receives training and experience. And although commanding, the *aksakal* is also presented as being obliged to transfer his knowledge to the young man. In this idealized model, old and young thus both enjoy privileges and have obligations towards one another which bind their asymmetrical yet reciprocal relation. The differences in age and status which the historian describes become embodied through the performance of specific interactional practices. While young people are compelled to be at the elders' disposal, elders are likewise expected to behave in ways deemed appropriate. This kind of interaction is conceptualized locally in terms of respect (*syi*; *urmat*). To put this in methodologically clear language, I suggest that being treated respectfully establishes an individual's claims to authority and that authority should be understood as the result of such co-emergent interactional practices. We can talk of elders having achieved authority when these co-emergent practices are not challenged in direct interactions.

This article describes the processes through which the authority of Kyrgyz elders is acknowledged and the rights and privileges elders enjoy. It is argued that working towards becoming an elder requires more than just being of a certain age. As they come of age, elders gradually learn to comply with and perform 'elderness' in the expected ways. Thus, socialization does not end once an individual has reached adolescence; actors are only socialized differently as they grow up. Borrowing a semantic construction from conversational analysis, elders are required to "do 'being elders'" (cf. Sacks 1984). Elders need to work at "being elders" and the acknowledgment of their authority should not be seen as an unproblematic automatism, but an accomplishment. This interactional perspective casts a new light on the hierarchical relationship between the young and old, because "being elder" cannot be taken for granted. Instead, an individual has to constantly work towards being recognized as an elder. The authority of an elder is evaluated and becomes visible by how successful he is in having his elderness acknowledged by others. This presupposes that elders are actively seeking opportunities to claim their authority. One way of doing this would be to perform high moral integrity. However, the young eventually challenge the old when claiming respect and authority for themselves. As they draw upon the same resources as their parents in order to be recognized as "head" (*bash*)[4], children find themselves competing with their parents.

In the given frame the article characterizes the types of interaction through which authority is situationally constituted. It first enumerates some of the fundamental rights elders enjoy in contemporary Talas, and then describes the obligations that come with these rights. Finally, it discusses a dispute case between a father and his son about access rights to land in order to show how the authority of elders can be challenged. In all three sections it draws upon field data gathered in two rural mountain villages in Talas, Northern Kyrgyzstan, between 2005 and 2008.

Respecting the Elders

As heads of their households, elders take decisions in regard to their property, land, and animals and they can to a great deal control the lives of their household members (cf. Abu-Lughod 1986: 80, Shahrani 1986). Their elevated status becomes visible for example in their right to name their grandchildren in the male line and, if they want to, raise them as their own children, who will call them "Father" (*ata*) and "Mother" (*apa*) and address their biological parents with "Uncle" (*baike*) and "Aunt" (*ezhe*).[5] Such requests by elders can hardly be refused and in fact I have not come across examples where parents would have denied these particular rights of their elders.[6] Within the household, the head (*bash*) will be treated in what are considered respectful ways, for example by being offered the honourable place opposite the door (*tör*). When meat is being served, the household head receives the head of the animal, a practice which was already noted in early ethnographies (see Grodekov 1889 p. 9). Other parts of the animal may be eaten by young household members only, for example the ears – "this way the young learn to listen to the elders", as an *aksakal* explained to me. Respect, in these cases, is the basis of the care the elders enjoy from their children and relatives.

The oldest *aksakals* of a descent group (*uruu*) are approached by their members, who come to ask for help and moral support, for blessings (*bata*) and mediation in dispute settlement (cf. Beyer 2006). Many current elders have held official positions during kolkhoz times: those who are currently members of the neotraditional court of elders (*aksakaldar sotu*), for example, have been kolkhoz directors, agronomists, journalists, or teachers. They are educated and possess a lot of technical knowledge related to land, irrigation, and animals – areas which are as central to much Kyrgyz life today, as they were during Soviet times, and around which disputes frequently arise. These elders are used to speaking in public and dealing with officials and politicians.

In their role as household heads or heads of descent groups, elders have gradually learnt to take over traditional roles and perform specific tasks of a *bash*. To summarize, they have expert knowledge, which they acquired during Soviet times and which remains crucial nowadays as the contemporary Kyrgyz education system is degrading. Some male elders have also taken on entirely new responsibilities by becoming judges of one of the neotraditional *aksakal* courts, which were set up in each village throughout the country (cf. Beyer 2007). In addition to that, elders are respected as veterans of the Second World War or the Afghanistan War. The fact that most of them perform Islam on a regular basis once they get older – made visible by praying (*namaz okuu*) and keeping the fast (*orozo*) – further demands the display of respectful behaviour from the younger generations. Whereas it would certainly be possible to delineate these different sources of knowledge into pre-Soviet (being *bash*), Soviet (being experts or veterans) and post-Soviet (being judges or being religious), these sources do not lead to a compartmentalization of the individual's personal histories. Being a technical expert, the head of a descent group and a pious Muslim are not contradictory or even separable characteristics of a contemporary elder in Talas. The authority which elders achieve in interactions thus cuts across the usual dichotomy of viewing the traditional against the modern, the leader against his followers and the past against the present. "Doing 'being elder'" is rather a practice of bricolage. I argue that elders continue to be respected nowadays because they have managed to accumulate different knowledge throughout the last decades and succeeded in presenting themselves as worthy of respect. This makes "being elder" look attractive in the eyes of the young who themselves strive towards it.

Obligations of Elders

The proverb "A beard is needed at a feast"[7] which I often heard as an answer when trying to find out why especially *aksakals* were invited to festivities, but also to sad events such as funerals, conveys well that the respect people accord to elders is only one side of the coin. On the one hand, elders enjoy privileges in everyday life and during festive events such as birth celebrations, marriages, funerals, and national holidays. But on the other hand, they also have to fulfil the expectations of other villagers by publicly approving and legitimizing these events (cf. Fortes 1969. p. 239, Holleman 1986). Thus, the elders' agency is directed by the expectations of others. A former Soviet judge, now an *aksakal*, explained to me that *aksakals* have to be generous, quiet, restrained, humble, and compromising. He also emphasized that *aksakals* are regarded as being responsible for the youth's behaviour and for those who have misbehaved in their community (20051021). Askar Ata[8], an *aksakal* court member from my field site, said they were required not to lie (20060514). Their work for people should be "for free", since it was "*aksakal*'s work", as an elder from another village on the other side of Talas province put it (20050608). "The judges of the *aksakal* court should not judge fairly because they are judges, but because they are *aksakals*", remarked Töröbek Ata, another member of the *aksakal* court (20060420). This short list gives an indication of how male elders should ideally behave in order to be considered good *aksakals*. Female elders, on the other hand, are exempt from these expectations as long as they have a husband. In general, women in Talas are characterized in opposite ways as compared to *aksakals*: gossipy, loud, and emotional. This is also what they say about themselves, laughingly. While these attributions are surely stereotypical, they are not judgmental. Women can display behaviour which would be inappropriate for *aksakals*, such as screaming and shouting in public. However, a shift in behaviour is required of them when they become widows and the head of their households, that is, responsible for the well-being and the standing of all household members. I never heard a widow scream and seldom did they gossip themselves although they were certainly listening to what other women had to tell. A key informant of mine, an eighty-two year-old woman, is such a female *bash*. She enjoys enormous respect not only within her household, but in the whole village. She is able to keep the household members together as "one", takes a central part in the life-cycle rituals of her extended family, her descent group, and her neighbourhood, and has a reputation for being one of the most religious elders in the village. She is even called *moldo* by the *aksakals* – a title usually given only to pious males. She resembles respected *aksakals* even more in the sense that she is home most of the time, attending to the sheer never-ending stream of relatives, neighbours, and other guests who come to see her, talk to her, and seek her advice. But along with her privileges come obligations, as female heads are supposed to act in ways that are usually expected from *aksakals*.[9]

In the following example she maintained the high moral ground at considerable material cost for her household. In spring 2006, after the potatoes had just been bedded out onto her land, a thief dared to dig out a large portion of them in order to plant them on his own land. He was found out, and with everyone in the village gossiping about him in very negative ways, he came to her house together with the sacks of potatoes he had managed to dig out. She refused to see him and had her youngest son deliver a message to him: "My mother said you should take these potatoes – she will not eat from what a thief has touched". The man was forced to take the sacks and leave. This example serves to show that by converting the potatoes into a non-returnable poisoned gift, she denied the thief's attempt to reconcile. She never lost another word about this incident. Her daughter-in-law (*kelin*), however, went on lamenting for some time, because she was already anticipating the problems lying ahead of her.[10] As this example shows, "doing 'being elder'" can get the actor entangled in a web of expectations (cf. Wrong 1994). The old woman acted according to her status as *bash*, displaying high moral integrity by sacrificing her and her family's only income, the potato harvest. The thief was humiliated not only because everyone in the village knew about his failed deed, but also because he had dared to steal the potatoes from one of the village's most respected individuals, who even went on to deprive him of the possibility to make up for his nefarious deed. As far as I could tell from the gossip going on afterwards, her reputation was strengthened throughout the village, since everyone acknowledged her virtuous behaviour. However, as an elder, she also did not have to worry about the practicalities following from her moral deed: her daughter-in-law had to find ways and money to cover the missing income in autumn when the festive season started.

As elders also hope to be remembered after their death as ancestors, they work at performing their authority in ways that prove them worthy of ancestorhood in the eyes of their relatives and fellow villagers (cf. Van der Geest 1998). Raising children, giving them an education, arranging their marriages, building houses for them, taking care of their grandchildren, and keeping a good reputation in the village are all practices through which an elder can show that he has led a successful and morally committed life and should therefore be remembered by others.

Challenging the Elders

So far, I have illustrated that the relation between the young and the old is ordered through a formalized mode of communication: while the young need to pay respect to their elders, these elders need to strive towards complying with an idealized image of being humble and wise. This social contract, however, can be challenged in several ways. Most frequently this occurs by means of indirect conversation: gossiping, vilifying, and reciting proverbs which portray elders in exactly the opposite way from the positive image of benevolence and wisdom. All these tactics give the younger generation the opportunity to reconcile hidden resentment with outward respect.[11] Another way to express disagreement with the commands of elders is to silently disapprove and simply do something else. Although there is little an old person can do in the face of disrespect, it turns out that young people themselves work to sustain the general principle of having to respect one's elders. Children, who are socialized into respecting their elders, habitually submit to their parents' wishes and demands. They do so, knowing that one day they will be in a position that allows them to command respect from others as well. The public demand that one has to respect one's elders acknowledges the future of the young: "Those who do not respect the old will not be respected when they are old themselves",[12] was an utterance I heard from young and old informants alike. Every male individual thus works throughout his life towards being recognized as a "head". Through the pursuit of these goals, the young perpetuate this domination by the elders (cf. Weber 1978: 212). In turn, they also learn to dominate their younger siblings who have to respectfully address them in a formal way, using the second person plural as well as titles usually reserved for the parents' generation (*baike* for older brothers and *ezhe* for older sisters). While coming of age, they also learn to shoulder the growing responsibilities, for example when having to take care of their younger siblings. This is how they also learn which behaviour commands respect from others.

However, young people will have to challenge their parents when (as sometimes happens) the latter continue to treat them like children. The following case shows how a nearly 50 year-old "son" had to rebel against his father who did not recognize the son as *bash.* The father, as the head of the household, had made use of his customary right to keep the land of all of his family members after they received their plots in the privatization schemes of 1993. Arstan Baike had set up his own household with the help of his parents after he got married. He has six children. His oldest son recently got married, brought a wife home, and they were expecting a child. Officially, Arstan Baike owned only 40 *sotik* of land (20 for himself and 20 for his wife) since none of his children were properly registered when the land had been privatized.[13] Even these 40 *sotik*, though, were still under the factual control of his elder father. Thus, Arstan Baike wanted to claim and exercise his right towards the 40 *sotik* of land his father had hitherto not handed over to him. He argued that he had many mouths to feed now and too little land. His father, however, systematically ignored the demands of his son to be recognized as *bash*, even though the latter was about to become a grandfather soon. In spring 2006, his father again sowed wheat on Arstan Baike's land plot, which the son had already cleared from stones, making it ready for a tractor to harrow. He had wanted to plant potatoes. When Arstan Baike saw how his father had crossed his plans again, he first confronted him personally, but failed to change the old man's mind. Finally, he approached the head of the court of elders, Myrzakul Ata, who is also a relative of the family.[14] With me in tow, Myrzakul Ata met the son and his mother on the respective land plot outside of Aral. The father had not come. "He does not understand", his wife simply said. Whereas Arstan Baike and his father had been fighting inside the house, as Arstan Baike later told me, there was no way that the father would bring this family dispute into the open. He could not allow his son to disrespect him in front of others, even if the "others" were only kinsmen such as Myrzakul Ata.[15]

The land dispute between mother and son was a lesson in how respecting one's elders (here, one's mother) can constrain an individual's actions. While the mother screamed at and cursed her son, accusing him of disrespecting his father and of being ungrateful for all that he had done for him, Arstan Baike tried to stay calm, not raising his voice, and arguing in a conciliatory way. He tried to get his mother to acknowledge that he, too, was a head and had to take responsibility for his family just as his father had done. But his mother would not listen. Instead, she compared his six children to the eleven children she had given birth to and kept on repeating that without his father, the son would own nothing, for the parents had paid for his marriage and built him and his wife a house:

> May you fall down deep into the ground together with your daughter-in-law! 'My son brought a daughter-in law' he says. Everyone brings a daughter-in-law! Or do you think you are the only one, who has a daughter-in-law? Do you think you did a great job by arranging the marriage of your son? I have 10, 15 daughters-in-law! We built houses for you all! Die instead of debating over the land with your father! (Mother, 20060417)

Myrzakul Ata had turned his head away, smoked a cigarette, and waited for things to calm down. He then took the woman's hand saying: "Come here, you have given birth to him", ignoring the next curse the old woman uttered towards her son. He continued telling her:

> You know you should have left the land to him and not plant anything. There is no need for conflict here.[16] The government gave the land to all of us. Everything is based on laws, you understand that, right? (20060417)

She did not answer. "I am trying to feed my family", said Arstan Baike instead: "Each person has to fight for his own life".[17] His mother cursed him again. This went on for thirty more minutes, leaving me standing by uncomfortably. Finally, the son gave in. "But from next year onwards", he said, "I will plant on my land". The only answer Myrzakul Ata had for him was to remind him that whatever he intended to do, he should not forget that "we are one people" and that such disputes should be kept "inside".[18] To me, he said, "I am glad I did not make this public. People would have said that we fought", referring to the fact that he was from the same descent group (*uruu*) as the disputing family. When I tried to talk with Arstan Baike a couple of days later on the street, he denied further problems saying "everything is quiet now".

This case shows that while household elders are expected to be benevolent, and not exploitative, in reality, things can look different. The father asserted his status as *bash* simply by not being present. This behaviour was also considered appropriate by Myrzakul Ata.

He himself reminded the son that family disputes should be kept "inside". While father and son could not openly resent each other, Arstan Baike's mother, however, did not seem to have lost face by showing up, demonstrating her discontent with what her son had done by screaming at him and even cursing him. While married women get away with such behaviour, for an old man to act this way would have been intolerable. This was the reason why Arstan Baike's father had not come. Approaching Myrzakul Ata was a desperate move of Arstan Baike, which, in the end, was not successful. Myrzakul Ata, likewise, would have had little influence over his absent fellow kinsman, who is older than him. Whereas state law prescribes formal equality between the father and son by categorizing both as landowners, their relation remained hierarchical with the father as *bash* deciding over his son's property (cf. Benda-Beckmann et.al. 2009: 4-5). In fact, Myrzakul Ata mentioned to Arstan Baike that he himself keeps the land plots of his own two sons as long as they live under his roof.[19] When I returned to Aral in 2008, Arstan Baike's son had left his household and moved to Talas with his wife and their child. Arstan Baike was cultivating his own land plot, as he had wanted to.

As this case has shown, paying respect to one's parents is a performative act with crucial material consequences. I suggest that Arstan Baike could not have approached Myrzakul Ata at an earlier stage in the dispute, which had been going on ever since he had left his fathers' house. He needed to become a grandfather to display enough compelling criteria in order to successfully establish his status as a *bash*. Thus, a male *bash* does not only need to be acknowledged by his household members or peers, but also by his own parents. In Talas, however, the situation has become complicated because acknowledging one's descendants as *bash* directly diminishes an actors' access to the most valuable material resource – land. We know from many other ethnographic cases that tensions between young and old are likely to arise over this issue (Fortes 1969, Parkin 1994). While Arstan Baike tried to reason in alignment with the provisions of the land reform, namely ownership on an individual basis,[20] his mother prioritised the principle of having to respect one's parents which also implies not to challenge the fact that land has always belonged to the *bash*.

However, at my field site such open conflict only seldom breaks out. In most of the cases I encountered during my fieldwork, children did show patience and tried to please their parents until the latter considered the younger generation worthy of being *bash*. Even when adult "children" like Arstan Baike successfully claimed their land from their parents (regardless that state law already gave them this right years before) they initially only gained economic independence from them. This autonomy, however, will allow them to eventually prove themselves worthy of respect.

Conclusion

In this article it has been suggested suggested that the decisive element of the inevitably hierarchical relation between young and old is the acknowledgement of the elders' authority. This is demonstrated through respectful behaviour on the side of the young generation, and the willingness on the side of the elders to present themselves as wise and knowledgeable, that is, beyond individual ambition. Kyrgyz are socialized into treating their elders with respect, and in turn they learn to act accordingly as they grow old. I have described granting and being granted respect as an interactional, life-long process everyone in Talas is engaged in and the suggestion is that being treated respectfully establishes an elder's claims to authority. This led me to argue that authority should be understood as an accomplishment and not as a simple result of having come of age or holding a certain position. There is therefore no fixed point in life when an actor has secured authority. Just as the young need to work towards having their authority recognized by others, the elders need to engage in "doing 'being elders'". This constrains their seeming autonomy. Since authority is relational and derives from how people interact with others (see Blumer 1969: 7), it should be seen as basic to human interactional behaviour rather than a capacity in itself (see Peabody 1968). The ideal relationship between the old and the young as it is transmitted through socialization depends on the mutual acknowledgment of each other's positions in everyday life.

We have seen that respect can be granted as a result of conversational work in performances and that authority is situationally achieved when an actor's normative and empirical claims are not challenged in direct interaction. These mutually constitutive performances not only lead to the acknowledgment of the elders' authority, but also perpetuate and consolidate the hierarchical relation between young and old, which manifests itself for example in forms of address or access rights to resources such as land. The young generation is socialized knowing that coming of age will lead to having authority, but only as long as one respects the elders today. While this social contract is challenged in specific interactions, as the land dispute between son and father showed, the principle as such is never questioned. This often leads actors – old and young alike – not to pursue their own interests to the utmost.

BIBLIOGRAPHY

David Parkin, *Palms, wine and witnesses: public spirit and private gain in an African farming community*. Prospect Heights: Waceland Pr, 1994 [1972].

Dennis Wrong, Dennis, *The problem of order: What unites and divides society*. New York: The Free Press, 1994.

Franz von Benda-Beckmann, Keebet von Benda-Beckmann and Anne Griffiths, Introduction to: *The power of law in a transnational world: anthropological enquiries*, edited by Franz von Benda-Beckmann, Keebet von Benda-Beckmann and Anne Griffiths. New York: Berghahn Books, 2009.

Harvey Sacks, Harvey. "On doing being ordinary". In: *Structures of social action: studies in conversation analysis*, edited by J. Maxwell Atkinson and John Heritage: Cambridge: Cambridge University Press, 1984.

Henri Dekker, *Property regimes in transition: land reform, food security, and economic development; a case study in the Kyrgyz Republic*. Aldershot: Ashgate, 2003.

Herbert Blumer, *Symbolic interactionism: perspective and method*. Berkeley, CA: University of California Press, 1969.

J. Holleman, J., "Trouble-cases and trouble-less cases in the study of customary law and legal reform". In: *Anthropology of law in the Netherlands: essays on legal pluralism*, edited by Keebet von Benda-Beckmann and Fons Strijbosch, pp. 110–131, 1986.

Judith Beyer, "Revitalisation, invention and continued existence of the Kyrgyz *aksakal* courts: Listening to pluralistic accounts of history". In: *Dynamics of plural legal orders. The Journal of Legal Pluralism and Unofficial Law*, edited by: Franz von Benda-Beckmann and Keebet von Benda-Beckmann. Volume 53/54. pp. 141–175, 2006.

— "Imagining the state in rural Kyrgyzstan: How perceptions of the state create customary law in the Kyrgyz *aksakal* courts". In: *Max Planck Institute for Social Anthropology Working Papers*. No. 95. Available online: http://www.eth.mpg.de/pubs/wps/pdf/mpi-eth-working-paper-0095.pdf, 2007.

Lila Abu-Lughod, *Veiled sentiments: honour and poetry in a Bedouin society*. Berkeley: Unversity of California Press, 1986.

Max Weber, Max. *Economy and society.* 2 Volumes. Berkeley.: University of California Press, 1978 [1956].

Meyer Fortes, *Kinship and the social order. The legacy of Lewis Henry Morgan*. London: Routledge, 1969.

N.I. Grodekov, *Kirgizy i karakirgizy Syr-Dariinskoi oblasti: Iuridicheskii byt.* Tashkent: Tipo-Litografiia S.I. Laxtina, Romonovskaia ul. Sob Dom., Vol. 1, 1889

Nazif Shahrani, "The Kirghiz khans: styles and substance of traditional local leadership in Central Asia". In: *Central Asian Survey*. 5/3, 4. pp. 255–271, 1986.

R.L. Peabody, "Authority". In: *International Encyclopedia of the Social Sciences.* Vol. 1., edited by David L. Sills and Robert K. Merton, pp 473-474, New York: Macmillan/Free Press, 1968.

Sjaak van der Geest, "Opanyin: The ideal of elder in the Akan culture of Ghana". In: *Canadian Journal of African Studies/Revue Canadienne des Études Africaines*. 32, 3, 1998. pp. 449–493, 1998.

NOTES

1. Parts of this article appear in my Ph-D dissertation entitled "According to *salt*. An ethnography of customary law in Talas, Kyrgyzstan" which I completed in 2009 at the Max Planck Institute for Social Anthropology in Halle/Saale, Germany. Field work took place between 2005 and 2008. Altogether, I spent 15 months in two rural mountain villages in Talas. My research focus was on the roles of elders, particularly those male elders (*aksakals*) who are part of a neotraditional court which came into existence in 1993 – the court of elders (*aksakaldar sotu*). My research project is financed by the Volkswagen Foundation and the Max Planck Institute for Social Anthropology. The first phase of my research project was financially supported by the Graduate School 'Society and Culture in Motion' at the Martin Luther University Halle-Wittenberg.
2. *Aksakaldardy syilash kerek* (lit. One has to respect the white beards; *aksakal* is the term people at my field site use to respectfully address male elders). While this proverb refers only to male elders, old women are equally respected. There are also other utterances which include males and females as for example "one has to respect one's parents". Throughout this article, I will use the term "elder" when speaking of all elders and the term *aksakal* when speaking of male elders only.

3. All terms are in Kyrgyz and in the singular form. The acronym "Russ" stands for the Russian language and is used whenever my informants use the Russian term instead of the Kyrgyz (or where there exists no Kyrgyz equivalent to the Russian word). The transliteration follows the standard ALA-LC Romanization tables. In addition I use the German Umlaute ö, ä and ü.
4. The *bash* is the oldest male person or the female widow heading a household. Only when both parents have died will the youngest son, who stays with his parents to take care of them, become *bash* himself. The head of a descent group (*uruu*) is also called *bash* and so are political leaders and heads of other organizational groups.
5. This is especially the case when there is only one son in the family who does not live with his parents, but – for example – lives in the capital Bishkek. If he has a child, it is likely that this child will be raised in the house of the grandparents who need a male relative to take care of them when they grow old. Likewise, grandparents can demand granddaughters from their sons if they feel they could use a helping hand in the household – or simply, because they enjoy being surrounded by their grandchildren.
6. The grandmother of a friend of mine who lives in the capital Bishkek is a huge fan of Jackie Chan movies. When one of her daughters-in-law gave birth to a son, she decided to name the child in honour of the martial arts actor who is a well-known figure in Kyrgyzstan. Whereas everyone tried to talk her out of this endeavour, she did not diverge from her decision.
7. *Sakal toido kerek.* Here, again, "beard" (*sakal*) is used as a pars pro toto for the male elder.
8. All names are anonymized.
9. In other parts of Kyrgyzstan, old women can be addressed with the term *aksakal* as well. However, this is not customary in Talas.
10. Potatoes are the main income for most villagers at my field site, whereas livestock serves mostly as capital. Potatoes are sold in autumn at the bazaar in Talas or to Kazakh traders roaming the villages with their trucks. Without this harvest, people do not have enough money to participate in life-cycle rituals that are predominantly held during these months when everyone has cash at hand.
11. Consider this proverb, for example: *Sakaly uzun kishinin akyly kyska* (A person who has a long beard has a short mind). This fundamental ambivalence towards elders is known from other contexts as well. See van der Geest (2002: 458) for Ghana where witchcraft accusations towards elders are put forward as a hidden way of airing frustration and dislike.

12. *Karyiany syilabagan, karyganda syi korboit. Or Zhakalaba atangdy, zhakalasang, seni da balang bir künü zhakalait* (Do not beat up your father, otherwise one day your son will beat you up).
13. 1 sotik is 0,1 ha.
14. They belong to the same descent group.
15. He could not have known that I would be at the meeting since the *aksakal* had decided spontaneously to take me along.
16. *Yr chyrdyn tük keregi zhok.*
17. *Ar bir adam öz – özü üchün küröshüshü kerek.*
18. *Biz özübüz. Özübüz özübüzdö kalsyn.*
19. He also keeps the land of another son who lives in Bishkek, but claims that should he want it, he would give it to him (20060417).
20. See Dekker (2003) for details on the land reform in Kyrgyzstan.

8

Muslim Travelers from Russia to the Ottoman Empire: Some thoughts on a Research Agenda

Norihiro Naganawa

On February 11, 2007 the President of the Russian Federation Vladimir Putin landed at King Khaled Airport in Saudi Arabia. This was the first visit of the head of the Russian state to the Kingdom. Although the Soviet Union established direct diplomatic relations with the Saudi polity in 1924, it was only in 1990 that they recovered from the severance in 1937. It is under Putin that the two largest providers of energy in the world converted rapprochement into real cooperation. The visit of the current King (then Prince) 'Abd al-'Azīz to Moscow in 2003 resulted in the creation of the Saudi-Russian Business Council (*Saudovsko-rossiiskii delovoi sovet*). Saudi Arabia was one of the first countries that supported the Russian initiative to become an observer of the Organization of Islamic Conference (OIC), which was realized in 2005. During his visit in 2007, the Russian president discussed with the Saudis joint projects in the sphere of transportation, extraction and refinement of oil and gas, the launch of satellites, and the investment of Saudi Arabia in the Russian economy. In that year, on November 23, Prince Sultan, son of 'Abd al-'Azīz, came to Moscow to see Putin at the Kremlin; they shared opinions concerning the situation in Palestine and Iraq, and cooperation in the sphere of energy and military technology.[1]

This historical visit of Putin to Saudi Arabia bore remarkable fruit for Russia's Muslim citizens, too. At least the Muslim representatives explained it as such. After Putin's visit, a Russian Muslim delegation dealing with the hajj succeeded in gaining another quota of 4,500 pilgrims to Mecca: until then Russia had held a quota of 20,500 pilgrims, and now 25,000 Russian Muslims would be eligible to carry out the hajj at the end of 2007.[2] Despite the pessimistic prognosis of some commentators,[3] the number of hajjis from Russia has increased significantly since the collapse of the Soviet Union. Whereas the Soviet Union after 1945 annually dispatched a delegation of 20-25 Muslims to Mecca, 1500 Soviet Muslims performed the hajj after the restoration of diplomatic relations with Saudi Arabia in 1990.[4] More than 3,000 Russian Muslims undertook the pilgrimage in 2000, 13,500 in 2006, 18,000 at the beginning of 2007,[5] and 24,326 in 2008.[6] Almost 80% of the pilgrims are from Dagestan: in the first hajj of 2007, for instance, there were 14,000 from Dagestan, 1300 from Chechen, 1200 from Tatarstan, 800 from Ingushetiia, 350 from Bashkiriia, and about 300 from other regions.[7]

This upsurge of aspiration for the hajj, one of the five pillars of Islam, led to the institutionalization of travel, where representatives of the Muslim community play a pivotal role. In order to coordinate operations of governmental organs to regulate this colossal annual event, Akhmad Bilalov, state deputy from Dagestan, has headed the Council on the Hajj within the Russian government since 2001.[8] Members of this council include central as well as regional Muslim Spiritual Boards (*Dukhovnye upravleniia musul'man*); in fact, it is they that distribute Russia's quota provided by the OIC to Muslim citizens according to each regional jurisdiction. Moreover, in July 2008, new Russian President Dmitrii Medvedev appointed Kamil' Sh. Iskhakov, former Kazan city head and the President's plenary representative in the Far East Federal Okrug, as the regular representative of the Russian Federation for the OIC.[9]

As the agenda of the Hajj Council shows, Russian authorities as well as the pilgrims themselves have to tackle complications of transportation, cooperation with tour companies, vaccination, medical care, insurance, and politics, either international or domestic, over distribution of the limited hajj quota. In addition, official organizers of the hajj have to contemplate the outward implications of their efforts: Akhmad Bilalov once said "[Muslims of the world] judge our country in general by Russian pilgrims; the hajj becomes ... a measure defining the image and face of the state."[10] However, a study of the mobility of the Russian Muslims has not sufficiently shed light on these interactive aspects of the state's commitment to the control of the hajj.

The historiography of the Cold War era describes border-crossing behaviors of Muslim intellectuals in particular as networking of pan-

Islamic and pan-Turkic movements subverting Russian imperial rule. Symbolically, this paradigm was buttressed, at least at its nascent stage, by Muslim émigré activists and scholars.[11] In the last decade, students of Russian Muslim societies have disclosed their vertically interdependent and interpenetrating relations with the state.[12] Only recently, making use of diplomatic documents of both Russian and Ottoman empires, some historians have begun to see such interactions in Muslim mobility across borders, too.[13]

The paper provides a research agenda to locate the new development of the hajj in contemporary Russia in historical perspective. I outline the Russian imperial entanglement with Muslim travelers at the turn of the nineteenth and the twentieth centuries, focusing on those from the Volga-Ural region to the Ottoman Empire. Author attempts to determine what their border-crossing experience and knowledge they brought home meant in the local Muslim politics of the Volga-Ural region, based on travelers' accounts and articles from local Muslim newspapers.

Study of Muslim travelers comprises a wide range of comparative studies of empire and exploration of interactions among empires as well as world order. Study of the modern hajj has revolved around sanitation, state security against anticolonial activities, transportation, and links between domestic and foreign policies concerning these matters. Along these lines, F. E. Peters integrated the pilgrimage accounts of both Muslims and Europeans into his comprehensive history of the hajj, although with his main interest directed to the Hijaz.[14] Michael Christopher Low reframes the hajj as Indian Ocean history: he furthers William Roff's pioneering work[15] by contextualizing the hajj's crucial role in pan-Islamic and anticolonial ties between India and the Ottoman Empire.[16] There are several works dealing with *hajji*s from the Russian Empire. Although they have a research agenda in common with the above-mentioned works, they lack reference to the experience of other empires and the combination of Muslim sources and archival documents.[17] The paper is a preliminary attempt to incorporate study of the Russian hajj into broader comparative studies.

In this paper I contend that the politics surrounding the traffic of Russia's Muslim subjects to the Ottoman lands and back consisted of multiple layers. The Russian government was concerned about its location in international relations, whose influence on the intra-bureaucratic debate around Muslim mobility was no less significant than that of the domestic challenge from the Muslim population. While the state was ready to make use of Muslim agency as diplomatic and administrative leverage, some Muslims were willing to play an intermediary role between the state and the Muslim communities. Last, but not least, border-crossing experience and expertise that travelers brought home were seeds of dispute in their native communities.

Roads to Mecca: World Order and Muslim Networking

In the second half of the nineteenth century pilgrims from the Russian Empire traveled mainly along three routes. Two of them owed their development to the linking of railways and steamship ports.[18] First of all, the Shiites of the southern Caucasus in particular entered Baghdad, traveled through Shiite holy places, and crossed the Arabian Peninsula. Secondly, the pilgrims left Samarkand and Bukhara, passed through Afghanistan to Bombay on foot and by train, and sailed either to Jidda or Yanbu by steamship. Since the 1880s, pilgrims from Turkestan, including those from Afghanistan and Chinese territory, could use the Trans-Caspian military railway, although it was expensive, traveling from Krasnovodsk to Baku by water and from Baku to the Black Sea ports by train. Some of those from Chinese Turkestan even posed as Russian subjects with the necessary documents issued at the Russian consulates; the Russian diplomats in their turn were ready to protect them before Ottoman officials.[19] The third route was the most common for the Muslim population of European Russia and Siberia: traveling to the Black Sea ports by train and sailing to Istanbul and from there through Suez to Jidda or Yanbu. The opening of the Tashkent-Orenburg railway in 1906 made this route the most economical for Turkestan Muslims, too.[20] The Russian consulate at Jidda in 1893 recorded 86,489 pilgrims passing through Jidda and Yanbu, of which 4,328 Russian subjects arrived from Bombay and 1,808 from Suez.[21]

Empires with a substantial number of Muslim subjects rigorously observed the annual hajj in order to prevent pilgrims from being infected with vicious political ideas and cholera, which equally subverted state security. Of course, for the Ottoman government, protection of pilgrims was vital in its demonstration of beneficent power to the Muslims of the world; the completion of the Hijaz Railroad in 1908 connecting Damascus and Medina offers the strongest evidence.[22] Thus, by the end of the nineteenth century, the Hijaz as the source of epidemic and anticolonial activities became a competitive site among the great powers in boosting prestige in the Muslim world. Eight international sanitary conferences were convened between 1851 and 1894, where the great powers' rivalry over influence in the Middle East as well as Britain's breach of international agreements often hampered joint action. The location of the Russian and Ottoman Empires at the periphery of Europe was a strategic asset for both states to fashion themselves as crucial partners in the protection of Europe from the cholera epidemic.[23]

Consulates based in Jidda played a crucial role in monitoring the sanitation and security of the colossal tide of hajjis; the first British vice consul at Jidda had already appeared in 1838, and a Dutch consul was appointed in 1872. Although the necessity to appoint Muslim consuls emerged in the middle of the 1860s among British diplomats, it was realized as the appointment of Indian surgeon Abdur Razzack as vice consul in 1881.[24] A Russian consulate was established in Jidda in 1891; it aimed not only at regulating hajj conditions for Muslim subjects, but also at "extending the fascination with our [Russia's] name into the Muslim East."[25] The first Russian consul at Jidda was Shagimardan Miriasovich Ibragimov, who had served in Turkestan for a long time. A dragoman of the consulate Shakirdzhan Ishaev commended Ibragimov for his attempts to guard compatriots from "locusts," or local wily guides and brokers.[26] The consulate provided safe custody for money and belongings of the pilgrims; if anyone died during the pilgrimage, the consulate would send them back to the heirs. Russia's protection was requested by those who originally had escaped military service, prosecution, and debt, and stayed in Mecca and Medina for a protracted period. The newly established Russian consulate at Jidda in its turn could depend on them for its operation in the holy places. Although cautioning not to promote the pilgrimage, the consulate also hoped that satisfying the hajji's needs would make it possible to reinforce its influence among them as well as to vie with the Ottoman authorities.[27]

The great powers' endeavor to forge international conventions for containment of an epidemic were closely connected to their imagination of the Muslim subjects' anti-colonial networking through the annual journey. But in reality communal barriers seemed to be high enough to hamper communications among the coreligionists. In Jidda, Mecca, and Medina, for instance, pilgrims were distributed among the guides (*muṭawwif* or *dalīl*) and their heads (*shaykh*) with different linguistic and cultural specialties, according to each client's respective country of origin. These hereditary guilds of pilgrimage guides, despite their corruption and abuses, provided pilgrims with guidance in performing the complex rituals of the hajj. Still, the British and Dutch attempted to keep them under surveillance, since they were likely to operate outside the Hijaz with the dubious political aims of pan-Islamic propaganda.[28]

Of course, there were guides specializing in the travels of Russian Muslim pilgrims according to their regional origin. Appointed by the written order of the sharif of Mecca, these guides also traveled around the Muslim regions of the Russian Empire in order to invite fellow believers to undertake the hajj. The main guide at Mecca, Mukhammad-Ali-Srudzhi, was a guide for "all Tatars and Kirgizs [Kazakhs] of the Russian Empire": he spoke Russian and knew "all famous Tatar merchants and rich men as well as sufi leaders and mullahs living in the Russian cities and the Kazakh steppe," keeping in touch with many of them.[29] Still, the pilgrims from Russia denounced these guilds for their bribery and indifference to the interests of "foreigners": in February 1907, the Kazakh pilgrims petitioned the Russian consul at Jidda to appoint a Kazakh as their guide as well as to establish a consul or vice-consul at Yanbu for protection of the hajjis.[30]

Russian Muslims created networks of lodges (*takīya* or tekke) familiar to fellow countrymen, rarely transcending communal limits.[31] One dragoman of the Russian consulate at Jidda, Shakirdzhan Ishaev, originally from Tashkent, considered one Tatar merchant of Istanbul, Mirza Salekh Mukhammed Karimov, to be the "kernel of all the abuses against Russia": Karimov worked as a mediator in the hajj and immigration (*mukhadzhirstvo*) to the Ottoman land, concealing bankrupt merchants. He managed a tekke that one Kazan merchant Iunusov donated for destitute Tatar hajjis.[32] In 1895, 126 Russian and Bukharan subjects lived in Mecca. There, Ishaev listed 24 tekkes, including five for the Kazan Tatars: one lodge that belonged to a Tatar merchant of Istanbul Duberdeev had its clean rooms distinguished from the others. "Sarts" from Central Asia organized the tekkes according to their regional belonging: Bukhara, Samarkand, Margelan, Andijan, Tashkent, and Namangan.[33] The Russian consulate at Jidda and the local Ottoman authorities vied for control of the tekkes: while the latter attempted to transfer them to be administered as pious endowments *(waqf)*, thereby depriving the consulate of the right of demesne, the consulate offered Russia's protection as well as participation in the personnel management of the tekkes.[34]

Muslim Agents between State and Travelers

Within the borders of the Russian Empire, the Muslim administration served as a channel to relay the government message to the Muslim community. In the Volga-Ural region, the Orenburg Spiritual Assembly based in Ufa disseminated not only admonitions of its head *(mufti)* as a top of regional Islamic authority, but also instructions of the Royal Anti-plague Commission established in January 1897. In the same year, when plague that had broken out in India was expected to reach the Hijaz, the Spiritual Assembly instructed the Muslim community to abstain from pilgrimage that year, "as the Holy Sharī'a strictly instructs that one beware of the possibility of plague infection and transmission."[35] In 1901, the head of the Spiritual Assembly, Mufti Sultanov announced that the Royal Anti-plague Commission permitted pilgrimage that year with the proviso that hajjis depart from one of the Black Sea ports and return to either Feodosiia or Batumi for disinfection in quarantine facilities.[36]

It was the Andijan uprising in 1898 that forced the Russian government to elaborate concrete regulations to handle the border-crossing mobility of the Muslim subjects. The impact of the uprising is comparable to that of the Sepoy Mutiny of 1857-58, which made British officials increasingly concerned with international webs of anticolonial radicalism.[37] After the uprising, the governor general of Turkestan S.M. Dukhovskoi, well known for his report on Islam in Turkestan submitted to the tsar in 1899, ordered specialists to compile a series of detailed studies of Muslim religious practices and beliefs; the first volume contained an article concerning the hajj, as the leader of the uprising Madali Ishan had also undertaken it. Its author V.I. Iarov-Ravskii claimed persuasively that the pilgrimage exacerbated Muslim fanaticism and political instability, with the Ottoman sultan and the sharif of Mecca at the summit uniting the Muslim world. He buttressed his arguments by citing not only an "anti-Muslim missionary" from Kazan, but also the renowned Dutch Orientalist Christiaan Snouck Hurgronje.[38]

However, the general staff made a different observation based on its own monitoring. In 1898, the War Ministry dispatched to the

Hijaz Muslim Staff Captain, Abd al-Aziz Davletshin, originally from Ufa province, and one Muslim doctor, Dalgat. Despite the concern of the Foreign Ministry over their security, the War Ministry insisted that they travel as "real pilgrims" without any preliminary contact with the Ottoman officials or the local Russian diplomats.[39] In his report, Davletshin gave assurance that the hajj did not lead to the political union of various Muslim peoples; on the contrary, he argued, disenchantment with the Ottoman state and its "caliph" during the hajj made the Russian subjects "fevered patriots" who would augment Russia's prestige in the Hijaz. He even contrasted it with hatred of the locals toward the British. Davletshin ended his report with a suggestion that instead of incompetent Ottoman officials, Muslim consuls or vice consuls of the European powers be positioned directly in Mecca to supervise all sanitary measures.[40] A dragoman of the Russian consulate at Jidda Shakirdzhan Ishaev had also made a similar observation in his report of the hajj of 1895: it was here in Mecca that the Tatars and Kazakhs in particular recognized the comfort of their own country as well as the complete negligence of the Ottoman government, although people from Turkestan expressed only their admiration for Mecca.[41]

Thus, elaborating on a bill concerning control of Muslim pilgrims from Russia, the Royal Anti-plague Commission grasped the two opposing observations of the hajj. However, the commission gave preference to Iarov-Ravskii's: "The hajj ... should definitely be recognized as a detrimental and unfavorable phenomenon from the national viewpoint." Still, taking into account the international conventions of Vienna (1892 and 1897) and Paris (1894), the commission deemed it essential to keep the hajj as an "inexorable and only tolerated evil" within rational limitations. It was also ready to collaborate with the Orenburg, Crimea, and Trans-Caucasus Muslim administrations in order to clarify the state measures to the Muslim communities. The Foreign Ministry in its turn cautioned against facilitating Muslim mobility so that Muslim subjects should not wrongly expect the government's protection of the hajj.[42]

In 1903, the Russian state promulgated temporary regulations for Muslim pilgrims. Muslim pilgrims should have special passports for foreign travel. Russian as well as foreign Muslim hajjis were to proceed through ports appointed by the Interior Ministry for sanitary purification: in the Black Sea, pilgrims could leave Odessa, Sevastopol', or Batumi, but they could return only to Feodosiia as the sole quarantine point. Quarantine officers were to send certificates of pilgrims' purification to governors of the pilgrims' provinces of residence. Violation of regulations was a matter of travelers' criminal responsibility.[43] Similar measures were already functioning for Orthodox pilgrims to Jerusalem; the new regulations seemed to contribute to the increase in the number of hajjis.[44]

The institutionalization of pilgrim transport could be reinforced with the help of the travel industry. The government of India approached the travel firm of Thomas Cook & Son to facilitate control of the pilgrimage.[45] In Russia, it was Sayyid Gani Sayyid 'Aẓimbāyūf from Tashkent who saw a business opportunity in the state administration of the hajj.[46] He successfully obtained the interior minister's consent to conduct the business, thanks to the mediation of 'Alī 'Askar Mīrzā Ṣirṭlanūf, Muslim state deputy from Ufa province. Sayyid 'Aẓimbāyūf's project deprived hajjis of much of their mobility. Hajjis were to come to certain fixed main stations of railroads as rendezvous points for departure: travelers from a part of Central Asia to Tashkent, those from Central Asia and Siberia to Samara, and those from Siberia, Kazan, and other Volga provinces to Penza. At these points, Sayyid 'Aẓimbāyūf planned to build guest lodges (*karawān sarāylar*) with mosques and separate rooms for women, which would be under the observation of the railroad authorities and the local police. Trains were to have cars specialized for hajjis. Sayyid 'Aẓimbāyūf's plan still allowed hajjis to choose either Odessa or Batumi for their departure by sea.

The order of the Odessa provisional governor general on August 9, 1908 buttressed Sayyid 'Aẓimbāyūf's initiative: it obliged pilgrims coming to Odessa to sojourn exclusively at Sayyid 'Aẓimbāyūf's "hajji lodge (*hājjī khāne*)." Other facilities were not eligible to accept hajjis without the governor general's sanction. When groups of hajjis arrived at Odessa by train, the guides among them had to inform the head of the station police of how many pilgrims there were and from where; receiving the report from the Odessa police authorities, the hajjikhane would send its representatives and sanitary doctor accompanied by the police to lead the hajjis directly to the lodge. They were practically forbidden from leaving it and were kept under the doctor's observation until their departure. Violators were either to be imprisoned for three months or fined three thousand rubles.[47]

Sayyid 'Aẓimbāyūf's monopoly of lodging and shipping as well as Ṣīrṭlānūf's collaboration with him aroused Muslims' indignation.[48]

The Astrakhan newspaper *Īdil* reported the hajjis' complaint that the agents of the hajjikhane at Odessa forced them to buy steamship tickets at unreasonable fares, taking advantage of the hajjis' segregation. The pilgrims sought help not only from the Muslim press but also from the Muslim deputies of the State Duma.[49] The organ of the Orenburg Spiritual Assembly *Ma'lūmāt* also addressed the pilgrims' discontent with being handled as "livestock for sale (*ṣātliq ḥayawānlar*)": excessive duties were levied on them at customs, and after disinfection in the fumigatory (*bakhūrkhāne*), they were obliged to throw away the dates and the *Zamzam* water brought from the holy cities as souvenirs. *Ma'lūmāt* gave assurance that the hajjis would pray for Russia's bliss in Mecca, if the Russian state treated them decently as Russian citizens (*Rūsiyaning ghrāzhdānlari*).[50]

In the increasingly interconnected world of the nineteenth century, state borders became "semipermeable membranes," open to European colonial and commercial enterprises and closed to the spread of the epidemic from the "Orient." In this world order, the hajjis were categorized as the main pernicious carriers of cholera. However, singling out the pilgrims as such justified the lowering of restraints on other groups of travelers. [51] The Crimean Muslim newspaper *Tarjumān* (Interpreter) was conscious of this asymmetrical treatment of the hajjis. It observed that the hajjis now gained passports not for the pilgrimage, but for sightseeing and trade.[52] *Tarjumān* contended that the hajjis brought such an enormous amount of money to the Russian railways and steamships that they were eligible to insist on refinement of their travel conditions: it estimated that eight to ten thousand hajjis from Russia, Iran, Central Asia, and Chinese Turkestan spent two million rubles on Russian transportation. *Tarjumān* warned that the pilgrims' escape of the restrictions in Odessa and the use of other foreign steamships would bring sanitary and economic harm to Russia.[53]

As Sayyid 'Aẓimbāyūf worked as the chief agent of "Dobrovol'nyi flot" based in Odessa, *Tarjumān* instead recommended the steamships of "Russkoe obshchestvo" based in Sevastopol'.[54] *Tarjumān* claimed that Sayyid 'Aẓimbāyūf's position as chief agent of the particular company was not compatible with his position as an observer from the Interior Ministry; as an official person, he had to guide the pilgrims to appropriate steamships. The introduction of rigorous control of the hajjis in Odessa almost coincided with the completion of the Hijaz Railroad connecting Damascus and Medina.

Tarjumān capitalized upon this in order to provide the steamship companies with his idea of linking Sevastopol' with Beirut through Istanbul. It argued that this new route would free the hajjis from the charge levied at the Suez Canal.[55]

Tarjumān even exhibited itself as a mediator of the Muslim community not only with the Russian but also with the Ottoman states. It appealed to its readers, saying that the newspaper would turn the attention of both governments' to all the hajjis' grievances against the local government and caravan heads in the Hijaz as well as railways, hajji lodges, and steamships in Russia. Endorsing the efficiency of the Hijaz Railroad, the newspaper insisted that the Ottoman government guarantee the safety of the caravan route between Medina and Mecca in order to facilitate the use of the new route. Estimating profits of 120 thousand lira from thirty and forty thousand hajjis using the new railroad (including eight to ten thousand from Russia), *Tarjumān* asserted that it would be Istanbul's duty as well as to its benefit not to cede the profits to the Suez Canal and the quarantine facilities.[56]

Border-crossing Experience and Local Politics

The successive revolutions of 1905 in Russia and 1908 in the Ottoman Empire made the domestic Russian authorities obsessing about "pan-Islamic" and "pan-Turkic" challenges from inside and outside. Tatar intellectuals' discourse regarding the unification of the Russian Muslims was convincing enough for the Russian authorities to believe in the penetration of global pan-Islamic movements in Russia. The efficient operation of the security services depended on the officers' capability to see concrete struggles within the context of a broader grasp of overall government strategy. They could justify the most severe measures for safeguarding the integrity of the empire against foreign threats.[57]

However, quite unlike the monolithic imagination of the officialdom, different groups of Muslim intellectuals related to the Ottoman Empire in different ways, depending on more immediate political concerns rooted in their own struggles at home. Modern travelogue writers usually sought to offer a critique of their own society and thereby transform the mentality towards social reform, providing their fellow people with cognizance of the self and others encountered during their voyages.[58] The Muslim press in the Volga-

Ural region, which progressively developed after the 1905 Revolution, also clearly reflected a wide variety of interactions with the Ottomans. Russian Muslims' intellectual borrowings from Istanbul and Cairo did not lead to servile imitation, but reinforcement or confirmation of a position already adopted by particular local clerics.[59] Moreover, contributors to local newspapers and periodicals often attempted to question the relevance of knowledge imported to this region, and to demonstrate a discrepancy between Muslims of European Russia and those of the Ottoman lands. Religious scholars (*'ulamā'*) and newly emerging intellectuals made competitive use of that comparison in order to reinforce their authority over "religious and communal (*dinī wa millī*)" discourses within the highly competitive local Muslim press.[60]

Hajj accounts, which began to be published in the 1880s, provided those wishing to visit holy cities with dry but practical description of the route, transportation, lodging, expenses, sights, and holy mausoleums.[61] A series of brochures named *Manāsik al-Ḥajj* furnished readers with the theological significance of the hajj, requirements in preparation, and meticulous details of rituals according to the Hanafi juridical literature.[62] By contrast, at the beginning of the twentieth century, some travelogue compilers began to pursue the obvious aim of contributing to Islamic reformist literature. They usually appropriated the "European" vantage in order to address their societies' backwardness, and prescribed remedies in Islamic terms. In the Volga-Ural Muslim press Muslim travelers from Turkestan were a typical object of reformist critique.

A travelogue written by Khair Allah al-'Uthmānī, imam of the first mosque in Qarghali near Orenburg and the former deputy of the second State Duma, is a standard reformist account. While al-'Uthmānī condemned the "Sarts" from Turkestan for their shameful behavior on their way to Odessa by train, he proudly depicted how he himself successfully managed scheming lodging agents and European steamship offices at Odessa, Istanbul, and Beirut. However, it seemed to al-'Uthmānī that the world changed at Suez: "We had traveled in the European world (*Yāwrūpā 'ālimī*) before we came to Suez. As soon as we stepped into Suez, we found ourselves in the pilgrims' world (*Ḥājjīlik 'ālimī*), victims of cheating deeds, like other pilgrims." In a steamship bound for Jidda, al-'Uthmānī enjoyed talks with two Frenchmen fluent in Arabic rather than with his "dirty and destitute" fellow believers from Java, India, and Kashghar. When the

Frenchmen ironically asked him if these people were well off enough to be eligible to undertake the hajj, al-'Uthmānī replied that it was their Islamic legal schools that allowed them to do. In addition, he even regarded these Muslim travelers as deviating from the religion and legal tradition in terms of hygiene.[63]

In marked contrast to the deep suspicion of the security police against the Muslim population, the Russian diplomatic representatives and the Muslim subjects abroad were involved in close interrelations. Russian Muslim immigrants invoked their citizenship as a means of receiving assistance from the Russian officials serving in the Ottoman Empire, who were in turn ready to offer them determined support.[64] Fātiḥ Karīmī, chief editor of the influential Orenburg newspaper *Waqt,* was a correspondent in Istanbul during the first Balkan War. Although the Orenburg governor regarded Karīmī as "a distinguished activist of the pan-Islamic movement and an irreconcilable opponent of the state order,"[65] Karīmī assured that industrious Russian Muslims devoting themselves to rescue activities in the Ottoman Empire would enhance Russia's prestige among the Ottomans; he argued that they would think that Russia was furnishing Muslims with "good discipline (*tarbiya*) and noble spirit (*'āl ḥiss*)." This kind of rhetoric had been observed in the reports of Staff Captain Davletshin as well as a dragoman of the Russian consulate at Jidda Ishaev in the 1890s: they made use of it in order to push forward proposals concerning improvement of hajj conditions. Karīmī in his turn employed this rhetoric as a remedy against pan-Islamic paranoia that obsessed Russian officials and publications.[66]

Conclusion

The Russian government saw Muslim subjects traveling to the Ottoman Empire and back as a challenge and leverage. On the one hand, regarding the Hijaz as the birthplace of epidemic and anticolonial subversion, Russian officials as well as their counterparts in other empires treated Muslim pilgrims as a menace to state security in sanitary and political terms. Just as the Sepoy Mutiny served as a spur for the British to caution against a network of radical Muslim activists, so did the Andijan uprising for the Russians. On the other hand, they were forced to recognize the hajj as an "inexorable and only tolerated evil," as excessive restrictions on the hajj could backfire, adversely affecting state stability. Elaboration of the regulations concerning hajj traffic at the turn of the century clearly revealed the Russian government's ambivalent stance toward Muslim mobility.

In addition, challenge also derived from the contemporary world order. In the second half of the nineteenth century, colonial powers attempted to control their subjects' hajj by means of organization of sanitation and tourism. The Ottoman government in its turn endeavored to maintain its paramount position as protector of Mecca and Medina, the epitome of which was the construction of the Hijaz Railroad. Thus, the Hijaz was the locus of competition among the great powers. The consulate at Jidda stood in the front line of monitoring the hygiene and political atmosphere among the hajjis, protecting the interests of each empire's subjects, and extending its influence to the Muslim world through the pilgrims.

As seen in the practice of the other great powers, Russia also employed Muslim agents so that they represented her imperial power abroad. The government tended to find appropriate figures among Muslims from Turkestan, who constituted the majority of the hajjis: Shagimardan Miriasovich Ibragimov was the first consul at Jidda; Shakirdzhan Ishaev was a dragoman of the consulate; Sayyid Ganī Sayyid 'Aẓimbāyūf was expected to assist the government in the control of hajj traffic. Staff Captain Abd al-Aziz Davletshin posed as a "real pilgrim" in order to provide the War Ministry with a detailed picture of the Hijaz and the pilgrims there.

The increased, if not willing, involvement of the Russian state in the hajj administration at the beginning of the twentieth century rendered not only the traditional channel of the Muslim administration but also the Muslim press enthusiastic about the role of mediator between the state and Muslim communities. It is true that the Orenburg Spiritual Assembly was one of the local branches of the huge machinery of the Interior Ministry. Still, it had two faces: while ready to underpin the state's anti-epidemic measures by communicating its intentions to the Muslim community, the Spiritual Assembly attempted to meet the need for hajj information as well as listen to the pilgrims' grievances. The Crimean newspaper *Tarjumān* even manifested itself as a mediator between the pilgrims and both the Russian and Ottoman states. Furthermore, the circulation of the printed word concerning the hajj contributed to inculcating the local Muslims with knowledge of Muhammad's life and the early history of Islam.[67]

Politics surrounding Muslim travelers between the Russian and Ottoman Empires arose not merely in negotiations with the state, but also inside the Muslim communities. Contrary to the Russian officials' speculation over Muslim unity created by their voyage, communal demarcations profoundly penetrated Muslim travelers. The encounter with Muslim "others" and border-crossing knowledge often brought controversy over various issues into the Volga-Ural Muslim community. To be sure, the revolutionary development of transportation led to the massive popularization of the hajj. But it seems unlikely that the ordinary masses commanded Arabic to communicate with the coreligionists in a significant manner. Rather, they might have to increasingly depend upon familiar networks of *tekkes* (lodging) as well as the *muṭawwif* (guide) system in the Hijaz, which operated following differences in the pilgrims' communal origins. Reformist travelers from the Volga-Ural region often made critical remarks about "Sarts," Kazakhs, and Ottoman society with a view to inclining readers to reassess their own societies. Furthermore, the demonstration of the potential of Muslim subjects to serve as leverage in the Ottoman lands gave travelers as well as the local population the prospect of alleviating the fierce discourse of Russian officialdom concerning the onerous challenge spawned by Muslim mobility.

Actually, what the enormous number of hajjis brings to Russia's Muslim communities today remains to be studied. As in other Islamic countries, tainted with favoritism, cronyism, and corruption, distribution of the limited quota of pilgrims may exert a certain influence on politics in the Muslim regions, making the travelers not so much "guests of God" as "guests of the state."[68] The Russian authorities attempt to prevent the pilgrims from meddling with ideologically biased literature including the Wahabite during the hajj.[69] However, in the past two decades Russia's Muslim Boards and regional secular authorities have fostered an indigenous "tolerant" tradition of Islam for their struggle against fundamentalism called "Wahabiism" in Russia: they have created the religious cadres through their own institutions of Islamic education, avoiding dependency upon foreign teachers and students who had studied abroad and began to denounce the local forms of Islam as heresy on their return home. Today some pilgrims from Tatarstan even denigrate the Wahabite way of life in Saudi Arabia, as they so internalize not only the concept of the regional tradition of a tolerant Islam, but also the existence of the Muslim community confined rigidly within the state borders, namely "the Russian *umma*."[70] The scrutiny of the entanglement of the holy travel to Mecca and local politics will equip us with a valuable angle to observe the dynamics of contemporary Muslim communities in Russia.

NOTES AND REFERENCES

1. [http://newsru.com/world/11feb2007/saud.html] See materials on the site of the General Consulate of the Russian Federation at Jidda, [http://www.jeddah.mid.ru/Albom/rech_putina.htm]; [http://www.jeddah.mid.ru/Albom/prince.htm] See also Grigorii G. Kosach's comment on this historical event, [http://i-r-p.ru/page/stream-exchange/index-10531.html]
2. See an article on the site of the Russia Muftis Council. [http://www.muslim.ru/1/news/1/290.htm]
3. R. Bianchi, *Guests of God: Pilgrimage and Politics in the Islamic World* (Oxford, 2004), p. 64.
4. E. A. Rezvan, "Khadzhzh iz Rossii," in *Vostok: istoriia i kul'tura* (St. Petersburg, 2000), pp. 139, 144; *Khadzh Rossiiskikh musul'man: sbornik putevykh zametok o khadzhe* (Nizhnii Novgorod, 2008), 73.
5. In 2007 the hajj took place twice, since the Muslim lunar calendar was shorter in that year.
6. [http://www.itar-tass.com/level2.html?NewsID=13401244&PageNum=0]
7. *Khadzh Rossiiskikh musul'man*, p. 73.
8. On works of this council, see an interview with Akhmed Bilalov on *Izvestiia*, [http://91.202.99.13/obshestvo /article3100390/]; some protocols of this council are available on [http://www.government.ru/content/coordinatingauthority/zhukov/religija/inf_mater iali/]
9. See an interview with Kamil' Iskhakov on *Rossiiskaia Gazeta*, [http://www.rg.ru/2008/09/26/ishakov.html]
10. [http://www.islam.ru/pressclub/smi/russia_hajj]
11. In the preface of his pioneering book, Serge A. Zenkovsky mentioned that he owed his work to "discussions and talks with participants in and eyewitnesses to…the Turkic national movement in Russia," such as Mustafa Chokaev, Ayaz Iskhaki, and Ahmed Zeki Velidi Togan. S.A. Zenkovsky, *Pan-Turkism and Islam in Russia* (Cambridge, Mass., 1960), pp. ix–x.
12. To name a few, S. A. Dudoignon, "Status, Strategies and Discourses of a Muslim "Clergy" under a Christian Law: Polemics about the Collection of the *Zakât* in Late Imperial Russia," in S.A. Dudoignon and H.

Komatsu, eds., *Islam in Politics in Russia and Central Asia (Early Eighteenth to Late Twentieth Centuries)* (London, 2001), pp. 43–73; Ch. Noack, "State Policy and its Impact on the Formation of a Muslim Identity in the Volga-Urals," in Dudoignon and Komatsu, *Islam in Politics*, pp. 3–26; A. Frank, *Islamic Historiography and 'Bulghar' Identity among the Tatars and Bashkirs of Russia* (Leiden, 1998); R. Crews, *For Prophet and Tsar: Islam and Empire in Russia and Central Asia* (Cambridge, Mass., 2006); D. Iu. Arapov, *Sistema gosudarstvennogo regulirovaniia islama v Rossiiskoi imperii (posledniaia tret' XVIII-nachalo XX vv.)* (Moscow, 2004).

13. M. Reynolds, *The Ottoman-Russian Struggle for Eastern Anatolia and the Caucasus, 1908-1918: Identity, Ideology and the Geopolitics of World Order* (PhD diss., Princeton University, 2003); E. Kane, *Pilgrims, Holy Places, and the Multi-confessional Empire: Russian Policy toward the Ottoman Empire under Tsar Nicholas I, 1825–1855* (PhD diss., Princeton University, 2005); J. Meyer, *Turkic Worlds: Community Representation and Collective Identity in the Russian and Ottoman Empires, 1870–1914* (PhD diss., Brown University, 2007). An article based on its Chapter 6 was published as "Immigration, Return, and the Politics of Citizenship: Russian Muslims in the Ottoman Empire, 1860–1914," *International Journal of Middle East Studies* 39 (2007), pp. 15–32.
14. F. E. Peters, *The Hajj: The Muslim Pilgrimage to Mecca and the Holy Places* (Princeton, 1994), chapter 6.
15. W. Roff, "Sanitation and Security: The Imperial Powers and the Nineteenth Century Hajj," *Arabian Studies* 6 (1982), pp. 143–160.
16. M. Christopher Low, "Empire and the Hajj: Pilgrims, Plagues, and Pan-Islam under British Surveillance, 1865–1908," *International Journal of Middle East Studies* 40 (2008), pp. 269–290.
17. D. Brower, "Russian Roads to Mecca: Religious Tolerance and Muslim Pilgrimage in the Russian Empire," *Slavic Review* 55/3 (1996), pp. 567–584; Rezvan, "Khadzhzh iz Rossii," pp. 129–146; D. M. Usmanova, *Musul'manskie predstaviteli v rossiiskom parlamente. 1906–1916* (Kazan, 2005), pp. 427–434; V. P. Litvinov, *Vneregional'noe palomnichestvo musul'man Turkestana (epokha Novogo vremeni)* (Elets, 2006).
18. The railroad age began in Odessa in 1865. P. Herlihy, *Odessa: a History, 1794–1914* (Cambridge, Mass., 1986), p. 216. On the ports of the Black Sea, see Ch. King, *The Black Sea: a History* (Oxford, 2004), pp. 196–197.
19. Litvinov, *Vneregional'noe palomnichestvo*, pp. 144–145, 147. See also AVPRI (Arkhiv vneshnei politiki Possiiskoi imperii), f.149 (Turetskii

stol), op.502b, d.3371, ll.30-31; *Otchet Shtabs-kapitana Davletshina o komandirovke v Khidzhaz* (St. Petersburg, 1899), p. 120.

20. Brower, "Russian Roads," p. 579.
21. V. I. Iarov-Ravskii, "Palomnichestvo (khadzh) v Mekku i Medinu," in *Sbornik marerialov po musul'manstvu* vol.1. (St. Petersburg, 1899), pp. 131, 136, 143.
22. The construction of the Hijaz Railroad resonated with the Muslim communities outside the Ottoman Empire in that they realized they belonged to the Islamic world. The Muslims of India keenly responded the Ottomans' appeals for donations to this enterprise. A. Özcan, *Pan-Islamism: Indian Muslims, the Ottomans and Britain, 1877–1924* (Leiden, 1997), pp. 108-111. On enthusiasm of Russian Muslims, see articles of an Astrakhan newspaper, *Īdil* September 2, 1908, 1; October 28, 1908, 2–3; October 31, 1908, 2–3. See also articles of an Orenburg journal, *Shūrā* 1 (1909), 7; 3 (1909), 68–69.
23. V. Huber, "The Unification of the Globe by Disease? The International Sanitary Conferences on Cholera, 1851-1894," *The Historical Journal 49/2* (2006), esp. pp. 461, 463–464, 475; see also Peters, *The Hajj,* pp. 301-305, 310. On pressure from European governments on Russia, see also Brower, "Russian Roads," pp. 577–578.
24. Roff, "Sanitation and Security," pp. 144, 147–148, 158; Christopher Low, "Empire and the Hajj," pp. 273, 282–284.
25. AVPRI, f.180, op.517/2, d.5322, l.97.
26. Ishaev, "Mekka," pp. 62-64. Ibragimov died of cholera on his way back to Jidda from the hajj in 1892.
27. AVPRI, f.149, op.502b, d.3371, ll.18ob.-19; f.180, op.517/2, d.5322, ll.102b, 117-117ob. See also Meyer, "Immigration," pp. 24–25.
28. Roff, "Sanitation and Security," pp. 155-156; Christopher Low, "Empire and the Hajj," p. 284. See also Peters, *The Hajj*, pp. 246-248, 277–279.
29. Sh. Ishaev, "Mekka, sviashchennyi gorod musul'man (Razskaz palomnika)," *Sredneaziatskii vestnik* November (Tashkent, 1896), pp. 73–74, 79. See a list of the guides for the Russian Muslims, Iarov-Ravskii, "Palomnichestvo," pp. 134–135.
30. AVPRI, f.149, op.502b, d.3371, ll.62-64ob. The Jidda consulate had also acknowledged the necessity of the consulate agent at Yanbu since the early years of its establishment. Ibid., l.19ob; AVPRI, f.180, op.517/2, d.5322, l.101.
31. An intelligence officer of the War Ministry reported that "even our Kazakhs and Tatars do not want to know each other." *Otchet Shtabs-kapitana Davletshina*, p. 117.
32. AVPRI, f.180, op.517/2, d.5322, ll.249-251ob.

33. AVPRI, f.180, op.517/2, d.5322, ll.201-201ob., 203-203ob., 236-236ob.
34. AVPRI, f.149, op.502b, d.3371, ll.31-32. In his list, Ishaev included two tekkes of the "former Kashghar khan Iakub Khan." The name seems to imply Ya'qub Bik. These lodges were then managed by one Sart called Seifuddin. In 1882, one subject of Iakub Khan attempted to acquire the property. However, the Ottoman government prevented it, since, as protector of the holy cities, it banned the acquisition of property and real estate in Hijaz by non-Ottoman Muslims. Selim Deringil argues that the Ottoman authorities considered non-Ottoman Muslims a very dangerous fifth column that could be brought to bear against them by the colonial powers. S. Deringil, "The Ottoman Empire and Russian Muslims: Brothers or Rivals?" *Central Asian Survey* 13/3 (1994), p. 414.
35. *Sbornik tsirkuliarov i inykh rukovodiashchikh rasporiazhenii po okrugu Orenburgskogo magometanskogo dukhovnogo sobraniia, 1836–1903 g.* (Kazan, 2004; orig. Ufa, 1905), pp. 93–96.
36. Ibid., pp. 136-137.
37. Christopher Low, "Empire and the Hajj," pp. 269, 274–277. The Dutch had established a relationship between returned hajjis and rebelliousness against colonial authority in 1840–50s. Roff, "Sanitation and Security," p. 146.
38. *Iarov-Ravskii*, "Palomnichestvo," pp. 136, 148-152, 156. See also RGVIA, f.1396 (Shtab Turkestanskogo voennogo okruga), op.2, d.1740; Brower, *Turkestan*, p. 97–99. M.A. Miropiev, "Religioznoe i politicheskoe znachenie khadzha ili sviashchennogo puteshestviia mukhameddan v Mekku," *Trudy studentov missioner protivo-musul'manskogo otdelen ia pri Kazanskoi dukhovnoi akademii* vyp.15 (Kazan, 1877). Hurgronje himself believed that the political unity of Islam had ended forever. Bianchi, *Guests of God*, p. 43. See also H. Benda, "Christiaan Snouck Hurgronje and the Foundations of Dutch Islamic Policy in Indonesia," *The Journal of Modern History* 30/4 (1958), pp. 338–347.
39. RGVIA, f.400 (Glavnyi shtab Voennogo ministerstva), op.1, d.2239, ll.13, 17-17ob.
40. *Otchet Shtabs-kapitana Davletshina*, pp. 117-119, 144. See also A. Marshall, *The Russian General Staff and Asia, 1800-1917* (London, 2006), p. 123. Davletshin was also highly critical of *Materials about Islam* compiled by Tashkent specialists at the initiative of Governor-General Dukhovskoi. D. Iu. Arapov, *Imperatorskaia Rossiia i musul'manskii mir: sbornik statei* (Moscow, 2006), pp. 228–241.
41. AVPRI, f.180, op.517/2, d.5322, ll.224-225ob. In his travel account to Mecca which appeared on *Sredneaziatskii vestnik*, Ishaev described how

his position as a representative of the Russian empire filled local Arabs and Turks with awe. Ishaev, "Mekka," pp. 74, 78.

42. RGVIA, f.400, op.1, d.2904, ll.26-26ob., 36-37ob., 40ob., 57ob., 145ob.
43. Arapov, *Islam v Rossiiskoi imperii,* pp. 260-261; TsGIARB, f.I-295, op.11, d.542, l.157; GAOO (Gosudarstvennyi arkhiv Orenburgskoi oblasti), f.10 (Kantseliariia orenburgskogo gubernatora), op.1, d.236. This GAOO file also contains many application forms for pilgrimage passports which were sent by Kazakhs of Ural'sk province to the Orenburg governor.
44. Rezvan, "Khadzhzh iz Rossii," p. 139.
45. Roff, "Sanitation and Security," p. 152; Christopher Low, "Empire and the Hajj," p. 284.
46. On the activities of Sayyid Gani Sayyid 'Aẓimbāyūf, see also Brower, "Russian Roads," pp. 581-583.
47. *Tarjumān* 19 August 1908, 1–2; 14 September 1908, 3.
48. Usmanova, *Musul'manskie predstaviteli,* pp. 431-432.
49. *Īdil 4* November 1908, 2. The same newspaper published a telegraph of the Astrakhan pilgrims from Odessa who were satisfied with Sayyid 'Aẓimbāyūf providing them with clean steamship and special foods for Muslims. *Idil 2*8 October 1908, 3.
50. *Ma'lūmāt* 17 (1908), 377-379.
51. Huber, "The Unification of the Globe," pp. 473–474, 476.
52. *Tarjumān* September 7, 1908, 3.
53. *Tarjumān* August 5, 1908, 1-2, 4; August 22, 1908, 1.
54. *Tarjumān* September 14, 1908, 3. On 13 October the newspaper published an advertisement of special steamships for the pilgrimage in Russian, Persian, Tatar, and Turkish. It offered round trip ticket to Hijaz, first class 250 ruble, second class 200 rubles, third class 100 rubles. The steamship company proposed to arrange a "hajji house (*ḥājjīsarāy*)" (30 kopeikas a day for one person).
55. *Tarjumān* August 22, 1908, 1; November 14, 1908, 1–2.
56. *Tarjumān* August 5, 1908, 1–2, 4; September 7, 1908, 3; November 14, 1908, 1–2.
57. R. Geraci, *Window on the East: National and Imperial Identities in Late Tsarist Russia (Ithaca,* 2001), pp. 277, 282.
58. A. Khalid, "Pan-Islamism in Practice: the Rhetoric of Muslim Unity and its Uses," in E. Özdalga, ed., *Late Ottoman Society: the Intellectual Legacy* (London, 2005), pp. 206–207.
59. S.A. Dudoignon, "Echoes to *al-Mandr* among the Muslims of the Russian Empire: A preliminary research note on Riza al-Din b. Fakhr al-Din and the *Šūrā* (1908-1918)," in S.A. Dudoignon et al., eds., *Intellectuals in*

the Modern Islamic World: Transmission, transformation, communication (London and New York, 2006), pp. 85–87.

60. One of the most controversial issues between Ottoman and Russian reformists was whether the holy Quran could be translated into the vernacular. Mūsā Bīgī, *Khalq naiarina bir nlcha mas'ala* (Kazan, 1912), esp. pp. 88–93; *Shūrā* 12 (1912), 356-360; Fatiḥ Karīmī, *Istānbūl maktūblarī* (Orenburg, 1913), pp. 219, 312–313, 324, 327.
61. Muḥammadī b. Ṣāliḥ al-'Umarī thumma al-Qazānī, *Safarnāma* (Kazan, 1890); 'Abd al-'Aziz b. Muḥammad b. Ahmad al-Ḥājṭarkhānī, *Ḥajjādme* (Astrakhan, 1910).
62. *Kitāb-i Manāsik al-Ḥajj (Kazan,* 1882); Zayn al-Dīn b. Sharaf al-Dīn al-Bulghārī, *Risāla-i Manāsik al-Ḥajj* (Kazan, 1901).
63. *Waqt* 24 June 1912, 2; 19 July 1912, 3; 28 September 1912, 3.
64. Meyer, "Immigration," pp. 23–24.
65. GAOO. f.10, op.4, d.10/9, l.35.
66. Karīmī, *Istānbūl maktūblarī,* 55–56, 416–417.
67. It is not accidental that the beginning of the twentieth century witnessed local Muslims attempting to forge the Prophet's birthday (*Maulid al-nabīy*) as a "national" holiday. See articles on a Kazan journal and newspaper, *Maktab* 2 (1914), 29–31; *Qūyāsh,* 22 January 1914, 1.
68. On other Islamic states, see Bianchi, *Guests of God*, pp. 5–6, 70–72, 75. On contemporary Russia, see *Khadzh Rossiiskikh musul'man*, p. 74.
69. See a proposal by the Hajj Council of the Russian government at the conference on the results of the 2003 hajj in Makhachkala at the end of May 2003 [http://www.islam.ru/pressclub/smi/russia_hajj/].
70. My interview with one teacher at the Russian Islamic University in Kazan on September 17, 2008. He carried out the hajj at the end of 2007.

9

Creation of the Composite Draft of the Buryat Heroic Epic 'Geser' in the Context of the Project of Nation Building*

Marina N. Baldano

The Buryat heroic epic 'Geser' – is the climax of the multi-faceted oral creativity of the Buryat people and an outstanding tribute to the epic poem of universal relevance. It is a unique product of the oral folk creativity, a representation of the moral and aesthetic ideals of the Buryat society, which is a kind of encyclopaedia of folk life.

The Buryats have always loved their epic, they named their children after their heroes, they organized sportive events in memory of their glorious gunners, bowed to the precious places which were connected to the legends about Geser. And today modern Buryat painters, writers and composers in their poetry and paintings, in musical compositions refer to the traditions of their mighty epic. It is fully a matter of course that heroic narrative, inhabiting practically the entire territory of the Baikal region for centuries, exerted a strong influence on the mentality of the Buryat people, and informed its national consciousness.

At the beginning of the twentieth century some Buryat academicians (scientists) like M. Hangalov, T. Zhamtsarano, B. Baradin and others, who had begun writing diverse versions of it, referred to Geser. The scientific and literary assimilation of national creativity that had begun came to a halt after the October Revolution. Simultaneously with the triumph of the Bolsheviks, a grand experiment began to create a 'new' national culture and identity, which was new in the sense that all of them were constructed in the context of a socialist ideology.

---

* Translated by Susmita Bhattacharya, Fellow, MAKAIAS, Kolkata and Aditi Bhaduri, Independent Researcher and Journalist, Kolkata.

At the head of this process of construction lay the ruling party, whose leadership, both at the centre and in the regions, determined the main parameters and criteria of nation construction. In the official discourse of the national-cultural and nation-state building, a new culture which was 'national in form, and socialist in content' began to be constructed. And it must be said that the interests of the national elite sometimes coincided with the decisions of the powers, and sometimes sharply differed. This happened with the epic 'Geser'.

In 1940 the Decade of Buryat-Mongal Art was celebrated in Moscow. The same year the government of the USSR adopted the decision to prepare the composite poetic version of the heroic epic Geser. The articles of S. Ignatyev and A. Khaklov, who were the secretaries of the Buryat Mongol oblast committee of the All Russia Communist Party (B), which were published in the central and local press, underscored the significance of the originality of the epic of the Buryat people in the spiritual cultures of the past and the present.

Power politics and the ambitions of the national elite coincided on this issue. However, in the words of J. Stalin, the Bolsheviks adopted measures, which were directed at the 'maximum development of the national cultures, so that it could drain itself to the end, and thereafter, a base was formed which would form an international socialist culture.'[1]

During this time the need to collect and study the primary verses of the epic Geser became acute. Active participation in the exercise to collect the primary material was undertaken by G. Belgayev, the Director of the institute for languages, literature and history (GIYLI), his deputy, B. Sanzhiyev, academic secretary N. Zugeev, coordinators D. Hiltukhin, T. Galzanov, N. Baldano, A. Shadaev[2]. The collection of material was further activated because of the celebrations in 1940 of the 500th anniversary of the Kalmyk epic 'Zhangar'. Already in the spring of 1941 a total of 115 thousand verses of 'Geser' was collected which till then had not been worked on.

On 6 May 1941 the Soviet Interior Committee (*sovnarkom*) of USSR came out with a ruling, signed by Stalin, on the celebration of the anniversary of the epic Geser in November of 1942, but the celebrations did not take place because of the Great Patriotic War. Many of the writers and coordinators of GIYLI were mobilized on the front, others directed their efforts and activities in accordance with the emergent needs of that time. However, work on the collection and the study of the verses of the epic did not stop. On the contrary, this work was given extra attention. N. Baldano's assignment at the front was delayed, he was assigned to compile a composite text of 'Geser', and he continued work on the study and collation of different versions of the epic.

The compilation of a composite version of the epic was, in essence, not so much of a literary project, as it was a project of nation construction. According to B. Dugarov, the most prominent Geseroved, 'the necessity of compiling a composite version of the epic Geser in the literary Buryat language, together with the scientific research and academic publications of the most authentic folk-tale variations of the Geseriads was understood by both the most scientific researchers of the epic, as well as by the representatives of the writers' workshop as far as the special significance of the particular *uliger* (tale) as the primary national achievement. Such an urgent assignment was conditioned by the ideology of promoting and development of the national literary and Buryat literary language like an oral artistic process, in which the heroic epic 'Geser' has from time immemorial for centuries of its existence in the different dialects and tongues of the Buryat-Mongal language and widely known to the Buryats, who live on both sides of the Baikal, have been called on to unite the great centuries of old oral tradition of epic words with the generally accepted literary language of the Buryats of the twentieth century'.[3]

N. Baldano was already experienced in the poetic research of folklores, which included such treasures of national creativity like 'Kharaasgai-mergen'. Work on Geser demanded maximum efficiency. Apart from this a series of most comprehensive folk-lore versions of Geser specialists, like those of P. Petrov, P.Tushemilov, had not yet been inducted into the scientific circle. Thus N. Baldano had to himself 'open' the primary sources, work in the archives, which stored the manuscripts of the texts, had to familiarize himself with the folklore narratives, touching upon the still living traditions of implementation of the ancient *uligers* (tales).

Here it should be mentioned, that no matter what a phenomenal memory the narrator had, within a century a variety of recitations and singing had appeared, thus the folklorists, philologists, and scholar had a huge work before them – of drafting a single narrative about Geser from a series of varied oral narratives, in order to publish its written version, which was initially to be an academic publication, and later a literary-artistic one.

In 1943 the poet M. Tarlovsky was assigned the task of translating the epic into Russian. N. Baldano and M. Tarlovsky prepared a tape for the Buryat-Mongol for the party *obkom*, which contained the summary and plot of the epic, which enabled the evaluation of Geser as a highly artistic and entirely ethnic creation. The notes were handed over to the Central Committee of the All Russian Communist Party (Bolshevik) by the secretary of the *obkom* B. Sanzhiev, who later got interested and worked hard for the publication of the epic. Then famous writers, poets and scholars led a highly visible propaganda about the epic, comparing the warriors of the Soviet Army to Geser. In July 1944 a conference of writers and narrators (those who narrate the *uliger)* the Buryat Mongol ASSR was held, with the participation of representatives of Moscow, Irkutsk, Chity, in which M. Shulukshin made a presentation with his thesis "On the publication of the Buryat-Mongol epic 'Geser'".[4]

In 1946 N Baldano presented a composite text of 25 thousand verses, which used material of most of the versions of the epic which were well known by then. However, it was particularly during this time, due to internal Soviet politics and national cultural politics, there was a sharp bend towards oppression. The programme of national-cultural reconstruction was supposed to remove and destroy entire layers of traditional, ethnic cultures of those, who, from the perspective of official ideology, were the "feudal-religious remnants" and were the 'culture of the exploitative classes'.

Towards the end of the 1940s, began the 'clerical' campaign in the scientific, academic institutions, and artistic collectives, which had created an unstable situation. In 1944 a regulation of the Central Committee of the Russian Communist Party (Bolshevik) was as follows: "On the conditions and measures for the improvement of the political and ideological work in the Tatar party organizations", in which the 'mistakes of nationalist character', 'embellishment of the Golden Hordes in the Khanate feudal epic about Edigey'[5] were greatly criticized. After the war open attacks on such treasures of folklores, like the Central Asian 'Alpamys', Karakalpak 'Krykkyz', Oguz 'Kitab-I dedem Korkut', began, as well as later on the Kyrgyz 'Manas', and on many other narratives of oral folk art and traditions. The representatives of the cultural elite, who were the main carriers and 'producers' of the remnants joined the race.

The ideological campaigns, the constant search for enemies and their exposure was supported in an atmosphere of fear. As an indication one may consider the discourse which revolved round the creative intelligentsia and the party leaders of the republic, the Buryat epic 'Geser', and the process was started by the Buryat-Mongol *obkom* of the All Russian Communist Party (Bolshevik) in 1948. At the meeting of Gesariads, held in May the same year, the head of the sector on literature and folklore of the Scientific Research Institute of Culture and Economics (NIIKE) M. Khamaganov observed, that the study and propagation of 'Geser' – is the work of 'bourgeois nationalists', the epic itself was characterised as a 'belligerent-feudal, *noyon* type and aristocratic', and giving it the status of national epic is being done with 'the aim of strengthening the fight against the Soviet nation'. 'Idealisation of the pre-revolutionary past, the identification of the pre-revolutionary and soviet patriotism, the representation of the Buryat nation as a single one which cannot be divided into classes in the feudal epoch, – the declaration mentioned – 'is an instrument of battle in anti-national aims. Geser is distinguished....by strong anti-Russian mood, the main idea of 'Geser' – is the education of the labouring masses about the pre-revolutionary subjugation to the khans and feudals'.[6] Though only few months earlier he wrote about Buryat folklore the following: 'From generation to generation was created oral national poetry, *uligers* (tales), in their tradition which are rich in social context and beauty. Folklores are an organic part of the Buryat-Mongol Soviet literature'.[7]

When the preparations for the meeting on 'Geser' were on, the 'work' was undertaken by individual enthusiasts of the epic, as a result of which they were forced to acknowledge 'the epic as unoriginal, and the form of Geser – devoid of any nobility'.

On 20-21 May 1948 a meeting was held that was represented by the members of the bureau of All Russian Communist Party (Bolshevik), responsible workers of the party *obkom*, the Council of Ministers of the BMASSR, workers of NIIKE, of the pedagogical institutes, writers, members of the press. The opinion of party was articulated by A. Kudryatsev, the first secretary of the party *obkom*. His participation practically excluded the possibility of free discussion of the problem, and his rejoinders and presentation were accepted as authoritative instructions. In the concluding words of A. Kudryatsev, referring to the opinion of all the participants, summing up the meeting, 'Geser' was announced a 'feudal-Khan epic, as if it had never existed in the Buryat nation, and the academic workers, working on its study and popularization were bourgeois nationalists or blind instruments of the nationalists'.[8]

On 24 May 1948 a party conference of the Council of Writers of the BMASSR on the above meeting was held, which evaluated the work of N. Baldano, A. Ulanov, T. Galsanov, A. Shadaev as their political mistake, 'which did not explain the earlier reality of the social roots of the epic'. Separately the 'political carelessness of N. Baldano, who had for long worked on the composite text of the epic.'

In 1949 a campaign against 'upstart cosmopolitans' was begun, which prompted destructive interference in the destinies of a number of academicians, who were working on literature and art. Regarding the epic itself, in February 1949 at the plenum of the Council of writers of the republic the presentation of the head of the government T. Galsanov 'Geser' was given the following ranking: 'The epic Geser was never the original Buryat-Mongol epic. It has its origins in the Tibetan-Mongolian version and some later layers, dictated first by Lamas, and thereafter by Shamans, in all cases by the *kulatsko-noyonatsky* elites in favour of the exploitative classes....The idea of 'Geser' is the negation of the inner contradictions, the class wars, its only instruction is the war against external forces...The political causes of the epic – is the orientation of the imperialistic East, the negation of the significance of material and spiritual culture of the Russian people, an anti-Russian direction, signified by the war of Geser – the heavenly envoy against the social evil – Mangathaev'.

N. Baldano was eliminated from work and sent on a 'creative vacation'. Nevertheless, he continued to work on the text. Under difficult circumstances he devoted more than thirty years to it.

The Central Committee of the Russian Communist Party (Bolshevik) did not outline its relation to the fact that the epic 'Geser' became an object of political manipulations. In this context it is interesting to note the opinion of the Buryat writer V. Mitypov, in which he emphasized the criticism of the republican party elite against 'Geser'. The negation of the epic's national significance was linked to 'the surplus vomits of the top local party officials, who are trying to convince Moscow of their Marxist affiliations and also about 'the threat of civil strife on their academic brethren, as they are consumed with personal ambitions'.[9]

In March 1951 a ruling of the CC of the VCP(B) was announced: 'On the shortcomings and mistakes in the work of the Buryat-Mongolian *obkom* of the All Russian Communist Party (Bolshevik)'. The republican leadership was changed – the Russian first secretary of the Buryat-Mongol party obkom A. Kudryatsev was replaced by

Buryat A. Khakhalov. As the Doctor of Historical Sciences A.A. Elaev writes, 'for the first time since 1937 the ethnic character of the head of the party obkom of the republic changed, which exerted a certain influence on the development of social and ethno-cultural processes in Buryatia'.[10]

In part, the change of head of the republic impacted on the destiny of the Buryat epic 'Geser': already in April 1951, on the request of the *obkom* of the party and on the instruction of the Central Committee of the All Russian Communist Party (Bolshevik) its essence was discussed in the Institute of Oriental Studies of the Academy of Sciences of USSR, and thereafter it was discussed in a joint academic session of the Institute of Oriental Studies and the Buryat-Mongal NIIKE in the city of Ulan Ude. The result was that 'its national character was acknowledged and its evaluation as a feudal-khan creation was rejected. The epic 'Geser' was acknowledged as the cultural heritage of the Buryat people.'[11] The rehabilitation of 'Geser', as the earlier attempt to discredit it ideologically proves once more that cultural material was actively used for political objectives.

At the same time it needs to be acknowledged that the Soviet modernization and cultural politics, with all its deformations, also had a positive impact on the preservation and development of lesser cultures. Among people with different levels of development, the significance of "national building" created within a short span of time "socialist nations", with the hallmark of highly developed ethnicities also marking their statehood. This is relevant for the Buryats too.

The composite text of the epic 'Geser' became a familiar phenomenon for the Buryat intelligentsia, it educated many new generations. First it was published in 1959 in the Buryat language, and in Russian translation by S. Lipkin and V. Soloukhin in 1968, 1973, 1986, 1988 and 2007. The 1000th anniversary of the epic 'Geser' was celebrated in 1991-1995. The ritual of hoisting the flag of Geser in the ethnic Buryat districts was carried out, which in turn played a definite role in the construction of an all-Buryat socio-cultural space.

NOTES AND REFERENCES

1. J. Stalin, *Marxism and the National-colonial question,* Moscow: Politizdat, 1939, p. 211.

2. National Archives of the Republic of Buryatia (NARB), F. 1, op. 1, d. 4829.
3. B.S. Dugarov, *Buryatskaya Geseriada – a song in time and space.* First article to "Abai Geser Bogdo Khan". Aginsk, 2007, pp. 7–8.
4. NARB, f. 1, op. 1, d. 4829.
5. *On the party and Soviet press*. Moscow, 1954, pp. 526–529.
6. NARB, f. 1, op. 1, d. 4764.
7. M.N. Khamaganov, 'Buryat-Mongolskaya Soviet Literature', *25 years of Buryat-Mongol ASSR*, Ulan Ude, 1948, p. 100.
8. A.A. Elaev, *Buryatsky Nation: The making, development, self-determination*, Moscow, 2000, p. 241.
9. V.G. Mitypov, 'The Mesopotamian Odyssey of the Buryat', *Ygai Zam,* 4 (2002), p. 4.
10. A.A. Elaev, *Buryatsky Nation: The making, development, self-determination*, Moscow, 2000, p. 242.
11. Essays on the History of the Buryat Organisation of the CPSU, Ulan Ude, 1970.

10

A Passage from India: Rahul Sankrityayana's Intercultural Quests

Jeta Sankrityayana

Among the many personalities crystallised within the crucible of India's struggle for freedom and social emancipation, Rahul Sankrityayana holds an inspiring place. A much-travelled linguistic scholar and a historian and philosopher of originality and distinction, he became one of the most influential Hindi litterateurs of his time. Yet unlike other scholars, the personal passage he chose for himself was not drawn from academic lessons but from an attempt to visualise the future course for his nation. Rahul Sankrityayana thus sought to understand India in a new light, drawing upon the common heritage it shares with its many cultural neighbours. And in his willingness to provoke and channel this intellectual discourse, he also lived the life of a political activist, emerging at the head of mass movements, chronicling their struggles, ever willing to learn from the struggles that had already been made by others. The literary corpus he left thus spans a considerable breadth, and is difficult to analyse without understanding his life. Rather than assessing his writing and his scholarly contribution in separate literary compartments, the present paper seeks to develop such an understanding by holistically re-evaluating his intellectual perspective and his quest.

The evaluation is presented in three subsequent sections. The first provides a short sketch of the life and times of Rahul Sankrityayana. The second assesses the process behind his active intellectual development, through selected readings from his writings. The third and last section briefly examines his intercultural quest in seeking to understand India against the backdrop of Eurasia, and the validity that this perspective still holds today.

The Life Passage

Rahul Sankrityayana was born into a family of middle Brahman peasantry in the small village of Pandaha in Azamgarh district, eastern Uttar Pradesh, in April 1893. He discarded his birth-name Kedarnath Pande while entering the Hindu monastic order at Parsa *math* [cloister] in northern Bihar in 1913, adopting the sacramental name of Swami Ramodardas. Stepping beyond Vaisnava orthodoxy, he later modified this into the non-denominational form Ramodar Sadhu. Finally, on being ordained a Theravadi Buddhist *bhikku* in 1930 in Sri Lanka, shortly after returning from his first Tibetan journey, he became Rahul Sankrityayana and has been known ever since by his admirers across India simply as Rahulji.

Behind every change of name is a critical transition within the formation of Rahul Sankrityayana's intellectual identity. For the young Kedar, formal education ended after a few years of Urdu school, when in 1907, he ran away from home at age 13 and fled to Kolkata, bent on exploring the external world. This act of rebellion was a protest against his marriage as a mere child of 10, in accordance with rural Indian custom, when he felt his freedom had been bartered away by his parents, who had sought to thwart his thirst for adventure and further learning. By 1910, he had already broken off ties with his family, wandering into the western Himalaya as a mendicant *sadhu*. However he returned to Varanasi to pursue a traditional education in Sanskrit and the philosophy of *Nyaya* [Logic] between 1911-12, where he was chosen as heir by the *mahant* [abbot] of Parsa. In 1913, he thus joined the Vaisnava order of Udasi *sanyasis* [Hindu monastic recluses] at age 20, renouncing worldly ties and encumbrances. Tiring rapidly however of the cloistered life and the lack of intellectual impetus at Parsa, he escaped to traverse across India mostly on foot, eventually joining another Vaisnava *math* as heir for a time, at Tirumishi in southern India, in order to further his studies in Sanskrit. In Ayodhya in 1914, where he was leading a movement against temple sacrifices and was assaulted by Saivite *sadhus*, he experienced a crisis of faith in orthodox Hinduism, and by 1915, had been drawn to the reformist ideology of the Arya Samaj, prompting him eventually to simplify his name to Ramodar Sadhu.

During his early years with the Arya Samaj, initially at Agra and later at Lahore between 1915-17, the young *sadhu* began to educate and engage himself in secular disciplines, while continuing his study of Sanskrit and Logic, along with Arabic and Persian. His first articles on social and political issues which were published in Hindi and Urdu, acknowledged the inspiration he received from the 1917 Russian Revolution. Drawing intellectual sustenance from his mentors, his growing interest in history led him to retrace the course of Indian civilisation from its spiritual and philosophical records. Thus using the journeys of Fa Xian (Fa Hsien) as a guide, he toured the dilapidated Buddhist shrines of north India in 1920, while gradually drifting away from his original intent of becoming a religious missionary. Meanwhile, the Jalianwala Bagh massacre in Amritsar in 1919 and the subsequent experience of Martial Law across Punjab led to the first stirrings of nationalistic feelings within him, and in 1921, he returned to northern Bihar to join the Non-Cooperation Movement in as a regional leader of the Indian National Congress, quickly rising to the position of District Secretary.

Rahulji's first political imprisonment at Buxar Jail for 6-months in 1922 was quickly followed by a longer 2-year incarceration at Hazaribagh Jail between 1924-25. Since the political programme of the Congress had by then retreated into hibernation, he used the time in between to travel through Nepal. In prison, he continued to write and to read extensively, also teaching himself Pali in order to read the Buddhist canonical texts in the original. Upon release, he travelled through Kashmir, Ladakh, the Kinnaur region of Himachal Pradesh and western Tibet in 1926, visiting old Buddhist monasteries along the way. Between 1927-28, the opportunity arose for him to join the Theravada Buddhist college at Vidyalankara Perivena in Sri Lanka as a Sanskrit teacher, where he utilised the rest of his time making an exhaustive personal study of the epigraphy of ancient languages, Buddhist history and the Pali *Tripitaka* [Three Canons]. While Rahulji's particular interest in the history Buddhist period emanated from the fact that the later Buddhist epistemological texts mentioned by refutation in the Advaita Vedanta works he had previously studied were lost, except in their Chinese or Tibetan translation, he was also beginning to view Buddhism as a historical tradition that had freed India from the tyranny of caste for the considerable period of ten centuries before the Brahmanical revival. Initially commencing his work as a major Buddhist scholar by restoring the *Abhidharmakosh* [Treasury of Higher Teachings] of Vasubandhu from Chinese to Sanskrit, he soon became aware of the importance of the Tibetan monasteries in preserving the works that had been lost in India.

Inspired now by the journey of Alexandra David-Neel, he made his first journey to Tibet in 1929, in disguise via Nepal, and stayed in Lhasa for the next 15-months, searching for and studying the canonical Buddhist texts preserved in their Tibetan versions. Making his way back to India with a vast collection of Tibetan scroll-paintings, block-printed texts and art-objects, he was ordained a Buddhist monk on his return to Sri Lanka and assumed the name Rahul Sankrityayana.

With Buddhism providing him with a complete intellectual break from the tradition-bound past, he returned briefly to political life in 1930, founding the Socialist Party of India, along with Acharya Narendra Deva and other nationalist leaders, while also making the first translation of Karl Marx's 'Communist Manifesto' into an Indian language. In 1932-33, while travelling through Europe, visiting France, England and Germany, lecturing on Buddhist philosophy, and exhibiting his collection of Tibetan paintings and art-objects, he tried in vain to visit Soviet Russia to see the socialist transformation there firsthand. Meanwhile, his involvement with the Buddhist heritage in Tibet continued to expand, and his second journey in 1933 through Ladakh, western Tibet and Kinnaur in Himachal Pradesh, where he was a guest of the Roerichs at Uruswati, was followed by another expedition into Tibet. This time, he discovered original palm-leaf manuscripts of lost Buddhist texts in their original Sanskrit, at the ancient monastery of Sakya in southern Tibet, and was conferred the honorific title of *'Mahapandita'* [Greatly-Learned One] by the Kashi Pandit Sabha – the Council of Brahmanical scholars at Varanasi – for opening new vistas for the study of ancient Sanskrit literature.

Through the 1930s, as Rahulji wrote extensively in Hindi on his travels as well as on the state of social transformation in the countries he had visited, a programme for the social and political transformation of India began to evolve within his mind. In 1935, he travelled through Malaya, Japan, Korea and the erstwhile state of Manchuria, reaching Moscow after crossing Siberian on the trans-Siberian Railway. Although he was unable to meet Academician S.F. Oldenburg there, who had just passed away, his return to India brought him through Azerbaijan and Iran, where he witnessed and wrote about the modernisation programme initiated under Reza Shah. In 1936, he made his third journey to Tibet, staying mostly in Sakya where the monastery had once been venue for the translation of Buddhist works into Tibetan. During this stay, he discovered, copied and photographed many more Sanskrit palm-leaf manuscripts, including an original copy of *Pramanavartika* [Critique of Evidence] of Dharmakirti (600 CE) – one of the most significant Buddhist logicians at the ancient monastery of Nalanda. This led in 1937 to his journey via Iran to the Institute of Oriental Studies at Leningrad (St. Petersburg) at the instance of Academician Th. Scherbatsky, who was among the most prominent Buddhist scholars of his time. After a short stay there, during which he met and married Elena Nazertovna Kozerovskaya, a scholar of the Mongolian language at the Faculty of Oriental Languages at Leningrad University, he returned in 1938 through Kazakhstan, Uzbekistan and Tajikistan in Soviet Central Asia, crossing the Amu Darya [Oxus] to enter India through Afghanistan. Later that same year, he led another expedition to Tibet, staying mainly at the old monasteries at Ngor and Sakya, where he had previously located many more lost Buddhist works. Soon after his return from Tibet, he re-entered political life through the Indian Left.

Soon becoming a prominent leader of the peasants' movement in India, he founded the Communist Party unit in Bihar, and was jailed again after he led the movement against the periodic eviction of tenant-farmers by large landlords. In 1940, he was elected President of the All-India Kisan Sabha [All-India Peasant's Congress], but was imprisoned between 1940-42 at Hazaribagh Jail and at the Deoli internment camp for Indian Leftists, in the Rajasthan desert. During this productive period, he wrote many of his important books, including the first two volumes of his autobiography *Meri Jeewan Yatra* [My Life's Journey], *Volga se Ganga* [From the Volga to the Ganga] – a Marxist interpretation of the history of India, conceptualised as a collection of stories, *Manav Samaj* [Human Society], and *Darsana-Digdarsana* [A Survey of Philosophy]. Following his release from prison in 1943 and the legalisation of the Communist Party in India, he went to the Party Headquarters in Mumbai, to work on the creation of Party literature in Hindi. In 1944, he left India for Iran on his way to Russia where he had been invited to teach at the Faculty of Oriental Languages at Leningrad University (now the State University of St. Petersburg). However, he was forced to stay on in Teheran for nearly eight months, till with the end of WW II, travel to Moscow became possible again.

Joining Elena and meeting his young son Igor – who had been born when Rahulji was in prison in India – for the first time, Rahulji taught Hindi and Sanskrit at the Faculty of Oriental Languages at Leningrad University for two years between 1945-47, where his colleagues included Academician A.P. Barannikov, V.M. Beskrovny, V.I. Kalyanov, while the students and researchers he assisted included the next generation of Russian indologists and linguistic scholars such as Tatyana Katenina, Tatyana Grek, Berta Volchok, A.M. Melnikov, A.S. Barkhudarov, I.D. Serebryakov and V.I. Balin. During this duration, Rahulji's own project at this time was to research the history of Central Asia from Russian sources, for which he collected a vast volume of books and other published materials, also interacting with the noted Russian archaeological scholars Professor A.N. Bernstam and Professor S.P. Tolstov, who had been closely involved in excavations in the Central Asian region. Drawing upon his close engagement through much of the 1930s in retracing the history of Buddhist civilisation, Rahulji by now perceived the pivotal influence of the region at various points through Indian history. Although he had hoped to accompany his reading of Russian archaeological texts with a tour of key historical sites in the region, the turning down of his request by the Soviet authorities brought him great personal disappointment. Meanwhile, political events in India had moved on rapidly after the conclusion of W II, and in July 1947, he set sail from Leningrad for India with his books, passing through Helsinki, Stockholm and London, landing at Bombay two days after India had become independent.

Upon his return, Rahulji threw himself energetically into new literary activities and the building of the Progressive Writers' Movement in India between 1947-48. In December 1948, he was elected President of the Akhil Bharatiya Hindi Sahitya Sammelan [All-India Hindi Literary Congress], but resigned his membership of the Communist Party of India over personal differences with the Party on the national language and nationality question. Even after this event, the retention of his Marxist outlook and commitment is evident in his writings between 1949-55. However, with this parting of ways with the Party denying him the possibility of returning to Russia in the foreseeable future, he took up residence for a while in the cool climate of the eastern Himalaya, at Kalimpong, while working with the Hindi Sahitya Sammelan and several Government Committees for the literary advancement of Hindi. His health had begun to deteriorate with age, and he now decided to find a home in the Himalaya. In late 1949, he left Kalimpong, and settled in Mussoorie (now in Uttarakhand). After a lifetime of wandering, Mussoorie thus became Rahulji's first permanent home, where he lived between 1950-59. Kamala who had joined him in Kalimpong as a literary assistant was now with him, and they were married in 1950. His daughter Jaya was born in 1953 and Jeta in 1955, shortly after which he also renewed his membership of the Communist Party of India.

Within the stability of a family home, Rahulji's literary output increased prolifically. Of his 164 published book-length works spanning a varied oeuvre of novels and stories, biographies, essays and travel-writing, historical, philosophical and anthropological writings, linguistic and lexicographic studies in Hindi, Sanskrit, Pali and Tibetan etc., 54 were written in Mussoorie. Among them was his two-volume *Madhya Asia ka Itihas* [History of Central Asia], for which he had spent 18 years compiling materials from Chinese, Mongol, Tibetan, Russian and Persian sources. Critically regarded as one of his most important works, this text was awarded the national prize for the best Hindi writing by the Sahitya Akademi [the Indian National Academy of Letters] in 1956. In its sweep from the Neolithic Age to the contemporary historical experience of the Central Asian region in the 19th and 20th centuries, this text sought to acquaint Indian readers with archaeological records and other source materials from which an important part of their own history had derived since the Vedic period.

In 1958, Rahulji travelled to China and toured its ancient Buddhist sites, including the Dunhuang caves. In China, his health suffered another setback and a cardiac attack prevented him from visiting Sakya in Tibet, where his work in restoring Sanskrit Buddhist texts was still unfinished. In 1959, he left Mussoorie and rejoined his old alma mater in Sri Lanka, which had been upgraded to Vidyalankara University, and taught there as Professor of Philosophy until 1961. The family had shifted by then to Darjeeling. In December 1961, a succession of cerebral strokes deprived him of his memory and he spent the last year of his life in a state of amnesia, of which eight months were spent at a Government hospital in Moscow. Finally, in April 1963, shortly after his return to Darjeeling in the terminal stages of his illness, he passed away at Darjeeling, reaching the end of a life that had taken him past many tangible as well as intangible frontiers, leaving behind his vision of India as a modern, self-aware and resurgent nation as his legacy.

The Intellectual Quest

Rahul Sankrityayana's life was inextricably bound with his times, which marked the renaissance of India. Leading him from place to place, and event to event, to the formation of the rationalistic outlook that survives with his writings, his life leaves many lessons that the modern Indian mind can draw upon. He was not born to privilege, and from humble beginnings, rose to considerable intellectual stature despite being denied the avenues for a formal education. Each transition his life made involved the challenge of accepting new perspectives and discarding the old. He wrote about this process in many places through his *Meri Jeewan Yatra* [MJY], which as he said was not an autobiography, but a record of his life's journey. Explaining this purpose at the outset, he wrote:

> "Why did I write 'My Life's Journey' [*Meri Jeewan Yatra*]? I had always kept feeling that if other travellers who traversed roads like mine had written of their own sojourn through life, I would have greatly benefited – not only by gaining foreknowledge but also by making an economy of time. I concede that any two of life's courses will never be exactly similar, yet there can be no doubt that all lives have to sail on the tides and impulses of identical outer and inner worlds. Why should I have chosen to write of my life's journey instead of writing an autobiography? Readers would have to read the book for an answer. I have, through my writing, attempted to sketch the varied paces and peculiarities of a world that the third generation after ours would have difficulty in imagining. In much the same manner as I have written on other themes without first teaching myself – formally – to write, I find myself to be as unlettered in the art of writing a life's journey. Formal education is of no mean value, but it has been my misfortune never to have received an opportunity for it". [*MJY*-I: foreword]

From early years spent in a sleepy Indian village, his passage forward commenced with the pursuit of traditional learning in Sanskrit and the Indian philosophies of *Nyaya* [Logic] and *Mimansa* [Contemplation]. He was not content however with absorbing these as a traditionalist, and used this initial training instead to set a course for his future intellectual life, striving to acquaint himself with other languages and competing philosophical systems. Meanwhile, through constant travel, he familiarised himself with social and economic realities across his country and began to perceive the intellectual quest as a vehicle for reform and social transformation. In doing so, he perceived that religious rituals and social institutions like caste were inimical to the progress of India. Nor were these absolute in any sense, since they had evolved from very different social dispensations that had existed in India in the past. Writing later, in an essay, this sense of deep frustration is strongly expressed:

> "The downfall of a nation, just as that of the individual, results from the errors of the past. The Hindu race has, for millennia, been entrapped by misfortunate affairs. The reasons for this can be its own errors of judgment. Of these errors, those primary are discrimination between the high and the low and between castes, blind servility to the Brahmans and their scripture, the oppression of ritual, and so on". [*Vividh Prasang*]

Gradually developing a materialistic outlook on the history of his nation, he began to explore the vanished Buddhist heritage of India as a source of useful information, viewing Buddhism essentially as a philosophy of social reform. His description about retracing the journeys of Fa Xian to historical Buddhist sites in 1920, long before the 20th century revival of Buddhism in India in which he was to play a major part, carries the flavour of this intellectual transition:

> "Accretion of respect over several years had etched an abiding reverence for the Buddha into my mind. The biographies I had read lately fuelled this into a resolve to visit the places associated with his life. I decided I should go there now...
>
> I visited Sarnath once more. The only sights then worth seeing were the ancient ruins and the Ashokan cenotaph. The Maha Bodhi Society functioned there from a small house in which it also ran a school. The route leading directly from Sarnath to Kasya would have taken me into the Azamgarh district, so I chose to detour instead through Chhapra, stopping en-route at Parsa for a couple of days....

Late in the evening I disembarked at the station at Deoria and passed the night at some temple in its main market. The next morning I was on the road to Kasya. It was either late April or early May. To me, a strong sun and weighty baggage are two possible impediments on a journey. I was free from worries on the second count, since a cloak-like *alfi* made from an old blanket reaching down to knee-length, along with two loin-cloths and a towel of coarse gauze were all I was carrying by way of clothes. For drinking-water I had a receptacle made out of a hollowed-out gourd. My head and feet were bare, although possibly I carried a book or two. Fear of heat however lingered for which the only restitution was not to stir over the day-hours between nine and four. I passed that afternoon at a roadside *madrasah* where there was a map of Gorakhpur district to examine and the teacher's offer of lunch. By evening I had located a new orchard of mangos to the left of the road, with a well and a brickwork platform within it. The landlord's brick dwelling and the others of the village stood at a sort distance, but having no wish to eat again I did not go there. The cool gusts of evening felt welcome as I stretched on the platform.

Hunger was nearer when I left the next morning and so when I heard that there was a cloister for Vaisnava recluses at a roadside village, I felt it prudent to first acquire a meal by going there.

The water-body of Ramabhar, or Mukut-bandhan where the Buddha was cremated, was located close by and some of the cloister's hutments in the cloister had been built by recycling old bricks from the ruin. The ascetics were saying that Mathakunwar was a prince, and that Rama was his sister. They also said the black basalt sculpture of the Buddha at Kusinagar was that of the prince Mathakunwar, and that the *stupa* that stood at the site of the Buddha's cremation was a memorial to the princess i.e. Rama-bhar. When I mentioned that I have to go on to Mathakunwar (Kusinagar), they exclaimed – Oh, so you are going to see the god of those Burma-people?

At Kasya I also stayed at a Vaisnava cloister. A few boys studying at the sub-divisional school also lived there, and when I asked them a few questions for the sake of entertainment, they gathered that I had also been to school which raised me considerably in their esteem.

It was past five in the evening when I reached the place of the Buddha's nirvana at Mathakunwar. The scorching sun of the day had lost its vigour and had been transmuted into a gentle gold, and the touch of the earth on my bare feet was now bearable. The *sheeshams* in their shrouds of fragile new leaves were spreading shade across the ground. I had read biographies of the Buddha, though not in the ancient language of the original. On stepping onto that soil, my heart was drawn back two and a half millennia to that great Indian who spread the name of his country all over the world making India the holy land for a third of all mankind.

Near the *sheeshams* past the ruin was a heap of white ashes from a funeral pyre, that lay there fresh and untouched. On asking, I was told that Mahavir Mahasthavir had just died and had been cremated here. It was a matter for regret that I could not meet Mahavir Swami. He had been the first North Indian for centuries to enter the *bhikku* order. Mahavir Singh was a relative of Kunwar Singh, and had been at his side in the liberation struggle of 1857. As happened later with several other brave men like him, he became a fugitive and had to live in disguise. As a wrestler, he found employ showing-off wrestling tricks in the courts of various princelings. Wandering in this manner he somehow reached Sri Lanka. A *bhikku* who tended him when he fell ill, introduced him to Buddhism. Just before Burma was annexed, he went there to become a *bhikku*. The Buddha's teachings which had made Mahavir Swami their apostle spoke also of their glorious past, and kindled in him an eagerness to make the memory of the Buddha flourish again in his benighted motherland. With this intent, he had established a small retreat in Kusinagar, and spent the remainder of his life there.

Mahasthavir Chandramani was not quite so old then. He had first been assistant and was now successor to Mahavir Swami. On meeting him I learned many things about the Buddha's life, and about the Mallas who had once inhabited Kusinagar. When he opened a portal and showed me to the huge reclining statue of the Buddha, my Arya Samajist leanings could not prevent my head, my heart and hands from bowing before it. I rationalised within myself – I am not offering idolatry before a God, I am expressing my tribute to an inspired Sage.

After stopping in Kasya for the night, I left again for Deoria the morning after … and then for Gorakhpur, where I stayed with another Vaisnava cloister. Although the heat had retreated when I left the train at Navgarh-Road, little remained of the day. Rummindei (Lumbini) still seemed far away when I sought direction…

The day had cooled when I reached Lumbini. The sides of a little water-tank were covered with shrubs of prickly gorse, and creepers and other vegetation. A small temple stood nearby, whose courtyard was stained with the blood of goats and fowls and other sacrificial animals. The statue inside was unidentifiable. To the rear of the temple stood the Ashokan column, with an edict of a few lines. The sight of the animal-sacrifice and its bloody desecration at the birthplace of Gautam Buddha, that apostle of compassion towards all living beings, came as a strong shock to the senses. No one was around. Sitting awhile, I reflected on the history of this place. In the distance, the white peaks of the Himalaya visible to the north seemed to beckon me to come. For a moment I did consider pressing on to Butwal, but sunset had neared, not leaving enough time for that destination to be reached...

I still had to go to Kapilavastu, and so had to postpone a journey to Butwal. In the morning, I set off for Tilaurakot (Kapilavastu). Although light on luggage I was walking slowly ... Learning of Piparahwa's being closer than Tilaurakot, I preferred to go there first. While in the caskets, stone chests and other artefacts excavated here that had appeared in photographs had been exquisite, the ruins were nondescript. In fact if I had not known of the ruins before from prior reading, I might not even have noticed them. At the edge of the trees a short distance from the Nepal frontier was a piece of land of uneven profile, on which the signs of excavation lay in broken brick-shards and a series of small pits. That the Sakyas had built a memorial over the crematorial remains of the best of their kin – the Buddha, the inscription on which had acquired the renown of being the oldest example of the Brahmi script of India, would scarcely have been apparent from the look of the place.

It was still daylight and so I chose to walk a little further towards Taulihava Bazaar and Tilaurakot. By evening I had reached the home of a prosperous Brahman, who had several head of cattle, several granaries and a very large house. While I was eating, the Brahman told me about places all around where heaps of ancient bricks lay in piles, and the next morning took me around his own village, showing me ancient foundations of ruined structures that had possibly been excavated by the Archaeological Survey....When I reached Taulihava Bazar finally, after stopping somewhere midway for food and rest, it was nearing five. In the vast expanse of the fortress, with evidence of past settlement spreading into the distance in the forms of bricks, water-tanks and mounds, it was not possible for me to locate the childhood home of the Buddha or Shuddhodana's palace. But the thought that amidst this red earth lay the dust of the Buddha's feet provided enough consolation. That same evening, I went to the Niglihava Tank to have look at the broken Ashokan column and its inscription and passed the night at a village nearby. My gaze was now fixed on snow peaks of the Himalaya, but it would first be necessary to glean some information about routes before trying to go there. It was not possible to enter the mountains of Nepal at will. There would be people there everywhere who asked questions...

I reached Balrampur by the morning train. I had already heard at Kusinara about Bhikku Varasambodhi who was resident there. He was building a hospice at that time of which only the walls stood, and had to supervise the construction. We spoke, sitting amidst the bricks of an unfinished cubicle...

I left for Sahet-Mahet while the day still retained its cool. A great many men and women at that time of year were bound on foot for the fair at Devipatan, and as such there were travellers all along the road. As evening neared, a village in view to the right of the road turned out to be inhabited by Brahmans, when I reached it. A woman ascetic lived amidst them, who was well-travelled among the religious shrines. I conversed with her about pilgrimages, and about Sanskrit with someone who knew its rudiments. After that there was little reason for them to deny a courteous welcome to the great *alfi*-clad ascetic with his water-gourd!

I reached Sahet-Mahet the next morning. My knowledge of the history of Jetavan and Sravasti then was only very basic. After cursory inspection of the old hutments and wells at Jetavan, I moved onwards to the ruins at Sravasti, and then traversed the jungle to a village in the north. This had a primary school, which provided me rest that afternoon as well as a meal that the teacher himself had prepared. At the end of the day, while returning to Balrampur, I met a Vaisnava recluse along the way. He did seem doubtful whether I really was a Vaisnava ascetic because of my appearance – although I often had to play the dual part of Vaisnava *bairagi* and Arya Samajist and therefore seldom carried the sandalwood smear across my forehead. Anyway, he made the ritual obeisance and then very politely asked me to rest at his hut. He himself was headed elsewhere with work to do, but he provided me with the location of the village and of his hut within it. After a short wait on reaching there, the resident holy man appeared and offered the best hospitality that it was possible to muster under village conditions". [*MJY*-I]

Seven years later, while teaching at Vidyalankara in 1927, his familiarity with Buddhist philosophy and history had expanded considerably, leading to an inner struggle with the traditional beliefs he had inherited from childhood. Describing this intellectual ferment, he wrote:

"As far as my own studies were concerned, within a month they had accelerated. I first commenced with the volumes of the *Suttapitaka.* Because of its affinities to Sanskrit, Pali was easy for me and I had even started learning it on my own while in India. I was using my own books for my readings and marked all geographical and historical references I found, which were then transcribed into my notebooks. I would be given an audience of two hours apiece by the Nayaka Mahasthavira and the Acharyas Pragyasara, Devananda and Pragyaloka, and yet my thirst remained unquenched. The Pali *Tripitakas* are a repository on the society, the politics, and the geography of India in Buddhist times. They heightened my search for history. The erudite prefaces in the *Tripitaka* editions from the Pali Text Society of London poured oil into this fire, and I found myself compelled to read the old volumes of the Pali Text Society's journal. After this, I made an elaborate investigation of the journals of the Royal Asiatic Society of Britain, and its branches in Ceylon, Bengal and Bombay. My acquaintance with the Brahmi script dated from my stay in Hazaribagh Jail, and here I was able to leaf through all the volumes of the *Epigraphica India.* With the elapse of six or seven months, my knowledge of research into the civilisation of India had increased to such volume and degree that when Professor Rudolf Otto of Marburg visited Vidyalankara, he was astonished to find that I had never been a student of any university after talking to me. However the credit for any such accomplishment on my part did not go entirely to these few months of study. I had the habit of sporadic reading from before. Pandit Bhagwandatt's guidance, at the DAV College at Lahore, had first drawn my eyes to research journals, but the utilitarian aspects in the knowledge of my forefathers only struck me here. My occasional readings of the Sanskrit books on philosophy and poetics, the information on geography and on the characteristics of regional language which I had gleaned from my wanderings – such knowledge as this now stirred my mind and memories to form a nascent scientific outlook.

I now savoured with relish, the simple penetrating rationality in the Buddha's precepts to time and society two millennia ago. Records of miracles and magical feats in the *Tripitakas* did not become objects for my derision, in spite of their being impossible, but were now material to be amused by. That 2500 years should have left no mark upon these volumes is quite improbable, I used to think. It was hardly feasible today to determine how many of such impossibilities might actually be attributable to the Buddha himself, but like embers buried in cinders, or like gems beneath the stones, the magical eloquence of the Buddha's true precepts that came in between drew my mind to them with tremendous force. When I came upon the Buddha's exhortation to the Kalamas – do not believe by deference to some book, or tradition, or to your elders; always decide upon belief by your own examination, and then stand firm – my heart suddenly exclaimed: here is the man whose faith in truth remains implacable, who understood the aegis of independent intellect within humankind. And when, in the *Majjhimanikaya*, I read – the precepts of Dhamma that I have given to you are like a ferry-boat, to help you disembark on the other side, and not headloads to bear on your heads – I realised that what I had been searching for in all my wanderings had now been found.

My mind was in this state on the one hand, in those early days; on the other, I was having infinite difficulty in explaining the concept of God to the students I was teaching. At this time all the beliefs of the Arya Samaj, and of my birth, were leaving me. That all Creation must have a Lord was the only faith I clung to, now. I had thought before that faith in God was a natural law, yet here I found that even my brightest pupils were bereft of it. Where I held God to be essential to the course of natural development and its daily manifestations, all these people were quite happy with the inevitability of these. That Buddhism is atheistic and negates God – I had read of this in Sanskrit texts, where it was a device for slander and an expression of hatred, that had long since ceased to affect me; but I had not known till now that I was being served an ultimatum to choose only one between God and the Buddha [the intellect]. My first effort was to make them compromise but this made pitfalls at every step. In a couple of months such an attempt began to seem quite worthless to me. Every evening I would take a walk along the railway track that led from Kelaniya to Talaimannar. I used to want to be alone, and often was. At such time the inner conflict within me would be so overpowering that there was cause for alarm that, in the heat of it, I might overlook a passing train. Fortunately, it was a dual track, and I used to walk keeping the train's approach in front of me. That God and the Buddha were incompatible was now quite clear to me, and it became clearer still that God was an illusionary construct, and the Buddha reality. For weeks thereafter, my heart suffered another disquiet – it seemed that an article of faith from times immemorial was now lost. But I always let the mind be my pathfinder and in a little while, was able to laugh at the thought of those imaginary confusions and fears, and at my own credulity". [*MJY*-II]

Having freed himself of this intellectual overburden, Rahulji was free to devote his time towards exploring the Buddhist heritage. Being well acquainted by now with the historical evolution of different philosophical schools within Buddhist thought, he was already aware that the Pali canonical texts compiled during the first synod did not include the Mahayana texts of later Buddhist schools, that could be found in translation in the Chinese and Tibetan *Tripitakas* which were later compilations. Through prior study of the Brahmanical *Nyaya* texts which refuted the propositions put forward by Buddhist logicians, he knew of the immense value of these later epistemological works which had originally been composed in Sanskrit but were no longer extant within India. After completing his Sanskrit restoration of Vasubandhu's *Abhidharmakosh* from its Chinese translation, Rahulji's imagination was captured by the challenge of rediscovering this Buddhist heritage, which had spread – along with trade – across the Silk Road during the age of the Sakas and Kusanas under whom many parts of northwestern India and Central Asia had formed a combined realm. In this historical context, he noted:

> "The civilisation of India crossed its frontiers with the spread of Buddhism.... After the loss of sovereignty, the lands which drew inspiration from the Indian heritage were cut off. To bring light to bear on these forgotten ties it is necessary to know Buddhism. If we really want to learn of the flourishing of India in ancient times, then the knowledge of that Greater India still extant in the major languages of Asia in the form of Buddhist literature, and its historical and geographical record can help us to shed our present insularity". [*Bauddha Sanskriti*]

Rahulji's life entered a new passage in 1929, with his journey to Tibet. Although this journey had all the hallmarks of intrepid adventure, it had a very serious scholarly purpose behind it. More startling success came during his second Tibetan journey in 1934, when he rediscovered a lost palm-leaf manuscript written in the original Sanskrit preserved in the collection at Sakya. Assessing the significance of this discovery towards recovering the lost cultural heritage of India, he wrote:

> "Of the more than four thousand lost manuscripts, if a few more are found in the Sanskrit, it can only be in Tibet. It is thus we conceive how great the hand of the Tibetan monasteries has been in the preservation of our heritage. At a certain epoch our *pandits* and the Tibetan *lotsawas* had, over centuries, translated these works from their Sanskrit, Prakrit or Apabhramsa into the Tibetan language. The time is coming when these will have to be retrieved into Sanskrit or Hindi – only then will our understanding of our heritage be complete". [*Vividh Prasang*]

But his encounter with the theocratic state in Tibet also had other intellectual fallouts, as he realised that the power of organised religion to institute progressive social change is circumscribed by the need to preserve the political structures of the state. Writing in London in 1932, he commented on these shifts in his personal standpoints:

> "The Arya Samaj had sufficed to banish my faith in astrology, ghosts and the various magics of spells and charms. My stay in Sri Lanka had even driven the hapless Creator into oblivion. After visiting Tibet, any faith still reposed on yoga, esoteria and other-worldly powers had come apart when I saw these claims for what they were, i.e. the mesmeric artifices contrived in self-hypnoses. Indeed, the difference between the materialist and me was solely that I still believed in the continuance of life's flow after the event of death. To me – for a long time – the Buddhist concept of *nirvana* was no more than extinction of that flow like a flame gone out". [*MJY*-II]

Musing on the paradox of trying to preserve static personal beliefs in a quickly-changing external world, he then likened the predicament in which India found itself to an encounter with a London subway:

> "For someone with a rural upbringing, even being in a city can pose a problem. London and Paris stood in even stronger contrast to the cities of Asia. The escalator formed a unique component of this. The measured consideration with which I had to address it fuelled thought. It occurred to me that the

> world is also self-propelled, like the escalator. It seizes one foot and impels us forward, while we still wish to dig the other into terra firma. And India was most afflicted amongst the sufferers of this malaise. Circumstances there had grasped a leg and were dragging the country into the future, but in matters of religion and society it wanted to hold on to its past. After reading geography, astronomy and the sciences, our people took the ritual dip and offered oblations to liberate the sun and moon held captive in an eclipse, reposed their trust in predictions of the future made by the misleading astrologies of the ancients, believed earnestly that the five Pandava brothers melted into the Himalayas en-route to heaven, and then holding onto the dispensations of sacred thread, hair-cue, body-cloth and caste-codes on defilement, sought to traverse the ocean of world experience that comprised the escalator". [*MJY*-II]

Two years later, in Lhasa in 1934, Rahulji wrote his socialist manifesto *Samyavad hi Kyon?* [Why Socialism?], making a complete transition towards the Marxist outlook that guided the rest of his life. By now, he believed that the goals of society and human existence should be secular and rational, rather than spiritual. Buddhism represented a materialist phase within a philosophical tradition that had sprung in continuity from the time of the Rigveda. Social transformation in India would only be possible through an active agenda of political change. Yet even while making this transition into philosophical rationalism, Rahulji continued to acknowledge his debt to Gautama Buddha as the guide and preceptor who had freed him to follow the path of the intellect. Thus as his leitmotif in *Meri Jeevan Yatra*, Rahulji affirmed that his life's course had remained true to the *sutra* teaching of the Buddha in the *Majjhimanikaya,* thus stating:

> "I took opinions for a ferry to cross to other shores, not as headloads that weight my mind".
> [leitmotif from *Meri Jeewan Yatra*]

Intercultural Perspective

Rahul Sankrityayana's writings over a lifetime span many genres, comprising both the conventional literary forms of the novel and the short story, as well as non-conventional forms like history, philosophy, cultural studies and politics written with a distinctive literary flourish. Nevertheless, a unique enquiry attaches to both the volume and variety of his literary activity. The partial outline below examines the intercultural perspective that informs his writing in a selection of his major literary works, with a more detailed reading of *Volga se Ganga* and *Madhya Asia ka Itihas*.

Among modern Hindi novelists, Rahulji excelled in the genre of the historical novel because of the authenticity of the facts he drew from the ancient period of Indian history. However, his purpose in writing these novels was to disseminate to Indian readers a less glorificatory awareness of their past, with particular effort to separate fact from myth. *Singha Senapati* [General Singha 1951] deals with primitive democracy in India, as existed in the Buddhist period among the Licchavis. *Jai Yaudheya* [Jai the Yaudheya 1956] describes life and times among the Yaudheya peoples, who were descendants of the Greek colonisers who had settled in India with the conquests of Alexander of Macedonia and had established their own democratic state till their absorption into the multicultural society of India destroyed it. *Divodas* [Divodas 1963] is a novel about the even earlier period of Aryan settlement in the area around the Indus, when the Vedas were compiled. *Vismrit Yatri* [Forgotten Traveller 1955] remembers the early Buddhist explorer Narendrayash, who had travelled over much of Asia during the Buddhist period. Much of the historical content in these novels appears unexpected to the average myth-laden and conservative Indian reader. Rahulji thus viewed his novels as a means of teaching history to otherwise reluctant people.

The novel *Madhur Swapna* [Pleasant Dream 1950] was the outcome of Rahulji's long and enforced stay in Iran in 1944-45, till the end of World War II permitted him to leave for Leningrad. The novel relates to the Sassanian period in Iranian history around the 5th century CE, when a people's revolt broke out centring around the teachings of the philosopher-saint Mazdak. The philosophy that Mazdak preached was the equality of wealth as the foundation of humanity and brotherhood, and the course of the revolt is followed until it is brutally quelled by the Hun emperor. Through the medium of the novel, Rahulji emphasises the parallel development of emancipatory ideas within contiguous human societies in Iran during the Hun invasions and in India during the early Buddhist period.

(i) The Volga se Ganga Stories

The collection *Volga se Ganga* [From Volga to Ganga 1943], the most widely translated among Rahulji's literary works, is an attempt to understand how Indian society came to be what it is over the course of history, through the medium of a story relating to each epoch of that evolution. Based on the imaginative reconstruction of events, on historical facts well known to the scholars of his time and on his readings of ancient Vedic and Buddhist texts, the eight thousand years spanned by these 20 stories mark the transition through 360 generations of one particular branch of the Indo-European peoples that had its primaeval home on the banks of the Volga in the Mesolithic Age, to its absorption into the syncretic civilisation of modern India. Even as the unseen process through which civilisation is created from accretion of the events witnessed by human societies have witnessed and the ideas that had arisen with them is made apparent, Rahulji's focus stays on establishing how progressive social thought within each generation becomes the foundation for every forward step that is made by the next. The saga he narrates is thus highly antithetical to popular but obscurantist beliefs in India that seek to ascribe mystical antecedents to its civilisation, and is firmly rooted instead in materialistic reinterpretations of history.

The stories initially trace the migrations of the Indo-Scythian peoples through the Oxus region in prehistoric times, the Aryan settlement during the Vedic period and its conflict with and ultimate ascendancy over the highly-civilised Indo-Mesopotamian culture of the Indus valley, although at the cost of inheriting its institutions of hereditary kingship and its feudal offshoots. The first four stories – 'Nisha', 'Diva', 'Amritashva' and 'Puruhuta' – are alternately placed in the upper and middle Volga basins, near Ferghana in the Pamirs, and in the valley of the Amu Darya in Tajikistan, between 6000 BCE and 2500 BCE, as the identity of the racial group evolves from Indo-European through Indo-Slav [the '*shatam*' family] to Indo-Iranian. Human struggle is born in the need to dominate and control, the initial context being the struggle for the position of matriarch in a time when the survival ethic demands that the group never be endangered for the sake of the individual. Over slow evolution, man is divided into several warring clans who vie with each other, living under the constant shadow of battle. Against this stream are the stirrings of consciousness of being one nation, which motivates the human community to move ahead, uniting its disparate elements into common cause and culture. Man learns to domesticate animals, and by giving herdsmanship the status of a vocation, curbs his former animal-like propensities. Organisation of human effort in more hospitable conditions develops the skills that enable man's various wants to be satisfied. The discovery of metals provides him with means of greatly enhancing his wealth, while the occupations of agriculture and herding provide the means of well-being. But although such activities are discovered through human struggle and endeavour, they support the proclivities of a section to turn indolent and parasitic through the foundation of slavery. The bifurcation of consciousness between lord and slave opens the doors to jealousy and conflict once again, whereby oppression is resultant. Against this backdrop, the great migrations take place: the westward wave leaves its scions in the Madras (Medes) and Purus (Persians); the wave eastwards in the Indian Aryas.

The next four stories – 'Purudhana', 'Angira', 'Sudas' and 'Pravahana' – have reference to the Vedic, Brahmanic, Mahabharata-Puranic and late pre-Buddhist ages. Over this period of 1300 years the development of man soars, but within its pace, the human community rapidly loses pastoral contentedness and peace of mind. Marriage is now taking the form of a social instrument, with no reference to the likes and will of the partners, while at an alternate level, the evolution of separate nationalities within humankind is taking form. The establishment of the cult of Indra [the Rain-God] and its eventual decline is also subsumed within the period of these stories; its formulation, and then its relegation in circumstances where it no longer serves the useful purposes of its founders takes place as people begin to show awareness of both their common good and its endangerment. Marked accentuation in this occurs when the Aryas come into social contiguity with the more-developed Asura nation which has ruled India. The gap between the poor and the wealthy widens immensely and the institutionalisation of separate classes into castes is endorsed by the composition of verses in the Rig Veda bearing reference to this, The institutions of kingship, generalship and priesthood that come into being indicate the parasitic nature of the evolving social organisation. With exploitation now reaching a new extreme, the illusionary doctrine of rebirth and the immortal soul emerges as a palliative. A core of protest exists, too small to light a fire.

In the incipient struggle for dominance between the two contiguous societies, there is a willingness to learn from, and to adopt the higher technical attainments of the Asuras, at the price of adopting their divided society. This becomes a clever device on the part of self-seekers among the hitherto pastoral Aryas to establish their own dominance within the community. The *rishis* [learned elders] admonish that while the modes of organisation are to be learnt from the Asuras, the prevalent divisions within education, ritual and society among them are to be resisted. Such precepts are however unable to prevent corruptions of Arya society by Asura imports, like the priesthood: the Rig Veda composed in these times bears evidence of subtle social engineering that provides justification for the neo-exploitative structures that have been adopted. The era is one where solid foundations are built for the social inequities that have survived in India till the present day, the exploitation of womenkind and their reduction to the status of chattels, and the formulation of a social order which shall perpetuate this. Drawing its later references from the Chhandogya and Brihadaranyak *upanishads*, the period is one where the Aryas eventually transform themselves beyond a forest-dwelling people and lay the foundations for an Aryan state. The simplicity of the old totemic Vedic gods has come to be questioned, and into their place are supplanted the complex philosophical structures of Brahmanism that render godhood unvisitable, and the thesis of rebirth as justificatory to the evolving hierarchies within Aryan society. The beginnings of Aryan domination and of assimilation of conquered peoples draw upon such structures, while the scriptural mysticism of monasticism, asceticism and contemplation cloud the social mind through the power of ritual.

The epoch then moves on to the rise of materialist philosophers among the unconquered peoples, and the refinement of their thinking into the philosophical and cultural flowerings of the Buddhist period. Interaction with the Bactrian Greeks of Gandhara brings about cross-fertilisation between the Indian and Greek philosophical discourse. Buddhism original evolves as a social synthesis between the inequalities rooted in organised statecraft and the promise of relief from them in the world to come. Although heretical in reference to the old beliefs, and revolutionary in terms of seeking solutions in the present instead of in the future in the next world, Buddhism leaves avenues towards becoming the new instrument of state by adherence to the doctrine of rebirth and by leaving slavery and servitude unquestioned, which deprives the new social philosophy of its power for coercive change. There is a realisation embodied in the period, that the state must be ethical and must be responsive to the people in a polity where despotic kingship is not yet entrenched and the king/ruler is still the chief among peoples, echoing the republican freedoms that have preceded the fledgling nation-state. The power of the merchant-classes, whose riches exceed those of the rulers, is extended with philanthropic favour to this new social dispensation because it promises the peace and stability within which they might prosper. This accelerates its acceptance by the society of the times. Social consolidation has by now produced the concepts of empire as the extension of dominance, and the enjoyment of wealth and luxury as its logical rewards.

The Brahman doctrine of the ways for personal salvation and of uplift from hell extends more keenness to the divisions that have begun to appear within society. Towards the end of the epoch, the Brahmanical formulation of caste institutions and the rule of their *yagya* [fire-sacrifice] rituals has been accompanied by the breakup of the Aryan nation into local republican principalities and states. Each set of local rulers seeks its own ends, leaving none to look after the commonweal. The result is a weakening of the nation-state from within, and its being forced to acknowledge the suzerainty of others around it in deference to their military strength or to the wiles of the Brahman priesthood. The relevance of Buddhism to the social milieu of Kusana times and the reasons for its wide acceptance by the people across their realm are next explored. The Kusana period is characterised by the presence of a resident Ionian (Bactrian) community in India, which is in the process of slow assimilation into Indian society. The Sanskrit poet Ashvaghosh who later becomes part of Kanishka's court, is drawn to the breadth, depth and intense compassion of Buddhism and emerges as its proponent through the medium of his poetry embodied in works like *Buddhacharit*, *Saundarnand* and *Sariputra-prakaran*. Drawing references from Ashvaghosh's *Vajra-suchi*, the foundations of the divisive system of caste that the Brahmans have established are questioned by pointing out the latent opportunism embodied in their annihilation of earlier Vedic concepts of equality.

Yet the passiveness of Buddhist culture, an asset to its spread over a large swathe of Asia, offers no protection against the relentless onslaughts of new invaders, and Buddhism gradually dies out in the land of its birth. The historical reasons for this decline are succinctly introduced into the fabric of the three stories covering this later epoch – 'Suparna Yaudheya', 'Durmukha' and 'Chakrapani' – which bridge a span of 800 years in the mediaeval period after the Hindu revival. The commencement of the period coincides with the decadent Brahmanism of the Gupta age, which has now taken on the form of a caste rather than a priestly vocation. The Brahmans openly proselytise and preach of their pre-eminence as defenders of the faith, preservers of ritual and upholders of social purity while sharing the spoils of their privileged hierarchical position and, in collusion with the rulers, destroy the last vestiges of primitive republicanism by investing the feudal classes with hereditary Kshatriyahood. The Yaudheyas, descended from the republican Greeks, align in opposition to these irreligious manipulations and thus forego the right to be recognised as Brahmans. In the midst of this social decline, there are individual protests by certain forward-thinkers who seek restitution against the social oppression of that age. However, the system that these thinkers condemn is now so well-entrenched within governance and society that these protests are eventually fruitless. Restitution cannot come from a monarch who has now become a ruler within a feudal system, and the protest might have been more effective if taken to the community at large. The king, the religious and social institutions and the priesthood that lives comfortably on its takings from rituals are mutually complementary, and can hardly be shaken at this late stage.

By the end of the Hindu period, realisation has dawned that liberation from the sequestrations and empty rituals imposed by the Brahmanical faith can only come through force of arms. Meanwhile, the force of Islam has taken firm root among the neighbouring Turkic peoples and is on its way to inspiring a new wave of conquests. In its incipient period, this new faith had survived within micro-communities, but with their gradual unification, has now acquired the strength to seek dominance with the sword. In contrast, the Hindu kings in India still adhere to their old ways of oppressing the common people, of extracting wealth founded on bondage and forced labour, and to lives of parasitic luxury. The social consciousness of the ruling classes is so immured in the pursuit of worldly pleasures that they have no inkling of what the future holds, leave alone of the need for awakening. Thus, the destruction of the democratic antecedents of Indian society and the rise of Brahmanism with its institution of caste are all instrumental in bringing about the subsequent 'Dark Age', where primary stress is laid on maintaining the purity of Hinduism in the face of new Muslim settlement.

But the enlightened and progressive efforts made to bridge the Hindu-Muslim divide within Indian society through this epoch, such as those made by the Sufi saints and the emperor Akbar are also explored. The next two stories – 'Baba Nur Din' and 'Suraiya' – thus relate to the establishment of the Muslim state in India. The entry of the Khilji Afghans demarcates the watershed between the time when India was considered the target for periodic plunder from the west and the time where it is subjected to territorial conquest and institutionalised Muslim rule. Social consciousness has by this time become alive to the evils of the feudal system and its functionaries, and the religious trappings worn by the feudal state have now become incapable of keeping the common people beguiled. It therefore becomes necessary now to win the hearts of the people and to build a firm foundation for the new Muslim state, based on their common well-being.

The prime instrument is to bridge the divide between the Hindu and Muslim faiths as an act of state, so that conversion to Islam may then take place as a result of free will, rather than under any form of compulsion. A restoration of human values and human dignity is sought through this period, and is embodied in the meditations of the Sufi philosophers who make common cause with the people. Imperial rule reaches a zenith under the Mughals, and the stability provided by the long rule of Akbar is the benign backdrop against which the state seeks to integrate Islam into the Indian consciousness. A serious attempt is made to remove the stigma of conquest from the newly-consolidated nation by an enlightened ruler who is not averse to placing reliance on personal merit rather than religious affiliations in selecting his counsellors, although rigid opinions among the priesthood – both Hindu and Muslim – eventually undo this policy. The country is open to peripheral contact with the European Renaissance by the advent of sea-trade with merchant-adventurers, and new ideas on the augmentation of nationhood percolate, which have the potential to transform the face of the old society. They die an untimely death with the demise of the ruler.

The next four stories – 'Rekha Bhagat', 'Mangal Singh', 'Safdar' and 'Sumer' – relate contextually to one and a half centuries of colonial subjugation experienced by India, commencing with the establishment of the *Diwani* of the East India Company and of the *zamindari* system of absentee landlordship, which together lay the foundation for the parallel regimes of Company rule and local rule by the *zamindar*. A third tier of exploitation of the common people emerges within this structure, representing the extortions and excesses of landlord's servants. Meanwhile, the wealth extracted from the peasantry goes towards enriching the country to which the colonial powers belong, and towards supporting the prodigal lifestyles of the *zamindars*. There are mutterings of protest and revolt, although these are initially too isolated to take on the form of a popular rebellion. However, the 1857 Uprising marks the first consolidated revolt against British rule in India. Although not a people's rebellion, but rather an attempt by the old feudal lords to re-establish their sway by uprooting the colonial power, the inspirational quality of the rebellion projects into future aspirations of the Indian people after the revolt is crushed and the old feudal powers are buried with it. As severe reprisals by the British take place, lessons are learnt: primary among them are the knowledge that internal dissensions will vitiate any struggle for freedom, that such a struggle cannot be effectively led by remnants of an old vanquished elite, and that the freedom of the people can never be achieved through the restoration of the mediaeval state.

The new nationalist movement gradually reorganises itself into the non-violent Gandhian mould. Against the backdrop of the civil disobedience movement, the contribution of Gandhi to the struggle for nationhood is critically assessed. His major success is seen in his ability to provide the middle-class idealism of nationalist politics with mass-outreach and a popular base, even though the expectations aroused are endangered by the element of economic and industrial obscurantism that tinges his philosophy. The times are viewed through the eyes of a member of India's privileged English-educated class, who is able to perceive the critical world events that have followed the growth of imperialism, and is thus able to see the developments in India as part of this continuity rather than as an isolated occurrence. The protagonist realises that a revolution cannot be the handiwork of one man, and nor can the middle class – which has the most to lose from it – become its vanguard. Realisation of this commits the protagonist to a path of action, and through disillusionment with the Gandhian struggle, to faith in the revolutionary potential of the people. The time of the last story is contemporary to the writing of the book, where the focal point relates to the true nature of freedom, since mere political liberation cannot be equated with social emancipation. The real problem continues to reside within India's social fabric and its preservation of the mummified strictures and exclusions of the past, through the sanction of organised religion. The hollowness of a nationalist struggle that serves the interests of the elite and the rich is brought out in the bitterness of an educated Dalit youth who will have to bear the brunt of these exclusions. No freedom wherein there is perpetuation of economic inequities through the rhetoric of religion can be a real freedom, and the Gandhian attempt to uplift the Dalit classes though a moral movement is seen as a mere facade. The steepening of social deprivations wrought by global wars are bringing such frustrations to a simmering-point, with the system providing no hope of amelioration. Elements of this situation still survive unchanged in India today.

Manav Samaj [Human Society 1943] is an exploration of the process by which human society took its present shape, and whether social forms are universal to every epoch and country, or follow historical or dialectical processes – a thesis that can be approached from both Marxist and Buddhist angles. As such, this book is a scholar's reference book on the course of social evolution, as much as *Volga se Ganga* is a fictionalised account of it. In fact, *Volga se Ganga* was written as a sequel to *Manav Samaj* and its purpose was to explain the central thesis of human evolution in the latter, to the non-scholarly reader.

(ii) The History of Central Asia

Rahul Sankrityayana's long-term interest in the Central Asian region was evident in his travels as well as in many of his previous writings, including *Volga se Ganga*, before he wrote *Madhya Asia ka Itihas* in 1956/57. His point of interest lay in the fact that it was through this region that ancient migrations had taken place and early trade-routes had passed, and it was along them that early travellers had crossed from one country to another, carrying their cultural and philosophical influences with them. It was also true that the historical course of development that Indo-European civilisation had followed tied in very closely with the early rise of the Xiongnu or Huns (Skt. Huna), their conflicts with the Scythians (Skt. Sakas) to their west and with the Chinese to their southeast, their subsequent warlike incursions into Persia, Russia and Europe, which led through a domino effect to the gradual migrations of other ancient peoples to India over two millennia. Rahulji also knew that it was the conversion of the Huna emperor Gusri Khan to Buddhism that really allowed Buddhism to spread over Asia along the Silk Road to the extent that it did. He spent many years gathering historical material on the region from Buddhist Sanskrit, Chinese, Mongol, Tibetan, Russian, Persian and Arabic sources before eventually writing this history. He also put the archaeological evidence collected by Russian scholars in the vicinity of Khwarezm and the Syr Darya to great use in understanding the historical complexity as well as the pivotal importance of this region to the histories of other surrounding nations, including India. Written in Hindi, Rahulji's *Madhya Asia ka Itihas* was intended to educate modern Indian readers about the part of their cultural heritage that derived from the penetration of the Yavanas, Sakas and Kusanas into India during the Buddhist epoch. It was also intended as a reply to many questions that had still remained unanswered in India, regarding the origins and historicity of the Arya people and their migrations, as well as sources of later Turk and Mughal settlement in India in the mediaeval and early modern age.

The task of writing this history had originally been assigned to Rahulji by the Party, just before he left for Russia in 1944. He conceived his project on a very large scale, sweeping from the prehistoric origins of the Scythians and their dominance during the Bronze Age over their ancient homelands; the subsequent coming of Achaemenid ascendancy (6th century BCE) under Darius and Cyrus, followed by the establishment of the Graeco-Bactrian state under the ascendancy of Macedonian and Seleucid rulers (4th to 2nd century BCE), when Central Asia came to be widely identified with Tokharistan; the resurgence of the Indo-Scythians under the Yuezhi (Yue-chi) and Kusanas (2nd century BCE to 5th century CE) till the Kusana empire was overrun by the outward movements of the Hephthals or White Huns from the Altai (5th to 6th century CE), soon to be followed by the establishment of the first Turkic Khaganate (6th century CE).

Establishment of Arab influence over Central Asia occurs almost contemporaneously with the foundation of Islam as a world religion. Its first source is the Ummayid caliphate at Damascus (7th and 8th centuries CE) followed by the Abbasid caliphate that rules from Baghdad and Khorasan (8th and 9th centuries CE). The collapse of the caliphates is followed by a brief spell when Tahirid and Saffarid influences extend beyond Iran (9th century), coinciding with which the Samanids (9th and 10th centuries CE) lay the foundation of the Tajik state. Meanwhile, the Turkic peoples begin their rise to nationhood under Mamluk rulers who form the Ghaznavid empire (10th to 11th centuries CE) and the Karakhanid rulers at Kashgar (10th to 12th centuries CE). From the north, the Oghuz Turks succeed to the power of the Ghaznavids, extending their Seljuk empire from Central Asia into Turkey (11th to 12th centuries CE). They are followed by the Karakhitais (12th and 13th centuries) who have emerged out of Mongol-dominated areas in the north and have displaced the Karakhanid khanate, while the Khwarezm Shahs (11th to 13th centuries CE) have established their ascendance in Iran. Over the next two centuries, however, the balance of power in the region shifts decisively to the Mongols.

Having united the confederations of the Mongols, Chengiz Khan embarks on a swathe of conquests through Central Asia (13th century CE) and is then succeeded by his son Chagatai Khan and his Golden Horde (13th to 14th centuries CE). However, while possessing overwhelming belligerence, the Mongols lack statecraft and their western empire passes into the hands of the Timurids (14th and 15th centuries CE), who are of mixed Mongol and Turkic lineage. The Timurid period is a precursor of the rise of Uzbek power in the region, reaching fruition under the Sheibanids (16th century CE) who descend past the Syr Darya and capture the domains of the Timurids in Central Asia, relegating the last Timurid ruler Babur to Afghanistan and to India, where he establishes the Moghul dynasty in 1526 CE. The legacy of the Uzbek state passes on to the Ashtarkhanids (17th and 18th centuries CE) who had formerly ruled the Tatar khanate of Astrakhan located to the north of the Caspian sea. After them, the emirate at Bukhara with its Tajik and Turkic territories is taken over by the Mangyts (18th to 20th centuries CE) in 1740 by enlisting help from Nadirshah in Iran, who later also annexe other territories controlled by Uzbek confederations. After gradual extension of Tsarist influence into Central Asia, the emirate is reduced to an appendage of the Russian empire in 1868, even though the Mangyt emirs retain local administrative powers. Ultimately, in 1920, the territories of Kazakhstan, Kyrgyzstan, Tajikistan, Uzbekistan and Turkmenistan, stretching from the shores of the Caspian to the borders of Xinjiang (Chinese Turkestan), are incorporated as republics into the Soviet Union and make the transition from ethnic homelands to socialist states.

Writing from his collection of the source materials that were extant in his time, Rahulji conceived his History of Central Asia as an effort to fill a critical gap in India's knowledge about its closest neighbours. Rather than being a chronicle of dynasties and kings, his text therefore expanded on this intercultural linkage that had existed both in the past and in the present. Exploring the ancient link between the Scythian and Indian peoples, as preserved in linguistic evidence, he remarked:

> Comparative analysis of words identical to each other in the vocabularies of Sanskrit and Russian sheds great light on the state of development of society in times when they were linked. Words like 'biltat' (H.bolna), 'dablyat' (H.dabna) tell us how many words unknown to Sanskrit but common to Prakrit, Apabhransa and the modern languages have their common roots far back in the Scythian-Aryan era. Similarly, onomatopoeic words like 'chheenkna' (sneezing) and 'khansna' (coughing) make their entry during this time. By analysing such words, we can describe the social complexion of the Aryans and Scythians at the time when they separated and moved out of their primordial homeland….
>
> The common vocabulary of those times does not include the name of any foodgrain, nor any cultivation-related word – the word 'igo' (Skt.yug) is there, but has always been used in the sense of 'yugal'=pair. This would imply that the common society had not then entered the agricultural stage. On the other hand the Indo-Aryans and Iranians were acquainted with agriculture at the time they lived as a common people, since words like 'jau'=barley; 'godhum'=wheat; 'maash'=udad [a lentil]; which differentiate grains and crops are present in the vocabularies of each. Words like 'gau'=cow; 'avi'=sheep=ewe are from the common Aryan-Scythian vocabulary, but there is no common word for milk; on the other hand the equivalence of 'ksheer' (Skt.) and 'sheer'(Pers.) is present in the common Aryan vocabulary. This would imply that if the Aryas and Sakas were already herders by the time they parted ways, the raising of livestock for milch purposes was still unknown. The indefiniteness of words attributing colours or descriptive

> of metals makes it apparent that they were still unacquainted with metals.
>
> Considering weaponry and tools, it becomes obvious that these were made of wood and stone, and that for the modelling of these the material 'taksh' was used. We later find that where Sanskrit applies 'taksh' in the sense of wood-modelling, the Russian 'tesaat' or 'tyosivaat' is descriptive of modelling in stone.
>
> All said and done, it is now apparent that when the Aryas and Sakas evolved into separate peoples and nations, they were still unacquainted with agriculture and the use of metals. Besides hunting ('aakhet') animals, they had probably just begun to rear them, in which the dog ('shvak') was definitely of assistance. This would have been in the Mesolithic, or early Neolithic age.
>
> ['The Russian Language & India'; appendix; *Madhya Asia ka Itihas*-I]

Expanding this perspective further into the shared histories, he observes:

> We could call the vast Scythian lands that spanned the continent of Eurasia from the Dunai (Danube) to the Tien Shan mountains at the commencement of the Bronze Age – the Shaka-dweepa [Land of the Sakas] in accordance with Indian terminologies, or Shakan-veija in Old Iranian, or Shaka-stan in terms of the later language. However, eastern Iran came to be known as Shaka-stan or Sistan in the second century BCE, following settlement by the Scythians. We can call this region the primordial Scythian homeland, and using the same terminology, can call the lands to the south of the Aral sea and the Syr Darya the Arya-dweepa, Aryan-veija, or Arya-stan. In Avestan times later, Aryan-veija was only a little province, which modern-day historians sometimes identify with Khorasan, Balkh (Bakhtar, or Bactria), Ajur-baijan, or sometimes Khwarezm. Hence to avoid confusion, it is better if we just speak of an Aryan homeland.

This distinction between Shaka-dweepa and Arya-dweepa did not survive too long. Attack by the Huns forced the Scythians to leave the eastern parts of Shaka-dweepa from 175 BCE onwards and over nearly six centuries that followed, the Huns and their descendants scattered the Scythians and reached the banks of the Danube. As a consequence of their great campaign, the eastern Scythian homeland had been converted into a Hun homeland by the fourth century CE; towards its western fringes, the Goths and Sarmaths (Scythian-offshoots) who had lived in the region of the Black Sea to the west of the Don had to flee their ancestral lands and go west or north. We also know that the total withdrawal from the eastern Scythian homeland led to one result – the destruction of the Greek-Bactrian state, the end of Ionian (Yavana) rule in India and to the permanent impress of the Scythians being left on the statecraft and social life of India". [*Madhya Asia ka Itihas* – I]

The idea of an original Aryan homeland outside India has come under a strongly motivated challenge in real times, even though the shared history of India and Central Asia throws up ample evidence of the constant movement of peoples between the two regions, stretching from ancient to mediaeval times. The evidence is amply represented in ancient Indian texts, and is essential towards understanding the cultural diversities within India:

> The Greeks were known to the Indians from times before Alexander (d.323 BCE). The Buddha, in a sutra from the *Majjhimanikaya*, mentions Kamboja (Northern Afghanistan) and Yavana (Ionia=Greece). The Greeks were also known to Panini (4 BCE). In the time after, the Ionians came to India in large numbers and established their rule in many parts of northern India in the second and third century BCE. Large tracts of northern India were under the sway of the Sakas (Scythians) from the first century BCE to the third century CE, while Punjab remained under Scythian rule till the fifth century CE, when they were displaced by the Hephthals, a branch of the Sakas (descendants of the Torman-Mihirakul dynasty) who by historical mistake have been classified as White Huns. Mihirakul was ejected from Malwa by Yashodharma, and with this the last Scythian kingdom vanished from India. Around the same time, Bahlik (Bakhtar=Bactria, or Balkh), Tushar and Sogd, were also snatched away from them by the Turks. But, over eight long centuries, the Ionians and Scythians had intimate connections

> in India and settled here by their thousands, and are now inseparably present among the Hindus as Shakdweepi Brahmins, as Chauhans, Banafars, etc. among the Rajputs and as the Jat-Gujjar tribes. [*Madhya Asia ka Itihas*-I]

While in Russia between 1945-47, Rahulji had fervently wished to visit each of the Central Asian republics in order to see the process through which they had evolved into modern states for himself. As was true for most of the journeys he made through his life, this curiosity about the Central Asian region rested on the belief that there was much that India could learn and adopt from the social transformations that had already occurred in countries which shared a similar cultural milieu. Since the opportunity to make these proposed visits did not materialise at that time, for political reasons, he had to limit himself to reporting on the social and economic progress he had witnessed during his earlier transit between Kazakhstan, Uzbekistan, Tajikistan, Afghanistan and India in 1937.

Putting to use his ability to read Farsi literature in the original, Rahulji nonetheless found alternate means to comprehend the renaissance that had occurred in Central Asia and to communicate it to Indian readers, by transliterating the Tajik novels of Sadruddin Aini (1878-1954) whose work had left a deep impression on him. These novels included *Dakhunda* (1948; Taj. *Dokhundo*), *Jo Das The* (1948; Taj. *Ghulomon*), *Anath* (1948; Taj. *Yatim*) and *Sudkhor ki Maut* (1952; Taj. *Marg-i-Sudkhur*). The similarity of cultural contexts, as well as the proximity of Tajikistan to India (which was even closer before 1947, when Pakistan was still a part of India), made it relatively easy for Indian readers to see reflections of their own social realities in Aini's novels. Narrating the Tajik transition from exploitation and abject suffering under the old feudal society of the Bukharan emirs, to struggle and emancipation under a new social dispensation that ensured equal rewards, the novels thus offered a valid social commentary that could be applied when visualising the future transition that needed to be accomplished by Indian society in its own struggle for emancipation and social justice. Rahulji believed that Indian readers would be able to benefit greatly from knowing these.

11

Linguistic Security during the Period of Acceleration of Economic and Socio-cultural Globalisation and Self-identification of Nationalities

Maria Gritsko

The term "globalisation" was already in use in the mid-eighties of the 20th century. Despite the general interest among researchers about globalization, its background, specificity and impact are not studied to a great extent. Among the numerous questions concerning globalisation, the issue that affects the world community most is "What is globalisation – a process containing alternatives and variants, or a process unambiguous, unidirectional, imperative; does this process lead to the creation of homogeneous integrity of the world or comprise some possibilities of different identities and different components of a mankind?"[1]

Problems of security and preservation of national and cultural identity in the modern globalising world is ambiguous. Globalisation as a natural-historical process of universalisation of diverse communications and relations in mankind is frequently considered to be the destructive factor for national interest and identity. We understand national identity "as the essence to what the person, social group, the people correlate themselves, what they connect themselves to and whether they feel sovereign and independent".[2] The basis of such national self-determination of nations and the ethnic self-determination of an individual are national culture and national language that express this culture.

The financial and economic crisis in the world shows the vulnerability and unstable character of world order and global interdependence. According to the famous literary essayist, mathematician and businessman Nassim Nicholas Taleb, "Globalization creates interlocking fragility, while reducing volatility and giving the appearance of stability... We have never lived before under the threat of a global collapse".[3] However even in such extreme conditions ethnic foundations remain firm. This fact testifies to their highest principles of a reality in mankind, than any "creation" of human activity.

Language and linguistic issues feature in several academic discussions. Language is not only the means of communication, but also is a tool of globalisation and sovereignty of world civilisations. The language of each ethnos has original features expressing uniqueness of a community or group of people. The language that expresses the common national-cultural symbols, attitudes and mythologies through centuries is a component of ethnicity. F. Hekkman gives the broadest definition of ethnicity: "Ethnicity is an indicator of real mutual relations at both the individual and collective levels, characterising the groups of people connected among themselves by the same ideas about genetic relationship and cultural-linguistic community, possessing collective historical experience".[4] Modern research on ethnicity tries to explain the nature of social and ethnic conflict, cultural interaction, political activism of ethnic minority and political changes in the postcolonial world testifies theories about ethnicity and ethnic self-identification. In Russian ethnology, the terms 'ethnicity' and 'ethnic identity', as well as other terms with the prefix 'ethno' are frequently used interchangeably and mean "the people as a national community". Most often ethnicity is considered as nationality (in terms of national identity), and ethnic identity as national identity (in terms of self-identification with the certain people.

These issues are significant in multiethnic communities in which the representatives of various ethnic groups differ in culture, religion and language. The modern geopolitical reality is that religion, culture and language have the strongest influence on international politics, economic and military relations. Having estimated threats and risks in the unstable world, the American consultative group called the Eurasia Group, specialising on the analysis of markets, indicates the danger of political radicalism and underlines that in some countries the threat of split of the country is often due to cultural, religious and linguistic factors.[5]

In Russia for instance, International Relations is a subject of debate among protagonists of the state and supporters of local administrative regions. Being a multinational state, for a long time Russia faced to the problem of relations between the people living in its territory. The influx of migrants from near abroad to 'safe areas' of Russia and big cities has caused social concern. Besides due to numerical imbalance between representatives of various nationalities, there is suspicion and misunderstanding, leading to extreme forms of xenophobia.

Thus, the modern geopolitical reality is that a great number of national conflicts are caused by extreme aspirations of nationalistic character. They are peculiar to many countries in which national minorities historically, and also after post-war geopolitical repartitions, consider themselves oppressed, suppressed by the dominating majority of the titular nation. Daisaku Ikeda, well-known Japanese religious and political figure underlines the latent force of oppressed nations: "Energy of nation cannot be destroyed either by military force or by forces of ideology.... Natural nationalist feelings are deep, as they are connected with traditional customs, culture and religion".[6] Thus because of their struggle for national and language independence, radical nationalist groups prosper. The intervention of other states or the interference of military-political blocks in internal affairs of the states has dissatisfied national minorities. For instance, the European Union, actually having united the states instead of the peoples, strengthened ethnic separatism in those territories where the borders of the states which have developed after the Second World War do not coincide with the ethnic borders. Among "flashpoints" in EU where weaponization has been till now the main source of dispute are included Basques which is a divided space between Spain and France and since 1965 has been conducting armed struggle for its independence with the help of ETA (Euskadi Ta Askatasuna: "the Basque Country and Freedom"), Ireland which through several centuries is contested between London and Dublin and which has been exposed to terrorist attacks of militant groups of the IRA (the Irish Republican Army), APU (Association of Protection of Ulster) and others.

Nevertheless the struggle of national minorities for sovereignty and negative aspects of this struggle are misinterpreted by the world community. This misinterpretation is one of the major reasons of international instability, an "arena" where religious and civilizational interests of different states and their unions clash. According to the Charter of the United nations, among 3,000 ethnic groups that exist in the modern world, 280 groups have the possibility of receiving sovereign status and would like to leave the state to which they now belong, and the demands of 70 of these groups have already become the reason of armed confrontations among member states of the United Nations.

In the Russian Federation, as well as in many other countries, the question about preserving national cultures amidst the complex process of globalisation, their interaction within a global framework and the polarized, hybrid and average mass culture (pretending to replace national cultures) is of great interest. Languages preserve national integrity and sovereignty. National cultures that are joined by centuries-old coexistence have much in common. Russia in its original form is multilateral and integrated, possessing the unified and many-sided features, reflected in the state language and in languages of the people living in Russia.

The population of Russia, according to population census of 2000, is 142.2 million. Besides Russians that constitute 79.8 per cent of the population, over 180 other nationalities live in the country. They speak more than 100 languages and dialects. In such a multinational state as Russia, a question on a unified state language is of great importance. Undoubtedly languages of the people of the Russian Federation are legislatively under protection of the state and have been given the status of national property, moreover the state takes measures on their maintenance and development; nevertheless a status of the Russian language as unified state language is the fundamental factor of communicative unity and integrity of the state.

Sustained development of the unified Russian language throughout last century (especially during the Soviet period) have resulted in the interaction among Russian-speaking people and can be emphasized as one of the achievements of language policy. The cultural diversity in the country was in every possible way supported by the state and represented the priorities of a national policy. However after disintegration of the USSR, Russia's interest about former union republics as well as distant neighbours has sharply decreased. That became the reason for the loss of international status of Russia. In the majority of the independent states of "near abroad" the restriction of the use of Russian in various spheres is being carried out. Without the official status of a state language, Russian has lost its initial position. As a result in these countries the new information field which does not correspond to social historical traditions and linguistic culture is taking shape. The results of such destructive linguistic policy in the countries, where Russian initially has not received the state language status (except Belarus), are expressed in weakening of economic, scientific and cultural contacts between Russia and these states that in turn leads to menacing and dangerous linguistic processes and negatively affects the state development and the international status of these countries. However, not all states on the post-Soviet territory have successfully replaced Russian with their national languages, especially with reference to its usage.

The restricted use of Russian is observed all over the world. In 1945, the newly created United Nations proclaimed 51 countries and five international languages: English, French, Spanish, Russian and Chinese. Since then all documents of the United Nations are published in these languages. However Russian is not used very often as a language of international dialogue. Representatives of Russia and the Commonwealth of Independent States (CIS) should submit all information either in English or in the official language of the countries where events take place. At international exhibitions and scientific conferences, Russian is considered the official language only when these events take place in the territory of Russia or the CIS countries. There are many cases of scientific research papers in Russian having hardly been recognized and only after their translation into English that they were fully presented to the world community.

By 1990 there were 350 million Russian speaking people in the world. In 2005 this number was reduced to 278 million people. According to the forecasts by 2015 the number of Russian speaking people will be reduced to 212 million, and by 2025-to 152 million.[7]

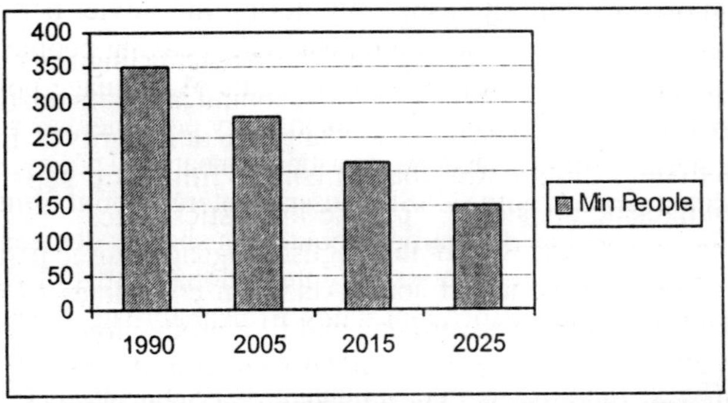

Figure 1. Russian Speaking People in the World in the Period from 1990 to 2025

Russian is the only leading world language that has been losing its position in the last 15 years. This tendency will continue in the next 20 years if proper attention is not given to the state language policy which can strengthen the position of the Russian language within the country and in the world.[8]

Global communicative and cultural contacts between the people outside and inside Russia, growing tendency to preserve the originality of the peoples, use of this tendency in geopolitical tussles lead to the actual problem of linguistic security. At the basis of linguistic security is the preservation and development of state sovereignty and the economic, social, ethnic or cultural-historical foundations.

In the socio-linguistic terms, linguistic security implies a series of measures for the realisation of positive linguistic processes, aborting the negative conditions of linguistic processes and their transformation into the positive ones, and also the prevention and liquidation of the dangerous linguistic processes. Such positive linguistic processes are "language variety", "linguistic policy", "linguistic development", "linguistic self-identification", "linguistic quality of languages", "linguistic methodology", "language ecology", "language hierarchy" – all that reflect positive tendencies in development and interaction among languages, promoting intensive cultural and political communication between people.

Public opinion in the post-Soviet states tries to understand the Eurasian space in the Russian, Soviet and post-Soviet periods which includes territories, states and people "from the Ukraine and Belorussia to Kuriles and from the Polar region to the branches of Tien Shan and Pamir".[9] The common basis and core of this union is the Russian language, Russian-speaking culture that have kept the cultural world of Eurasia intact.

The negative processes highlight the menacing linguistic situation leading to intrastate complications and complicate state relations and are characterised by such terms as "language unipolarity", "linguistic nationalism", "linguistic chauvinism", "linguistic separatism", "ethnolinguistic divisions", "pseudo-linguistics", etc.

The overall expansion of the English language caused particularly by an aggressive policy of some American companies to promote mass culture (through advertising and film production, grammatical constructions) may be considered as an example of deliberate intention of "language unipolarity". The advancing role of the mass media and the Internet has contributed to the popularity of English as language of the masses. The influence of mass-media on the life of the people is indicated as follows: "Mass-media become the secular religion to a great extent replacing the common history, national culture, true religion, family and friends as the main force creating our opinion about the reality".[10]

The use of this mass language gives it the chance of a global language in the near future. However according to British statistics, today 372 million people speak English and 350 million people use it as a second language. Almost an equivalent number of people speak Hindi but about 1,113 million people speak Chinese.[11] It should be also mentioned, that considerable financial expenses are required for studying any foreign language, therefore English at the moment is still not available to the majority of people, so "language, which is unknown to 92 per cent of a world's population, it not the world language".[12]

One might cite the example of India to explain "linguistic nationalism". Numerous attempts to create a standard national language in the polyethnic state that recognizes at least 24 languages have not yielded results. Hindi is the official and intermediate language in India. However, English is still used as the official language in management, policy-oriented and general education as well as in communicative spheres despite the fact that English is spoken by only 2 per cent of the population.

The dangerous socio-linguistic processes can threaten state sovereignty and lead to international tension. Extreme stages of the dangerous socio-linguistic processes can be – "linguistic racism", "linguistic mutiny", "linguistic terrorism", "linguistic aggression", "language war". In Ukraine where 60 per cent of population speaks Russian, it has a minority status. According to the State Committee statistics of Ukraine,[13] Russian language has almost been pushed out of daily use, business communication and in the realm of education, culture and history. According to 2001 census, the number of Russian-speaking citizens of Ukraine is the largest and yet their language is not recognised as official.[14] In such a situation it is appropriate to talk not simply about the linguistic chauvinism implying therefore the infringement of linguistic rights of the Russian-speaking people and also about the current trend of linguistic racism whereby the political elite carries out a policy of eradication of Russian for the purpose of revision of history and escalating political tension with Russia. Analysing the present language situation in Ukraine it should be noted that language polarisation prevails among the population. As a result many inhabitants of Ukraine name themselves "ukrainorus" that testifies to the impossibility of clear elf-identification at the cultural-language level. Special attention should be given to the fact that through linguistic agendas nationalist groups can motivate the population.

Moreover, numerous attempts have been made by the Ministry for Foreign Affairs of the Russian Federation to protect Russian from discrimination in Ukraine and to give it the status of state language, as well as to recognise that "bilingualism is historically developed phenomenon, therefore to eradicate Russian by such methods is simply counterproductive",[15] that Ukraine will not interfere with Russian internal affairs, and stop playing the "language card" and control internal politics in Ukraine and respect the laws of Ukraine according to international standards".[16]

In conditions of globalisation, a socio-linguistic aspect is associated with the cultural self-identification of the people of Russia, and, in particular, of Siberia. The Siberian region of Russia (here the Siberian Federal district is considered) can become an object of studying this problem of national self-identification.

Because of its geographical position, huge territory, the historical importance for Russia, natural-resource base of the world value, the developed economy and science, intercontinental transport possibilities, base of economic, political and socio-cultural contacts to the neighbouring states on the post-Soviet space and to the countries of South East Asia the Siberian region evokes enormous interest. "The development of self-identity in the regions, territorially located at the historical crossroad of cultures always has particular specificity".[17]

Thus it is important to investigate identity problems in connection with a region which is territorially located at the crossroads of culture and civilisation. The Russian Siberian multinational self-identity, idealized by such concepts as "western" and "eastern" nationalism and frequently discussed upon by the world linguistic community,[18] is significant from the point of view of linguistic, ethno-religious, political, social and economic and historical criteria. Along with the research of traditional aspects of preservation of self-identification of nationalities of Siberia it is necessary to look at a problem through the prism of interaction of a unified state language and the languages of nationalities of Siberia, and evaluate the problems of linguistic security.

The Siberian Federal District has a population of 20.06 million and a territory which is 30 per cent of the entire Russian territory. It has 12 subdivisions of the Russian Federation. Four of them have national language identification except for the nation-wide Russian language (in the Altai republic the Russian and Altai languages have equal rights in usage; in Tuva, Khakassia and Buryatia republics the Tuvan, Khakass and Buryat languages have the status of official languages besides Russian).

Table 1. The Siberian Federal District: National Structure of the Population (%)[19]

Russians	87.38
Buryats	2.13
Ukrainians	1.86
Germans	1.54
Tatars	1.26
Tuvinians	1.20
Kazakhs	0.62
Belorussians	0.41
Khakases	0.36
Altai	0.33
Chuvashes	0.31
Azerbaijani	0.30
Armenians	0.30

In the republics of the Siberian Federal district questions on teaching, preservation and development of ethnic languages are more and more discussed; there are doubts concerning the prevalence of a unified state Russian language that inevitably leads to conflict situations, sporadic outburst of linguistic separatism.

Despite the external "peace" in the linguistic situation, in the Russian society there are "hot poles" – nationalist aspirations of a part of the national elite and extreme radical type. The Russian state can resist centrifugal forces of one republic or area. But if there are too many dangerous regions, what will happen then? It is calculated that the outbreak of centrifugal tendencies might surpass the durability of a construction as a whole. And Russia will collapse".[20]

The absence of attention to the problem of linguistic security weakens the efficiency of language policy. Proponents of alternative languages belonging to different nationalities under the pretext of protection of their ethnic languages can "rise" against the state language and stir up interethnic hostility.[21] As a rule, requirements of linguistic sovereignty or the requirements in other areas of the symbiosis of ethnoses finally concentrate on political aspirations. Thus political aspirations will be hidden unless the right time approaches and language sovereignty can play the role of "the trigger mechanism" and consequently infringe upon linguistic security.

Today the socio-linguistic processes in areas with Siberian ethnoses are analyzed poorly that can also pose a threat to linguistic security. The available facts of political life indicate the weakening of economic and cultural contacts between the nationalities of Siberia; moreover for some Siberian ethnoses that live territorially far from the Central European part of the country are close to China and Mongolia (Buryatiya, Tuva) in the ethnocultural sense. It is correct to speak about the presence of national-separatist tendencies of the ethnic elite. Slogans of nationalists from some ethnic minority groups are hardly different from slogans of nationalists of the Russian majority. The youth considers Russians as "newcomers" who should always make way for "the indigenous nation" or "go back to their Russia". For example, the large-scale migration of Russians from Tuva in the early nineties was the outcome of this sentiment. Nationalism is expressed due to the discrimination of personnel in the national republics. Practically everywhere the top elite consists only of representatives of the titular nation though there is a sizeable proportion of representatives belonging to non-titular nationalities. In the post-Soviet territory and inside the territory of the Russian Federation the problem of ethnicity has been especially focused upon in the last few years. It is known that ethnicity due to its reaction to external circumstances tends to become the major ideological tool of a race for power: "The ethnicity issue is especially sensitive to changes in the interethnic atmosphere and its actualisation as a form of intragroup and intergroup influence conducts to the growth of interethnic intensity and disintegration in a multiethnic society".[22]

It is also impossible to ignore the indigenous minorities of the North of Siberia. In the Siberian Federal District territory about 70,000 people of 18 national indigenous peoples of the North and Siberia live (it is more than one third of the 45 indigenous peoples of the North and Siberia living in the Russian Federation).[23] The Khanti, Mansi, Nenets, Shors, Telengits, Chelkans, Kumandins are the most numerous ethnic groups speaking mainly in the Turkic and Finno-Ugric languages and dialects. Most of these indigenous peoples live in the territory of the

Altai. A great number of independent and mixed nationalities can be found here but their exact number is difficult to determine. Their traditions and customs are very much alike and almost all of them practice shamanism. Nowadays scientific and cultural elite of northern people has united into the Russian Association of Indigenous Peoples of the North and prefers to have close active cultural and spiritual cooperation with foreign countries what leads to the growing intensity between the Siberian Russian ethnos and the North ethnoses.

Research marks the uncertain position of the Russian population in the republics and the autonomies of the Russian Federation. The sovereignty of national republics amounts to the strengthening of Russian sovereignty and this contradiction is clearly evident in the North Caucasus, especially in the Chechen Republic, and also in Bashkiria, Tatarstan and Yakutia. In territory of the Siberian Federal district the similar situation is observed in the republic Tuva, mountain part of the Altai region. As observed recently, "it is rather probable that in the near future in these former autonomous republics there will be a sharp problem of protection of the rights of Russians as national minority".[24]

In the given situation, the modern socio-linguistic and "pure linguistic" analysis calls for something more than merely a simplified description of the language situations in various territories. Essentially linguistic methods investigate crucial world problems, problems of globalisation and ethnicity, problems of relations between civilisations, "polarity" of the world etc. Finally, all these problems are reduced to existence of an individual in the boundless boiling mix of world problems.

The problems of linguistic security reflect the problems of external and internal policy, economy, culture, historical development, an entire spectrum of interrelations in the world by the linguistic method. It concerns the interaction of languages and cultures in Russia, as relations of Russia with its near and far neighbours, partners and competitors. Scientific research of these issues, a preliminary assessment of possible tendencies and situations needs to be done in the interest of the world community, the states and the individual.

NOTES AND REFERENCES

1. Tchernyak E., *Sud'i i zagovorschik,* Moscow: Mysl', 1984, p. 52.
2. Koksharov N.V., "Diskurs natsionalizma (Bibliography review)". Available from http://www.orenburg.ru

3. Taleb N., *The Black Swan: The Impact of the Highly Improbable*, New York: Random House, 2007. ISBN 978-1-4000-6351-5.
4. Heckmann F., *Ethnische Minderheiten, Volk und Nation: Soziologie inter-ethnischer Beziehungen*, Stuttgart, Ferdinand Enke Verlag, 1992, p. 8.
5. "Amerikantsy otsenili ugrozy dlja Rossii", *Vlast'/Den'gi*, 29.4.2009, No. 77 (2347). Available from htpp://www.vedomosti.ru
6. Daisaku Ikeda., *Na vstrechu novomu globalizmu*, Tokyo, 26 January, 1989.
7. Aref'ev A.L., "Skol'ko lyudei govoryat i budut govorit' po-russki", 2006. Available from: http://demoscope.ru/weekly/2006/0251/tema01.php
8. See for details: Gritsko M.I., "2007-god russkogo yazyka", *Nauka v Sibiri*, No. 30 (9 August) 2007.
9. Nazarbaev N.A., From the speech at the meeting of professors and students in the Moscow State University (the first official visit of the President of Kazakh to the Russian Federation), March, 29, 1994.
10. Turou L., "Budushchee kapitalizma. Kak ekonomika segodnyashnego dnya formiruet mir zavtrashnij", In *Novaya postindustrialnaya volna na zapade*, Ìoscow: Academia, 1999, p. 218.
11. According to the data from: Udovik S.L., *Globalizatsiya: semioticheskie podhody*, "Refl-book", "Vakler", 2002, p. 257.
12. Huntington S.P., "Zahid: unikalnist' versus universalizm", *Filosofs'ka dumka*, 1999, N1-2, p. 94.
13. Statistics is available from http://www.ukrcensus.gov.ua
14. Aref'ev A.L., "Skol'ko lyudei govoryat i budut govorit' po-russki", 2006. Available from http://demoscope.ru/weekly/2006/0251/tema01.php
15. The official comment of the Department of Information and Press of the Ministry of Foreign Affairs of the Russian Federation in connection with a question of "Novosti" news agency concerning continuing discrimination of the Russian language in Ukraine, 27.9.2006. Available from http://www.mid.ru
16. Statement of the Press Service of the Ministry of Foreign Affairs of Ukraine in connection with the official comment of the Department of Information and Press of the Ministry of Foreign Affairs of the Russian Federation of September 27, 2006, on so called discrimination of the Russian language in Ukraine (eng.). Available from: http://www.mfa.gov.ua
17. E.G. Vodichev, M.I. Gritsko, "Linguistic security and Self-identification in the Global world (Siberian region as an example)", *Siberia in Focus. Proceedings of the conference-Eurasia: Regional Perspectives –*

Maulana Abul Kalam Azad Institute of Asian Studies, Kolkata, Towards Freedom, 2007, p. 170.

18. Anderson B., "Zapadnyj natsionalizm i vostochnyj natsionalizm: est' li mezhdu nimi raznitsa?", *Russkij zhurnal*, 2001, No. 11 (19 December). Available from http://old.russ.ru/politics/20011219-and.html/
19. According to the data from the official Website of the Siberian Federal District. Available from http://www.sibfo.ru/passport/sfo.php
20. Kuryanovitch N., "S akuloj luchshe borot'sya na beregu", *Politichesky Zhurnal*, 26 September, 2005, No. 31 (82), p. 82.
21. Savelyev A.N., *Natsiya i gosudarstvo. Teoriya konservativnoy rekonstrukzii*, Moscow: Logos, 2005.
22. "Etnichnost' i etnicheskaya identichnost': problema sootnosheniya ponyatij i podhody k ih issledovaniyu". Available from: http://student.km.ru
23. According to the data from an official Web-site of the Siberian Federal District. Available from http://www.sibfo.ru/passport/sfo.php
24. Sokolovsky S.V., *Prava men'shinstv. Antropologicheskie, sotsiologicheskie i mezhdunarodno-pravovye aspekty*, Ìoscow: Moskovsky obschestvenny nauchny fond, 1997. Available from: http://polbu.ru/sokolovsky_prava/

12

The Role of Language in Forming Modern Society in Kazakhstan

Anna Yessengaliyeva

Preservation of a stable international world order and consent within poly-ethnic states should be promoted by language policy. Language policy is the state policy on development of languages of the people occupying the territory of the given state. Language policy is pursued in the language environment, i.e., in the environment that nurtures the language. It is directed towards change of language behaviour of native speakers, i.e., language policy is carried out in relation to representatives of language groups. Efficiency and productivity of a language policy depends on regulation of language behaviour of the subjects and objects of language policy. The state, other official state structures form the subject of language policy. As object of language policy native speakers, representatives of language groups react to the policy.

Mastering a language is an ongoing process. And development of language is closely connected with the history of the society, that public situation in which this language is used, and those social functions which language carries out. Among these three functions of language, named by scientists as means of dialogue it would be incorrect to allocate significance to any one. They are equally important and strongly interconnected. Language, as one of the main characteristics of the society, has communicative function. Communicative function is the basic social function of language representing language as the force, providing existence and development of a society. Accumulative (gnosiological) function of language – means of preservation of the saved up experience and knowledge for the future generations, and besides, means of interethnic development. Expressive function – the unity of expression and transferring of feelings, emotions, and wills of the speaker, some information – represents language as means of expression of ideas. It is necessary to emphasize, that the quantity of people speaking a language and the quantity of persons of the given nationality do not coincide. And the wide circulation of any language makes these languages carry out additional functions. And then it can become a language of interethnic dialogue. Similarly, world languages, which carry out the role of intermediary, emerge. Language is not only the carrier of culture and its greatest phenomenon, but also the major political tool. This political function of language has assumed (in the USSR, and then on the post-Soviet territory), "overwhelming" position last ten years of the last millennium.

After the collapse of the USSR the Central Asian region has drawn the attention of different forces and states. A search for national self-identity and economic self-sufficiency was an important factor that made the newly independent states turn first to the countries which were geographically, culturally and ethnically close to them. Serious influence on the language policy of Central Asian countries was rendered by political shifts and business factors. The question of language still remains an important political issue for the countries. A number of factors still influence the language policy of the countries of the Central Asia. One of the most important variables here is the status of titular languages during Soviet times. In Uzbekistan, in higher educational institutions most of the teaching was conducted in the Uzbek language even during Soviet times, but if one looks at Kazakhstan and Kyrgyzstan there the volume of high school teaching in the Kazakh or Uzbek languages was rather insignificant. Another important factor is geopolitics. With the change of diplomatic course the language policy too can undergo changes. The economy also influences aspects of cultural life thanks to which there are distinctions in the language policy of Kyrgyzstan and Kazakhstan. Rich reserves of natural resources of Kazakhstan have allowed it to promote faster in the field of national language development whereas Kyrgyzstan which does not have natural resources, experiences difficulties with distribution of the Kirghiz language. The strongest factor defining language policy is demography. Existing demographic tendencies give the grounds to believe that in due course its value will increase.

With independence each state has made a national language its state language. Since the time Kazakhstan gained its independence, the purpose of creating modern democratic society has become an integral component of the strategic course of the state. A rich and unique experience of peaceful coexistence of nations, civilizations, cultures and various faiths on the historical land of Kazakhs is accumulated in one state. This heritage defines the roots of our unity and helps us to see our future clearly. Today the basic principles of the State National Policy of Kazakhstan are: Equality of rights and freedoms of people and citizens regardless of their race, nationality, language, religious denomination, belonging to social groups and social unions. As subjects of the language policy the President of the Republic of Kazakhstan, the Government of Kazakhstan, and the official state structures have to act accordingly.

At the same time complexity of carrying out a purposeful and consecutive language policy requires the definition of the objects of a language policy. In the given role some groups within the population is defined as "carriers of a language policy"[1]. In the first language group, in our opinion, are Kazakh people, born till 1995. The second language group, consists of Kazakh people, born after 1995. The first group is characterized by their inability to adapt to the new language environment; representatives of the given group perceive change of the language environment painful. The second language group is represented by the youth who are ready to adapt the newly created language environment, simultaneously participating in the creation of this language environment.

Language policy is formulated in reaction to a language situation or a language problem. Therefore it is possible to identify a language situation or a problem as the source of a language policy. "The language policy is a set of acts of the state intended for the development of the state and of the ethnic languages of a society.[2] Language policy can promote regulation of interethnic relations or lead to its aggravation in a given region. According to A.A. Tsutsiyeva of the Institute of Humanitarian and Social Researches RSO: "it is possible to name the basic purpose of language policy maintenance of conditions for language functioning as the cultural factor promoting national integration"[3]. As the interests underlying the language policy, it is possible to designate interests of representatives of language groups, and also the state interests in language sphere at the given stage of national development. The language policy, as well as any type of a state policy, is defined by official procedures. So, for example, in Kazakhstan means of a language policy are Acts,

Decrees of President RK, governmental orders RK, decisions *akims* areas, cities, orders of Ministers of Education, Cultures, the Information and the Public Consent, regulating relations in language sphere. There are various kinds and types of a language policy. The types of the language policies are assimilation, cultural pluralism and autonomism.

Language assimilation by radically-etatistic methods means suppression of language of smaller language groups by representatives of the largest language group. At the time of the Russian empire the imperial language policy was directed towards increase of the status of Russian, suppression of languages of ethnic minority even in their republics. Subsequently, in the Soviet Union language policy has had the further development, has accepted the hypertrophied forms. Universal "russification"[4] in the USSR has led to cultural degradation of national languages in language groups, as a result of such policy languages of many "ethnic minority"[4] are now forgotten by representatives of ethnic minority. Such native speakers began to be named "Russian-speaking"[4].

Cultural pluralism in the tideway of radically-etatistic policy means support of languages of all language groups. Cultural pluralism can be liberal, thus authorities show tolerance in relation to language minority. In Kazakhstan special attention, in our opinion, is given to the decision of language problems, as positive examples of a policy of the state in the mentioned sphere it is possible to define the Concept of the language policy, the Law on languages in the Republic of Kazakhstan. Language policy of Kazakhstan will get increasing political and ideological importance. The strategically important direction of work of State bodies of Kazakhstan is to realize Governmental policy about preserving and strengthening international and interfaith accord.

Formation of language policy of the Republic of Kazakhstan is carried out by a number of documents concerning its standard-legal regulation accepted by Parliament RK, President RK and Government RK. It is the Law "On languages in the Republic of Kazakhstan" [5] (from July, 15th, 1997), the Decree of the President of the Republic of Kazakhstan "About the Government programme of functioning and development of languages for 2001-2010"[6] (it is confirmed by the Decree of President RK N.A. Nazarbayev from February, 7th, 2001 № 550), "the Concept of a language policy of the Republic of Kazakhstan"[7] (is accepted by the order of the President of the Republic of Kazakhstan from November, 4th, 1996 N 3186). Language "self-determination" has found real reflection in Law RK accepted in September 1989 on languages. In it the state language status for the first time has been legislatively given to the Kazakh language, Russian has received the status of language of international dialogue. A new direction of a language policy occurred in Kazakhstan in 1997 with the acceptance of the new Law" On languages in the Republic of Kazakhstan "in which it has been recognized that" in the state organizations and local governments Russian can be used at the same level with Kazakh"[5] (Law item 5 "On languages in the Republic of Kazakhstan"). In the Law on Languages in the Republic of Kazakhstan, Kazakh language is defined as a state language of Kazakhstan. At the same time, use of the Russian language, is accepted as official.

In February, 1989 at the plenum of the Central Committee of Communist Party of the Republic two state languages had been accepted: Kazakh and Russian. This decision was made taking into consideration the demographic situation in republic, and also the danger of split of a society in case of the instalment of one language, the language of the "titular" nation[9]. But after the First Congress of Councils of People's Deputies of the USSR in June, 1989 G.V. Kolbin was withdrawn. N.A. Nazarbayev became the First Secretary of a Communist Party of Kazakhstan. Under his instructions orientation of the law on language varied, and in August a bill was put for "national"[8] discussion where the state language had been declared one – the Kazakh language. A month of discussions showed that the Kazakh people were deeply divided. From all letters which have come to the Supreme body of the Kazakh Soviet Socialist Republic and the central newspaper of republic "Kazakhstan truth"[9], 98 per cent written by Kazakhs, were for one state language, and 98 per cent of references from Russian authors and the mixed collectives – were for another one. As the majority of the population of republic was Russian-speaking – the opinion on necessity of two state languages prevailed. Deputies of local councils have also expressed their desire for two state languages. These opinions were brought to Alma-Ata by the deputies of the Supreme Council who called for the statement of the Law on languages. A short session was held under the powerful pressure of the Kazakh nationalists. It was promised that the January, 1990 Law on Languages in the USSR where the state language was Russian language would be changed. Then it would be passed to each of Union republics. Kazakh, was made the state language leaving Russian with the uncertain position of "language of international dialogue".[10] Only 25 from 500 deputies have voted against division of a society into "the state" part – Kazakhs, and "not state", Russian-speaking. Russian became a symbol of "the colonial past".[11]

East Kazakhstan was not reconciled to the cancellation of the state status of Russian and here ideas of Russian autonomy began to sound. But the language policy of the Kazakhstan authorities, considering lessons of Transdniestria region, was more flexible, than in Moldova or in Baltic. Introduction of the law on languages was postponed for half a year. And further performance of programmes on expansion of functioning of the Kazakh language was spent cautiously enough, with numerous promises of returning to Russian its official status. New edition of the Law on languages of 1997 has removed the status of is used on a level with state in the state organizations and local governments. "The Concept of a language policy of Republic Kazakhstan" was elaborated by the government of Kazakhstan on November 7, 1996. In "the Concept of a language policy of the Republic of Kazakhstan" following purposes of the state language policy, such as "working out of strategy of a state policy in the field of preservation and functional development of languages in a transition period, definition of problems of the state on creation of conditions for development of the Kazakh language as state"[8] have been defined. Carrying out of actions for formation of machinery of government of functioning of languages in Republic Kazakhstan territory became the Primary goal of the Concept of a language policy. Its main goals are the maintenance of the international world and the consent in the polyethnic state. Under the Concept language has been defined as "a basis of national culture", and the language policy in Kazakhstan should be directed towards "harmonious sustainable development of separate ethnoses"[7].

Concept issues: definition according to the Constitution of Republic Kazakhstan of priority directions of language development, development of the mechanism of functioning. Necessity of change of an existing language situation for Kazakhstan became the primary goal of a new language policy: "Despite measures taken it is not possible to realize the official status of the Kazakh language. The principal cause is that this status is only declared till now, but is not supported adequately by the mechanism that would provide its universal study and use. Office-work and office dialogue in a state language has secondary character"[7].Thus, it is further indicated in the Concept, that the state language carries out the most important functions in the state and public life. However, despite measures, it is not possible to fully realize the official status of the Kazakh language. Therefore in the concept of a language policy the main principles that define a state language place in political practice are allocated.

First of all, it is language on which all acts of the given state are accepted. Answers to references of citizens also are given in a state language. The state policy concerning creation of conditions for development of languages should be focused on updating of real-life hierarchy of languages in a direction of priority development of a state language. State problems in relation to state and to other languages will be various. The state undertakes to create all conditions for realization of the status of a state language. In the Concept of a language policy of the Republic of Kazakhstan civil servants, workers of sphere of a science, culture of formation, public health services and service of the population require possession of the state language. Real maintenance of conditions for development of languages of the people of Kazakhstan means creation of possibilities for mastering the native language by all interested persons. It can be effective with active participation in it of the national-cultural centers, capable of expressing cultural-language interests of ethnoses.

The state language is used in the working of all state structures, organizations, in armed forces. It is the basic language of legal proceedings in the country. Besides, in a state language all transactions physical and the legal bodies, made in writing are necessarily stated. In public funds of the mass information state language application is obligatory. For the purpose of creation of the corresponding language environment the volume of transfers on the state channels in other languages should not exceed volume of transfers in the state language. Reception on public service is carried out in the state language. State structures of all levels and their heads bear the basic responsibility for realization of the status of the Kazakh language. Mastering of the state language is a component of Kazakh patriotism.

The change of language policy in Kazakhstan has been connected with the impossibility of the exclusive domination of the Kazakh language as state language in the polyethnic state. And the new policy of formation of a machinery of government for the development of a parity of application of all languages in the republic became the most comprehensible. In the newly created language space problems of the further functional development of the linguistic base of the Kazakh language as the state language began to occupy a priority place. In a language policy of Kazakhstan serious reforms are expected. Alongside with Kazakh, the state language of Kazakhstan, and Russian, the language of interethnic dialogue and intercourse, the English language should become one of official languages not only at the international level, but also inside the country. English is the language of successful integration to the global economy. Three languages will get almost equal status. This is a necessity caused, politically and economically. To strengthen the positions in the world community helps the knowledge of world or international languages. Today the most widespread all over the world is the English language. It got the international value in 19th century and since then has gathered increasing force. Its role in present conditions of breath-taking scientific and technical universal progress, a powerful stream of information, a general computerization and internationalization has become global.

In the modern world the English and Russian languages have a special position not only because of their extension in the area, but also because of variety and scale of functions carried out by them. It is pleasant, that when developing a language policy our government takes into account real opportunities of development of a society and a language. Though the development of a language does not depend on the will of people, nevertheless, the society can influence the development of the language, accelerating or slowing down separate tendencies and directions in its development. This year has been declared as the Year of a State Language. The desire to learn Kazakh is expressed by almost all levels of population, the government allocates decent sums for language development: in the budget it is 2 billions 700 million tenge.

It is now possible to discuss the results of these policies. Language, develops. And the state considers the problem of language as a problem of development and formation. That is, today it is one of the most essential problems of the country. The development of separate ethnoses also assumes implementation of the language policy and promoting preservation of language on the basis of national culture – ethnos language. It creates conditions for interaction and mutual aid of cultures and their further development in the Republic. New sociopolitical realities of Kazakhstan as sovereign state demands that the language policy should meet the requirements of the polyethnic population of the country. Coordination of efforts of state structures, public associations, religious and other organizations is necessary for carrying out of a uniform language policy in the country. In Kazakhstan there are more than 170 nationalities. The Assembly of Peoples of Kazakhstan has significantly contributed to the process of turning multinational into strategic advantage thus avoiding interethnic tensions and xenophobia. This deliberative body was established in 1995 on the initiative of the President of Kazakhstan. For the last twelve years the Assembly of Peoples of Kazakhstan has been the public institution for interethnic harmonization.

The achievements of all nationalities of our country their openness to dialogue, innovations, interconnection and prosperity have become the common national wealth. The state gives great attention to development of languages of the people living in Kazakhstan. In particular, in the Republic there now operates more than 170 Sunday schools for the study of native language, traditions and customs. Today one of the directions of enlarging functions of the state language is imposition of business correspondence in the governmental language. For realization of this question various electronic dictionaries and computer programmes are being held. At the present time the work on issuing computer programmes by the system programme software of the Kazakh language, coding state standard information, supporting the Kazakh language in the web "Internet", multilanguage electronical dictionaries, checking texts in the Kazakh language is being held. Republican seminar-counsel about problems of using industrial terms and imposition of business correspondence in the state language, presentation of electronical cultural-historical fond of ancient-Turk writing monuments is being held as well.

The courses for learning the state language for members of the republican and regional national-cultural centers who are constantly being taught at Sunday schools are organized. 4 republican and 15 regional national newspapers publish, 6 national theaters (the Kazakh, Russian, German, Uigur, Korean and Uzbek) work in Kazakhstan. Today 7483 printed and electronic media outlets are registered in Kazakhstan. 2493 among them are in action. From the registered mass media outlets 2479 is printed media outlets within which 320 media outlets or 13 per cent publish in the national language. The state support of the national newspapers has found a reflection in purchasing services for leading state informational policy through magazines and newspapers. Activities of the national newspapers is being contributed to the interpretation of the issues of international accord, internal political stability, increase of the population's interest to the state activities of the Assembly of the People of the Republic of Kazakhstan, support of the state programme "Cultural heritage". Among printed mass media outlets publishing in other languages, 4 of them are accomplishing the state order according to the results of the competition. Among them: Uigur republican newspaper "Uigur Avazi", German newspaper "Deutsche Allgemeine Zeitung", Korean national newspapers "Kore ilbo", Ukrainian newspapers "Ukrainian news". Due to modernization of the television of the TV channel "Kazakhstan" on the basis of the national programmes a united programme "We are the citizens of Kazakhstan" was created with the duration of 20 minutes with the daily broadcasting in different languages.

The main difficulty in the future of language policy in Kazakhstan is "creating the optimal linguistic space state", requiring "clear definitions of a functional parity of languages in which the state language should take a worthy place".[7] The matter is that the parity of actual use of Russian and Kazakh languages does not correspond to the given requirement. In practice the actual indicator of use of Russian corresponds to level of application of a state language, and the Kazakh language an official language. "Definitions of a functional parity of languages at which the state language should take a worthy place".[7] For change of the developed language situation carrying out of a large-scale state policy on actual investment of the Kazakh language with the status state is required. Official state structures had been during the last years developed the Government programme of functioning and development of languages for 2001-2010. It's paramount value has been "expansion and strengthening of socially-communicative functions of a state language; preservation thus common cultural functions of Russian and the further development of languages of ethnic groups".[6]

In the given direction of development of a language policy a number of issues have been taken into account. Among them "maintenance of functioning of a state language as government language; perfection of standard-legal base; maintenance of functioning of a state language as the basic language of office-work in all state structures, the organizations and local governments with definition of the schedule of transition of office-work on a state language (with instructions of concrete terms and actions); with a view of realization of articles 7 and 93 Constitution of the Republic of Kazakhstan the organization in scales of Republic of uniform system of courses on free training of citizens to a state language at the expense of means republican and local budgets, the organizations, and also other sources of financing; maintenance of functioning of Russian as the language officially used in the state organizations and local governments; scientifically-lingware Russian functioning; rendering of the state support in training of representatives ethnic общностей (diasporas) to native languages".[6] In the listed directions of a language policy priority place is given to the further development of standard-legal maintenance, expansion, deepening of terminological and linguistic base of the Kazakh language.

At the present stage application of the Kazakh language there are a number of tasks, among which – a low level of development of modern Kazakh language as a whole, development problems "its possibilities in display new socio-cultural realities by interaction with other world languages, and use in it of internal potential of language".[6] In our opinion, the Kazakh language de jure has official status of state language, but de facto it has not found such status. Till now Kazakh is not used in higher education. At the same time, recently in such spheres as the legislation, the government, science, culture, mass media the Kazakh language has begun to be applied more actively. For example, in the government sphere the requirement of knowledge of a state language becomes one of the requirements of employment for the future civil servants. Nevertheless, there are certain complexities. According to sociological research "the Language situation in the Republic of Kazakhstan", held in April-May, 2008 (2000 respondents interrogated in all regions of the country) by Institute of comparative social researches "ICSR-Kazakhstan" together with Department on development of languages of the Republic of Kazakhstan by the basic language of dialogue among civil servants is Russian (75, 4% of answers of respondents), 21, 9 per cent interrogated use the Kazakh language only[12]. The exception is in the "titular territories" of West Kazakhstan, Atyrausky, Kyzylordinsky, South Kazakhstan, Mangistausky. Here the Kazakh language in government sphere is the basic language of dialogue, accordingly indicators fluctuate for respondents southern (51, 0%) and western (25, 5%) republic areas (according to the same interrogation)[12].

The degree of readiness of the higher official bodies to the actual creation of the new language environment, which is based on use of a state language of the Republic of Kazakhstan as a unique state official language, requires examination. The other part of the given problem consists in definition of readiness of the population of Kazakhstan to adapt to the newly created language environment. From outside the state structures creation of the language environment will demand new reforms in an education sphere, cultures, sciences, and the government. The principal cause is that this status has only recently been declared but is not supported adequately by the mechanism, which would provide its universal study and use. Office-work and office dialogue in a state language has secondary character. Problems of the Kazakh language are not settled by necessity of acquisition by it of the real state status. The problem is of its development and enrichment. Considered process of reforming will result not only in necessity of financial investments from the state treasury in the specified spheres, but also huge activity on a bookmark of the base to normal functioning, development, state language distribution, or formation of the state structures carrying out of actions on institutionalization a state language.

Under institutionalization process of adjustment, carrying out of the actions directed towards organizational registration of the political phenomenon is understood. Institutionalization of language means creation of the machinery of government, capable of providing functional regulation, constant development, expansion and enrichment of linguistic base of all languages in Republic Kazakhstan territory. At the initial stage institutionalization a state language in Kazakhstan following official bodies were created:

- The state terminological commission at the Government of Kazakhstan (it is confirmed by the governmental order of the Republic of Kazakhstan from April, 21, 1998 N 367)[13];
- The republican state enterprise "the Republican center of the advanced training to a state language" (the Governmental order of the Republic of Kazakhstan from October, 9, 1999 N 1545)[14].

Each of considered official bodies has functional features. "The state terminological commission at the Government of the Republic of Kazakhstan (further – the Commission) is an advisory body, developing offers in the field of terminological lexicon of the Kazakh language on all branches of economy, a science, technique, culture"[15] (the Governmental order of Republic Kazakhstan from April, 21, 1998). The basic purpose of activity of the Republican centre of the advanced training to a state language is "the organization of creation of all necessary organizational and material conditions, and also methodical and scientific maintenance of intensive training of civil servants to the Kazakh language"[14] (the Governmental order of Republic Kazakhstan from October, 9, 1999).

The basic document, and also the newly created machinery of government, called to regulate process institutionalization in the Republic of Kazakhstan state language it is possible to define the Government programme of functioning and development of languages for 2001-2010. The programme is calculated for 10 years, includes stage-by-stage realization of a new language policy in Kazakhstan, the minimum settlement requirement for budgetary funds on Programme realization makes 3087,7 million tenge. The Programme budget is included by annual deductions from republican and local budgets. The programme is realized in several directions: standard legal maintenance, state language development in sphere of the government, the legislation, legal proceedings, office-work, in Armed forces and law enforcement bodies, the international activity, language development in an education sphere and training to languages, scientific maintenance of language development, language development in sphere of culture and mass media, and also sphere of public health services and population service.

On the basis of settlement indicators for 2009, the minimum requirement for the budgetary funds necessary for realization of the Programme is 274,5 million tenge. The greatest financial assignments are necessary for carrying out actions in sphere of culture, mass media and population service (32%); for Programme realization in an education sphere and training to languages (26%); for functioning of languages in sphere of the government and office-work, the legislation and legal proceedings (25%). The least expenses are necessary in is standard-legal maintenance (5%) and scientifically – the lingware (12%)[15]. Carrying out of a language policy should promote preservation of the civil consent in Kazakhstan, to friendship strengthening between representatives of various ethnoses and the people living in Kazakhstan, to stability and world preservation. Therefore institutionalization of a state language should have stage-by-stage, gradual character. The idea of giving to the Kazakh language the status of a state language is capable of becoming a basis of Kazakh patriotism and the national idea necessary for rallying Kazakhstani people as the uniform nation. Kazakhstan patriotism should adopt the best lines based on uniform citizenship, freedom, independence for all citizens.

Now in Kazakhstan there exists a wide variety of languages. Languages of the people of ethnic groups of the country are inadequate. Despite measures it is not possible to fully realize the state status of the Kazakh language. What is important is an expansion of its possibilities by interaction with other world languages, and use in it of the internal potential of language. It is impossible to be reconciled with the tendency to provide "cleanliness" of language, having refused the loans, which have taken root in it and international terms. There is today the necessity of objective, scientific studying of language processes for different regions and creation of optimum language environment. It is thus necessary to consider the actual distribution of language and its real possibilities in terms of expansion of public functions.

NOTES AND REFERENCES

1. I.G. Zholamanova, "Kazakh language: problems not carriers", in *Science of Kazakhstan* (Almata, 1994), no. 7, April, p. 19.
2. A.B. Dokuchayeva, *About language: From emotions to common sense*, (Alma-Ata: Thought Press, 1993), no. 9, p. 25.
3. A.A Tsutsiyeva, *Problem of language-problem of the people* (Shymkent: Panorama 1994), p. 23.
4. B.H. Khassanov, *Mechanism of introduction and realizations of the Law on languages in the Kazakh Soviet Socialist Republic and a way of introduction of language to various spheres of a life* (Almaty, 2004), p. 52–53.
5. The Law "On languages in the Republic of Kazakhstan", from July, 15th, 1997 no. 151, Pages of Parliament of the Republic of Kazakhstan, 1997, no. 13–14, art. 202.
6. "About the Government programme of functioning and development of languages for 2001–2010", the Decree of the President of the Republic of Kazakhstan from February, 7th, 2001 no. 550.
7. "Concept of a language policy of the Republic of Kazakhstan", the Order of the President of Kazakhstan from November, 4th, 1996 no. 3186.

8. G.M. Mendikulova, *Kazakh Diaspora: history and the present* (Almaty, 2008), p. 65.
9. *The Kazakhstan truth*, no. 91, 1994.
10. *Ibid.*
11. *Business world of Kazakhstan*, no. 1, 1997.
12. *New Generation*, no. 20, 2008.
13. The Governmental Order of the Republic of Kazakhstan from April, 21st, 1998 no. 367.
14. The Governmental Order of the Republic of Kazakhstan from October, 9th, 1999.
15. "About the Plan of measures for 2009-2010 on realization of the Government programme of functioning and development of languages for 2001-2010", the Governmental Order of the Republic of Kazakhstan from December, 24, 2008, no. 1246.

13

Language Socialisation and the Benefits of Bilingualism Today

S.A. Meiramova

According to Bambi Schieffelin and Elinor Ochs[1] the notion of language socialization (further LS) is premised on two assumptions about the nature of language, culture, and socialization. First, the process of acquiring language is deeply affected by the process of becoming a competent member of a society, and second, the process of becoming a competent member of society is realized to a large extent through language, by acquiring knowledge of its functions, social distribution, and interpretations in and across socially defined situations. This is largely achieved through participation in exchanges of language in particular social situations. From this perspective, language is seen as a source for the students to acquire the ways and world views of their culture.

Heath[2] once argued: "all language learning is culture learning". Promoting the same viewpoint, Agar[3] coined the terms *languaculture* to emphasize that language and culture are so tightly interwoven that neither should be studied in isolation from the other, otherwise both concepts will be distorted. Such a belief in the inextricably entwined nexus between language and culture forms the basic premise of language socialization theory. In LS, language and culture co-constitute and co-contextualize each other. We have mentioned above that according to Schieffelin and Ochs' point of view language learning is regarded as the simultaneous acquisition of both linguistic knowledge and sociocultural knowledge. In the languacultural acquisition process, language is "the primary symbolic medium through which cultural knowledge is communicated and instantiated, negotiated and contested, reproduced and transformed" by Garret and Baquedano-Lopez[4]; while culturally based practices, settings and interactions are the primary vehicles which powerfully and necessarily affect both language teaching and learning processes according to Poole[5].

Language socialization theory cautions against regarding language only as an intra-psychological cognitive representation and development. Instead, LS argues that knowledge, including knowledge of language, is not only transmitted but also used, acquired and created through concrete interactive practices in specific historical, political, and sociocultural contexts because there is no context-free learning. Knowledge should be properly viewed as inter-psychologically distributed and constructed. Thus, a complete and valid interpretation of many significant aspects of language acquisition and performance in immediate contexts (micro) cannot be fulfilled apart from the relevant sociocultural and political contexts (macro), which mediate "which linguistic forms are available or taught and how they are represented".

Moreover, language socialization can occur either implicitly or explicitly. Implicit language socialization occurs when learners come to perceive sociocultural meaning transmitted to them indirectly through conversation. On the other hand, explicit language socialization takes place when experts (teachers) overtly convey sociocultural meanings to learners. Practice shows that implicit socialization may be more effective than explicit socialization, since learners or students cannot readily contradict the way in which language is used in society, whereas they can challenge an explicit mention of some norm of society. Since language is a means by which we communicate, and it is more than just a means of communication because it conveys a wealth of information other than the primary content of the message. By this we mean that language serves multiple functions. We use it to exchange, share, report, and define experiences. It structures meaning, determines how we see things, is the carrier of our culture, and affects our worldviews. Schieffelin and Ochs[6] consider socialization to be an interactional display (covert or overt) to a novice of expected ways of thinking, feeling, and acting ... through their participation in social interactions, students come to internalize and gain performance competence in these sociocultural defined contexts". We take for granted the noncontroversial and obvious sense of this statement, that the development of intelligence and knowledge is facilitated (to an extent) by students' communication with others.

It should be noted here that the paradigm of intercultural communication has developed two broad domains of interests: (a) the comparative examination of communicative similarities and differences across cultures, and (b) the communicative adaptations made by individuals when they move between cultures. The former, the pre-eminent line of inquiry in cross-cultural communication, attempts to link variations in communication behaviour to cultural contexts. It provides the conceptual tools needed to understand culture, communication, and the ways in which culture influences communications. The latter is relatively a new area, which seeks to understand changes in individual communication behaviour that are related to the process of acculturation and communicative interactions. This approach, young as it is, has provided a substantial body of literature dealing with stages, patterns and outcomes of adjustment. Understanding the two domains in the literature of intercultural communication helps to comprehend daily events in the multicultural world from the depth of socio-cultural, especially cross-cultural level. Generally speaking, the first approach provides theoretical support to understand where cross-cultural misunderstanding occurs, and how such misunderstanding can be minimized in future intercultural encounters. The second approach provides cross-cultural adaptation models, which can serve as informative indexes to understand cross-cultural newcomers' dynamic status of intercultural transformation.

Intercultural transformation presupposes that an individual has to pass through the stage of marginality, which is actually the peripheral position of a person in society. Marginality is usually referred to in connection with aliens and immigrants. By Issayev's[7] definition a 'transitional personality' is seen as an isolated, lonely, and unprotected person, no longer rooted in his/her native soil and searching in vain for an opportunity to take root in a new medium, non-equivalent to the old one. It is worth noting that for marginal persons it is extremely difficult to enter a new society because they find themselves on the crossroads between two different cultures. On the one hand, the old roots still hold them tightly; the old world image is clear and familiar, their actions are guided by customary values. On the other hand, the old notions are no longer unquestionable; the images and ideas of the new life turn out to be attractive. As J. Nehru once wrote: "I have become a queer mixture of the East and the West, out of place everywhere, at home nowhere. Perhaps my thoughts and approach are more akin to what is called

Western than Eastern, but India clings to me, as she does to all her children. I cannot get rid of either that past inheritance or my recent acquisitions. They are both part of me, and they create in me a feeling of spiritual loneliness. I am a stranger and alien in the West. But in my own country also, sometimes, I have an exile's feeling".

In general, intercultural transformation may be regarded as a painful process of transition of quantitative changes into qualitative ones. A long stay in a different culture does not automatically provide for this transition: immigrants can live in their communities for years and never have enough exposure to the new culture in order to form an intercultural personality. There are numerous jokes in this concern, true life situations when an American enters a Russian store in Brighton Beach and the owner shouts to her husband: "Senya, come here, we have a foreign customer, he cannot speak Russian!"

According to M. Magomed-Eminov, the process of personality transformation is the transition of unconscious mental content into a conscious state, the realization of a previously subconscious incentive, the actualization of an unused potential, and the awakening of profound energy and resources. The process of active transformation in intercultural communication requires a high intensity of intercultural contacts on both a quantitative and a qualitative level. The degree of the individual's assimilation depends on the initial attitude – willingness or unwillingness to become part of the new culture, degree of participation in the life of community, as well as the state policy in relation to immigrants (including language policy).

Because of intercultural transformation, an individual undergoes profound changes. It is worth here to pay our attention to M. Bennet's[8] *developmental model*, which envisages the transition from the ethnocentric stages (isolation and denial of cultural differences) to the ethnorelative stages, i.e. (a) acceptance of another culture through the formation of respect for behavioural and value differences, (b) adaptation (empathy and pluralism), and (c) integration. Furthermore, Bennet points out the interconnection and interrelation of the cognitive, affective, and behavioural dimensions, but warns that "the separateness of these dimensions is not always clear for each stage, nor should it be, since development is multidimensional".

Many works focus on the problem of losing one's cultural identity (*cultural loss*) in connection with the American multiculturalism and the problem of immigration (e.g. in: Lambert 1972: 180; Armitage, Hoffman 1989: 204). The transformation can, on the one hand, be expressed in the gradual loss of unique cultural traits and blind imitation of an alien culture, or, on the other hand, in the formation of an intercultural personality with different levels of cultural, linguistic, and communicative competence: from the monocultural stage through marginality to the bicultural or multicultural stage. Actually, the survey shows that the formation of a truly bicultural personality is possible only if an individual is born in a bilingual family or enters a new culture from the very childhood. It is proved and the practice show that truly bilingual people flit easily between tongues.

I think intercultural transformation does not necessarily require full bilingualism. Significantly more important is cognitive flexibility, cultural awareness, and the knowledge of the ways to overcome them. The readiness of personality for intercultural transformation depends on the stability of the nervous system, educational level, personal qualities, and linguistic abilities. For some people the process of intercultural transformation lasts for months, for others it takes years, for still others it never ends. The traditional Kazakh and Russian inclination for self-criticism accelerates this process. For Americans, on the contrary, transformation proceeds slowly because of their self-righteousness and ethnocentrism.

There are many terms of American scholars to denote the highest stages of intercultural personality development: *intercultural person* (Dahl[9]), *multicultural man* (Adler), *mediating person* (Bochner[10]), etc. They also employ the concepts of *maturity* (Heath), *ethnorelativism* (as opposed to *ethnocentrism*-Bennet), *transnationalism* (Martin), *global identity* (Dahl), and *transnational feeling* (Dahl).Thus it is possible to maintain that for adequate intercultural communication it is necessary not only to master the language, but also to learn how to think and feel as a native speaker, i.e. to acquire what I.I. Khaleyeva calls the formation of a *'secondary linguistic personality'*. Success in language mastering means all the cultural baggage accompanying its use. For successful intercultural contacts it is also important that intercultural personalities should be formed not unilaterally, but in both contacting cultures, i.e., that the cultures should be constantly moving towards each other. In this way, acquisition of literacy and reading skills will be faster in the first language, and these transfer readily to the second language. Moreover, several studies analysis show that students in well-designed bilingual education programmes acquire academic second language as well as, and often even better than, students in programmes that use the second language only.

In this connection it is worth noting that the perception of the foreign world by the learners and its representation in the learners' imagination which may vary considerably from the officially sanctioned picture. We know from experience that students quite often do not learn what they are supposed to learn, that they do not simply adopt the pre-formed and "prescribed" view of the target world presented in their textbooks, but in their minds create (or already have created) their own images and fantasies about the foreign world which are unstable and which in the process of learning the target language (and gathering more knowledge or experience of the foreign world outside the classroom) may undergo remarkable changes. Therefore, it is interesting to know what influences the view of the foreign world in the learner's mind and what leads to changes of the images of the world of the target language in the process of learning. We can thus state that there are changing and unstable concepts of the foreign world at both ends: in the presentation of socio-cultural content (teaching) and in the perception of the foreign world in the learner's mind (learning). These are what we call *interim worlds*.

Moreover, if we manage to activate such socio-cultural categories for foundation, metaphorically speaking, "building bridges" between our own world and the foreign world which enable us to venture into the foreign world in our imagination then we can expand our own experiences, realise similarities and negotiate possible differences. In addition, this may decrease a possible discrepancy and tension between the own view of the foreign world (interim world II) and the pre-conceived picture that is presented in the "official interpretation" of the foreign world (interim world I). So, we can suggest some considerations for developing one's own socio-cultural and personal identity to deal successfully with the two worlds a few qualifications:

- empathy
- role distance
- tolerance of ambiguity
- awareness and representation of identity (cf. Krappmann, 1969).

Considering them in detail we can state that:

Empathy implies venturing into the foreign world and trying to understand it "from within", i.e. try to understand "the others" in their own socio-cultural contexts and realising that what may look "strange" to one may be "normal" for them. Empathy helps us to understand the "otherness" of the people of the world of the target language in their own world.

Role distance means another change of perspectives, the "view from outside" upon our own world which helps us to realise that not all people share our view of our own world and, as a consequence, may have opinions about us which to us appear as prejudices. Role distance helps us to gain a different perspective upon ourselves.

Tolerance of ambiguity is the development of strategies of negotiating ambiguity, e.g. signalling non-comprehension and, maybe, embarrassment; inviting interpretation and help; referring to "safe clues" in a critical situation or context; tracing roots back to safe ground"; explaining one's own position; asking for and giving reasons. It is essential to understand from the beginning that in foreign language teaching process such breakdowns in comprehension and communication are quite natural and will occur again and again at all stages of foreign language learning and use. Such awareness will help the learners to sustain interest, gain calmness and overcome "dumbfoundedness" in critical situations.

Awareness and representation of identity means the socio-cultural foundations of one's own world that influence their view of the world, regulate their day-to-day life (routines, rituals, life style, etc.), shaping their mentality (value systems, traditions, attitudes, judgements) and their capability of relating this self-awareness to others in the foreign language (explaining one's own world to others). The learners' own world and socio-cultural experience, which form their own outlook in life, play an essential part in their perception and evaluation of socio-cultural phenomena of the foreign world. Therefore, their own world must not be excluded from foreign language teaching but can be used a reference point for the selection of topics and the design of tasks.

Let us define bilingualism and types of bilingualism. Bilingualism is using two languages and regular switching from one language to another depending on situation of communication. Multilingualism is using two or more languages. Ambilingualism is perfect using of both languages. Semilingualism is using languages partially. The study of bilingualism has not been exempted from the scholarly tendency to create dichotomies. Popular ones include coordinate compound bilingualism (Weinreich, 1953), early subtractive bilingualism (Lambert, 1985), simultaneous successive bilingualism (McLaughlin, 1984), additive subtractive bilingualism (Lambert, 1975), and elite folk bilingualism (Skutnabb-Kangas, 1981). While such distinctions have served a purpose in drawing attention to certain aspects of bilingualism, perhaps the most important lesson to be learned from these distinctions is that some of them refer to characteristics of individuals (the first three mentioned), and others to characteristics of social groups (the latter two). Linguists and psychologists have paid primary attention to the individual mental and cognitive properties of bilinguals; linguists and sociologists have attempted primarily to characterize social groups in terms of configuration of the languages with respect to robustness, prestige, and other sociological and institutional features.

As for the cognitive effects of bilingualism more and more scientists' research is made in order to understand the complex phenomena of it. At first blush, the bilingual would seem to be the ideal experimental subject for the modern neuropsychologists. In the bilingual, we have personified the essence of the experiment with two competing channels: one brain, two simultaneous systems, no fancy experimental technology necessary, and no problem with finding controls matched for age, gender, education or handedness. However, it turns that no two bilinguals looks to be the same on any scale. Therefore, the subject of bilingualism is to distinct negative and positive impact on the individual.

Looking at the cognitive dimension of bilingualism and literacy acquisition, there are three key skills needed for successful literacy acquisition – oral language proficiency, phonological awareness (metalinguistic awareness), and understanding of the symbolic nature of print. We should note that the cognitive developmental path to literacy is not the same for bilingual and monolingual students, and identifies two broad consequences of bilingualism in relation to literacy: first, both the ability to read and some of the components of reading that prepare students for that ability transfer across languages and systems. Therefore, students who have learned skills in one language can potentially benefit from that mastery by applying them to the other. Even though such transfer is neither automatic nor assured, it does happen, and the consequences are always salutary. Second, the differences between monolinguals and bilinguals that occur are invariably to the benefit of the bilinguals. To my mind knowing more has never been a disadvantage when compared to knowing less. As experience states, there is no evidence of a bilingual disadvantage in literacy development, and, moreover, there appear to be broader educational and cognitive advantages of bilingualism that last across the lifespan.

As for societal bilingualism, there is a range of possibilities. The United States, for example, is widely recognized as monolingual when judged in terms of its interest and success in study of foreign languages. Yet, being a nation of immigrants, it has been host to a broad representation of languages spoken throughout the world, most of which are lost within two or three generations in a process of assimilation. During this process, bilingualism plays a prominent role.

Widespread multilingualism is one form of language contact. Multilingualism was more common in the past than is usually supposed. In early times, when most people were members of small language communities, it was necessary to know two or more languages for trade or any other dealings outside one's own town or village, and this holds true today in places of high linguistic diversity such as Sub-Saharan Africa and India. Linguist Eckerd Wolff estimates that 50 per cent of the population of Africa is multilingual. In multilingual societies, not all speakers need to be multilingual; linguists classify the community according to the functional distribution of the language involved:

- *Diglossia*: if there is structural functional distribution of the language involved, the society is termed "diglossic". Typical diglossic areas are those areas in Europe where regional language is used in informal, usually oral, contexts, while the state language is used in more formal situations. Frisia (with Frisian and German/Dutch) and Lusatia (with Sorbia and German) are well-known examples. Some writers limit diglossia to situations where the languages are closely related, and could be considered dialects of each other.
- *Ambilingualism*: a region is called ambilingual if this functional distribution is not observed. In a typical ambilingual area it is nearly impossible to say which language is used when in a given setting. True ambilingualism is rare. Ambilingual tendencies can be found in Luxembourg, or in border regions with many cross-border contacts.

> *Bipart-lingualism*: If more than one language can be heard in a small area, but if the much majority of speakers are monolinguals, who have little contact with speakers from neighbouring ethnic groups, an area is called "bipart-lingual". The typical example is Balkans.

As for multilingualism between different language speakers here, we can say that whenever two people meet, negotiations take place. If they want to express solidarity and sympathy, they tend to seek common features in their behaviour. If speakers wish to express distance towards or even dislike of the person they are speaking to, the reverse is true, and differences are sought. This mechanism also extends to language, as has been described by Howard Giles' Accommodation Theory. Various, but not nearly all, multilingual tends to use code switching, the term that describes the process of "swapping" between languages. In many cases, code switching is motivated by the wish to express loyalty to more than one cultural group, as holds for many immigrant communities in the New World. Code switching may also function as strategy where proficiency is lacking. Such strategies are common if the vocabulary of one of the languages is not elaborated for certain fields, or if the speakers have not developed proficiency in certain lexical domains, as in case immigrant languages. This code switching appears in many forms. If a speaker has a positive attitude towards both languages and towards code switching, many switches can be found, even within the same sentence. If, however, the speaker is reluctant to use code-switching, as in case of a lack of proficiency, he might knowingly or unknowingly try to camouflage his attempt by converting elements of one language into elements of other language. This results in speakers using words like *courier noir* in French, instead word for blackmail, *chantage.* Bilingual interaction can even take place without the speakers switching. In certain areas, it is not uncommon for speakers to consistently use a different language. This phenomenon is found amongst others, in Scandinavia. Speakers of Swedish and Norwegian can easily communicate with each other speaking their respective language. It is usually called non-convergent discourse, a term introduced by the Dutch linguist Reitze Jonkman. Reasons for native language literacy include sociopolitical as well as socio-cultural identity arguments. While these two camps may occupy much of the debate which language students will learn to read, a great emphasis on the linguistic aspects of the argument are necessary. In spite of the political turmoil precipitated by this debate, researches continue to espouse a linguistic basis for this logic. This rationale is based upon the work of John Cummins.

It is necessary to mention that there are three types of models. Firstly, *sequential model*: in this model, learners receive literacy instruction in native language until they acquire "threshold" literacy proficiency. The transition into the community language class is then made. Secondly, *bilingual model*: in this model, language and the community language simultaneously taught. The advantage is literacy in two languages as the outcome. However, teacher training must be high in both languages and in techniques in teaching a second language. Thirdly, *coordinate model*: this model posits equal time be sent separately in both instruction of the native language and the community language. The native language class however focuses on basic literacy while the community language class focuses on listening or speaking skills. Being a bilingual does not necessarily mean that you can speak, for example, English and French.

Nowadays, in the era of globalization at least six important aspects are interlaced. There are political, economical, educational, informative lingual and cultural. The political side is expressed with a growth of national and transcontinental political organization. The economical aspect is shown by the global stream of trade, investment and transcontinental location of goods in different countries. The educational aspect is expressed with the creation of unified and global educational expansions. The informational aspect is shown in the growth of rapid using and delivery of information, owing to inculcation of a new informational technology. The lingual side is expressed with the appearance of the English language, which plays the main role in communication between people in the definite geographical area.

We can confirm that the idea of globalization and peoples ambitions to learn and cooperate on the definite language courses some negative influence on the many side of the life as for instance the sphere of upbringing and education of rising generation. Experiences of some Kazakhstani scientists show the following negative points in the process of globalization. They conclude that globalization has caused irreparable damage to any nationality and its feature. Therewith, the informational lingual inequality is formed as the English language with the opportunities creates new problems.

In addition, giving some example, scientists explain that those countries and people who are capable of international lingual environment purposes and effectively, get advantages before those who do not capable to do the same. The next remark includes that globalization displaced the whole series of the language which have played a definite role recently with purpose of exchange information between people, so, the English language penetration into the countries of the Middle East displaced the Arabic language and in the Latin America-Spanish language. Therefore, we see the great influence of English on society today. On the other hand, the idea of globalization and the people's ambitions to the cooperative solution of corresponding problems and difficulties are coursed more positive features. Most people will agree that there are questions, which we have to solve with efforts of many countries or all humankind. Further, English is learned by people of different age, because they realize that to know English is very important and in many countries, it already became equal to official language. Thus, the globalization of the English language equalizes people who speak it and it provide for opportunity of free intercultural, and international social interaction.

In conclusion, I would like to say that great attention should be paid to a new approach to the developmental study of language and culture described by Bambi Schieffelin and Elinor Ochs which focuses upon the interconnections between students' acquisition of language and their acquisition of culture. To their mind students' acquisition of language and their acquisition of culture are processes that have usually been studied separately due to the fact that students are both socialized through language and socialized to use language in culturally specific ways. The contributors emphasize the salient language behaviours of students and others, and show how these are embedded in broader patterns of social behaviour and cultural knowledge. They reveal that various features of discourse – phonological, morpho-syntactic, lexical, pragmatic, and conversational – carry sociocultural information, and that language use is a major resource for conveying and displaying socio-cultural knowledge. As students acquire language, so they are also acquiring a world view. This innovative approach to the study of language acquisition and socialization will appeal widely to linguists, psychologists, specialists in communication studies, and educationists.

NOTES AND REFERENCES

1. B.B. Schieffelin, E. Ochs. *Language socialization across cultures,* Melbourne, Australia: Cambridge University Press, 1986.
2. S.B. Heath, *Ways with words: Language, life and work in communities and classrooms,* Cambridge: Cambridge University Press, 1983.
3. M. Agar, *Language shock: Understanding the culture of conversation,* New York: W. Morrow, 1994.
4. P.B. Garret and P. Baquedano-Lopez, *Language socialization: Reproduction and continuity, transformation and change.* Annual Review of Anthropology 31, (2002): 339–362.
5. D. Poole, *Language socialization on the second language classroom,* Lang. Learning,(1992): 593–616.
6. B.B. Schieffelin, E. Ochs. *Language socialization across cultures,* Melbourne, Australia: Cambridge University Press, 1986.
7. M.K. Issayev, *The peculiarities of English,* Bulletin of KUIRWL, № 1. Almaty, 2000, pp. 5–6.
8. M.J. Bennet, "Towards Ethnorelativism: A Developmental Model of Intercultural Sensitivity." *Education for the Intercultural Experience,* ed. by R.M. Paige. USA: Intercultural Press, 1993. 21–71.
9 S. Dahl, *Communications and Culture Transformation. Cultural Diversity, Globalization and Cultural Convergence.* Project presented to the European University, Barcelona. June 1998.
10. Bochner S., "Problems in Culture Learning." in *Overseas Students in Australia,* ed. by S. Bochner, P. Wicks. Sydney: New South Wales University Press, 1972. 33-41.

SELECT BIBLIOGRAPHY

B.B. Schieffelin, E.Ochs. *Language socialization across cultures,* Cambridge: Cambridge UP, 1996.

S.B. Heath, *Ways with words: Language, life and work in communities and classrooms,* Cambridge: Cambridge University Press, 1983.

M. Agar, *Language shock: Understanding the culture of conversation,* New York: W. Morrow, 1994.

P.B. Garret and P. Baquedano-Lopez, *Language socialization: Reproduction and continuity, transformation and change.* Annual Review of Anthropology 31, (2002): 339–362.

D. Poole, *Language socialization on the second language classroom,* Lang. Learning, (1992): 593–616.

B.B. Schieffelin, E. Ochs. *Language socialization across cultures,* Melbourne, Australia: Cambridge University Press, 1986.

M.K. Issayev, *The peculiarities of English,* Bulletin of KUIRWL, №1. Almaty, 2000, pp. 5–6.

M.J. Bennet, "Towards Ethnorelativism: A Developmental Model of Intercultural Sensitivity." *Education for the Intercultural Experience*, ed. by R.M. Paige. USA: Intercultural Press, 1993. 21–71.

E.B. Berry, Epstein M.N. *Transcultural Experiments: Russian and American Models of Creative Communication.* New York: St. Martin's Press, 1999.

S. Bochner, "Problems in Culture Learning." *Overseas Students in Australia*, ed. by S. Bochner, P. Wicks. Sydney: New South Wales University Press, 1972. 33 – 41.

D. Crystal, *The Cambridge Encyclopedia of Language*. New York; Port Chester; Melbourne; Sydney; Cambridge: Cambridge University Press, 1987.

S. Dahl, *Communications and Culture Transformation. Cultural Diversity, Globalization and Cultural Convergence*. Project presented to the European University, Barcelona. June 1998.

L. Damen, *Culture Learning: The Fifth Dimension in the Language Classroom*. USA.: Addison-Wesley Publishing Company, 1987.

R.M. Paige (ed.). *Education for the Intercultural Experience*, USA: Intercultural Press, 1993.

W.B. Gudykunst W.B., Ting-Toomey S., Chua, E. *Culture and Interpersonal Communication*. Newbury Park, CA: Sage, 1988.

14

Tajikistan in a Changing Eurasia: Reorientation?

Muzaffar Olimov and Saodat Olimova

Along with global developments in Eurasia in recent decades, there have been changes in the position, identity, and orientation of previously isolated countries lying in the "heart" of Eurasia, such as Tajikistan.

Previously Tajikistan was oriented toward the north. Now it turns to the south and the east. Integration into the international transportation network, construction of new roads, bridges and tunnels, the growth of international trade, transport and migration sharply increased the level of interaction with the world and especially with neighbors in Eurasia – China, Afghanistan, Iran, India, Pakistan. For example, from 2002 to 2006 the volume of trade between Tajikistan and China grew nearly 25 times. The intensification of trade contact as well as political, cultural and human contact with the outside world has expanded the understanding of other countries, people, culture and the identity of the Tajik people. In turn, these changes affect the position of Tajikistan in dealing with regional and international players.

The revitalization of the foreign policy of Tajikistan in the past few years has led us to ponder about the following questions:

Whether there have been changes in foreign policy orientations of Tajikistan in recent years? What are the factors (socio-cultural, economic, political and military) that determine the foreign policy orientation of Tajikistan?

The sources of this work are the following:

- Secondary sources: press materials in Tajikistan, historical essays, scientific literature.

We used also results of public opinion polls, which were conducted by the Center "Sharq" in October 2006 (1800 respondents were asked) and November 2007 (2000 respondents were asked). These polls used the methods of the national representative sample and of personal interviews. The percentage of errors is 2.8 per cent.

- Secondary data: Surveys of public opinion. October 2006 (1800 respondents were asked), November 2007 (2000 respondents were asked). Research Center SHARQ, Survey on base of national representative sample, percentage of error is 2.5 per cent.

Currently in Tajikistan, there are some criteria that influence the character of foreign policy:

1. Construction of the nation-state hypothesis.
2. The formation of bilateral relationship with the former metropolis – Russia.
3. Participation of Tajikistan in the development of relations within the Central Asian region in the formation of regional identity in general.
4. Tajikistan's identity as an integral part of the Islamic world.
5. Tajikistan's identity as an integral part of the Iranian world.
6. Participation of Tajikistan in the new "big game" in Central Asia (CA)
7. Possibility of conversion of Tajikistan into a buffer zone of China.

All these criteria project the political, economic, cultural and social life of Tajikistan. To determine the possible directions of development in Tajikistan, we have to understand how the world sees the people of Tajikistan; what collective perceptions of friends and foes are; who are the partners and patrons of Tajikistan, who played role in the elite formation in Tajikistan.

Tajik-Russian Relations

To determine the prospects for Tajik-Russian relations we have to identify the main aspects of the Russian presence in Tajikistan since 1991, developments in the Tajik-Russian relations, and the phases of these developments.

The image of Russia as the "elder brother" in the community of the republics of the USSR was replaced by the image of metropolis. Then it transformed into the image of military and political suzerain, and, finally, into the image of a much more powerful partner.

The main content of the relations between the Republic of Tajikistan (RT) and the Russian Federation (RF) in this period is the so-called "divorce", which means the division of responsibilities and property of the erstwhile USSR. Russia also participated in the civil conflict in Tajikistan and in its settlement as a "third party". All these events took place when Tajik economy and social sphere were collapsing.

It is possible to define several types of relationships between Russia and Tajikistan in the first five years after the collapse of the USSR:

- The so-called "divorce", i.e. relationships which dominated after the collapse of the USSR and during transformation of existing relations within the USSR;
- Political-military presence of Russia in Tajikistan, including the deployment of the 201 Motorised Division and the border guards of Russia;
- The participation of Russia in the settlement of the civil conflict in Tajikistan;
- Relations between Tajikistan and Russia within the framework of CIS;
- The preservation of new informal contacts between individuals, government agencies, various organizations in both countries;
- The formation of new informal connections (migrant networks, NGOs).

By 1996 the "divorce" was almost complete. By this time a relatively stable configuration of the Tajik-Russian relations was formed. The dominant factor in this process was military and political cooperation. At the same time, for the majority of Tajik people Russia was perceived as the center. In 1996 the Movement for the restoration of the Soviet Union was very popular in Tajikistan; about one and half million people signed the petition supporting this idea. It means that at least half of adult citizen supported it. Adults retained Soviet passports, children used Soviet textbooks at schools, and Russian

TV channels in 1998 were the main source of information for 72 per cent of the population of Tajikistan[1].

1996-2003: Formation of Tajikistan's Foreign Policy

The signing of the Peace Accord on June 27 of 1997 in Moscow set the stage of nation-building in Tajikistan. After the presidential elections (1999) and parliamentary elections (2000), the country began to recover from the shock of the 1990's. The pace of economic growth from 2000 to 2003 was more than 8 per cent annually. The poverty rate from 1999 to 2003 fell from 83 per cent to 64 per cent[2].

The international situation changed as well. In the aftermath of September 11 terrorist attacks, international attention increased in Central Asia. The active participation of Tajikistan in anti-terror campaign intensified interaction with Tajikistan. Despite the fact that Russia was the only guarantor of stability and a strategic partner of Tajikistan, the country began to formulate its own foreign policy, which was independent from the Russian foreign policy.

The main content of the Tajik-Russian relations in this period are:

- High levels of military and political cooperation;
- Labour migration from Tajikistan to Russia (about 300,000-400,000 people);
- Tension between Russia and Tajikistan in 2003 resulting from Tajikistan's attempt to establish closer ties with the West. Withdrawal of Russian troops from Tajikistan's border.

2004 to Present Time: From Unconditional Submission to Realization of National Interests

The official visit of President V.V. Putin in October 2004 opened a new phase in relations between Tajikistan and Russia. Since then, large-scale cooperation between Tajikistan and Russia increased. The main components of this cooperation are not only military and political ties or cooperation in the field of security, but also economic projects.

Nevertheless, Tajik "multi-vector foreign policy" irritated Russia. On the one hand, the visit of the Russian president Dmitry Medvedev on August 29, 2008 gave new life to Tajik-Russian relations. On the other hand, it exacerbated existing differences and contradictions. The most critical are the issues of military-technical cooperation and the question of participation of Russia in the completion of Rogun hydroelectric power plant. The situation in the sphere of construction of Rogun power plant is much more difficult, than the situation in the spheres of political and military cooperation. Despite the successful construction of Sangtuda 1 hydroelectric power plant by the Russian company RAO EES, the Tajik-Russian agreement about construction of Rogun hydroelectric power plant has not been successfully implemented.

The main content of the Tajik-Russian relations during this phase are:

– Military-Political Cooperation: Recent events have shown that Russia is beginning to play an increasingly prominent role in world affairs. This change is especially noticed with the strengthening of Russian military presence in Tajikistan. Thus, during President Medvedev's visit to the country, an agreement on the joint use of Aini military airport in Hissar was reached. The main goal of Russian squadrons at the Aini airfield will be to support operations launched from Russian military bases, including its base in Tajikistan. In addition, the military and technical upgradation of the Russian military base in Tajikistan (former 201 Rifles Division) will result in the Tajik National army receiving the old armaments of the Russian military base, estimated at $1 billion. The allocation of these weapons to Tajikistan is expected to significantly strengthen its armed forces[3].
– Cooperation in the field of security;
– Economic projects:
  1. The construction of Sangtuda 1 hydroelectric power station (670 MW) is the largest joint venture with the share of Russian capital of 75 per cent.
  2. Labour migration from Tajikistan to Russia – 500,000 people.
  3. Remittances from Russia to Tajikistan – more than $ 1.5 billion a year.

Tajik-Chinese Relations

The evolution of relationship between Tajikistan and China is very significant. In the Soviet period there were almost no relations between the Tajik SSR and China. During the succeeding years, China's relations with Tajikistan were limited to the framework of resolution of border disputes with Tajikistan. This period began since Tajikistan's independence and lasted until 1997, when the civil war formally came to an end.

From 1997 to 2002, relations have developed steadily and slowly. The relationship between China and Tajikistan took place only within the Shanghai Five and then within the Shanghai Cooperation Organization (SCO).

The situation has changed since the events of September 11 2001, when China became actively interested in the countries of Central Asia. Since that time, the active development of the Tajik-Chinese relationships has begun. China has strengthened its economic presence in Tajikistan, and became the top five leading trade partner of Tajikistan. From 2002 to 2006, the volume of trade between the two countries has grown almost 25 times. In 2006 it reached 323 million US dollars.

In January 2007 the People's Republic of China and the Republic of Tajikistan signed the Treaty on Good-Neighborliness, Friendship and Cooperation. The main element of the treaty was the principle of combined development based on principles of mutual respect for each other's choices, mutual favour and complementarity and mutual assistance. The combined development also included the fight against international terrorism, separatism extremism, and illegal drug trafficking.

The main components of Tajik-Chinese relations are:

Borders

The 430-kilometer Tajik-Chinese border is the outcome of division of the territory of the Pamirs between the Russian Empire and Tsin China. In 2001, after a long period of expertise and coordination Tajikistan agreed to transfer to China the disputed territories. The transferred territory included more than 1,000 square km. In June 2006, the border demarcation work began that was to continue till the end of 2008.

One of the most important outcomes of resolution of border problem for the two countries is the emergence of direct transport corridor Tashkurgan-Khorog via Kulma pass (4,363 m) at Sarykol Ridge. It provides *direct* access to Tajikistan from Xinjiang and access to Pakistan and to the Indian Ocean. The first result was the rapid development of border trade between Xinjiang and the Gorno-Badakhshan Autonomous Region (GBAO).

Economic Relations

Tajik-Chinese relations began to develop rapidly after the signing of the Treaty on Good-neighborliness, Friendship and Cooperation on 15 January, 2007. With the help of China large infrastructure projects within the framework of the SCO were carried out. In 2006, within the framework of the SCO Tajikistan obtained from China's a preferential loan of 608 million dollars. It was mainly used for the construction of high voltage lines LEP-500 "South-North" and LEP-220 "Lolazor-Khatlon" in the Khatlon region, and also for the construction of a tunnel under Shar-Shar pass on the road between Dushanbe-Kulyab[4]. The Export-Import Bank of China loaned to Tajikistan funds within the framework of SCO, to finance a project to build the highway from Tajikistan to Uzbekistan.

In the area of hydropower development Tajikistan is the main partner of China among all Central Asian states. There are currently plans to build several hydro and thermal power plants with participation of China.

There were some factors which affected the growth of interest of private Chinese businesses in Tajikistan. Some of these factors were the increasing activity of the Chinese capital owners in the developing of Tajik market, and opening the office of the State Development Bank of China in Dushanbe. More than 50 joint projects are being undertaken in Tajikistan. There are over 40 enterprises with Chinese participation. The number of these enterprises is growing every day[5]. The number of Chinese citizens in Tajikistan is growing because of development of trade with China. (See the following table):

Migration

	2006 to 2007	*2008*
Chinese migrants in Tajikistan	More than 3000 people	More than 34 000 people
Tajik migrants in China	4 200 people	More than 8000 people
Tajik students in China	About 100 people	200 people

Sources: Ministry of Internal Affairs of Tajikistan, Ministry of Foreign Affairs of Tajikistan

Relationships between Tajikistan and EU

The European Union is a new partner in Tajikistan's foreign relations. Relations with the European countries have been developing since 1991, when Tajikistan became an independent country. However, the interest of EU in Central Asian countries was low, because European countries was had internal problems to deal with such as, for instance, the Balkan crisis. In 1998, after military actions broke out in the south of Kyrgyzstan, the Europeans finally realized that Central Asia and Europe had similar problems. In March 1999 the European Parliament adopted a resolution "On the EU strategy for the development of relations with the independent states of Central Asia". The main concern in Europe at that time was the strategic scenario and security situation of the Central Asian region. Tajikistan began to cooperate with the EU later than other countries in the region. The development of relations with the EU was slow, because Tajikistan was in the state of military conflict for a long period of time. For the same reason the first European institutions operating in Tajikistan were OSCE and other humanitarian assistance organizations. After September 11, Tajikistan was the focus of attention from the European Union because of security concerns, which affected not only USA but also Europe. Therefore, in 2001 the EU structures in Tajikistan started to take more active part. But a real breakthrough in the relations between Tajikistan and the EU took place in 2007, when the EU adopted a new strategy for Central Asia. Tajikistan enthusiastically adopted the document, hoping to diversify its foreign policy and foreign economic relations, the growth of foreign investment, technical and humanitarian assistance.[6]

The interaction with the EU has been very productive in the framework of financial cooperation, as stipulated in the EU Strategy for 2007-2013. This strategy specifies three main priorities: effective governance and economic reform, poverty reduction and regional cooperation. Tajikistan is also cooperating with the EU in projects related to combating terrorism, extremism, organized crime, drug trafficking and proliferation of WMD and environmental issues. Intensive work is being conducted in the field of border management. On 17-18 September 2008, the first Security Forum "The European Union – Central Asia" took place. The forum focused on the following topics: political and military threat, drug trafficking and border management, energy security and environment. All these issues are linked with the new concept of cooperative security. One of the first activities planned to take place after the forum was the government-supported conference "Border management and combating illicit drug trafficking in Central Asia", which was held in Dushanbe in 21-22 October 2008. Participants at the conference included representatives of governments of the Central Asian republics and the EU, the European Commission, OSCE, OONODS, UNDP, France, Germany and Finland. The goal of the conference was to define measures aimed at helping the countries of Central Asia to strengthen their institutional commitments in regional cooperation and to establish mechanisms for coordination.[7]

Implementation of the EU strategy for Central Asia has already produced tangible results. Particularly intensive political dialogue on bilateral and regional levels between the EU and Tajikistan took place.

On November 24, the European Commission's delegation arrived in Dushanbe. As a part of this visit there was a meeting of the Joint Committee of European Union and Tajikistan, where issues of development of cooperation between Tajikistan and the EU were covered. The discussed issues included the implementation of the EU strategy in Tajikistan. The priority areas of cooperation between European Commission and Tajikistan are social protection, health, private sector development, public financial management and poverty reduction. At the meeting of the Joint EU-Tajikistan Commission, issues such as border management, human rights and democracy, and development of small and medium-sized businesses were discussed.

Tajikistan would receive 66 million Euros in technical assistance projects and grants from the funds allocated by the European Union (EU) between 2007 and 2010 and implement the new EU strategy for Central Asia.

On December 4, the European Commission (EC) and the Government of Tajikistan signed the second financial arrangement in the amount of 14 million euros to support the Tajik government reforms in social protection. This arrangement complements the first financial agreement of the amount of 9 million euros, which was signed by the parties in January 2008. This programme is expected to contribute to the effectiveness of state budget expenditures in social sector through improved financial management and accountability. It will also help to establish modern and sustainable system of social protection and a reliable system of statistical standards in the social field.

The main features of cooperation between Tajikistan and the EU are:

Military Cooperation

- French military air force base in Dushanbe is used for support of military operations in Afghanistan.
- Participation of Tajikistan in NATO programme "Partnership for Peace"

Cooperation in the Field of Security: The Strategic Areas of Cooperation are:

- political and military threats
- drug trafficking and border management
- energy security
- environmental issues
- the problem of Afghanistan
- the problem of Iran.

Economic Cooperation

- The EU is the biggest trade partner of Tajikistan
- The reconstruction of the Dushanbe airport – funding and technical assistance of France

Public Opinion on the Changes in Foreign Policy Orientations of Tajikistan[8]

The public in Tajikistan has the most positive attitude toward Russia and Iran (see table below)

		China	*Russia*	*Iran*	*France*
1.	Very friendly	33.6	79.5	69.6	16.3
2.	More likely to be positive	48.2	18.0	26.4	63.2
3.	More likely to be negative	16.1	1.9	3.1	12.9
4.	Very negative	2.1	0.3	0.2	0.9
5.	No idea	–	0.3	0.7	6.7
	Total	100.0	100.0	100.0	100.0

Public opinion polls in Tajikistan show the controversial attitude toward China and European countries. Tajik public believes that the degree of Chinese impact is low. Only 8 per cent believe that currently

China has the greatest influence on RT. 89 per cent believe that Russia provides the greatest influence on RT, and 9 per cent believe that Iran provides the greatest influence on Tajikistan. But when we asked about countries that would have the greatest impact on the RT in the 10 years, the results were different. 50.8 per cent believe that Russia will still have the biggest influence, 22 per cent believe that China will have the biggest influence, and 16.7 per cent believe that Iran will have the biggest influence. Thus, we can conclude that the public believes a greater role of China and Iran and the declining influence of Russia.

When we assess military images of China and Russia we witness different result. Tajik people still do not trust China. Only 6 per cent of respondents believe that China is the closest ally of Tajikistan, while 59 per cent indicate that the closest ally of Tajikistan is Russia. 11 per cent believe that Iran is the closest ally[9]. At the same time, public opinion of Tajikistan believes that China does not represent a threat to Tajikistan's security and stability in Central Asia. Only 3 per cent have a fear of China, while 13 per cent have a fear of Russia. In general, we can assume that the military image of China has a neutral shade. In popular consciousness, China is viewed neither as an ally nor as an enemy. It seems that the Tajik society is not aware of the growing presence of Chinese in the country yet and that the Tajik society has not formed an attitude towards the new reality. The Tajik society is accumulating the new information now.

Referring to the image of China, reflected in public opinion polls, we should not forget that there is an enormous difference between mass consciousness and the conscience of political, economic, military and intellectual elite. On the one hand this difference is caused by various foreign policy orientations of different elite groups. On the other hand it is caused by the different levels of interaction among different social groups within China, including elite groups. The Tajik ruling elite has the most positive attitude to China. This elite is even ready to replace Russia with China. The common attitude of China and the elite of Tajikistan towards pan-Turkism also plays a very important role. The fear of the Uighur separatism helps the foster negative attitude toward pan-Turkism in China. Tajikistan is the only Iranian-speaking country in the region, and therefore, the political elites Of Tajikistan are afraid of Turkish ethno-political community. Thus, Tajikistan identifies itself with China against the Turkish national movements.

There is also negativism toward China in Tajikistan. The intelligentsia from northern Tajikistan, and which is oriented toward Iran, has the most negative attitude toward China. These people cannot forget China's claim to the Ferghana Valley and the lessons of defeat of Kashgar ruler Yaqub-Beg (1865-1877)[10]. Another group which has negative attitude toward China and increasing Chinese influence in Tajikistan is the group of Islamists from different areas of Tajikistan. It can be assumed that their position will become a major obstacle for advancing China's interests in Tajikistan.

Conclusions

The Georgian conflict, the global financial and economic crisis, the war in Gaza and the energy competition between Russia and Ukraine have changed the balance of power in the world, especially in Eurasia. The positions of China and Russia have become stronger in the modern world. The deepening tensions between Russia on one side and the EU and the US on the other side increasingly affect Tajikistan. One the one hand Tajikistan tries to establish partnership relations with Russia. On the other hand Tajikistan develops relations with the EU. Relations with China have become even more active.

Each country dominates its own sector in Tajikistan and almost does not compete with other countries. Russia remains the main military and political partner of Tajikistan, the host country for Tajik migrants, and economic partner in energy projects. China is a powerful neighbor and the fast-growing economic partner of Tajikistan. The European Union has provided great assistance to the state in the post-Civil War period especially in the economic reform sector and poverty reduction programmes. The US and the NATO, based in Afghanistan, provide security to Tajikistan.

It is the most difficult to predict changes in Tajikistan-Russia and Tajikistan-China relations, since both Russia and China are playing an ever increasing role in the world.

On the one hand the military-political and economic presence of Russia in Tajikistan have been strengthened. At the same time, relations with China are developing very rapidly. Does the intensification of relations with China reflect the rivalry between Russia and China, or their co-operation? The realities of life in Tajikistan are forced to think about this issue, because China often replaces Russia as initiator of projects. It is clear that in case of implementation of agreements, which are already signed, China will become one of the major foreign economic and possibly political partners of Tajikistan replacing Russia. At the same time, the EU is actively contributing to the modernization of Tajikistan by fostering young Tajik elite. In any case, the question whether Tajikistan is going to change its priorities and in which direction is still not certain.

NOTES AND REFERENCES

1. S. Olimova, M.Olimov. *Tadjikistan na poroge peremen*. Moscow: "NIOPIK" 1999, p. 40.
2. World Bank. Renew estimation of poverty in Tajikistan. Main report. (2004). p. 2
3. Alexey Matveev, *Voennaia mosh-za schet Moskvi* ("Military power – at the expense of Moscow"). in *Voenno-promishlenniy kurer*, 2007, No 42 (208). http://www.centrasia.ru/newsA.php4?st=1193799180
4. Akram Abdukahharov. "*Investicii iz Podnebesnoj, Tajikistan*". http://www.stan.tv/news/6935/?print=1 on 11/09/2008
5. Tajikistan Ambassador in China: Tajik-China trade-economic relations are increasing. – http://russian.china.org.cn
6. See: European Community Regional Strategy Paper for Assistance to Central Asia for the period 2007–2013. http://ec.europa.eu/external_relations/ceeca/c_asia/index.htm.
7. See: Conference "*Upravlenie granitsami i borba s ne zakonnoi torgovlei narkotikami v Tsentralnoi Azii*". Newspaper "Asia-Plus" 2008, October 23.
8. The attitude of the citizens of Tajikistan toward China, Russia, Iran, France. The materials of survey. May 2008. Research Center SHARQ, Dushanbe. Survey based on national representative sample, 1000 respondents, percent of error – 2.5 per cent.
9. The materials of the survey of November 2007 by SHARQ, Dushanbe. Survey on the basis of national representative sample-2000 respondents, percent of error – 2.5 per cent.
10. À.D.Vasilev, 'Interrelations Ottoman Empire and State of Yaqub-Bek', *Vostok\ Oriens*, 2007, No. 2, p. 15–22; E.V.Bunakov, 'On issue political and economic contacts of the Central Asian properties of Russian Tsar with Eastern Turkistan under government Yaqub-Bek (1865–1877)', *Bulletin Uzbek SSR of the Academy of Sciences*, 1945, No. 5.

15

Post-Soviet Migration of Mongolian-Kazakhs to Kazakhstan

Sharad K. Soni

Today the most accepted definition of migration, which includes the movement of refugees, displaced persons, uprooted people as well as economic migrants, is the crossing of the boundary of a political or administrative unit for a certain minimum period of time. However, classical theories, while elaborating on migration, lay more emphasis on "a rational decision made by an individual to move from a less advantageous situation, to a more advantageous one after weighing risks and benefits".[1] Recent trends, especially in the Eurasian region, show that migration generally results from the decision making of collectives, such as families or households "based on little more than an ill-defined sense that life will offer more elsewhere, with very little information about the reality the migrant will face".[2] The migration of ethnic Kazakhs of Mongolia (or the Mongolian-Kazakhs as they are generally known) to Kazakhstan, the country of their origin, in the early 1990s i.e., in the post-Soviet period has been a classic example of such decision-making where decision was largely based on the perception that life will offer more in terms of economic opportunity in the newly independent Central Asian Republic of Kazakhstan with little or absolutely no information about the reality they would face there. The growing feeling of nationalism among both the Buddhist Mongols and Muslim Kazakhs in Mongolia soon after the break up of the former Soviet Union too contributed much to set in motion the migration process of Mongolian-Kazakhs to Kazakhstan.

It is in this context that this paper not only highlights the background of the origin of Kazakhs in Mongolia but also seeks to analyse the causes and consequences of their migration to Kazakhstan and re-migration back to Mongolia, as well as their status in both Kazakhstan and Mongolia, besides examining whether issues related to Mongolian-Kazakhs still remain to be a key factor in facilitating both the ongoing and future development of ties between Mongolia and Kazakhstan. Some of the facts highlighted in the following paragraphs are based on author's personal experiences acquired during a field study trip undertaken in 2006 to Western Mongolia, especially the Bayan-Ölgii *aimag* (province).

Historical Background of the Mongolian-Kazakhs

Kazakh diaspora in Mongolia is said to have originated from frequent waves of migration due to various reasons the ethnic Kazakhs were confronted with in different period of time. Historically, Kazakhs are of Turkic descent,[3] belonging to the nomadic tribes who in the sixth century AD migrated eastwards from their original homeland in Mongolia.[4] They developed a distinct ethnic identity in the early sixteenth century when one of the Kazakh princes, Kasym Khan succeeded in uniting the main tribal groupings.[5] It was during the seventeenth-nineteenth centuries that Russian imperial expansion led to the displacement of a large number of Kazakhs. While moving eastwards and beyond some Kazakh tribes pushed into the high pastures of Tien Shan (Heavenly) mountains and into Xinjiang region of northwest China where they continued to live a pastoral nomadic life-style until the Manchus put pressure on their precious grazing lands. In fact, for the Qing rulers Xinjiang was the first line of defence in the northwest China against foreign intrusion and "the concern for defence was directed both at the Uighurs, Kazakhs, and other tribes of Central Asia and at the Russians who continued their relentless drive to the east".[6]

However, Xinjiang could not remain isolated from the troubles besetting China due to the Taipei rebellion and other uprisings of the 1850s. China required additional revenue to tackle such uprisings and, therefore, the Qing court raised the taxes on the non-Chinese peoples of the Xinjiang region, which resulted in bringing the predominantly Muslim population to the verge of rebellion.[7] This might have been one of the reasons that led to the Kazakh migration elsewhere in order to escape the trouble in the region. Besides, heavy snowfall during the close of the nineteenth century also caused the exodus of a few Kazakh families from Xinjiang to the east of the Altai mountains.[8] Whatever might have been the reasons it is believed that beginning in the 1860s the Kazakhs from Xinjiang started migrating across the high Altai Mountain passes to enter into the Mongolian territory and settled down in the western part particularly in the areas today known as Bayan-Ölgii *aimag* (province).[9] Later, some small groups of Kazakhs from the Russian Altai and eastern Kazakhstan fleeing the October revolution of 1917 and the civil war of 1920s in Russia too entered into western Mongolia. It is to be noted that in 1921 when Bogdo Gegen's theocracy was proclaimed in Mongolia,[10] a few Kazakhs who were living there expressed their allegiance to him.[11] Further in the 1930s and 1940s there had been few other major Kazakh movements from Xinjiang into Mongolia because of the frequent riots in Xinjiang.[12]

Evidently, most of the Kazakhs came to Mongolia in the pre-1940 period and also well before the communists came to power in China, since already in 1940 the Mongolian government created a separate administrative unit for the Kazakh minority i.e., the *aimag* of Bayan-Ölgii. An ever-growing influx of Kazakh refugees into Mongolia began to be witnessed as a result of turbulence in Xinjiang due to the civil war, rebellions and revolts between 1930s and 1940s,[13] and it was Bayan-Ölgii *aimag* that remained a true destination for taking refuge to the fleeing Kazakhs. In July 1942 itself an estimated 359 people from 69 Kazakh families were reported to have fled to Mongolia where "they sought asylum because they were victims of pillage and robbery, and they applied for Mongolian citizenship".[14] This was followed by another wave of Kazakh migration on a large scale and "within several months more than 2,200 people from 330 families fled to Mongolia and settled down in different areas".[15] However, at the same time China was alleged of attacking Kazakhs fleeing from Xinjiang in to Mongolian territory which was protested in 1944 by the former Soviet Union but the Chinese denied the charges.[16] Over the years by establishing themselves in Mongolia, the Kazakhs not only considered the country as their home but their extended family also seasonally grazed livestock there which contributed greatly to the benefit of the whole nation.

Apart from Kazakhs there are also a few other ethnic minorities who live in Mongolia. Demographically, Mongolia's total population in 2008 has been recorded as 29,96,081 (about 3 million)[17], a slow but steady growth since the last census was conducted in 2000, which itself had recorded the figure as 23,73,493 (about 2.4 million). This figure is the quadruple of what was the total population at the beginning of the twentieth century, i.e., half a million. The major ethnic group in the country is Khalkha Mongols who make up a total number of 19,34,674 (a little over 1.9 million) or 81.5 per cent of the entire population. Among the remaining ethnic groups, Kazakhs have the largest share with a total number of 1,02,983 or 4.3 per cent of the entire population followed by Durved, Bayad (Bait), Buriad (Buryat), Dariganga, Dzakhchin, and Uriankhai (Tuvan) each representing between 1.1 and 2.8 per cent of the total population.[18] Table 1 presents the comparative figures for total population of Mongolia by main ethnic groups as recorded by 1989 and 2000 censuses.

Table 1: Population of Mongolia by Ethnic Group

	1989 Census		*2000 Census*	
Population	*Number ('000)*	*%age*	*Number ('000)*	*%age*
Ethnic Group				
Khalkha	1610.4	78.8	1934.7	81.5
Kazakh	120.5	5.9	103.0	4.3
Durved	55.2	2.7	66.7	2.8
Bayad (Bait)	39.2	1.9	50.8	2.1
Buriad (Buryat)	35.4	1.7	40.6	1.7
Dariganga	29.0	1.4	31.9	1.3
Dzakhchin	23.0	1.1	29.8	1.3
Uriankhai (Tuvan)	21.3	1.0	25.2	1.1
Other ethnic groups	53.1	2.6	82.6	3.5
Total by ethnic groups	**1987.1**	**97.1**	**2365.3**	**99.6**
Total Mongolian Citizens (both ethnic and other groups)	1987.3	97.2	2365.4	99.7
Foreign Citizens	**56.7**	**2.8**	**8.1**	**0.3**
Total Population ('000)	**2044.0**	**100.00**	**2373.5**	**100.00**

Source: 2000 Population and Housing Census of Mongolia: The Main Results, National Statistical Office of Mongolia, Ulaanbaatar.

Main Areas of Kazakh Concentration in Mongolia

The ethnic Kazakhs in Mongolia are today concentrated mostly in the country's western region that includes five provinces (*aimags*) – Bayan-Ölgii, Khovd, Uvs, Zavkhan and Gobi-Altai. In sharp contrast to the rest of the country, Western Mongolian population is comprised mainly of the Western Mongolian groups of Oirats and Turkic speaking minorities such as Kazakhs. Under the Manchu-Chinese rule, Mongolia (then known as Outer Mongolia) was divided into four *aimags* of the Khalkha Mongols and the special district of Kobdo (also known as Sain Jayagato Khan *aimag*) in the far northwest, each divided into several banner (*khoshuu*). While the *khoshuu* of the four Khalkha *aimags* were hereditary territories of the Mongolian nobility, the special district of Kobdo, was inhabited mostly by the specific ethnic or tribal groups belonging to the old Western Mongol confederation.[19] Following the establishment of the People's Republic in Mongolia in 1924, the *khoshuu* were abandoned and the *aimags* gradually split up into *sums* (districts) and these in turn into *bag* (the smallest Mongol administrative unit). In 1931 the special district of Kobdo was divided into two *aimags* – the Khovd and the Uvs. Further in 1938 when the question of the national minorities in Khovd *aimag* came under discussion of the Mongolian government, it was eventually decided to establish "a completely new democratic administration" for the Kazakh dominated area.[20] Following this decision, in 1940, out of the western parts of Khovd and Uvs *aimags* the Bayan-Ölgii *aimag* was formed as a separate administrative unit for the Kazakh national minority".[21]

Having a population of 99,112 and covering an area of 45,800 sq. kms. the Bayan-Ölgii *aimag* comprises 2.9 per cent of the whole Mongolian territory with 13 territorial administrative units.[22] Bayan-Ölgii *aimag*, alone accounts for more than 78.4 per cent of the Kazakh population, thus, apart from being the most numerous, the Kazakhs are the only minority in Mongolia forming the majority of one *aimag*. Moreover, 88.7 per cent of the total population of Bayan-Ölgii city is composed of Kazakhs. Besides, Kazakhs also comprise over 10 per cent of the population in neighbouring Khovd, living primarily in the *aimag* centre, Khovd *sum* (district) where they are a dominant majority, and in Buyant *sum* where they comprise about one-third of the population, and as a smaller minority in other *sums*. In this area, the Kazakhs are said to have started coming in the 1930s, partly from Xinjiang and partly from Bayan-Ölgii.[23] While the majority of Kazakhs continue to live in the traditional *aimags* to the extreme west, more recent migration eastward to the urban areas has resulted in significant growth in their numbers, especially in Mongolia's capital Ulaanbaatar. At the time of the 2000 census, 6.3 per cent of country's total Kazakh population lived in Ulaanbaatar alone with significant and growing settlement in Darkhan-Uul, Tuv, Selenge, Orkhon, Khentii and Uvs *aimags*.[24] In Ulaanbaatar, whereas the number of Kazakhs increased from 3,200 in 1969 to 5,600 in 1979, it further grew in 1989 to reach the figure of 9,000 thus becoming the second largest ethnic group in the Mongolian capital.[25]

The Kazakhs also live in the industrial cities of Choibalson, Darkhan and Erdenet as well as in the coal mining area of Nalaikh District, in *Khoroo*-4 (sub-district) which is 90 per cent Kazakh dominated area located near Ulaanbaatar. Most of them are employed in factories besides being in different occupations and working as state-employees in the *aimag* centres. They are said to have left Bayan-Ölgii in the 1960s and 1970s in search of employment due to overpopulation in this western *aimag*. A disproportionate number of Kazakhs are also traced among the relatively highly paid workers in the coal mines of north-central Mongolia. These Kazakhs may have come to this area either due to "limited opportunities in the narrow valleys of Bayan-Ölgii *aimag* or government efforts to favour a potentially restive minority, or both".[26] Though a sizeable number of Mongolian-Kazakhs in the post-Soviet period migrated to Kazakhstan, they still constitute the most numerous ethnic minority group in Mongolia. In fact, a higher birth rate among Kazakhs than any other ethnic groups has been the single most factor for increased percentage of their population until 1989 when a decline began to be witnessed. Whereas the Kazakh population registered an increase from 4.3 per cent in 1956 to 5.9 per cent in 1989, in 2000 it reduced to 4.3 per cent i.e., coming back again to the 1956 level (when the census was conducted for the first time by an established organisation).

As recorded by the 2000 Population and Housing Census of Mongolia, the total number of Kazakhs in the country stands at 1,02,983, of which 51,869 are males and 51,114 are females.[27] This figure has further been divided into urban and rural areas. The Kazakhs living in urban areas account for 36,294 including 18,202 males and 18,092 females, while in rural areas they number 66,689 inclusive of 33,667 males and 33,022 females.[28] The statistics reveal that although difference between number of Kazakh males and females is very less, there is much difference between Kazakhs living in urban and rural areas. The higher Kazakh concentration in rural areas points to pastoralism as still being the most prevalent occupation among the Kazakhs, though side by side agriculture is also being practiced. These pastoral Kazakhs are said to be "typical" of most herders in the western

Mongol region. The *yadilbay* variety of livestock is the prevalent Kazakh breed, which alone accounts for more than 30 per cent of the total livestock.[29] Table 2 shows the total number and percentage of Kazakh population in Mongolia during the census years 1956, 1963,1969,1979,1989 and 2000. The difference in ethnic Kazakh population after 1989 occurred primarily due to their migration from Mongolia to Kazakhstan in the early 1990s. There has been a decline of almost 17,500 in the number of ethnic Kazakhs in 2000 while compared to 1989 census figure, though the overall Mongolia's resident population increased.[30] Significantly, there has been a corresponding increase in the proportion claiming Khalkha ethnicity, from about 79 per cent in 1989 to about 82 per cent in 2000 (Table 1).

Table 2: Population of Mongolian-Kazakhs by Census Year

Year	Total Number	Percentage of Total Population
1956	36,700	4.3
1963	47,700	4.7
1969	62,800	5.2
1979	84,300	5.3
1989	1,20,500	5.9
2000	1,03,000	4.3

Sources: X. Nyambuu, *Mongolin ugsaatni züy. udirtgal* [Ethnography of Mongolia and the Mongols: An introduction], Ulaanbaatar, 1992, p. 24 for the figures of 1956 and 1963; *National Economy of the MPR For 65 Years*, Ulaanbaatar, 1986, p. 90 for the figures of 1969 and 1979; *2000 Population and Housing Census of Mongolia* for the figures of 1989 and 2000.

Table 3: Mongolian-Kazakh Population by Age Group (2000)

Age group	Percentage of Kazakh citizens	Percentage of total Mongolian citizens
0-14	42.5	35.8
15-24	20.6	21.1
25-34	15.5	17.0
35-44	10.1	12.6
45-54	04.6	05.9
55+	06.7	07.6
Total	100	100

Source: 2000 Population and Housing Census of Mongolia: The Main Results, National Statistical Office of Mongolia, Ulaanbaatar.

The percentage increase in the Khalkha majority seems to be largely due to the decline in the number of both the Kazakhs as well as the foreign citizens in the period of democratization in Mongolia. In the age structure, it is noticeable that unlike other ethnic groups the Kazakh population is much younger. Table 3 shows that 42.5 per cent of the Kazakh population falls under 15 years of age as against 35.8 per cent of the overall Mongolian citizens in the same age group. The higher fertility rate among Kazakh ethnic group appears to be one of the reasons for the predominance of age group ranging from zero to fourteen years old. However, in the age group 15 to 24, the Kazakh population is 21 per cent which is more or less same as the figure of all Mongolian citizens. Similarly in the age group 25 to 34, Kazakhs form 15.5 per cent as against 17 per cent figure for all Mongolian citizens; in the age group 35 to 44, Kazakhs – 10.1 per cent and all Mongolian citizens – 12.6 per cent; in the age group 45 to 54, Kazakhs – 4.6 per cent and all Mongolian citizens – 5.9 per cent; and in the age group over 55, Kazakhs – 6.7 per cent and all Mongolian citizens – 7.6 per cent.

Mongolian-Kazakh Migration to Kazakhstan

Generally, there are two aspects which influence people to migrate from one place to another – the "push" and "pull" factors. Push factors are those that force people to move due to civil wars or wars in general in the country where they stay, as well as political or religious oppression, climate changes, lack of jobs or simply poverty. On the other hand, pull factors are those which encourage people to move to the target country and that include peace and safety, better job, better education, social security or simply better standard of living as well as political and religious freedom. Evidently, the "pull" factors rather than "push" factors, particularly better economic opportunity in target country basically influenced Mongolian-Kazakhs to move from Mongolia to Kazakhstan.

It all began in the early 1990s, when a sizeable number of Mongolian-Kazakhs decided to move to the newly independent Central Asian Republic of Kazakhstan. Their decision came in the wake of Soviet-style reforms and restructuring through *Iltod* and *Orchilan baigalalt* in Mongolia and the ensuing economic crisis the country had witnessed in the same period. In this stride they were encouraged by Kazakhstan government's call for return of diasporic Kazakhs to their country of origin or what they call as their "historic homeland" as described by Article 1 of the Law on Immigration adopted in June 1992. Significantly, Kazakhs from Mongolia were among the first to heed the call for repatriation, and only within the first 2 years of independence, i.e., in 1991 and 1992 a total of 60,000 Mongolian-Kazakhs migrated to Kazakhstan. According to a study conducted in 1992 by the Kazakhstan Institute of Strategic Studies, these Mongolian-Kazakhs expressed their willingness to make their future residence in Eastern Kazakhstan (possibly due to the fact that this area is nearer to Mongolian-Kazakh dominated Bayan-Ölgii *aimag*), Karaganda, Almaty, Kokchetav and Kustanay regions. It is to be noted that with the collapse of the former Soviet Union and the attainment of political independence in 1991, Kazakhstan emerged as a "multiethnic" state in which ethnic Kazakhs constituted less than 50 per cent of the population. In this regard, recently a research undertaken in the Almaty region during December 2006-September 2007 on the role of ethnic Kazakh returnees from Mongolia in shaping conceptions and practices of citizenship and national belonging in post-Soviet Kazakhstan published its report on the IREX (Individual Advanced Research Opportunities Programme) website.[31] The report quotes some scholars as pointing out that the "political elites in Kazakhstan have walked somewhat of a tightrope: trying not to alienate ethnic Russians and other non-Kazakh 'Kazakhstanis', while at the same time fostering expectations of Kazakhstan as the homeland of Kazakhs", and that the "return migrants are caught in the resulting social and political ambivalences".

Though the motivation for Kazakhstan's policy of repatriation was a perceived need to increase the number of ethnic Kazakhs, it has never been officially acknowledged. However, there is no denying the fact that such motivation remained "closely linked to the process of nation building, preservation of national identity and culture as well as internal stability".[32] This became clear at the First World *Kurultai* (assembly) of Kazakh people held in 1992 when the authorities urged ethnic Kazakhs wherever they were to return to Kazakhstan and promised them a number of benefits with simplification in citizenship procedure. As a result, the first annual quota for ethnic Kazakhs willing to return to Kazakhstan was set in 1993 which provided for repatriation of 10,000 families or approximately 40,000 persons (Table 4). But in the following years it was reduced to 7000 families in 1994 and 5000 families in 1995. A sharp decline in the immigration quota was revealed in 1999 when

Table 4
Quota for Repatriation of Ethnic Kazakhs

Year	*Households*
1993	10,000
1994	7,000
1995	5,000
1996	4,000
1997	2,200
1998	3,000
1999	500
2000	500
2001	600
2002	2,655
2003	5,000
2004	10,000
2005	15,000

Source: *Status of Oralmans in Kazakhstan: Overview*, Almaty: UNDP Kazakhstan, 2006.

the Kazakh government fixed it for only 500 families and the quota remained same even in 2000. This decline in the immigration quota seems to have been influenced by unchecked migration of a large number of ethnic Kazakhs. The Kazakh ethnic immigrant is known as *oralman* meaning "one who came back" or "returnee" from across Asia and Europe into their homeland. Until 1996, an estimated 154,941 ethnic Kazakhs returned to Kazakhstan that included 84,828 persons from other CIS countries, 62,126 from Mongolia, 640 from China and 418 from Afghanistan.[33] However, official data for the period from the end of 1992 to the beginning of 2001 put the figure at a total of approximately 181,400 immigrant Kazakhs, of which 158,400 came under immigration quota.[34] These migrants included 106,800 from other CIS countries; 63,900 from Mongolia; 4,800 from Iran; 2,600 from Turkey; 1,100 from China; 771 from Pakistan and 83 from Saudi Arabia.[35] During the period 1991-2003, it was estimated that approximately 260,000 ethnic Kazakhs returned to Kazakhstan,[36] while in 2005 the official figure reached to 277,000.[37] But, according to a study commissioned by the UNDP in Kazakhstan, as of October 2005, the total number of *oralmans* living in Kazakhstan was 464,426 persons representing 117,698 families.[38] This figure is much higher than the official one as it also includes those ethnic Kazakh immigrants who arrived outside the quota system. The study further provides the figures of the *oralmans* coming from the major source countries during 1991-2005 as 285,409 from Uzbekistan, 71,507 from Mongolia, 41,787 from Turkmenistan, 22,117 from China and 18, 632 from Russia.[39]

It is estimated that roughly 5 million ethnic Kazakhs live outside Kazakhstan in more than 40 countries,[40] including those returned to their homeland. But what is striking to point out is that despite an allocation of each year quota for the number of Kazakhs eligible to return to Kazakhstan, the arrival figure far exceeds the quota. According to International Organisation for Migration (IOM), in 2001, more than 10,000 families of *oralmans* arrived in Kazakhstan as against permissible limit of 600 families or 3000 persons.[41] The migration quota is normally fixed on the basis of financial situation of Kazakhstan and there is also no denying of the fact that the desire to migrate is mainly connected with economic considerations as Kazakh economy is getting better year by year, especially since 2002. Having been described as the "economic power house of Central Asia", Kazakhstan registered a "double-digit growth" over the three years period before GDP was forecast to rise 8 per cent in 2003.[42] Evidently, better economic condition has once again shown signs of positive response from the Kazakh government on several concrete problems related to migration issues. On 23 October 2002, in his opening remarks at the Second World *Kurultai* of Kazakhs, President Nursultan Nazarbayev stressed on the need to increase quotas for immigration. As such in accordance with 2003 quota 5,000 families of ethnic Kazakhs were allowed to settle permanently which further increased to 10,000 families in 2004 (Table 4). Since the quota of immigration of *oralmans* is fixed annually by the President of the Republic of Kazakhstan, it was raised to 15,000 families for the period 2005-2007 by a Presidential Decree of 27 December 2004. Nazarbayev's statement provides a clear view of his government policy on resolving the problems of *oralmans* when he said:

> ...the number of those, desiring to come to historic homeplace is much higher. But everyone should understand that the state is unable to resolve all their problems. People come to Kazakhstan over quotas. And the authority branches got a task to do everything possible for the citizens to settle. Kazakhstan has overcome the hardships of transitional period. The country's economic strength has grown. But to

> make the state richer and stronger is the task [of] those residing in the republic and abroad [and they] have to resolve it together.[43]

While commending the Kazakhs living in Mongolia he said that they have preserved their traditions and "*oralmans* from that country have brought to Kazakhstan many interesting traditions".[44] Since the biggest number of ethnic Kazakhs who migrated to Kazakhstan comes from Mongolia, it is noteworthy that both Mongolia and Kazakhstan have concluded several agreements to facilitate the migration of Mongolian-Kazakhs to Kazakhstan and provide them opportunities for employment and housing.[45] Despite problems they faced simultaneously at several fronts in terms of living a professionally secured life, they started working as herdsmen in the rural areas of Kazakhstan since this was considered to be the most suitable job for Kazakhs from Mongolia. Some of the Mongolian-Kazakh migrants obtained the status of foreign workers in Kazakhstan and so retained their Mongolian citizenship as well. In 1995, an inter-state accord was signed between Mongolia and Kazakhstan by which Kazakhs were given a legal right to live in either of the two countries they had chosen.[46] Perhaps such an accord generated for the first time an opportunity to the Kazakhs living in Mongolia to settle down in a place of their choice. However, some Mongolian scholars demanded that if Mongolian-Kazakhs go to Kazakhstan, they should abandon their claims to their land in Mongolia.[47] And in fact, in the initial period of migration process thousands of Kazakhs sold off their assets in Mongolia with a view to settle in Kazakhstan.[48]

Re-migration of Mongolian-Kazakhs Back to Mongolia

Though both the Mongolian and Kazakh governments are seriously involved in negotiating the simplification of procedure for settling citizenship issues and the visa regime for Mongolian-Kazakhs, the pace of their migration process has now reduced due to the emergence of quite a new phenomenon i.e., re-migration back to Mongolia since 1994 but in a lesser number. As there are no reliable figures, it is very difficult to estimate the number of these Kazakhs who came back to Mongolia. Even though between 10,000 and 20,000 of them are estimated to have returned to Mongolia during 1994 and 1995. The experiences of Mongolian-Kazakhs living in Almaty now reveal that what was begun as "a nationalist euphoria" and "a spirit of patriotism" that spread among the Kazakh intelligentsia in Mongolia with Kazakhstan's independence has turned in to disappointments and hardships they have been experiencing in Kazakhstan for over 16 years now. They relate their experiences by describing, "we have forgotten what we came here [Kazakhstan] for in the first place".[49] As a well known scholar on the subject, Alexander Diener too points out, "for many of those diasporic Kazakhs heeding the call of migration to their historical territory, the Republic of Kazakhstan differs greatly from the homeland they imagined [This was particularly true for the Mongolian-Kazakhs]".[50] These "repatriates" often discovered their dreams of an ethnic homecoming shattered by the reality of Kazakhstan's "multicultural and largely Russified society".[51] Within Kazakhstan they found themselves politically, socially, economically and even culturally marginalized, and hence their integration into new society remained low.

Local communities in Kazakhstan, which generally demonstrated tolerance to newcomers in the nineteenth and twentieth centuries, demonstrated different attitude to the *oralmans* in general and Mongolian-Kazakhs in particular. According to a survey conducted in 2005 by the independent analytical Centre for Social Technologies (CST), the attitude of local communities towards *oralmans* has been found to be 34 per cent as good, 25 per cent as tolerable, 22.5 per cent as indifferent, and 10.1 per cent as bad.[52] In addition, legal obstacles have a significant impact on the growth of a high level of unemployment experienced by the *oralmans* because in order to be legally employed they must receive citizenship, or at least residency, which they find very difficult to get.[53] It is more so because though the Law on Population Migration adopted in 1997 (with amendments in 2001, 2002 and 2004) does provide a definition of *oralman* status, it does not define the rights and responsibilities entitled through such distinction, thus precluding the application of other laws, such as the Labour Code of Kazakhstan. Language barrier is another obstacle faced by these repatriates as those who do not speak Russian (officially recognized language and its wide use throughout the country for everyday communication) have problems in finding employment, particularly in the northern regions.[54] While *oralmans* share the same cultural roots as Kazakhs in Kazakhstan, differences in cultural practices and norms do exist: *oralmans* have conserved the traditional Kazakh culture and lifestyle, whereas Kazakhs in Kazakhstan have adapted, first to influences brought about during the Soviet period, and more recently to changes occurring through the transition to market economy.[55]

These obstacles indeed have had adverse impact on the socio-economic status of Mongolian-Kazakhs within Kazakhstan. While they continue to repatriate from Mongolia every year, most of them agree that "repatriation has lost much of its initial sense of euphoria and promise, as well as its mass character after 1993".[56] In fact, those repatriates who have returned to Mongolia since then, were carrying negative reports of their experiences in Kazakhstan, thus discouraging further repatriation among those remaining in Mongolia.[57] Nevertheless, due to the worsening economic situation in Mongolia in 1996 emigration to Kazakhstan again started mostly from the *aimag* centre of Bayan-Ölgii, though this time not on a large scale. It is evident from the fact that while 60,000 Mongolian-Kazakhs migrated to Kazakhstan in just two years during 1991 and 1992, the figure increased further but only by a margin of 3,900 until 2001 and 11,607 till 2005 to total the figure merely as 71,507 in 14 years or so since 1991. Interestingly, on 21 June 2000, President Nazarbayev issued a special decree granting Kazakh citizenship to 1882 Mongolian-Kazakhs who settled down in Kazakhstan after emigrating from Mongolia in the early 1990s.[58] However, this number is nothing but an eyewash given the fact that an estimated 30,000 immigrant Mongolian-Kazakhs are still awaiting their documents to be fully processed for Kazakh citizenship.

On the other hand, the status of ethnic Kazakhs as a minority within the State of Mongolia appears to be free from any systematic discrimination. Presently they enjoy equal rights with their Mongol peers within the country, as had been the case in the past. There has never been any instance of ethnic inspired suppression of Kazakhs by the Mongolian government. Considering their status as being the only one community having a limited cultural and political autonomy it seems that somehow they enjoy superior socio-economic and political privileges compared to other minority communities. In all Kazakh majority areas, the local administration has largely been dominated by ethnic Kazakhs. They always have some representatives in the *State Great Khural* (Mongolian Parliament), apart from occupying senior ranks in various government institutions. They are known to have well preserved their native language, culture, tradition, customs and rites. They are the only ethnic minority group in Mongolia for whom the medium of instruction in schools is their own language as can be witnessed in the whole of Bayan-Ölgii as well as in the Khovd-*sum*. It has been revealed that while maintaining their linguistic and cultural identity, the Mongolian-Kazakhs have a far greater advantage over Kazakhs of Kazakhstan. It is more so because the Mongolian-Kazakhs have their own newspaper and periodicals in Kazakh language as well as Kazakh radio and television broadcasts, theatre and music.[59]

The written forms of Kazakhstani Kazakh and Mongolian Kazakh are same largely due to the fact that most of the Kazakh language books and printed materials used by Mongolian Kazakhs are imported from Kazakhstan. However, it is significant to note that the spoken varieties of Kazakh in Mongolia and Kazakhstan have several characteristic differences, particularly the phonological differences.[60] Bilingual Kazakhs i.e. those who have expertise in both the Mongolian and Kazakh languages, join the Mongols in professional and bureaucratic life on an equal footing. Like Mongolians, the Kazakhs are also very traditional which can be seen through the architectural style of the Bayan-Ölgii city that reflects a significant Central Asian influence. Instead of having a typical Mongolian market the city has a *bazaar* where many buildings are designed and built by Kazakh architects. Not only eagle hunting and herding but also felt making and the sewing of sophisticated wall hangings are all examples of the exciting Kazakh culture that is flourishing in Western Mongolia. Kazakhs of the Altai region have traditionally hunted from horseback with trained golden eagles and, therefore, pictures of eagle-bearing Kazakhs are common in Mongolian tourist literature. Though the practice of eagle hunting has existed for over 2,000 years as a Kazakh tradition, today it is widely practiced only among Mongolian-Kazakhs.

So far as religious life of Mongolian-Kazakhs is concerned, today it is evident that religion has a growing influence in the whole Mongolian society but there is little evidence of religious activity among the Mongolian-Kazakhs, who are originally Sunni Muslims. There are still only few strong adherents to Islam among the Kazakhs and the number of people praying regularly in mosques is very small.[61] The process of building mosques in Mongolia started in early 1990s. The largest mosque in the Bayan-Ölgii *aimag* was financed by Saudi Arabia,[62] followed by the establishment of a few other mosques. However, at the same time it cannot be denied that resurgence of Islam elsewhere in Central Asia soon after its independence has had no impact on Mongolian-Kazakhs. It is evident from the fact that since the beginning of democratisation in Mongolia there has been a worsening situation in ethnic relations due to increasing nationalism among Kazakhs and Mongols alike. Some Kazakhs then demanded autonomy or even independence for Bayan-Ölgii *aimag*,[63] which if at all happens in future once again, may not be conducive for harmonious relations between overall Kazakh minority and Mongol majority in the country.

Nevertheless, the re-migration of Mongolian-Kazakhs from Kazakhstan has again not been hindered by the Mongolian government, which always had an ambiguous attitude against the emigration of the Kazakhs who are esteemed as hard workers. What is significant to note here is that most of the Kazakhs do not hesitate in considering Mongolia as their native country, and, therefore, homesickness has often been cited as being one of the main reasons for their re-migration back to Mongolia.[64] But according to a survey conducted among the Mongolian Kazakhs both in Mongolia as well as Kazakhstan, a clear divergence in individual and community identity has been revealed between the two geographic camps. The preliminary findings of the research conclude the following:

> Those remaining in Mongolia express high levels of territorialisation to both Mongolia as a whole and to smaller scales of place within Mongolia (i.e. the Kazakh *aimag* of Bayan-Ölgii, specific *summons*/counties or towns and cities), while those that have migrated to Kazakhstan express a commitment to remain in Kazakhstan but retain strong attachments to smaller scales of place in Mongolia.[65]

Conclusion

Despite the fact that Kazakhstan's policy on its diaspora has focussed on bringing ethnic Kazakhs to the territory of Kazakhstan for preserving its national identity, the socio-economic integration of these immigrants into local communities of Kazakhstan has remained a significant challenge at various fronts. This needs to be addressed first and foremost at the government level by adopting such viable immigration policies, which could benefit the new comers in terms of their social, economic and cultural integration. It is more so because, as revealed by the study commissioned by the UNDP in Kazakhstan, the complexity of the legal procedures generated by different government agencies dealing with migration and quota system and a general lack of inter-agency coordination represent a considerable obstacle in the integration process. Significantly, the International Organization for Migration (IOM) has been contributing much to the successful integration of ethnic Kazakh returnees and to a greater respect of the rights of migrants by facilitating the development and adoption of a number of national strategic papers and plans including the Sectoral Programme of Migration Policy of the Republic of Kazakhstan (2001-2010).[66] But the successful implementation of such policies is yet to be seen. In the absence of transparent legal procedures it would be a very difficult task to convince the *oralmans* to stay in the country of their origin. Given the lack of a secure socio-economic life in their ethnic homeland, Kazakhstan, several Mongolian-Kazakhs have already returned to the country from where they migrated earlier.

Within Mongolia there has been peaceful co-existence between the Mongols and the Kazakhs for a long time. Yet, there are indications that the Mongols now are not disinclined towards Kazakh migration as they think that this will relieve them of potential inter-ethnic and inter-religious tensions between Muslim Kazakhs and Buddhist Mongols. However, considering the fact that the Kazakh community in Mongolia can easily be accessed through their rather tight and intimate social networks, dominant Muslim Kazakh factor particularly in Bayan-Ölgii *aimag* would remain intact as ever, which would not allow the Buddhist Mongols to outnumber Kazakhs at least in this western part of the country. Besides, unlike early 1990s today there are few Mongolian-Kazakhs who are inclined to migrate to Kazakhstan, but it is hard to predict as economic situation in Mongolia is not conducive while that of Kazakhstan is becoming better year after year. Possibly "push" factors, such as unstable economic condition in Mongolia compared with growth in Kazakhstan may accelerate the migration process of Mongolian-Kazakhs, though nothing concrete can be predicted at the moment. In any case, Mongolian-Kazakhs may prefer to keep their options open as long as possible. However, it is also to be pointed out that on the diplomatic front, issues related to Mongolian-Kazakh diaspora would remain a key factor in the smooth sailing of friendly ties between Mongolia and Kazakhstan. It is evident from the fact that just a few years back one of the reports of the Kazakh Foreign Affairs Ministry acknowledged that the issue of migration of Mongolia's ethnic

Kazakhs as continuing to be the "key problem" in Mongolia-Kazakhstan relations.[67]

NOTES AND REFERENCES

1. "Mobility and Migration", *http: www. youandaids.org/Themes/migration.asp*
2. *Ibid.*
3. Tsedendambyn Batbayar and Sharad K. Soni, *Modern Mongolia: A Concise Histrory*, New Delhi: Pentagon Press, 2007, p. 2.
4. Shirin Akiner, "Kazakhstan; An Overview", UNHCR Emergency and Security Service, Writenet Paper, no. 3 (June 2002), p. 1.
5. *Ibid.*
6. Morris Rossabi, *China and Inner Asia; From 1368 to the Present Day*, London: Thames and Hudson, 1975, pp. 167-168.
7. *Ibid*, pp. 170–171.
8. Baabar, *Twentieth Century Mongolia,* Cambridge: The White Horse Press, 1999, p. 396.
9. See Peter Finke, "The Kazaks of Western Mongolia", In *Contemporary Kazaks:Cultural and Social Perspectives,* edited by Ingvar Svanberg. New York: St. Martin Press, 1999, pp. 109-110. According to another view, the Kazakhs in Mongolia are mostly Abak-kerei and Naiman Kazakhs who settled in the Altai and Khovd regions, where they rented pasture from the lords of Mongolia during the 1860s as per the Tarbagatai protocol concluded between Tsarist Russia and the Qing Dynasty, see Ts. Baatar, "Present Situation of Kazakh-Mongolian Community", *The Mongolian Journal of International Affairs*, nos.8-9 (2002): 95.
10. For more on the events in 1921 directly related to Bogdo Gegen who was also called the *Khutukhtu,* the religious head of Mongolia, see Sharad K. Soni, *Mongolia-Russia Relations: Kiakhta to Vladivostok*, Delhi: Shipra Publications, 2002, pp. 48–52.
11. Baabar (1999), p. 396.
12. For more details, see Linda Benson and Ingvar Svanberg, "The Kazakhs in Xinjiang", In *The Kazakhs of China: Essays on an Ethnic Minority,* edited by Linda Benson and Ingvar Svanberg, Uppsala, 1988, pp. 1–106.
13. For more on the situation in Xinjiang during this period, see K. Warikoo, "Muslim Separatism in Xinjiang", *Himalayan and Central Asian Studies* 4, nos. 3–4 (July-December 2000), pp. 32–34.
14. Baabar (1999), p. 397.
15. *Ibid.*

16. Robert R. Rupen, *Mongols of the Twentieth Century*, Bloomington, 1964, Part 1, p. 258.
17. "CIA-The World Fact Book: Mongolia", https://www.cia.gov/library/publications/the-world-factbook/print/mg.html
18. For main ethnic groups comprising the whole population of Mongolia, see *2000 Population and Housing Census of Mongolia: The Main Results*, Ulaanbaatar: National Statistical Office of Mongolia, 2000, p. 50.
19. Owen Lattimore, "Mongolia", *China Year Book* (1938), p. 26.
20. B. Shirendyb et al, *History of the Mongolian People's Republic*, Translated by William A. Brown and Urgunge Onon, Cambridge, Massachusetts: Harvard University, 1976, p. 343.
21. *Ibid.*, p. 344.
22. Yerlan Arynov, "The Kazakh Diaspora in Mongolia", Translated from Kazakh by Paul D. Buell, *http://userpage.fu-berlin.de/~corff/in/Landeskunde/kazakh*
23. Peter Finke, "Common Property to Open Access: Changing Pastoral Land Tenure in Post-Socialist Mongolia", 2000, *http://dlc.dlib.indiana.edu/documents*
24. *2000 Population and Housing Census of Mongolia: The Main Results*, p. 51.
25. Dashzhav, *Ulaanbaatar xotin xün am* [Population of the Town of Ulaanbaatar], Ulaanbaatar, 1994, p. 30.
26. "Mongols and Kazakhs", *http://drlee.org/mongol/r43.html*
27. *2000 Population and Housing Census of Mongolia: The Main Results*, p. 128.
28. *Ibid.*, pp. 129–30.
29. Yerlan Arynov, "The Kazakh Diaspora in Mongolia", Translated from Kazakh by Paul D. Buell, *http://userpage.fu-berlin.de/~corff/in/Landeskunde/kazakh*
30. *2000 Population and Housing Census of Mongolia: The Main Results*, *op.cit*, p. 50.
31. See Anna Genina, "Mongolian-Kazakh Oralmander: Repatriation, Citizenship, and National Belonging in Kazakhstan", *http://www.irex.org/programmes/iaro/research/06-07/Genina.pdf*
32. *Status of Oralmans in Kazakhstan: Overview* (Almaty: UNDP Kazakhstan, 2006), p. 8.
33. "US Committee for Refugees: 1997 Country Reports: Kazakhstan", *http://www.refugees.org/world/countryrpt/scasia/1997/kazakhstan.html*
34. "Large Group of Repatriates Receives Kazakh Citizenship but Problems Remain Acute", *KIBHR Information Newsletter*, no. 3 (1-8 April 2001), *http://www.bureau.kz/bulletin_eng.html*

35. *Ibid.*
36. See Alfred Kueppers, "Ethnic Kazakhs Find Titular Homeland to be Economic Haven" (22 April 2003), *http://www.eurasianet.org/departments/culture/articles/eav042203.shtml*
37. See "Kazakhstan: The Challenge of Sustaining Returnees", *http;//www.irinnews.org/report.asp?ReportID=45782& SelectRegion =Central_Asia*
38. *Status of Oralmans in Kazakhstan* (2006), p. 13.
39. *Ibid.*
40. President Nazarbaev's Speech at the Third World *Kurultai* of Kazakhs held in Astana on 25 September 2005.
41. Kueppers (22 April 2003).
42. *Ibid.*
43. *Ibid.*
44. *Ibid.*
45. Sharad K. Soni "Perspectives on Mongolia-Central Asia Relations", *Jadavpur Journal of International Relations* (1995), p. 176.
46. *Summary of World Broadcasts*, FE/2214, 30 January 1995.
47. See Suchandna Chatterjee, *Mind and Vision: Perceptions of Reform in Kazakhstan and Kyrgyzstan,* New Delhi: Bookwell, 2006, p. 24.
48. K. Warikoo, "Emerging Order in Central Asia", *World Focus* 14, nos.3–4 (1993), p. 8.
49. Genina, *op.cit.*
50. Alexander C. Diener, Kazakhstan's Kin State Diaspora: Settlement Planning and the *Oralman* Dilemma", *Europe-Asia Studies* 57, no. 2 (March 2005), p. 327.
51. *Ibid*, pp. 327-328.
52. *Status of Oralmans in Kazakhstan* (2006), p. 24.
53. *Ibid*, pp. 15–16.
54. *Ibid*, p. 23.
55. *Ibid.*
56. Anna Genina, "Mongolian-Kazakh Oralmander: Repatriation, Citizenship, and National Belonging in Kazakhstan", *http://www.irex.org/programs/iaro/research/06-07/Genina.pdf*
57. *Ibid.*
58. See "Kazakh Report" (23 June 2000), *http://www.rferl.org/bd/ka/reports/archives/2000/06/230600.html*
59. Alan J.K. Sanders, *Mongolia: Politics, Economics and Society*, London: Frances Printer, 1987, p. 46.
60. See Andrew Shimunek, "Brief Field Notes on Ulaanbaatar Kazakhs", *Mongol Survey*, no. 17 (Winter-Spring 2006), pp. 21–22.
61. Finke (1999), p. 136.

62. Shirin Akiner, ed., *Mongolia Today*, London and New York: Keegan Paul International, 1991, p. xxiv.
63. Henry G. Schwarz, "Mongolia in the Era of Ethnicity", *Mongolica* 9, no. 30 (1999), pp. 662–663.
64. Finke, (1999), p. 138.
65. See Alexander C. Diener, "One Homeland or Two?: Territorialisation of Identity and the Repatriation Decision among the Mongolian-Kazakh Diaspora", *http://www.irex.org/programmes/iaro/research/01Diener.pdf*
66. See "UN in Kazakhstan-International Organization for Migration", *http://www.un.kz/script_site.php?id=127#207*
67. See Justin Burke, "BBC 06/11/01: Mongolian Envoy Examines Kazakh-Mongolian Relations", *http://www.eurasianet.org/resource/mongolia/hypermail/200106/0003.html*

16

New Russian 'Middle East Concept' in Eurasia

P.L. Dash

After one and half decades of soul searching, Russia is back with a bang to Eurasia. The pro-western foreign policy of the initial Yeltsin years failed to provide the depth Russia required to fathom its strategic balance on its eastern flanks. It was a lopsided diplomacy that received no popular applause from the Russians. Then, with the advent of Evgeny Primakov, first as Russian Foreign Minister and then as Prime Minister, there was a discernible balance by 1996 in Russian foreign policy between the orient and the occident. The China card began to play as determining a role as the India card. And the much hyped Russia-India China (RIC) triangle finally emerged to overwhelm Eurasian geopolitical analyses. When Putin's Russia finally took the Chinese bull by the horns to resolve the Russo-Chinese boundary conflicts, nagging their bilateral relations since the border firing in late 1960s, it seemed a slew of problems still remained unresolved. Russia's Japan card has been like Emerson's poem "Fable" that depicts the tale between a high mountain and a little squirrel, where the little one prevails. The island dispute over the Kuriles continues to persist and improvement in bilateral relations is made hostage to resolution of territorial disputes, where the Fable is evident as:

> "If I am not as large as you
> You are not so small as I.
> And half not spry
> Talents differ,
> All is well and wisely put
> If I cannot carry forest on my back
> Neither can you crack a nut".

This being so, on 4-5 November, 2008, an international conference was held at Issyk Kul in Kyrgyzstan. A social organisation called Alexander Knyazev organised this conference that excluded the US, NATO and other extra regional powers. Thus, indeed by nature a regional conference by the CIS countries to deliberate on the evolving pattern of foreign relations in the context of global transformations in the emerging system of international relations, the conference gathered together academics and policy planners from Russia and other Central Asian countries, SCO representatives to discuss political and security issues as well as issues of economic cooperation. Central and vital to the conference was the thesis put forward by the Russian representative, Yuri Krupnov, on a "New Middle East: Focused Integration on Afghanistan, Central Asia and Siberia". This is the concept under discussion in this paper that argues against the forces of globalization grossly assigning it in favour of a Russo-Centric approach.

Roots of the New Concept

The genesis and growth of this concept that Russia is a Eurasian power has been taking place slowly but steadily in the mindset of the Russian intellectual circle. In a clear departure from those who pursued a west-centric foreign policy in the inceptive post-Soviet years of Russia's independence under the leadership of Yeltsin-Kozyrev combine, there is a sizeable group of Russian scholars, who rejected the Atlanticist notion and tried to propound a thesis of laying greater emphasis on the orient rather than on the occident. Foremost among them was academician Evgeny Primakov, a West Asian expert, who assumed the reign of Russian diplomacy in the midst of reigning chaos. Primakov's foreign policy overtures hinted at the emergence and viability of an alliance between Russia-India – China (RIC) to counter the growing influence of the US to chart out the architecture of a unipolar world – a notion Russia has been repeatedly rejecting in favour of multipolarity. From here stems Russia's rejection of globalisation as a means of unipolarity and the increasing quest to find a solution to the growing aura of globalisation led by the US.

At the root of this reorientation lay a fundamental shift in US policy toward Russia and NATO. In the wee years of the velvet revolution, particularly from the fall of the Berlin Wall in October, 1989 to the disintegration of the Soviet Union in December 1991, the US had pledged not to take advantage of Moscow's weakness, further democracy in the space what was once known as Eastern Block and not to extend NATO eastward so as to avoid military confrontation with Russia. This promise of 1990 held no good for the Russians in subsequent years, when Poland, Hungary and the Czech Republic were taken in as NATO members, while Russia was plainly told that "it would never be able to join". Michael Mandelbaum writes: "NATO expansion seemed to break a Western promise and tell Russians that to have a say in Europe's affairs, they need to be able to assert themselves militarily. Georgia was the result".[1]

The US activities and military entanglement, first in Central Asia by leasing out military bases and logistics from the countries of the region who were the Russian prefectures in Soviet yesteryears, and then overt military involvement in Afghanistan in 2001 and Iraq in 2003 were further evidence that sent a clear and loud message to Russia to worry about the rapidly changing political contours across Trans-Caucasus and Central Asia. Further the tacit US support in staging coloured revolutions in all regions bordering Russia – Rose revolution in Georgia in the Caucasus, Orange revolution in the Ukraine in the Russian west and Tulip revolution in Kyrgyzstan in Central Asia – overshadowed the gains of velvet revolution that had given these countries independence with the promise to build democracy. As the US began unilaterally pursuing its goals in Iraq in utter defiance of the UN and international community, many countries including Russia, lost their investments in Iraq that had taken place under Saddam Husain. The US unilateral bombardment of Syria also conveyed the message that the US military ambitions are steadily growing in the region. NATO's eastward expansion to include Georgia and the Ukraine as members further infuriated Russia and the final straw came when Putin vehemently opposed the US missile defence deployment system in Poland. Through the second term of Putin between 2004-08, Russia gradually developed a feeling inimical to the ambitions and pursuits of the US.

Furthermore, the operationalisation of the Baku-Tbilisi-Ceyhan oil pipeline and Baku-Tbilisi-Erzurum gas pipeline, bypassing Russia and Iran in 2006 to transport Caspian and Central Asian energy to the world market enhanced Russian apprehensions as a major energy power to think of alternative transportation linkages. These pipelines were hailed in the West as a fantastic success of stoic political commitment.[2] Russian intellectuals began seriously pondering about an alternative strategy that would provide her with a theoretical postulate to express her foreign policy overtures in the countries of the near abroad and beyond. The seriousness of the matter reverberated across the region when Russia witnessed US and NATO warship cruising along the Black Sea waters to extend humanitarian aid to Georgia at the grave moment of a brewing war in that country. All these developments of recent years were evidence that the geopolitical equations in Eurasia have taken a swift turn that Russia can no longer ignore.[3] The Bear has now to assert itself in the domain of its own periphery across all eleven time zones spreading over Eurasia.

A Russian antithesis to the US hegemony in the Middle East, Caspian/Caucasian/Central Asian regions was thus certainly in the waiting. The final straw in the evolution of such a strategy was the Georgian onslaught on South Ossetia that escalated into a five-day bloody war between Georgia and Russia in August, 2008. This conflict discernibly demonstrated the position of vying powers: Georgia, the US and West on the one hand and Russia, South Ossetia and Abkhazia on the other. At the end of the conflict, when Russian president Dmitry Medvedev recognised the independence of South Ossetia and Abkhazia, the tectonic plate of geopolitics across Trans-Caucasus had suddenly, dramatically altered. Apparently, the domino effect of Kosovo was strongly felt in the region. With the declaration of independence and their recognition by Russia, South Ossetia and Abkhazia ceased to be Georgian territories. They became independent political entities under strong Russian protection that further implied that Russia was no longer interested in annexing these Georgian enclaves as it had been accused of in the past one and half decades. Forced by Georgian administrative apathy often leading to repression, these two enclaves have been repeatedly requesting Russia to accord them political and diplomatic recognition as independent states. The last act of Georgian defeat by Russian forces starkly exposed three things: the Georgian vulnerability in a volatile region, the American ambitions to nurture and foster Georgia as a regional, frontline surrogate in Trans-Caucasus; and finally the US led NATO's goals to use Saakashvili as a pliant front man to derive strategic mileage along the Russian underbelly. It also nakedly exposed how Georgia and the US lightly took Russia as a worthless weakling.

All these machinations suddenly evaporated as the Georgian defeat dawned over the horizon. The aura of confidence vanished with that crushing defeat, perhaps not to be repeated anytime in

Georgia in foreseeable future or anywhere else in the Caucasus. Although Russia faced a virtual isolation in the venture, it had its own tale to tell. Not many countries of the world came forward to approve of Medvedev's action in Georgia. Western democracies unanimously condemned the Russian venture. US president Bush exhorted the Russian president not to recognise the independence of South Ossetia and Abkhazia. Surprisingly, support poured from unexpected quarters from distant Latin America. Nicaragua's Daniel Ortega was first to recognise followed by Hamas of the PLO to be further followed by Cuba's Castro and Ecuador's Rafael Correa. Venezuelan president Hugo Chavez also hailed Russia's return as a great power and announced joint Russian Venezuelan naval maneuvers in the Caribbean.[4]

Looking Beyond Georgia

The operational perimeter of the slowly evolving Russian concept of a New Middle East in Eurasia stretches far beyond Georgia in all directions. It encompasses the Trans-Caucasian underbelly of the Russian Federation, the Caspian Basin countries including Iran, the very confluence of civilizations, where West Asia meets with South and Central Asia, Pakistan, India and Western China, all Central Asian countries including Kazakhstan and Mongolia and the entire stretch of Southern Russia from the Volga Basin to Angara Basin. This is the core of the concept to embrace as many important countries as possible to work out Eurasian elements that they possess. In this region China and India are two most populous countries of the world. Secondly they are emerging economies that constitute the future of economic hub. Thirdly, Central Asia has emerged as the geopolitical pivot in Asia. Fourthly, the Caspian Basin is beset with incalculable significance in terms of transport corridors and pipelines taking shape in that realm, Fifthly, volatile Caucasus is largely anchored to Russia, where shape of things to come is predictably under Russian control. Sixthly, the region is so pregnant with the concept of regional cooperation that it has everything from Black Sea cooperation Council to APEC and the interlaying space is filled by a host of regional organisations. Altogether over a dozen active and potential regional organisations are strewn over the region trying to vie in a space that is politically unstable, economically volatile, ethno-nationally fractured and religiously in perennial ferment.

A glance at the list of these regional organisations would amply convince anyone that Russia would find any semblance of harmony in the region in its favour a tough nut to crack. They include the Shanghai Cooperation Council (SCO), the Commonwealth of Independent States (CIS), Caspian Cooperation Organisation (CCO), Organisation of Central Asian Cooperation (OCAC), North Atlantic Treaty Organisation (NATO), Organisation on Security and Cooperation in Europe (OSCE), European Union (EU), Council of Europe (COU), Black Sea Economic Cooperation (BSEC), Eurasian Economic Community (EURASEC), Economic Cooperation Organisation (ECO), Organisation for Democracy and Economic Development called GUAM, Organisation of Collective Security Treaty (OCST), Asia Pacific Economic Cooperation (APEC) Seventhly, the region is home to enormous oil and gas deposits and has the supply channels to nearly all energy needy countries of the world. And bizarrely, the region is also home to intractable conflicts such as the Russia-Georgia conflict, Azerbaijan-Armenian conflict, Azerbaijan-Iran conflict, US-Iran conflict, India-Pakistan conflict, India-China conflict, Uzbek-Tajik conflict, Sino-Russian conflicts (largely settled now) plus water disputes, ethnic disputes and other bickering perennially nagging. To find harmony in such a region to pursue a new postulate to ensure regional cooperation that would serve an antithesis to proliferating globalisation will certainly merit intense intellectual discourse in the years to come.

And finally, the US remains a potential geopolitical anchor in the region. It leads NATO that unleashes an ambitious eastward extension project that constantly rubs salt on Russia's injured ego. The August 2008 Russia-Georgia conflict over South Ossetia could be interpreted in a manner that would pit Georgia verses the West and Georgia verses the rest in Eurasia. In character, content and intent all the above cited organisations vastly differ from one another. However, NATO and its activities in Eurasia unmistakably pick up issues unpalatable to Russia. Yet Russia desires to carry them all into the evolving concept of New Middle East in Eurasia; not knowing how to reconcile their differences and not knowing how to address the vast amount of hostility each neighbour harbours and nurtures against the other.

The desire of the Russian Federation to serve as a vast, geopolitical and geostrategic anchor for all differing elements of its Eurasian concept stems from the fact that Eurasia has common enemies and common ills to which a common solution could be found. The post-9/11 scenario has forcefully reinforced the idea of this commonness where even the US has found common grounds to fight the menace of terrorism jointly with all other countries of Eurasia. Yet, what we see in practice is a different Russia largely renting inconsonance on many issues of vital significance with the US. Nearly a year into the presidency, despite a unique tandem holding good the Putin-Medvedev duumvirate, there is hardly anything clarity that could be termed a "Medvedev Doctrine". Knitting together all that has emerged in recent months, one finds the irony of indecisions. On the one hand, Medvedev has repeatedly talked of ending corruption in Russia, taking his country's economy beyond oil and gas industry, instituting the rule of law, ensuring freedom for the Russians so they participate actively in building their country and integrating Russia into the world economy. On the other, in the same breadth of voice, Medvedev has been highly critical of Washington. "He has lambasted Washington for destabilizing the world's finances, blamed the United States for provoking the August war with Georgia and laid claim to Russia's privileged interests in its neighbourhood", while proposing at the same time "a massive shift in the global architecture which would give Russia a pronounced say in world affairs".[5]

While Medvedev has sounded liberal at home and hawkish abroad, he has certainly pronounced his country's claim to a greater Russian role in the evolving and emerging architecture of international relations. Prime Minister Putin has given him company in his endeavour. Hence the need to evolve a new Eurasian policy to define clearly what Russia means by its neighbourhood interests. Medvedev's desire is not entirely intriguing. It is rather a welcome gesture from a leader visualizing his country's interest far onto the future, which other Russian leaders save Putin had failed to evince in recent years. In the delineated space of Eurasian Middle East, Russia wishes to forbid forever US and European meddling in its near abroad. With the help of SCO, it desires to build a solid NATO like block. And slowly build up Russian image as major financial hub in Europe to wean away the sheen from the US predominance. For this to be achieved Russia would most likely use oil and gas as a financial and diplomatic weapon. Russia considers the concept of a unipolar world antiquated and advocates that new power centres are emerging to ensure multi-polarity.[6]

The emphasis on the emergence of Brazil, Russia, India and China (BRIC) and particularly Russia, India and China (RIC) – three countries with potential emerging economies in Eurasia – has precipitated the urgency for Russia to visualize a greater Eurasian role for her in the shape of things to come. Problems must persist, but at the same time efforts must also persist with clarity of objectives in the midst of an incredible divide galore as detailed below.

A Dozen Divide Galore

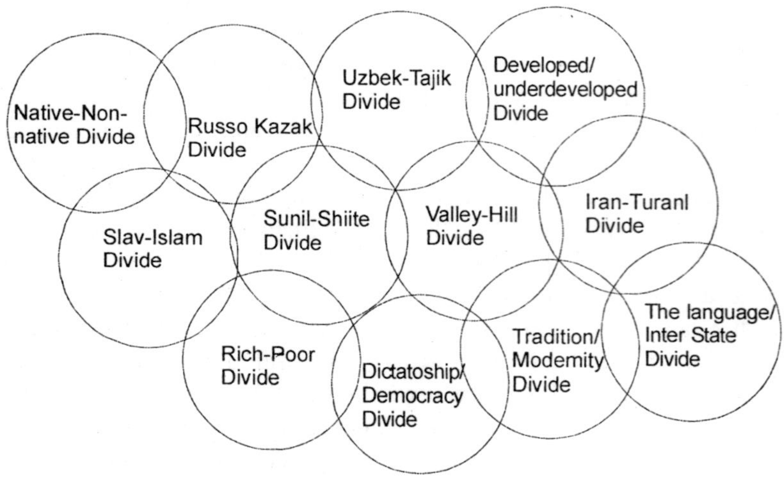

So much of positive accolades for Soviet help alongside innumerable nuances of grievance against Russia are a contrast in itself that constitute the anger and anguish of a clear divide in post-Soviet Eurasia. Bound by age old geographical proximity, Russia's umbilical cord extends to Caucasus, Central Asia and beyond to the Far East across Eurasia to the region in general and to each of its individual countries in particular that push all of them together to a realm of shared history of coexistence often studded with conflicts. The cycle of conflict and cooperation is so intricately interwoven with hostility and friendship that a post-Soviet narrative caption once succinctly put it: "The Soul is Uzbek, the Language is Russian and the army is Soviet". Precisely, this is what expresses the extant reality. Until yesterday, all these countries were Sovietizing; earlier they were Russifying, and now they are globalizing by being busy in their nation building process, and at the same time, facing the challenges of globalization, while Russia is busy in putting them in the framework of a new world architecture called "New Middle East" in Eurasia. Since the divide is obvious and ominous, time has come countries of Eurasia ought to choose upholding sovereignty of their nationhood in consonance with the challenging tasks of globalization; maybe within the ambit of the New Middle East project or slip to illusory, US led democracy building, which has proven to be a costly affair in many countries such as Somalia, Kosovo, Haiti, Afghanistan and Iraq.

New Geopolitical Contour

In addition, the region encompassing Russia's New Middle East from Saudi Arabia to Mongolia and from Astrakhan to New Delhi is host to all important religions of the world. Christianity in its varied strands including Russian Orthodoxy, all factions of Islam, Zoroastrianism, Confucianism, Buddhism, Hinduism, *et al.* At a time when religious sentiments are invoked to flare up fissiparous politics, Russia's endeavour to obtain a coordinated New Middle East in Eurasia is as commendable as it seems implausible. Moreover the region is rich with energy – a fungible commodity sought after by all for economic growth. The concentration of energy resources on the map of the New Middle East makes it a potential candidate for rivalry because large energy reserves are concentrated in the Persian Gulf, the Caspian basin and the Russian Federation. From the fringes to the core it would remain a competitive arena for energy trade, pipeline politics and geostrategic jockeying.

The Eurasian Middle East encompasses the resource rich Urals. Although it has not taken into consideration the linkages with the Far Eastern sector, the organic linkages of the Far East as an integral part of Eurasia are imperative. Of the vast resources at the disposal of the countries of the region energy demand and supply could be singled out as the determining factor in geopolitics in the years to come. The way energy politics and diplomacy has been conducted in the post-Soviet years in the Caucasian-Caspian/Central Asian and Far Eastern sector is a telling testimony of at least four big powers afield in the region. Russia as a major energy supplier cannot afford to ignore the presence of other three potential contenders: the US, India and China. The energy needs of the later two countries with their impressive sustained growth of 8 percent per annum for the past decade has precipitated the urgency to have a viable look-east energy policy that could connect the energy hungry India and China with production centres across Eurasia.

So far, all pipeline connections, whether from the Persian Gulf or from the Russian Federation, looked westward because demand was there for energy over the years. That demands stay put. However, new regions of growth have emerged with additional demands and they have to be met because energy is the locomotive of growth to facilitate welfare of the people that cannot be overlooked. This implies that sooner or later, there is a need to construct pipelines, particularly in the direction of China and India. Besides, all countries of Eurasia are not equally endowed with reserves of energy. Even within Central Asia-Tajikistan and Kyrgyzstan have enough hydro resources and no hydrocarbon reserves that compel them to depend on their resource rich neighbours such as Kazakhstan, Turkmenistan, Uzbekistan and Russia. The asymmetry is evident in Trans-Caucasus too where Georgia and Armenia are energy poor, whereas Azerbaijan is very rich. Similarly Russia is rich in energy reserves, while China is poor and so on.

Although many pipeline proposals have been tabled over the past one and half decades, none sans the Baku-Tbilisi-Ceyhan, once again a westward looking pipeline, has materialised primarily because of lack of desire to invest in risky regions and secondarily because there is apparent lack of political will and the tertiary cause could be attributed to a treacherous terrain, creating clear North-South divide on both sides of such mountains as the Himalayas, Hindukush, Pamir and Albert and Caucasian range. What signifies the growing requirement of a continuous flow energy supply to the East is the rise of Asian economies. The more will be their growth, the more they will require energy. And it will come from the Persian/Caspian regions and from the Siberian oil and gas fields of Russia. A resurgent Russia's overarching position in Eurasia from the Caucasus in ferment to an Asia on the upswing is a crucial factor in ensuring energy securities of many countries including those of India and China. There are two clear directions where Russia will play its inevitable role. In a way it has already been playing this role in post-Soviet years. First, in the years to come, Russia in collaboration with Kazakhstan, Turkmenistan, Azerbaijan and Iran will have to construct a supply network of the non-OPEC oil producing countries to connect to the OPEC network with a view to ensuring sustained and reasonable energy flow to the Asian economies. Secondly, if a cooperative platform will seem improbable, mainly due to political instability and economic volatility, Russia would throw open oil and gas fields in its Siberian and Far Eastern flanks to collaborative exploitation in order to meet the growing need of Asian economies. Such indications are already evident in various phases of Sakhalin projects, in construction of new pipelines to China from Siberia and to Japan from the Far East and in expressing willingness to join emerging Kazakh pipeline systems to ensure supply of energy to China. This is a complex Russian approach that encompasses the entire Eurasian continent in a new supplier group of energy led by Russia, and this fits into the concept of a New Middle East in Eurasia that shows Russia's tangible, forward looking approach to energy security of Eurasia.[7]

In the emerging energy supply and pipeline architecture across Eurasia, Russia's potential and pivotal role cannot be ignored. From the Caspian/Black/Baltic Sea directions to Western Siberia and beyond right up to peninsular Sakhalin and pan-Okhotsk area, Russia spreads over its pipeline network. In the years to come, Russia is likely to develop oil industry infrastructure in accessible areas of Siberia to harness energy and other resources and export them to needy areas in the Asian Far East. Such conclusion is derived from the target Russia has set for oil production till 2020: 445-490 million tonnes in the year 2010 and 450-520 tonnes in the year 2020 compared to 379 tonnes in 2003.[8] Capacity enhancement for transportation of oil and gas will lead to infrastructure augmentation in various directions. And this is most likely to happen in areas so far least exploited. However, beyond the control of Russia will be a plethora of unstable regimes from Caucasus to Central Asia to Afghanistan and Pakistan. This aspect would jeopardise as much the process of infrastructure building as the very process of nation state building based on participatory democracy.

Dilemma of Democracy

When new political parties, still not very strong to stand on their feet, toe the line of a president who has unlimited powers, nascent democracy becomes a mockery because everybody enjoys office at the mercy of the President. In many of the countries in Eurasia, particularly those successor to the USSR, the political situation grew dilemmatic within a triangular circumference involving three clear pressure groups: the president and his close cronies, the coterie, encircling the president, comprising a couple of thousand bureaucrats, military and policemen to maintain law and order and the old Soviet apparatchiks, whose residual influence still matters. The last folk, disheartened and disoriented, normally considered a spent force, but often yet reckoned with as an expertise pool because they still wield considerable influence of bygone years, wherever they live. They do not normally side with the President and favour the people. Finally, the grassroots comprising of millions with strong, esoteric political inclination try to serve their motherland. The President is located at the upper tip of the triangle, thereby administering political pressure in the system of governance. The base of the triangle is occupied by people at one end, and old apparatchiks at the other end. The pressure from above is invariably heavy on the base due to the cycle of policy implementation that may be liked or disliked. The quality of pro-people policies assuages political pressure to a great extent. Alternatively, the wider the schism between the rulers and the ruled, the heavier is this pressure of the grassroots from below on the rulers.

On the three spectrums of a parallel triangle, all three angles are occupied by three differing elements: the pro-Russian elite, the pro-native nationalists and the globalization Gurus. Each of them remains preoccupied with their respective agendas that tangibly affect the society and politics. All these elements on the second triangle are normally watchful about the way the government conducts itself, they are disappointed with the growing pace of corruption, the malfeasance of the government to meet the increasing demands of the people. All these elements tend to side with the people with socio-economic demands to ameliorate the societal conditions in favour of a civil society.

One could observe a series of contradictory tendencies evident in the democratization process in the countries of Eurasia in the last seventeen plus years. First of all there is a discernible divide between the capital and the countryside. This could otherwise be called the urban rural divide that authorities in every country try to ignore, sidestep or render lip sympathy to. Secondly, there is a certain degree of difference between the past Sovietised political system and the present new political system. For instance, what Yeltsin wanted to preserve was a unified economic zone with a singular defence and currency arrangement to be overseen by the Kremlin. The Central Asians wished to obtain sovereignty in all spheres of governance and management including defence, diplomacy, economic development and social progress without Russian mediation. This clearly implied that Russia wanted an integrated system to prevail, while the Central Asians and the Caucasians endeavoured to devise a sovereign governance style of their own. In the emerging scheme of a Eurasian New Middle East, this aspect may severely undermine coherence, governance compatibility and mutual cooperation.

Past emotions of clinging to a union that existed for decades clashed with present political dispensation that yearned for increasing autonomy and independence. Although it has been hugely difficult for the Central Asians to bid adieu to Russia and embrace Western capitalism, they have preferred independence to Russian meddling. However, when the debate over a strong state verses a soft state took centre stage and a viable, unifying, political model was searched in the periphery and beyond, it was finally observed that many successor states preferred their native national model to slowly evolve to aping any other model, no matter whether Turkish, Iranian, Chinese, Indian, American or Russian.

In such a scenario, all countries of the region looked beyond Russia and found that all countries in their neighbourhood have been undergoing economic reforms: India, China, Turkey, Russia *et al.* Most interestingly, if these countries do not tend to change their political system, why should Central Asians and Caucasians? This very thought convinced the leaders and the led alike that there is little urgency for political leadership change. The system would evolve slowly over the years and what must be the focus of the moment are economic reforms to salvage the countries from doldrums. This thought was further corroborated by another prevailing idea: there is no democracy in the surroundings. China, Russia, Mongolia, Afghanistan, Pakistan, the three Caucasian countries do not necessarily pass through Western democracy. Then, logically, why should Central Asia? The existing regimes and system could mutate gradually, evolve a country specific, people savvy democracy over a period of time and lead Central Eurasia to prosperity.

The essence of the economic clash in all countries of Central Asia was between a deep-rooted public sector bequeathed from the Soviet era and a fragile private sector slowly emerging in the jungle of misrule and maladministration. There was no rule of law in place to regulate private economic activities, no proper taxation law to regulate profit repatriation, no knowledge to open a letter of credit, no clear rules on ownership issues, no proper banking mechanism and so many other lacunae. It was incumbent upon the political leadership to devise rules and promulgate regulations to control the country, its economic activities and face the challenges of globalisation. While intra-republic rivalry prevailed on chalking out regional regulations for an integrated approach to the challenges of globalisation, country specific rules gradually emerged to regulate internal and international conduct of each state. And we see many of them do well in the recent past in projecting themselves in the international arena. In this respect all countries are different, their approaches to resolving issues are also different and outlook to the future varies from one another. Even among such bigger countries as Kazakhstan, one could find forward looking policies and in Uzbekistan inward looking tendencies to corroborate native nationalism. This brings us to the platform of debating a strong state versus the soft state and it is but common knowledge to gauze where both strong and soft states stand internationally. The Russian endeavour for a New Middle East in Eurasia, particularly across the post-Soviet space may not strike a balance between the soft and the strong state, thereby jeopardising implementation of the very concept itself.

Analysis and Conclusion

What began as a geostrategic, geo-economic and geopolitical project by the Movement for Development by its Chairman, Yurii Krupnov and worked out jointly by like-minded intellectuals, who focus largely on a Russia rebound, the New Middle East Concept soon turned out to be a highly debatable, diplomatic strategy for a resurgent Russia. This project cannot altogether be ignored, nor sidestepped, nor overlooked. It has cast its niche in the government to debate, discuss and adopt the strategy as a national agenda to pursue the concept in the years to come. Krupnov has urged the Russian leadership to seriously consider the proposal and take appropriate diplomatic initiatives to ensure unification of the Eurasian space under the leadership of Russia. Russia must take the initiatives of uniting such divergent countries as India and Pakistan, Azerbaijan and Armenia, Turkey and Georgia, Tajikistan and Uzbekistan, China and Mongolia and a host of small countries lying across the Eurasian space. The hallmark of the Russian endeavour ought to be focused on the industrialization of Afghanistan and its resource-rich but cash-poor states of Central Asia. It also must lay emphasis on the deplorably developed Siberian flanks. As Chairman of the Observation Council of the Institute of Demography, Migration and Regional Development,

Krupnov insists that there is an urgency to channelize the resources of Siberia to the benefit of Eurasia, and for this to materialise, his proposal includes a bypass transport lane from the main North South Transport Corridor from St. Petersburg to Mumbai via the Caspian and Iran. The bypass he proposes must connect St. Petersburg with Siberia and Siberia with the Caspia via Kazakhstan to join with the mainstream of North-South Corridor in Iran further down south to the Persian Gulf and onto India.

The Russian eastern flanks have never so far looked in the southern direction. And looking westward at St. Petersburg for ages has not rewarded the Siberian peoples adequately. Therefore infrastructure building in Siberia is a prerequisite of the New Middle East. Krupnov's outline of the Eurasian New Middle East, as elucidated through an online conference in late 2008, premises on the sweeping anti-US sentiments in Iraq, Iran, Afghanistan and Pakistan – the underbelly of the Caucasus and Central Asia – and push the Russian agenda effectively. The assumption that the concept has a future is further based on the recent recession and declining US role in the world economy and market. On the contrary Russian popularity and proximity may replace or may tangibly offset the US agenda for a unipolar world. Deployment of 60,000 foreign troops in Afghanistan on the ninth year of their active military entanglement has brought nothing for America and NATO as it did exactly similar disservice to the 100,000 Soviet troops involved in Afghanistan for nearly a decade in the 1980s.[9] Similarly, doling out $10 billion to Pakistan from 9/11 to Mumbai terror act for its cooperation in the fight against terror has brought the US to naught.

The unstable nature of the Afghan political imbroglio and countries in its proximity provide no crimson hopes for immediate US success in the region. Although the US, Russia and China have spent the past few years in positioning themselves in the region, none has achieved a firm foothold. Therefore as Martha Brill Olcott, noted by "invoking the nineteenth century competition between Russia and England does not do justice to the complexity of the evolving geo-political situation in Central Asia"[10] The US cannot ensure peace in the region. The industrialisation of Afghanistan and other countries less developed is the need of the hour. That time of geopolitical jockeying has passed by. The post-Soviet age demands infrastructure building, capacity building and democracy building. Many developmental goals ought to be addressed instead of geopolitical jockeying and a resurgent Russia must undertake this mission as a responsible power to wean away countries in Eurasia from the US hegemony.

The complicity of Pakistan first in the Indian embassy bombing in Kabul and in Mumbai terror attack as well as the blunt revelation by British Prime Minister, Gordon Brown that the origin of two third of all terrorist acts in Britain have been traced to Pakistan, throw a chilling proposition to doubt and question whether the US could still sustain 75 percent of its supply to allied forces in Afghanistan via Pakistan. The Pakistan double speak is a telling instance of betrayal that the US must understand and address so that the Army-ISI nexus within Pakistan must feel the heat and stop encouraging the sources of terror.[11] Therefore the US is back to Eurasia for help. It had sought Russia's help when it ventured into Afghanistan because Russia was then the only country that had detailed information on the geographical contour of Afghanistan as well as a lot of political information to share with the US. Russia could now also be a reliable partner in the US Afghan venture, should it ever succeed. Afghanistan or no Afghanistan, Russia for the US is a force that cannot be wised off. Therefore, post 26/11, the US has been seriously exploring the possibility of a Ukraine-Georgia-Azerbaijan Turkmenistan route to replace the lopsided dependence on Pakistan for NATO supply, and for this too, Russia remains indispensible. This was precisely why the US announced recently a land-transit deal with Russia in order to minimize its lopsided logistics dependence on Pakistan.

However indispensible Russia may seem in the whole architecture of emerging international shape of things to come in Eurasia, the idea of New Middle East swims against the mainstream tide of reigning globalisation. An inward looking Russia may find it hard to put in place effective counter measures against US proliferation into Eurasia. Although democracy deficit in Russia's influence zone may pose a challenge to US penetration, a cooperative rather than a competitive platform is the need of the hour for the New Middle East concept to succeed. However, in its present form the concept is an antithesis to globalisation, an alternative anathema to western style democracy being implanted in the region and a pertinent answer to Huntington's theory of Clash of Civilisations. A unified Eurasia under the Russian umbrella could seem an answer to the eastward extension of NATO and political penetration of the US, but at the same time, the US interests must not be excluded altogether.

NOTES AND REFERENCES

1. Michael Mandelbaum, "Stop Baiting the Bear," *Newsweek*, Special Edition, Issues 2009, p. 33.
2. Brenda Shaffer, "From Pipedream to Pipeline: A Caspian Success Story," *Current History*, October, 2005, pp. 343–346.
3. For details, see, Sanjay Kumar Pandey, "Russian Foreign Policy Under Putin," *World Focus*, New Delhi, August, 2008, pp. 311–315.
4. The *Newsweek*, September 8, 2008, p. 5.
5. Owen Matthews and Anna Nemtsova, "The Medvedev Doctrine," *News Week*, December 1, 2008, p. 36.
6. *Ibid.*, p. 37.
7. See Tabata, Shinichiro (Ed.) *Energy and Environment in Slavic Eurasia: Toward the Establishment of the Network of Environmental Studies in the Pan-Akhotsk Region*, Slavic Research Centre, Hokkaido University, Sapporo, 2008, Chapter 1, pp. 3–66.
8. Igor Tomberg, "Geopolitics of Pipeline Communication System in Eurasia," *World Affairs*, Vol. X, No. 1, Spring, 2006, p. 69.
9. Krupnov and other Russian sources cite the presence of 60,000 allied NATO troops stationed in Afghanistan, while other reports indicate the presence of 30,000 US troops and 35,000 allied troops in Afghanistan. See Brahma Chellany, "Pay-offs won't Pay: America's New Afghan Strategy could compound problems," *The Times of India*, January 2, 2009, p. 16.
10. Martha Brill Olcott, "The Great Powers in Central Asia," *Current History*, October 2005, p. 331.
11. Shaun Gregory, "It is Time for Army-ISI to Feel the Heat," *Sunday Times of India*, January 4, 2009, p. 12.

17

Energy: The New Vector in Alliances in Eurasia

Sreemati Ganguli

Energy has gained a strategic significance in the post-Cold War context in the post-Soviet space, here referred to as Eurasia. There is geo-economics and there is geo-politics concerning energy as a product, as a marketable commodity and as the driving force of economic growth the world over. The virgin newness of the proven, possible and probable energy resources of Eurasia has catapulted the region into the centre of these geo-strategic activities. Eurasia in the post-disintegration era has been a witness to a whole lot of new pipeline projects. The yet untapped energy riches of the region, its land-lockedness, the need for the post-Soviet energy-producing states to reach out to the wider global market for energy revenues to re-structure their economies, and the growing demand for energy the world over as the driving force for economic growth – all these factors have enhanced the significance of this region for global energy security. Pipelines are the carriers of this energy from the producer states to the markets across transit territories, initiating a complex and intertwined process of competition as well as cooperation, countering as well as balancing.

In the post-Cold War era, there has been a paradigmatic shift in the concept of security as non-traditional components of security gain wider attention and focus. The concept of energy security is such a non-traditional one and is a significant component of a country's over-all security parameters. Energy security means, for the producing countries, a secure access to markets, whereas for the consumer countries, it is a question of gaining sufficient and uninterrupted supplies of energy. Given the contemporary model of energy-driven economic growth, energy security is essentially linked with economic security of states and thus, is integrally linked with global security. Energy pipelines are said to be economic lifelines, as they create a bond of intra-or inter-regional interdependency among the producers, the transit states and the market states. This article tries to present the energy-scenario in post-Cold War Eurasia from these two perspectives – the need for energy security and the resultant interdependence that makes energy alliances in the region crucial. This article identifies three such alliances – one built-up around Russia, the other centering the Baku-Tbilisi-Ceyhan Pipeline, as a counterweight to the first one, and the third one is the evolving SCO Energy Club. These alliances are not self-declared ones, like OPEC, apart from the SCO Energy Club. And, OPEC is only a club of oil producers, but these alliances, as the article will show, consists of energy producers, markets as also transit states.

Alliance around Russia

In May 1995, President Boris Yeltsin issued a Decree on Russia's Energy Strategy till 2010[1], the first official recognition of using energy as an instrument to build up cooperation among the CIS states. This Strategy projected the national 'fuel and energy' complex as a preferred ' instrument for the conduct of (Russia's) domestic and foreign policies'. This view is also represented in President Putin's so-called Ph.D. dissertation at St. Petersburg's State Mining Institute, titled 'Mineral Raw Materials in the Strategy of Development of the Russian Economy' and later, in published abstract of his thesis, where he argued that Russia's natural resource base would secure both national economic development to turn Russia into a leading economic power and its position in the global scenario and harped on the need for state regulation in development, investment and export operations in the energy sector.[2] Later, in his May 2004 Address to the Federal Assembly, he talked about the need for a well-developed transport infrastructure, as this is 'capable of turning Russia's geographical features into a real competitive advantage for the country'[3].

With the reserves of approximately 34 per cent of world's gas and nearly 12 per cent of world's oil reserves, and with energy accounting for 70 per cent of the country's export earnings and nearly 40 per cent of its entire economy, it is quite natural for Russia to view energy as a strategic instrument. Russia tries to link this approach with that of using energy as one of its soft power capabilities to re-structure its relations with the states in Eurasia. Energy pipelines, built during the Soviet era, and with additions of new and modifications of the old ones during the post-Soviet era give Russia a unique advantage in this sphere. Some of the important pipelines are: the Atyrau-Samara line that is connected with the larger Druzhba pipeline system, the newly-built Caspian Pipeline Consortium from Tengiz-Novorossisk, the Central Asia-Centre gas pipeline to connect Turkmenistan with Russia through Uzbekistan and Kazakhstan, the planned Prikaspiisky gas pipeline with Kazakhstan and Turkmenistan, the Baku-Novorossisk oil pipeline with Azerbaijan, the newly built Gazli-Kagan gas pipeline with Uzbekistan to connect Bukhara-Khiva region with the Central Asia-Centre and Bukhara-Urals main pipeline etc. Russia also offered Kazakhstan to join the Baltic oil pipeline system from Timan-Siberia and Urals-Volga region to the Baltic town of Primorsk on the Gulf of Finland.

The March 2002 Statement of Intent on Cooperation in Energy Policy and Measures to Defend the Interests of Natural Gas Producers[4] by Russia, Turkmenistan, Kazakhstan, and Uzbekistan enabled them to undertake a common energy security strategy through coordination of their export, import and investment. Through this arrangement, Russia benefited from secure supply of gas as its own gas fields were depleting and new fields like Zapolyarnoe would reach peak production by 2006 and Arctic fields by 2020.Also this arrangement made these states dependent on Russian pipeline network to reach European gas markets.

The four energy agreements of Russia with Turkmenistan, Uzbekistan, Kyrgyzstan and Tajikistan in 2003 had a 25-year long vista and included a broad range of partnerships: gas exports, joint exploration of oil and gas fields, development of new pipelines as well as restoration of the existing outmoded energy installations of the CARs. This arrangement also proposed to upgrade Central Asian gas pipeline system and to connect the system ultimately with the Russian gas pipelines to create a unified structure for all gas exports from Central Asia. We may quote Roy Allison in this context as he commented that Russia perceives the energy resources of the Central Asian states as 'both a strategic asset and a strategic instrument in the region'[5] to project its pre-eminence in the region.

In a significant move, Russia shifted its earlier stance over the legal status of the Caspian Sea (that the Caspian should be exploited jointly by all the littoral states) to accept the Kazakh view that the seabed should be divided along the median line. According to this modified median line principle, Kazakhstan was allocated 29 per cent share in the Caspian Sea, Azerbaijan and Turkmenistan – over 19 per cent, Russia – 18.5 per cent and Iran – 14 per cent. In spite of the loss of 1.5 per cent share (as under the condominium principle, each littoral state would be entitled to equal 20 per cent share), Russia made the pragmatic policy choice to help the process of official demarcation of the national sectors in the Caspian Sea as well as to project itself in a role of a mediator in the region to avert possible international arbitration in the dispute. The formal demarcation of the Northern Caspian Sea among Russia, Kazakhstan and Uzbekistan was declared in the 2003 Almaty Meet of the Special Working Group on the Legal Status of the Caspian Sea. All these moves show Russia's endeavours to make itself relevant in the energy scenario of the region, and through this, to build up a bond of interdependence in the region.

The energy pipelines are essential to this approach. Russia's Gas dispute with Ukraine over pricing of gas and the resultant stopping of gas supplies in January 2006 is the other facet of this approach, whereby energy pipelines are used to deal with non-compliant states.

Russia tries to use energy to become geopolitically relevant in the region and apart from bilateral security measures with the CIS states and multilateral security initiatives like the CSTO, energy is used effectively by Russia to promote its interests in the region, considered to be of vital strategic significance for Russia. As Robert L. Larsson pointed out that ' Russia has strategic priorities to keep its influence over the CIS and its energy policy is one of the means used for this reason….Russia uses its energy policy to create growth, extend influence, avert geopolitical and macroeconomic threats and to reduce the risk of being blackmailed'[6].

The financial crisis of 2008-09 and the sharp drop in energy prices (from $147 a barrel in July 2008 to around $50 a barrel in early 2009) portend a grim picture. It led to cutbacks in the expenditure on exploration and production of energy and so, many high cost developmental projects were cancelled or postponed. The downward demand revision also influenced global energy price behaviour. This crisis has important implications for Russia, as its economy depends largely on energy revenues. Its stock market experienced a steep decline, investors pulled tens of billions of dollars out of the country in anticipation of worse situation and the growth projection of the economy shows negative trends, after nearly a decade of high growth[7].

The Stabilization Fund, established in 2004, was meant to regularize the management of resource revenues and the accountability in regard to resource rents. It was also expected to reduce budgetary dependence on resource rents, as Finance Minister Kudrin suggested that $1 decrease in the price of a barrel of oil translated into a 0.5 per cent reduction in Russian national GDP, and also it was projected as a safeguard against 'Dutch Disease', which entails inflation and appreciation of national currency as a result of excessive revenues got from export of natural resources[8]. But despite all such measures Russian economy suffered badly and the most prominent reason is its over-dependence on one source of income, the energy revenue. This is not a very healthy trend for Russia, after the Soviet experience, as Fiona Hill analyzed – '(O)ne of the prevailing theories behind the decline of the Soviet economy that ultimately led to the collapse of the USSR is that it was precipitated by an oil production decline, combined both with a dramatic drop in world oil prices after record highs in the wake of the 1970s OPEC oil embargo, and by the mismanagement and misuse of oil resources.'[9] The future energy policy orientation of Russia, after this crisis, is expected to determine its relations with the alliance around it and also with the other ones in the Eurasian space.

BTC (Baku-Tbilisi-Ceyhan) Project

The Baku-Tbilisi-Ceyhan oil Pipeline is a unique example of an energy-alliance in Eurasia. This 1760 kms long Pipeline connects the Azeri-Chirag – Guneshli fields of Azerbaijan in the Caspian to the Mediterranean Sea port of Ceyhan. Though the initial document on the construction of this Pipeline was signed between Azerbaijan and Turkey in March 1993, but the initiative got momentum only after the Ankara Declaration of October 1998 by Turkey, Georgia, Azerbaijan, Kazakhstan and Uzbekistan. The presence of the US Energy Secretary Bill Richardson as the witness there marked the US interest for the pipeline. The Inter-Governmental Agreement on the construction was signed by Georgia, Azerbaijan and Turkey in November 1999 during the Istanbul Meet of the OSCE, whereas the construction formally started in April 2003 and was inaugurated in May 2005. In 2006, Kazakhstan agreed to join the Project. The estimated cost of this Pipeline is $3 billion but it is a part of a larger $12 billion upstream project of developing the Shah Deniz gas fields of Azerbaijan and of constructing the Baku-Tbilisi-Erzurum pipeline to carry gas from this field. At its peak volume, it is expected to carry 1 million barrels of oil per day. Kazakhstan joined the Project in 2006.

This Pipeline-project is promoted by a conglomerate of international oil companies: British Petroleum (30.1%), SOCAR (25%) of Azerbaijan, Unocal, Chevron (8.9%), Conocophilips (2.5%), and Hess Corporation (2.3%) of the USA, StatoilHydro of Norway (8.71%), TPAO (6.53%) of Turkey, ENI/Agip (5%) of Italy, Total (5%) of France, and Itochu (3.4%) and Impex (2.5%) of Japan. The costs are mostly funded by external agencies like the World Bank, the EBRD, and again, a conglomerate of export credit agencies of seven countries and a syndicate of fifteen commercial banks.

The economic benefits of the Project are, to a great extent, expected and projected. During the construction phase, 10,000 short-term jobs were created and operation of the pipeline would require some thousands of long-term employees. Once fully operational, Azerbaijan is expected to get $29 billion annually in oil revenues, for Georgia the expected transit fees are $62.5 million annually, whereas for Turkey $200 millions annually in the initial phase, and an increased annual rate of $290 millions later.

This Project has some unique and significant features:

The 50-meter wide corridor of the Pipeline is termed as a 'virtual state within a state', as it is ruled by the Inter-Governmental Agreement of the participating states. Interestingly, this Agreement allows the international energy companies, involved in the Project, to demand compensation if any legislation (including environmental, social or human rights laws) of these countries interferes with the functioning of the Project[10].

Second, this is the first Pipeline project that is guarded by a special protection force, the 'Caspian Guards' against possible terrorist or any other kind of attack. This force is established under an US initiative and is a coordinated effort among the US Central Command and the Azerbaijan-Georgian and Israeli army.

Third, environmental concerns are closely tied with this Project in more ways than one. BTC has been promoted by Turkey and the US as the most environmentally safe, as it is scheduled to reduce the ever-increasing tanker traffic in the Bosporous straits, through which is already being used by such oil projects like Baku-Supsa, Atyrau-Samara, and the CPC project of Atyrau-Novorossiysk. But this has been a highly politicized debate as Russia, and to a certain extent,

Kazakhstan have raised questions on whether it is genuine concern for environmental safety on part of Ankara or it is a pretext to promote the BTC as it provides an alternative route bypassing the straits and also, whether this decision violates the 1936 Montreaux Convention, allowing free passage for 'innocent shipping' through this international waterway.

The Significance of BTC Pipeline as an Alliance

First, the BTC is promoted as an integral part and the most important pillar of the East-West super highway or an integrated transport network to link Central Asia and the Caucasus with the Middle East and Europe. This Project, along with the US-sponsored East-West Energy Corridors and the EU-sponsored TRACECA Project, tries to provide alternative transport and trade options to the Eurasian states. The success of this Project will help develop some other projects like the Turkey-Greece-Italy gas pipeline and the Turkey-Austria gas pipeline. The Energy Corridor, of which this Project is an integral part, is set to reduce the 'strategic dependence' of the EU on Russian gas. As forecasts for 2020 suggests that EU's dependence on gas import will increase from 40 per cent at present to 70-80 per cent, Russian gas exports to the EU in the same period will increase from 26 per cent to 40-50 per cent[11]. Cornell commented, in this connection, that 'BTC will palpably increase the mutual interdependence between Europe and the South Caucasus by adding a million barrels of oil a day to the European market and the fact that the oil 'is neither Russian nor OPEC in origin' will serve to diversify European energy sources[12].

Second, this Project is a crucial part of the US' energy diplomacy. The Report[13] by the US National Energy Policy Development Group laid stress on securing more energy from diversified foreign sources so as to support the economic growth of the US and to maintain the interdependence of the energy security of America and those of Europe and Japan. This Pipeline is expected to lessen the US dependence on OPEC oil and on the other hand, the importance of the Caspian region as an energy-exporter is bound to increase, as according to the BP Statistical Review of World Energy, the proven oil reserves of the five Caspian littoral states is 216.4 billion barrels, while total estimated gas reserves are estimated at 2819.2 trillion cubic feet.

Third, this Project proves to be beneficial for all the three participating countries: for Turkey, the gains are securing new supply options of oil as well as positioning itself as an important transit state for energy flows from the Caspian to the European market; for Georgia a steady source of oil and also transit fees are guaranteed; and for Azerbaijan new markets in Middle East and Europe ensure 'economic benefits and political capital', to quote President Ibrahim Aliyev. This Project also provides these countries with energy interdependence, as Georgia and Turkey get Azerbaijani oil. In this interdependence scenario, Israel is the new entrant. Israel is totally dependent on energy imports, as it does not possess significant energy reserves. Turkey and Azerbaijan have emerged as its new sources for energy supplies in the 1990's, apart from its traditional sources like Russia and Egypt. The prospects of getting oil from the BTC Project (as Ceyhan is only 600 km away from Israeli territory) and the pro-US policies of all the four countries are conducive to develop this alliance[14].

Fourth, the exclusion of Iran from this Project is another notable feature. US sanctions on Iran under the ILSA; the unwillingness of the US administration to make any project of its backing vulnerable to possible Iranian maneuverings as any project through Iran has to go through the Persian Gulf and the Strait of Hormuz, one of the world's most important energy chokepoint, and to deny Iran any advantage of providing the Caspian states with an alternative route to the South – all these factors played a crucial role in this move. Peuch commented that 'the real reason behind the US policy towards Tehran is perhaps that the White House is reluctant to see Iran turn into a regional power which could pose a potential military threat to Israel and compete with Turkey in the Middle Eastern oil market'[15].

Fifth, the most significant feature is that this Pipeline represents the Multiple Export Pipeline concept of the US government, or the so-called 'anti-monopoly' concept, meaning not to allow Russia to have an unilateral advantage over the transport of energy resources of the region to the external market, thereby gaining a geo-economic as well as geo-political clout over both the producing states in the region and over the global market.[16].So, it is notable, to quote Svante Cornell that the BTC Pipeline 'is clearly the most strategic project that America has supported outside the security sector in the former Soviet space'[17]. Oktav also commented that Baku-Ceyhan project 'is essentially, from Washington's perspective, a matter of geo-strategic and political significance rather than an economic one'[18]. Stanislav Zhiznin stated that in the 1998 Ankara Summit, the 'BTC pipeline was regarded as a strategic pipeline and political factors played a leading role in the declaration'[19]. The emphasis on the strategic aspect of the BTC project points to another angle of these energy-alliances – there is much more than only economics involved in the formation and workings of them.

The SCO Energy Club

The third such alliance may be the proposed Energy Club under the aegis of the SCO. The proposal was first mooted in the 2006 Shanghai Summit by the Russian President Vladimir Putin to coordinate energy policies of the member-states and to increase energy cooperation among them. And the proposal was endorsed in the Prime Ministerial Summit of the SCO in Tajikistan in late-2006. Before the 2007 SCO Summit in Bishkek, Kazakhstan presented a plan for an Asian Energy Strategy. It was followed by the formal signing of the SCO Energy Charter, at the August 2007 Bishkek Summit, to address energy cooperation among the members.

This initiative is a natural corollary to such developments and trends like the eastern vector of Russia's foreign as well as energy policy; the growing energy demand of the Chinese economy (as in 2005 the need for oil doubled from 3 million barrels per day to 6 million barrels per day and China became the second largest net importer of energy after the US, and as the International Energy Agency suggested that by 2030 the volume of imported crude for China would reach more than 80 per cent of its total energy requirements); the need for China to get steady and secure energy supplies from sources that are so close to its territory; whereas for Central Asian states the advantage is of reaching the growing Chinese market.

For China, there are various imperatives for building up such an alliance – China's search for alternative energy sources, apart from the traditional ones like Saudi Arabia, Iran, Angola, Oman, Yemen, Sudan etc. and the need to avoid single-supplier dependence as in 2006 China imported nearly 46 per cent of its oil requirements from the Middle-East. The political volatility and instability in the Middle East during and after the US-led Operation Iraqi Freedom and the need to reduce the dependence on the US naval protection of critical maritime routes to import energy are other pressing needs for China to opt for energy supplies from Eurasia. As Vitaly Kozyrev[20] noted that 'the energy potential of China's northern "backyard"(meaning Russia and Central Asia) provides it with additional options to advance its energy security interests'. It also enables China to further its geopolitical influence in Central Asia, considered as a 'geoeconomic extension' of its territory. In other words, China's growing relations with the energy-producing states of Central Asia 'reflects its perceived "energy vulnerabilities" and a desire to ensure energy security by diversifying supply away from Middle Eastern sources'[21]. And this strategy is in perfect harmony with its so-called 'Grand West Development' programme. To Russia, China is an integral part of its Asian energy market and the 'Chinese alternative' approach provides Russia with a better bargaining advantage against other buyers like the EU and Japan. There are a number of agreements between Russian companies like Gazprom, Rosneft and Transneft and CNPC on the development of energy cooperation between these two states. Significantly, the 2006 Sino-Russian Joint Declaration, signed during Putin's visit to China, spelt out the essential points of Sino-Russian energy cooperation – this cooperation was considered as an important part of their strategic partnership, but at the same time it allowed their respective rights to diversify markets and sources of energy supply as both the states adopted 'a pluralistic strategy' in their energy relations.[22] This mutual recognition of pursuing respective interests is vital for the growth of the SCO Energy Club, as unlike the other alliances discussed here, this alliance accommodates two powers in the region – one, the traditional and the other, growing.

There are a whole lot of proposed pipeline projects among the SCO members, like the Kovykta gas pipeline project from Irkutsk to North-East China and the Altai gas pipeline project from West Siberia to Xinjiang and from there to Shanghai. There are other proposed trans-Central Asian gas pipeline projects: Turkmenistan-Uzbekistan-Kazakhstan-China; Uzbek-Chinese gas pipeline deal of 2007 to build a 530 km pipeline, with an estimated capacity of 30 bcm annually; and the Almaty-Urumqui project. China is also helping the reconstruction of the Uzbekistan-Kazakhstan gas pipeline.

But the two most important pipelines, in this context, are: first, the Atasu-Alashankou oil pipeline between Kazakhstan and China with the current capacity of 200,000 barrels a day. This programme is a part of the 3000 km long Kazakh-China Transnational Pipeline network, involving Russia and other Central Asian states as well. The second one is the Angarsk-Nakhodka oil pipeline, which is now renamed as the East Siberia-Pacific Ocean line. This Project is to carry oil in two stretches – one from Taishet to Skovorodino and then to Daquing in China, and second branch from Skovorodino to the Russian port of Nakhodka to transport oil to Japan. The fact that half the oil pumped through the Atasu-Alashankou line would come from Russia points to a closer China-Russia-Kazakhstan energy cooperation, 'the nightmare scenario' for the US This Project also poses major strategic gains for China as it is for the first time that China has secured 'a source of imported energy not vulnerable to US aircraft carrier battle groups, as is the case with present oil deliveries from the Persian Gulf and Sudan'[23]. On the other hand, the Angarsk-Nakhodka line shows Russia's balancing of China – it does not afford to lose the Chinese market, as Russia is the fifth largest energy exporter to China and also it does not afford to let China have an economic advantage as a monopolist consumer of energy resources of Siberia.

Kazakhstan has emerged as a growing power in this alliance in a number of ways. It acquired an indispensable place in both Russian and Chinese energy strategy by allowing Russian oil to flow through its pipeline to China. It also acts as a transit state for Turkmenistan and Uzbekistan to reach Chinese energy market. Also it wants to establish a Russo-Kazakh oil cartel to coordinate exports to Asian and European markets. Interestingly, while China is not averse to the idea of such a cartel as that would be conducive to Chinese strategy to safeguard half of its oil imports from the 'strategic northern rear', but it is apprehensive of a Russian-led Gas OPEC, as suggested by Gazprom. While President Putin had to downplay the idea of a formal gas cartel, Vladimir Milov, former Russian Energy Minister, termed the prospect of such a cartel as unrealistic, to allay Chinese apprehensions[24].

The concept of an evolving Energy Club provides SCO with another dimension, apart from its present status as a security cum economic cooperation organization in the region. Notably, the nature of the member-states of the SCO presents a geo-economic combination of energy producers like Russia, Kazakhstan and Uzbekistan with energy consumers like China, whereas Tajikistan and Kyrgyzstan are both producers of hydro-electricity and energy markets as well. The possible inclusion of observer countries like Iran, India and Pakistan will help widen this concept of Energy Club under SCO format. And, if the SCO Energy Club can be re-structured and re-organized in such a way, it has the potentials of becoming a formidable energy-alliance in Eurasia.

Conclusion

Energy Pipelines exhibit an interesting compromise formula of geo-politics and geo-economics. This is evident in the choice of routes, of participants in the projects and more so, in the denial of participation of a state or a group of states in a particular project. We may refer to such Projects in this regard – the North European Gas Project or the Nord Stream Project (to bring gas from Russia to Britain, Germany, France and Netherlands) which bypasses Belarus, Poland and the Baltic Republics to lessen Russia's dependence on non-Russian Baltic ports and other transit states, and the EU's Nabucco project to carry gas from Turkey to Austria via Bulgaria, Romania and Hungary that bypasses Russia to provide an alternative route for the European market.

Energy Alliances are also a blend of geo-economic and geo-political interests, as are evident from their formation and workings. This is most evident in the BTC Project – this alliance is built up around a single pipeline, unlike the other alliances discussed here. The geo-economics of export potentials of energy and the geo-politics of forging an alliance of a group of states, that follow pro-US orientations in their foreign policies (that both Georgia and Azerbaijan are members of GUAM is no coincidence), through providing them with an alternative pipeline route, the first of its kind in Eurasia to bypass Russian territory, are blended strategically. So the formation of counter-alliances is a natural corollary as Oktav noted that while the BTC 'solidified a strategic alliance among Azerbaijan, Georgia, Turkey and the US, it 'fuelled, in a way, the rapprochement between Russia, Iran and Armenia'.[25]

There are some interesting points in inter-Alliance relations: with the promotion of the Blue Stream line, Russia tries to reduce the economic imperatives to build a new pipeline from the Shah Deniz gas fields in Azerbaijan. Russia also tries to expand the capacity of the CPC line and tie it with the Bourgas-Alexandroupolis line (between Russia-Bulgaria-Greece) under the March 2007 arrangement and provide another option to producers to reach European market. Turkey's efforts to lessen its dependence on Russia are balanced by the success of the Blue Stream that carries gas from Russia to Ankara via a sub-sea pipeline across the Black Sea from Dzubga to Samsun. This pipeline is bound to increase Turkey's dependence on Russian energy, as Russia, at present, supplies 60 per cent of Turkey's gas and 20 per cent of oil requirements. There is another planned project to carry Russian gas to Israel through an extension of the Blue Stream. Also, despite Sino-Russian competition for gaining energy leverage in the region, the SCO Energy Club presents a sort of convergence of interests among them – first, interdependence of Russia, the producer and the transit state, and China, the market and, most important, the provision of an alternate market, apart from those offered by the West, for the Central Asian states

But the most important point is the urge of the energy producing countries to reach out to market that prompts them to be a part of as many pipeline projects as possible, that somewhat blurs geopolitical boundaries of the alliances. As Kazakhstan participates in all the alliances, Uzbekistan joins both Russia and China in energy initiatives, and Azerbaijan's involvement as the main supplier of BTC project does not bar it from continuing energy relations with Russia through the Baku-Novorossiysk oil pipeline. Turkmenistan presents a slightly different case – it is a part of the alliance around Russia, and is not a part of SCO Energy Club, though it is developing bilateral energy relations with China through Turkmen-China gas pipeline project; it is not a part of BTC project but is a part of a bigger project, with possible greater implications for the region – the Trans-Caspian Pipeline to carry gas to Central Europe, bypassing both Iran and Russia.

For some scholars, 'pipeline geopolitics' is not a correct expression to analyze the context where these pipelines operate as 'the reality is not only "geopolitics" but rather economics, which is a complex competitive interaction among effectiveness, possibility and cost'[26] that regulates the environment. This article attempts to show, on the other hand, the complex inter-linkages between geopolitics and geo-economics in determination of energy alliances that are centered round one or multiple energy pipelines. So the ultimate significance lies in the fact that energy pipelines have become the pivot, around which new alliances are being evolved in Eurasia, a region where there have been only security and economic alliances so far. And energy, apart from being the driving force for economic growth, has become a vector in new alliance-building processes in Eurasia.

NOTES AND REFERENCES

1. *Rossiskaya Gazeta*, 16 May 1995.
2. See Martha Brill Olcott, *The Energy Dimension in Russian Global*

Strategy, The James A. Baker III Institute for Public Policy of Rice University, 2004.

3. Annual Address to the Federal Assembly of the Russian Federation, May 2004, www. Kremlin.ru.eng/speeches
4. Sergei Blagov, 'Efforts to Produce Eurasian OPEC Fall Short at CIS Summit' 1 March 2002, www.eurasianet.org
5. Roy Allison, 'Strategic Reassertion in Russia's Central Asia Policy', *International Affairs*, 80(2), March 2004, p. 290.
6. Robert L. Larsson, *Russia's Energy Policy: Security Dimensions and Russia's Reliability as an Energy Supplier,* Report to the Swedish Defence Research Academy, 2006, p. 5.
7. See Andrew Gould, 'Fossil Fuels Expert Round Table: How Will A World Recession Affect Oil and Gas Investment, Supply and Demand?', April 2009, www.chathamhouse.org
8. See A Vatansever, ' Russia's Growing Dependence on Oil and Its Venture into A Stabilisation Fund', March 2005, www.iajs.org
9. Fionna Hill, *Energy Empire: Oil, Gas and Russia's Revival,* London, Foreign Policy Centre, 2004.
10. Peter Symonds, 'Oil Pipeline Completed', 31 May 2005, www.countercurrents.org
11. A.Arbatov-M. Belova-V.Feygin, 'Russian Hydrocarbons and World Markets', *Russia in Global Affairs*, 1, Jan-March 2006.
12. S.Cornell-M.Tsereteli-V.Socor, 'Geostrategic Implications of the Baku-Tbilisi-Ceyhan Pipeline', in SF Starr-S E Cornell, eds, The Baku-Tbilisi-Ceyhan Pipeline: Oil Window to the West, 2005, www.silkroadstudies.org
13. Cited in OZ Oktav, 'American Policies Towards the Caspian Sea and the Baku-Tbilisi-Ceyhan Pipeline' *Perceptions,* Spring 2005.
14. See A. Muurinson, 'Azerbaijan-Turkey-Israel Relations: The Energy Factor', September 2008, www.meriajournal.com/en
15. J.C. Peuch, 'Private and National Interests in the Caspian Region', in B.Gokay, ed, *The Politics of Caspian Oil,* London, Palgrave Publishers, 2001, p. 176.
16. As it is noted by some scholars that the objective of the US is 'to deny a single state, other than the US itself, or coalition of partners not including the US, the capability to set conditions for accessing the energy resources of West and CEA'. See M P Amineh-H Houweling, 'The Geopolitics of Power Projection in US foreign Policy: From Colonization to Globalization', in MP Amineh-H Houweling, eds., *Central Eurasia in Global Politics: Conflict, Security and Development,* Leiden, KB NV, 2005, p. 25.

17. S. Cornell, 'Geostrategic Implications of the Baku-Tbilisi-Ceyhan Pipeline'.
18. OZ Oktav, 'American Policies Towards the Caspian Sea and the Baku-Tbilisi-Ceyhan Pipeline'.
19. S.Zhiznin, 'Fundamentals of Energy Diplomacy', 2003, cited in G.Xuetang, 'The Energy Security in Central Eurasia:the Geopolitical Implications to China's Energy Strategy', *China and Eurasia Forum Quarterly,* 4(4), 2006.
20. V Kozyrev, 'China's Continental Energy Strategy: Russia and Central Asia', in GB Collins-AS Erickson, eds, *China's Energy Strategy The Impact on Beijing's Maritime Policies*, Annapolis, Naval Institute Press, 2008.
21. G. Xuetang, 'The Energy Security in Central Eurasia'.
22. 'Joint Declaration of the Russian Federation and the People's Republic of China', *www.kremlin.ru/en*
23. Both the quotations are from F W Engdahl, 'China lays down gauntlet in energy war', *Asia Times Online,* December 2005.
24. S Boykewich, 'A New OPEC in the Making?', *The Moscow Times*, n.3437, June 2006.
25. O Z Oktav, 'American Policies Towards the Caspian Sea and the Baku-Tbilisi-Ceyhan Pipeline'.
26. M Masumi, 'The Russian Energy Outlook and Its Influence on East Asia', *Acta Slavica Iaponica*, Tomus 25, 2007.

18

Central Asia and Caucasus: New Paradigms

Abdolmajid Eskandari

Disintegration of the former Soviet Union has had varied global impacts in particular on the Central Asian and Caucasus regions. It has created a new environment in which new parameters should be taken into consideration. The Soviet legacy still weighs on the newly established republics but this event has brought about many new changes in different levels. "The main change is the fact that there has been an abrupt shift from a centralized system into an open or so-called the market system".[1] New independent republics have emerged and there is a need for new arrangements. The Central Asian and Caucasus states were for many decades cut off from their historic and natural contacts with countries outside the former block. Gradually those contacts are being re-established. Central Asia and Caucasus region is once again going to serve as a bridge between the east and the west. The stability of the region is important for the establishment of a sustainable development. The transition period has inevitable consequences on political, cultural, social, economic and other aspects of people's life. So, it is natural to observe certain ups and downs in the structure of the new states and it needs time to have a stable structure in place. The issues related to this region are interlinked with each other and each component is a function of other components, though every country in the region has its own specific situation. So, in order to have a true understanding of the situation, it is necessary to have a comprehensive study.

New Changes

Privatization of the economies of new republics is progressing and the region is becoming an attractive market for different countries.[2]

This issue has created certain imbalances in the livelihood of different layers of the society in the region. The West in facing problems with leaders trained in the former system and with structures that still exist. In most of the new republics the administrative elites have not changed but as a matter of fact, the necessities of age will produce them. In the course of time, it seems that a new generation of leaders will emerge out of new structure, which will inevitably emerge.[3] These changes will take place normally but there are efforts to speed up the process by imposing certain changes. Due to the fact that the nature of such changes have no natural roots in the society and are imposed, they can not create a basic change in the society.

The fact is that in many of these countries, there has not been a fundamental change in its real sense in the whole system, but a change mainly at the surface level has taken place as far as the socio-cultural and political aspects are concerned. Change has only provided a historical opportunity for the region to make great steps but it will be a long process and its objectives cannot be materialized instantly.

Shaping a New Identity and a Sense of Belonging

The newly independent republics are shaping their own identities and future and make their direct contact with the international community. It is natural for each country to have its own specific model. Reviewing the course of these models, it seems that each republic has its own way of contact with the world. Some are trying to abandon all the past and old heritages and some others, while moving towards the west, keep an eye on the former identity as well since they think it will be a mistake to distance themselves from the past abruptly. The behaviour of these countries is not similar and is more a function of their geopolitical situation. Restoration of ethnic identity and culture is in the making. There are efforts to re-build language, traditions, and religious and spiritual rituals which will help restore culture, ethnic and national identity and reinforce the sense of belonging as a pillar for national integrity.[4]

Central Asia and Caucasus had been a forgotten region and is now the centre of focus. This has added a new dimension to the issues of the region. There are historical and cultural linkages with neighbouring countries, which can serve as a base for reviving multilateral collaboration. The countries in the region have had cultural interaction and some of these ties are still found in the memories of people.

Ethnic Identity

"The region is a living museum of ancient races and ethnic groups, with a diversity of cultures, languages and religions".[5] The arrangements of these ethnic groups have been within the format of ideological stance of the former Soviet Union and this has created many problems when rearranged within new a framework. The variety of ethnic groups sometimes adds fuel to the crises if not managed properly. Cultural and ethnic identity is not a cloth to be taken away in a day and night, but is has deep roots in the history of the people and this has made the issue more complex. It will take time until the people of each new state with various cultures and ethnical root find a sense of a belonging beyond limited ethnic identity. The formation of this sense is necessary to maintain the integrity of the new independent states. There is a fear that over-emphasis on business competition may endanger respect to ethical values and commercialization creating an imbalance as far as cultural identity and value system are concerned.

New Game

The region is again caught in the new games of great powers. [6] The new players wish to have a control over the course of events. The region wishes to throw away the old skin and the western companies with advanced technology are promoting their presence in the region. It is necessary for the countries in the region not to be entangled in the new game whose disadvantages in a pessimistic view might be the blood and oil. The region has great possibilities for economic development, but it also contains the potential for conflict. One of the great challenges of the twenty-first century will be to ensure that the region becomes "an engine for growth, not for conflict". [7] One way to escape from such problems is to emphasize on regionalism.

Energy

Oil and gas reservoirs and the resulting competition are new realities of the region. Various powers are attempting to have more influence.

In a logical estimation, these gas and oil reservoirs can reach other countries through Iranian territory most economically, but the policy supported by US intends to route it through other uneconomic routes such as BTC whose future is not clear, given the recent conflicts in the region. The plan entitled" East-West Energy Transfer Corridor" has been devised with trans-Caspian pipelines to transfer energy from eastern Caspian to the west of the sea, circle Iran and avoid Russia. It is a policy, which tries to ignore the reality of two important powers of the region that exist.

The region with high reservoir of hydrocarbon reserves is landlocked and therefore the issue of energy transfer will necessarily involve the construction of onshore facilities and pipelines. The term "pipeline diplomacy"[8] has entered the political lexicon of the region. China and India as two important powers of the region with a fast growing economy are potential consumers of the energy in the region.

Iran, the shortest route to the sea for the land-locked Caspian energy and swap arrangement should be considered. Energy transfer on the east-west route is not economic and the present fields cannot meet the supply to make it viable. It also traverses the earthquake-prone zone of the Caspian, and ignores the fact that the habitat of this closed sea will be seriously threatened.[9] In the context of SWAP arrangement, Iran could emerge as a main consumer country in the Caspian region. This arrangement is practiced at present with Turkmenistan. Everything without Iran has been the US attitude so far which in practice has not been efficient and despite that Iran enjoys a constructive relation with the countries of the Central Asia and Caucasus.

Global Economic Crises

After the emergence of global crises, doubts are prevailing about the efficiency of the market economy. This crisis, in the view of some scholars took roots in the imbalance between the loans and real money deposited in banks. Now it has become clear that the western model is not unproblematic. The financial disintegration revealed many deficiencies. Some personalities even go further and believe that these signs are confirming the death of the ideology of unlimited free market.It has become evident that as a result of no real work and over-concentration on service sector, the economic ideas have not met their objectives. As a result, there is a need to pause before subscribing to any prevailing model. Some scholars propose a new Eurasian model whose focus is on regional cooperation as a mechanism to ensure sustainable development.

Challenges

Observing human rights based on world standards in the newly established republics is of great importance and it is sometimes ignored or overemphasized for certain intentions by powers outside the region. In many cases, the violation of human rights is a pretext and used as a mechanism to impose pressure.

A legal statute of the Caspian Sea is still an issue demanding long-standing negotiations and is an issue which emphasizes the multilateral agreement of respective countries. So far, the countries of the region have agreed not to let any forces attack the other neighbouring countries and this is an important step in establishing peace. The problem of drug trafficking is an issue which still demands collective will to overcome. The narcotic passing the region is a threat endangering the health and wealth of people. A large proportion of the opium is still illegally produced in Afghanistan and transferred to the region which is a potential threat imposing heavy prices on the economy of the region.[10]

Widespread of corruption and poverty, street children and similar such phenomenon are the consequences of system changes which sometimes make the people of the region feel a nostalgia for the past centralized system with all its deficiencies. The new financial crises in the west will have good lessons for the countries of the region to take right decisions while thinking about choosing an appropriate economic model.

Cooperation

When it comes to the cooperation between the neighbouring countries, it should be emphasized that one of the mechanisms to solve different problems of the region is regional cooperation. The construction of dams of friendship between Iran and Turkmenistan, "dam of Sangtoodeh 2 (Sangab) in Tajikistan, hydro-electrical power stations, manufacturing cars with the technical help of Iranian engineers in Tajikistan",[11] the mediatory role of Iran in the case of Armenia and Azerbaijan disputes and the case of helping with the settlement of the Tajikistan internal conflict in the past, linking the railway of these countries such as Kazakhstan to the nationwide railway of Iran for the transit of goods, progressing business relations between the private sectors of the countries of the region and academic cooperation are all examples that pragmatic bilateral and multilateral relations are of great significance. Dialogue and cooperation will ensure security and peace. Raising awareness and long-term cultural programmes will prevent from the formation of reactionary and extremist groups. Creating wrong image of the neighbouring countries pave way for the interference of the powers outside the region. So, there is a high need for mutual exchange programme in different areas to show that the fabricated images are not true and the nations in the region are in pursuance of peace and cooperation.

Turkey and Iran as two important neighbours of the region enjoy historical ties with the newly established republics and have found an opportunity to explore new political and economic roles in the region. Turkey shares ethnic and linguistic ties with the Turkic states of the Central Asia.[12] Iran also shares a common language with Tajikistan and common religion with other countries in the region, which can serve as a good base to expand bilateral ties. Iran has followed a pragmatic policy in its ties with Tajikistan, Turkmenistan, Uzbekistan, Kazakhstan, and Kyrgyzstan. Turkey remains active through small businesses and also in the private education sphere.

Imposing Barriers

Seeking to maximize its presence in the region, the US policy has aimed at limiting the cooperation and influence of Iran in the region. So far, in practice many countries of the region have ignored that and adopted their own independent stance for the sake of their national interests and respecting the principle of good neighbourhood. It is necessary for the new republics to reinforce ties with their neighbouring countries as a proven mechanism of sustainable development. Iran tries to neutralize the fabricated obstacles by promoting cooperation and dialogue. Iran views the Caspian as a unified region, the fate of which must lie in the hands of the regional countries. 'The history of the region is tied with Iran during pre-and post Islamic eras. The history of the region in cases such as Silk Road[13] proves that it is possible to establish such routes of cooperates and many problems are common and the key to solve them is cooperation'.[14]

Conclusion

It seems that the ideological competition between the two blocks of the east and the west has changed into an economic competition. Most of the countries of the Caucasus and Central Asia are trying to make the transition to democracy amid different conditions. The new opportunity is a chance for the region to overcome the historical backwardness and utilize the new facilities to promote nation welfare. If the leaders of the region use the situation efficiently, there will be no regret about the collapse of the former system and nostalgia for the past. The basic shift in the economic structure has had different impacts on the countries in the region. Some people feel they have lost and the ruling elites gained from the transition and some borne the transition difficulties in the hope of a thriving state for their new generation. Iran tries to emphasize its cultural and economic connections with the countries in the region and adopt a pragmatic constructive policy.

Central Asia and Caucasus have the opportunity to become a hub for the new transcontinental links that are beginning to grow across Eurasia from east to west and north to south. Much can – and must – be done in each country to address many serious challenges. The countries of the region will not flourish as long as rigid borders divide them, impeding cross-border cooperation and economic integration among themselves and with the rest of the world. This does not mean recreating the centrally planned integration in the sense of the past system, but creating conditions that allow people to connect across borders and help markets work across borders through trade and investment, linked infrastructure, shared water and energy, common environmental and health protection, and a free flow of ideas and experiences.

However, to realize this opportunity, the countries of the Central Asian and Caucasus region will need to cooperate to create conditions that will allow the region to flourish as a peaceful and prosperous area, attract investment and expertise needed to build on its natural and human resource base.

The key to sustainable development of the region is collaboration. In any scenario either in the present or in the future, the geopolitical situation of Iran is undeniable. Transition from a closed political system of the past into the open system of the future is both a difficult job and involves threat for the region. To minimize the threat, education and experience will help. Democracy cannot be imported and it requires people with a belief in it and there is no way to transplant it through imposed changes. If it is to be institutionalized, it has to be learnt by practice and experience. The educational system and in particular the higher education system should educate people and train people for the new conditions and this will institutionalize democracy as a political culture in a long-term period.

NOTES AND REFERENCES

1. http://uk.geocities.com/balihar_sanghera/mtispostcommunismand transition.html
2. http://www.isn-inc.com/news/news.aspx?nid=13&cid=7
3. http://www.reliefweb.int/rw/rwb.nsf/db900SID/KHII-6ZR48L?Open Document, See also Jyotinder Nath Dixit, "Emerging International Security Environment," published in *India and Central Asia,* Editors K. Santhanam, Ramakant Dwivedi, 2004.
4. http://www.eurasianet.org/departments/insight/articles/eav071306b.shtml
5. Seyed Hossein Sifzadeh, "Caucasus: Democratic Development and Identity Crisis," *Amu Darya Journal*, Fall 1999.
6. http://cns.miis.edu/cres/nuriyev.htm
7. Michal W. Cotter, The New Face of Central Asia, (*Caucasian Review of International Affairs*, Vol. 2 (2) Spring, 2008, at http://cria-online.org/3_5.html
8. Nasser Saghafi-Ameri, Said Naqi-Zadeh, "Pipeline Policy Symbol of Strategic Challenges in the Caspian Sea Region", *AMU DARYA*, The Iranian Journal of Central Asian Studies, Fall 1999, Vol. 4, No. 3 Published quarterly by the Center for the Study of Central Asia and the Caucasus.
9. Sudha Mahalingam, "India-Central Asia Energy Cooperation," *India and Central Asia, Advancing the Common Interest*, Editors, K. Santhanam Ramakant Dwivedi, 2004.
10. Nancy Lubin, "Drug Trafficking in Central Asia: A Matter of Survival for some," *Eurasia Insight*, 5/09/01, http://www.eurasianet.org/
11. Tajikistan, www.jamejamonline.ir, 2009.
12. Ruben Safrastyan, "The Concept of Eurasia and Turkey's Regional Strategies", *Global Politician*, 2005 at http://www.globalpoliti cian.com/2761-turkey
13. Eduard Shevardnadze, *Great Silk Route*, Georgian Transport System Publishers, 1999.
14. Iran and the Caucasus International Conference (Abstracts), Iran and the Caucasus Unity and Diversity, June 6-8,2008, AIU, Yerevan, Armenia.

19

Competing Geopolitical Interests and Conflicts in the Caucasus

Ajay Patnaik

With the war between Russia and Georgia in 2008, geopolitics of the Caucasus has moved full circle. Though conflicts in the Caucasus had already started towards the end the Soviet period, the polarised geopolitics of the region accentuated in the late 1990s with the arrival of the US as a major player in the Caucasus/Caspian region. The war between Russia and a US surrogate state in the region was the logical outcome of that polarisation. The post-Soviet geopolitics of the Caucasus regions is influenced by the external context as much as by issues of ethnicity and territorial conflicts. The involvement of the US in the troubled waters of the Caucasus-Caspian region intensified the existing fault lines. While controlling the energy resources of the region remains an important geopolitical objective, the internal conflicts in the region have also created huge opportunity for the US to give shape to its strategy of containment of Russia and encircling Iran.

Energy as a Geopolitical Instrument

The Caspian-Caucasus region is important from the point of view of energy. In the Caucasus, Azerbaijan has enormous oil and gas resources. In Central Asia, three out of five countries have huge hydrocarbon reserve, of which Kazakhstan and Turkmenistan are Caspian states. As a result, the Caspian-Caucasus region has been a theatre for intense American engagement. Taking energy to Europe has been traditionally through Russian pipelines. But the containment strategy that began in the post-Cold War period with the NATO decision to expand to the former Soviet sphere of influence including the Baltic republics of the former USSR could not be effective if Russia controled the supply lines. That is why the US decided to open a new pipeline BTC to the Turkey's Black Sea port of Ceyhan from the Caspian coastal city of Baku in Azerbaijan through Georgia.

Taking energy to the West, by passing Russia, is not only expensive but required shaping the geopolitics of the regions involved. Geographically, these land locked countries share borders with larger markets and countries, which can provide access to the sea. Azerbaijan and Turkmenistan are next to Iran and can use the Gulf ports of Iran, through either pipelines or swap arrangements. Kazakhstan is on the border of Russia and China. Russia already takes away a bulk of Kazakh gas. China has recently built a pipeline to Kazakhstan. The only way some of these countries could be persuaded was to draw them close to the US orbit and away from Russia. Though Central Asia was reluctant except for Uzbekistan for a brief period, Caucasus proved to be more receptive to the US geopolitical moves, given the existing fault lines in the region and Russia's strained relations with some of the states there. Russia's preoccupation in Chechnya was an additional incentive.

The same objective of creating a grouping that promotes American geopolitical objectives was behind the move to form a regional security grouping in 1999 called GUAM (which included Georgia, Ukraine, Azerbaijan and Moldova). Since the BTC pipeline is long and through a difficult terrain, the viability of the route would depend on continuous and growing supply of energy through it. At a time when Russia was aggressively pursuing its energy diplomacy under Putin, the West could protect its own interests in the region by effecting strong control over the ruling establishment. The change of regime in Georgia through the so called "Rose Revolution" has to be understood in this back ground.

The US Containment Strategy

Energy, however, is not the only factor that drives the US and its allies towards the Caucasus and Caspian. The geographical location of this region is near states that the US considers threats to its security as well as global hegemony – Iran and Russia. Containment of Russia from the West and the South has been a major underlining objective since the end of early bonhomie of the Yeltsin period and Iran remains an immediate target for which bases around Caspian and Caucasus would be extremely important.

From the time when Washington under Clinton created a Caspian task force headed by then Deputy Secretary of State, Strobe Talbott, (with representatives from Energy and Commerce Departments, the National Security Council and the CIA) the aim was to marginalise Russia in the region.[1] US policy subsequently veered round to integrate the Caucasian/Central Asian states into the Euro-Atlantic orbit by increasing US involvement including military engagement, promoting regimes and policies that are US-friendly and encourage free market, trade liberalisation and Western investments.[2] According to Stephen Blank, since the days of the Clinton administration, the US National Security Strategy has made the integration of the former Soviet republics into Western economic, political and military institutions and practices a fundamental policy objective. Blank further underlines, "Notwithstanding its rhetoric about win-win outcomes, in practice the growing involvement in the Caspian region is in the highest degree strategic or even geopolitical and aims to enhance US and no other state's influence. It combines all the traditional instruments of power, superior economic potential and military prowess, and a commitment to integrating the area more fully into the West in terms of both defence and economics", he states.[3]

According to M. Bhadrakumar, a strategic specialist in India, "The geopolitics of energy lies at the core of the conflict in the Caucasus. The US suffered a series of major reverses in the past two-year period in the "great game" over Caspian energy. Moscow's success in getting Turkmenistan to commit its entire gas production to Gazprom, Russia's state-controlled energy giant, for export was a stunning blow to the US' energy diplomacy. Moscow has now made a similar offer to Azerbaijan to buy all its gas on highly attractive terms that the Western companies cannot match. Similarly, the US failed to get Kazakhstan to jettison its close ties with Russia, especially the arrangement to route its oil exports primarily through Russian pipelines". "Washington cannot accept a situation where Russia remains Europe's principal energy partner, as that would enable Moscow to build up rapidly the sinews of a broad-based economic and political partnership with major European powers, which are eventually bound to challenge the US' trans-Atlantic leadership", adds Bhadrakumar.[4]

The current Washington strategy, however, according to Engdahl, targets many Eurasian former Soviet republics which per se have no known oil or gas reserves. What they do have, instead, is strategic military or geopolitical significance for the Washington policy of dominating the future of Eurasia. From the location of the countries that are target for various US-sponsored Colour Revolutions the US intentions are unmistakeably clear. To the east of the Caspian Sea, Washington in one degree or another today controls Pakistan, Afghanistan, potentially Kyrgyzstan and Kazakhstan. These serve as a potential US-controlled barrier or buffer zone between China and Russian, Caspian and Iranian energy sources, adds Engdahl.[5]

Coloured Revolutions

The ouster of leadership in three CIS countries in a space of less than two years through what is known as "coloured revolutions" has added a new dimension to the competition for influence in the post-Soviet space, also referred to as the "New Great Game". The involvement of external powers in facilitating regime changes in the former Soviet republics has complicated the situation. Since the US has strong geopolitical interests in the Central Asian as well as the Caspian region and their neighbourhood, its use of democracy plank has to be seen in the context of advancing those goals. Regimes have gained or lost American favour depending on their usefulness in promoting the US strategic interests in the region. Issues of democracy and human rights have been sidelined or ignored in countries that are American allies though gross violations on these scores have been reported.

US-inspired regime changes have prompted other powers, especially Russia, to focus on this region as an arena of geopolitical competition. This has been demonstrated quite amply in the case of Georgia. While Georgia would naturally seek to reintegrate its breakaway territories, the process has been made more difficult by the changes in the geopolitics of the region and its neighbourhood. The regime change in Georgia in 2004 was the first in the CIS to hoist to power a pro-Western and blatantly anti-Russian leadership. Georgia has been the key link for the US to create the alternative BTC pipeline that takes Azerbaijani oil to Turkey avoiding the Russian pipeline system. Georgia is also the leading force behind the US-sponsored regional organisation called GUAM, which includes countries that have either witnessed Georgia like regime change or have problematic relationship with Russia. Georgia has become a forward post to advance the US geopolitical strategy in the Caspian/ Caucasian region.

Russia and its Caucasian Neighbours

The hostility of the pro-US regime in Georgia towards Russia does not augur well for the solution to the conflicts there. While Georgia's relations with Russia deteriorated on the issues of Abkhazia and South Ossetia, Russia has done a Kosovo in Georgia in retaliation by recognising the two break away regions. Given NATO advancement to Russia's borders and Georgia's vigorous attempts to be accepted as a NATO member, there would be no urgency on the part of Russia to solve the crisis and let these two buffer regions of Georgia along Russia's borders become future anti-Russian outposts.

Russia's relation with Azerbaijan has also been problematic, though not as bad as it is with Georgia. As Azerbaijan lost ground in its war with Armenia, it started accusing Russia of taking side and being helpful to Armenia. Since the mid-1990s Azerbaijan's frustration, following from losses in its conflict with Armenia, was reflected in its attitude to Russia. It accused Russia of transferring weapons to Armenia. Even Russian Duma's initiative to invite parliamentarians from Armenia, Azerbaijan and a delegation from Nagorno-Karabakh were considered as an unfriendly act and interference in the internal affairs of Azerbaijan. Russia tried to address Azerbaijan's concerns through some high profile visits like that of the Head of Russian Federal Security Services (Sergei Stepashin), Head of Russia's Federal Border Services (Andrei Nikolaev), Deputy Foreign Minister Albert Chernishev and Russian Federation Council Speaker Vladimir Shumeiko to Azerbaijan during June-July 1995. Agreements were signed on the defence of Russia-Azerbaijan border, and cultural and scientific co-operation. The issue of easing restrictions on the Russia-Azerbaijan border was discussed. Russia also offered drafts of two agreements – "Concerning citizens of one country, permanently residing on the territory of the other country", and, "Concerning the principles of organized resettlement". Even during these high profile visits Azerbaijan's Karabakh-centric approach to the relationship was visible. While agreeing in principle to hand over the Gabbalin military base to Russia, there were expectations from Azerbaijani side that "Russians will start to make concessions on the Karabakh matter and will help Azerbaijan in recovering lands occupied by Armenians".[6]

The US push into the Caspian and its neighbourhood damaged the improving Azerbaijan-Russia relations. Azerbaijan was instrumental to the creation of the BTC pipeline, GUUAM, as well as stationing of American troops, trainers and equipment in the Caspian. Azerbaijan has made no secret of its wish to join the NATO and host US troops and bases. With the US and NATO troops and bases already there in Central Asia, Russia has had natural security worries. There is a growing feeling in the Russian security establishment that "the US is systematically appropriating Russia's geopolitical space".[7] According to the Office of Research, US Department of State, there is not much hope of co-operative security management through a broad partnership between Russia and the US or NATO. In this context, some are of the opinion that Russia's 'changing strategic calculus' is not just a reflection of shifting political current in Moscow or the mindset of the policy-making community there. This rupture is also due to the broader deterioration in Russia-American relationship, for which "US policies and attitudes bear some responsibility".[8]

Iran and the Caucasus

The creation of independent states in the Caspian region brought new challenges and opportunities for Iran, which has historical and cultural ties with the region since ancient times. Its geographical location close to the region has its advantage. It shares Caspian Sea with Kazakhstan and has a long border with Turkmenistan. Oil and gas industry of Iran could take advantage of energy resources in countries like Kazakhstan and Turkmenistan, which can also benefit from shortest access to international markets through Iran's Persian Gulf ports.[9] However, Iran's image as a radical Islamic country and American hostility to the Islamic republic handicapped Iran's advantage as an immediate neighbour located between the Persian Gulf and the Caspian Sea. The US military presence in Afghanistan and Central Asia added to Iran's security worries.[10]

Iran tried without much success through multilateral regional organisations like Economic Co-operation Organisation (ECO) to improve relations with the Muslim-majority states in the CIS. Competition with Turkey frustrated its efforts to economically integrate those new states with Iran. Both formed regional groupings to counter each other's influence. Iran initiated Caspian Sea Council, while Turkey formed the Black Sea Common Market. Another organisation formed in April 1992, Caspian Sea Littoral States Co-operation Organisation (CSLSCO), which includes Iran, Russia, Kazakhstan, Turkmenistan and Azerbaijan (Caspian littoral states), has not made much headway. On the other hand, Iran has achieved relatively better success in its bilateral dealings with post-Soviet Caspian republics.

However, Iran's relation with Azerbaijan deteriorated due to its reluctance to be guided by religious considerations and help Azerbaijan against Armenia. Iran's policy towards the conflict, it seems, has been guided by ethnic considerations. One-third of Iran's population is Azeri and Baku's support for irredentist activities of Azeri nationalists in Iran has angered Tehran. Despite these problems, Iran-Azerbaijan relations were moving in positive direction and till the beginning of 1995 Iran was the leading external economic partner of Azerbaijan. Iran was also a participant in the "contract of the century", that was awarded to an international oil consortium formed to explore Azerbaijan's Caspian oil resources. Iran helped Azerbaijan during a difficult period of its war with Armenia when Tehran negotiated a ceasefire on 21 March 1992, following Armenia's successes in the battlefield. Peace talks were held in Teheran in May 1992, which failed, however, as Armenia captured Shusha and thus expanded its control beyond Karabakh.

Relations between the two took a dramatic downturn when under the US pressure Azerbaijan decided to drop Iran as a partner in the consortium and provide instead more shares to US and Turkish companies. (Exxon was given 5 percent share by transferring Azerbaijan's share and Turkish Petroleum's share was increased from 1.7 to 5 percent). This move confirmed that American moves in the Caspian could only be *zero sum* for Iran. Instantly Iran raised the issue of legality of the Consortium since the delineation of the Caspian Sea was yet unresolved. Reacting to Azerbaijan's decision to keep Iran out of the Consortium, Iran's then foreign minister Ali Akber Velayeti said, "Abrogation of the Iran-Azerbaijan agreement about Iran joining the consortium does not serve the interests of Azerbaijan. Until the question of the legal status of the Caspian Sea has been finally solved, the agreement on the consortium is invalid and cannot be implemented unilaterally".[11]

Differing claims over oil fields have been based on different positions on the division of the Caspian. Threat of force has accompanied such claims. One such occasion was in July 2001, when Iran demonstrated naval force and violated Azerbaijan's air space several times a week to prevent a British Petroleum geological vessel from prospecting at the disputed Alov-Shirag-Araz area of the Caspian Sea. Iran even signed a communication of understanding with Armenia on 5 March 2002, intended as a foundational agreement for bilateral military co-operation. Simultaneously, Tehran declared the intention to implement its own understanding of the demarcation of the Caspian and prospect or prevent others from prospecting Caspian resources accordingly. This was bound to aggravate conflict in the South Caspian, where Iran, Azerbaijan and Turkmenistan have disputed claims.[12]

Iran has been worried about the US using Azerbaijani territory for attack against Iran. The US State Department started pressing in 1999 for removing Section 907 of the Freedom Support Act that prevented sale of weapons to Azerbaijan (and also Armenia). Both Secretary Madeline Albright and her Deputy Strobe Talbott testified before the Congress and argued that this Section prevents American military assistance to regional states and, thus, impede US objectives in the region. Then US Special Advisor and Secretary of State for Caspian Basin Energy Diplomacy, Richard Morningstar, in his testimony to a Senate subcommittee also presented similar arguments.[13] Iran tried to mend fences with Azerbaijan by offering political support for Azerbaijan's claim over Karabakh and in May 2004 defence ministers of both countries signed a non-aggression pact agreeing not to allow a third party to use their territories for an attack against the other.[14] Despite all these efforts, Azerbaijan's military collaboration with the US increased. Baku's willingness to offer the US access to military bases in Azerbaijan prompted Iran to raise the issue of legal aspects of division of the Caspian and increase its military profile there. Iran also initiated bilateral military co-operation with Armenia during Iranian Defence Minister Ali Shamkhani's visit to Yeravan on 5 March 2006, when a memorandum of understanding to that effect was signed between the two countries.[15]

Post-9/11 Geopolitics

Since September 2001, the United States used the fight against international terrorism to legitimise its military presence and force projection in the post-Soviet space. Unsure that the local leadership would toe the US policy and serve its geopolitical interests, sponsored "regime changes" were orchestrated with some success in key states like Georgia, Ukraine and Kyrgyzstan. These developments have augmented the US influence and presence not only in states that witnessed the installation of pro-US regimes, but also in other states in the neighbourhood. States in Caspian have come under intense US pressure to move away from Russia and accept American protection against 'America's enemies' in the region. Countries like Azerbaijan, which for their own reason have been moving closer to the US, have grabbed this opportunity in the hope of settling 'old scores', with regional neighbours. This has facilitated the growth of US political, economic and military influence in the Caspian and the Caucasus regions.

During US Defence Secretary Rumsfeld's visit to Baku in April 2005, an agreement was reached to locate the US "temporarily deployed mobile forces" in Azerbaijan, according to government sources there. In 2005 there were 250-300 US troops on various missions and a few aircrafts, logistic and special operation forces in Azerbaijan. Apart from training the Caspian Guard, a large command of mainly Azerbaijani troops under direct American supervision, the mission of current US troops is to prepare logistical and other facilities for major US military contingent in the future. The Caspian Guard Command, where the US officers hold supervisory positions and some American special operations troops to protect the facility, will cover for surveillance and detection not only in Azerbaijan but also border areas of Iran and Russia (including Chechnya) and the Caspian Sea with its heavy oil traffic.[16]

However, keeping Russia out of the security architecture in the Caspian and Caucasus would weaken the long-term stability of the region. GUAM (after the departure of Uzbekistan) comprises mostly of states that have been embroiled in conflicts and lack the resources to solve these by themselves. Aligning with the NATO would further isolate Russia and could complicate the efforts to find peaceful solutions to intra-and inter-state conflicts in the Caspian/Caucasus region. According to Fiona Hill, Russia perceives itself as a country caught between an expanding NATO on its west and a chaotic world on its south. Azerbaijan and Georgia's proximity to the US means that Russia has lost in the Caucasus its strategic defensive structures against NATO's southern flank in Turkey. The Atlantic Alliance's willingness to use force in the extended European arena has made Russia even more worried and angry about Azerbaijan's and Georgia's intention to join the Alliance. For Russia, southern tier is its most sensitive frontier, and Central Asia and Caucasus are its most important security priority.[17]

Russia is a major world power and has a shared geography, history, ethno-cultural and economic links with these regions. It is impossible to dislodge Russia from its "near abroad". The US moves there would only put pressure on Russia to project its power more forcefully. Since 2002, following US stationing of troops and bases in Central Asia, Moscow has shown a greater willingness to prevent the erosion of Russia's influence in the CIS. Apart from the Collective Security Treaty Organisation (CSTO), which in 2003 decided to have a joint military command in Moscow, a rapid reaction force for Central Asia, a combined air-defence system and a coordinated foreign, security and defence policy. Russia has successfully negotiated for a permanent base in Tajikistan. This base would station Russia's 5,500 servicemen in the 201st Motorised Division, which had been guarding the Tajik-Afghan border. Russian troops and aircraft are also stationed in the newly created air base in Kant in Kyrgyzstan for use by CSTO's Rapid Reaction Force. Russia has acquired for use many strategic military facilities in Kazakhstan such as Sary-Shagan test site, the Engels air base and the Kputsin Yar test site. In June 2004 presidents of the two countries agreed to extend Russia's lease of Baikonur cosmodrome (where 70 percent of Russia's space launches take place) till 2050, to reinforce bilateral military co-operation, including defence purchases, and even joint use of troops in the interest of security of both countries.

Worried about growing naval might of other Caspian states and the future possibility of American naval presence in some form, Russia has increased its military presence in the Caspian which is even stronger than that deployed by the erstwhile USSR. In August 2002 Caspian Sea witnessed the biggest naval exercise since Soviet collapse, involving 60 warships and 10,000 military personnel held.[18] For Iran, building a strong Caspian navy is a strategic priority emanating from increasing American involvement there. The US is training Kazakhstan's and Turkmenistan's coast guards. Azerbaijan has the potential to help project American military and political influence both into Central Asia and West Asia. Iran's sea and land border with Azerbaijan makes it feel even more vulnerable to the US designs and moves. Given Iran's fear of a possible US assault on its country, Azerbaijan's military overtures to the United States has prompted Iran to take countermeasures to secure itself from future aggression. Iran even showed for the first time its willingness to work jointly with Russia in the Caspian, including the creation of a Rapid Reaction Force.[19]

By aggressively moving to these regions of primary security concern to Russia and Iran, the US has converted the Caspian region (which includes states of Central Asia and Caucasus) into an arena of intense geopolitical competition and in the process has shaken the edifice of inter and-intra-regional stability in and around the Caspian.

Conclusion

While going ahead with the strategic preference for certain states as the key to achieving its geopolitical objectives in the Caspian, the US did not take into account the impact such security alliance would have on the ongoing conflicts in the region. American military assistance has pushed some of the beneficiaries to opt for military solutions to the ongoing inter-ethnic and inter-state disputes. Arming both Azerbaijan and Armenia would keep the conflict situation alive in the region, Though the waiver of the Section 907 sanctions of the US Freedom Support Act for Azerbaijan was designed to bolster the latter's maritime power vis-à-vis Iran, the flow of the US arms to both Armenia and Azerbaijan keeps their confidence in a military solution going. Georgia in recent years has looked less bent on seeking political solutions and more on flexing its military muscle based on the new found strength of being America's closest ally in the Caucasus region. Following regime change, Georgia's attempt under a new leadership to take the crisis resolution out of Russia-Georgia-Abkhazia framework while working against Russian interests in tandem with the US in the Caspian/Caucasus has created complications for resolving the conflict. Georgia's attempt to use force from time to time kept the conflict situation simmering. The Russia-Georgia conflict of August 2008 was a result of the latter's eagerness to use force which only turned the "frozen conflict" into an open war but has also made reintegration of Georgia's break away regions virtually impossible.

Without peaceful resolution of the conflicts through mutual dialogue and negotiations, the "frozen conflicts" or "no peace-no war" situations in the Caspian and Caucasus regions do not ensure stability. Though the OSCE is in charge of mediation in the Nagorno-Karabakh and South Ossetian conflicts and the UN that of the Abkhazian conflict, these conflicts are no where nearer to resolution. West's attempt to weaken Russia's influence in the region has not helped. It was Russia that was instrumental in the signing of a lasting cease-fire in South Ossetia (1992) and Nagorno-Karabakh (1994).

However, the US-backed "revolutions" in some CIS states in recent years have facilitated greater Western intervention in the CIS and intensified polarisation of post-Soviet republics. Russia has reasons to feel that this trend of "regime change" by orchestrated protests affects negatively its interests in the post-Soviet space. It may also feel encircled by states whose present regimes are close to the West and aspire for NATO membership. Other states in the Caspian, Caucasus and Central Asian regions will seek to protect their interests by joining either the Russia-led or the US-led military-security groupings. There are dangers that such a polarisation might deepen inter-ethnic, clan/tribal and regional divisions, which could complicate any attempt at conflict resolution.

NOTES AND REFERENCES

1. R. Hrair Dekmejian and Hovan H. Simonian, *Troubled Waters: The Geopolitics of the Caspian Region*, I.B. Tauris, London, 2001, p. 134; S. Neil Macfarlane, "The United States and regionalism in Central Asia", *International Affairs*, Vol. 80, No. 3, May 2004, p. 450.
2. For example, Strobe Talbott's address, "A farewell to Flashman: American Policy in the Caucasus and Central Asia", delivered at Central Asia and Caucasus Institute, John Hopkins School of Advanced International Studies on 21 July 1997, http://www.state.gov/www/regions/nis/970721talbott.html; Testimony to the Congress on 17 March 1999 by Adviser on the CIS to the US Secretary of State, Sestanovich; and, Testimony before the Senate Foreign Relations Committee on 22 July 1997 by Stuart Eizenstat, Under Secretary of State for European Affairs, cited in Bradfort R. Mcguinn and Mohiaddin Mesbahi, "American drive to the Caspian" in Hoosang Amirahmadi (ed.), *The Caspian Region at a Cross Road*, Macmillan, London, 2000, p. 189.
3. Stephen Blank, "The United States and Central Asia", *Journal of International Affairs*, Vol. 56, No. 2, Spring 2003, p. 136.
4. *Front Line*, Vol. 25, Issue 18: Aug. 30-Sep. 12, 2008.

5. F. William Engdahl, "Colour Revolutions, Geopolitics and the Baku Pipeline" *Global Research*, June 25, 2005 http://www.globalresearch.ca/index.php?context=va&aid=518
6. Vladislav Shorokhov, "Energy resources of Azerbaijan: Political stability and regional relations, *Caucasus Regional Studies*, Vol. 1, No. 1, 1996, http://poli.vub.ac.be/publi/crs/
7. *Vremya Novostei*, 3 October 2003, cited in Vitaly Naumkin, "Russian policy towards Kazakhstan", in Robert Levgold (ed.), *Thinking Strategically: The Major Powers, Kazakhstan and the Central Asian nexus*, MIT Press, Cambridge, 2003
8. "Russia tops US in Central Asia", *Opinion Analysis*, Office of Research, Department of State, Washington DC, 31 May 2002, pp. 1–14.
9. Abbas Maleki, "Relations between Iran and Central Asian republics", *Central Asia and Caucasus Review*, Vol. 1, No. 1, 1992.
10. Olga Oliker points to the silence on the part of Iran to Uzbekistan's persecution of Islamic groups and Persian-Speakers as an indication of Iran's shifting focus from ideology to economic opportunities and regional stability. Olga Oliker, "Conflict in Central Asia and South Caucasus: Implications of foreign interests and involvement", in Olga Oliker and Thomas S. Szayna (eds.), *Faultlines of Conflict in Central Asia and the South Caucasus*, Rand, Santa Monica, 2003, pp. 209–212; Shireen Hunter suggests that Iran should come to terms with reality and must reach a *modus vivendi* with the US to achieve its goals in Central Asia. Shireen Hunter, "Iran's pragmatic regional policy", *Journal of International Affairs*, Vol. 56, No. 2, 2003, pp. 146–147.
11. Vladislav Shorokov, "Energy resources of Azerbaijan: Political stability and regional relations, *Caucasus Regional Studies*, Volume 1, Number 1, 1996, http://poli.vub.ac.be/publi/crs.
12. *RFE/RL Newsline*, 6 March 2002; Vladislav Shorokov, *ibid.*; Shannon O' Lear, "Resources and conflict in the Caspian Sea", *Geopolitics*, Vol. 9, No. 1, Spring 2004; Brenda Shaffer, "Iran's international Azerbaijani challenge: Implications for policy in the Caucasus", in Moshe Grammar (ed.), *The Caspian Region: A Re-emerging Region*, Vol. I, Routledge, London and New York, 2004; There were about 20 million Azeris in Iran in 2002. "South Caspian and the Caspian: A view from Baku", summary of SOCAR (Azerbaijani state oil company) first Vice-President's remarks at the School of Advanced International Studies (SAIS) in Washington DC on 22 October 2002.
13. Deputy Secretary Strobe Talbott, "A Farewell to Flashman: American Policy in the Caucasus and Central Asia", Address at John Hopkins School of Advanced International Studies, Baltimore, Maryland, 21 July 1997. http://www/regions/nis/970721 talbott.html; Ambassador Richard

L. Morningstar, Special Advisor to the President and Secretary of State for Caspian Basin Energy Diplomacy during his testimony before the Senate Subcommittee on International Economic Policy, Exports and Trade Promotion, 3 March 1999.

14. *Iran Daily*, 17 May 2005; IRNA, 15 June 2005.
15. "Armenia, Iran sign defense Cooperation", *RFE/RL Newsline*, http://www.hri.org/news/balkans/rferl/2002/02-03-06.rferl.html
16. *STRATFOR*, Strategic Forecasting Inc., 15 April 2005.
17. Fiona Hill, "The Caucasus and Central Asia", *Policy Brief*, No. 80, The Brooking Institution, May 2001.
18. *RFE/RL, Central Asia Report*, 19 January 2004; cited in Roy Allison, "Strategic reassertion in Russia's Central Asian policy," *International Affairs*, 80, 2, 2004; Alec Rasizade, "The great game of Caspian energy: ambitions and realities", *Journal of Southern Europe and the Balkans*, Vol. 7, Number 1, April 2005.
19. Stephen Blank, *Eurasia Daily Monitor*, Vol. 2, Issue 106, 1 June 2005; *IRNA*, 3 May 2005; *RIA NOVOSTI*, 4 May 2005.

20

Central Asia: Challenges of Regional and International Cooperation

Mirzokhid Rakhimov

By accepting differentiations – you will find unity
—Rabindra Nath Tagor

Regional Security Challenges in Central Asia

It is well known that international relations between the end of the 20th and the beginning of the 21st centuries is characterized by uncertainty. The bipolar system has become a thing of the past and that requires revising and reassessing the activity of all international institutes established in the last century. Contributing to this process globalization exerts increasingly profound influence on socioeconomic, military-political and other spheres of life of mankind including the principles of international co-existence. Central Asia faced considerable political, social, cultural changes in the 20th century. With the beginning of the 21st century began a new stage of geopolitical changes and dynamics of international relations in Central Asia. There are many factors, which make Central Asia an important region in the world arena. Among than is firstly, the availability of rich energy resources in Central Asia and the Caspian region, secondly, geopolitical location of Central Asia among such regional powers as Russia, China, India, Iran and the interest shown by the US, the EU and major international actors and thirdly, issue of Afghanistan, can also be regarded as a source of possible threats to neighbouring countries and other countries of the world because of the illegal drug production and trafficking, and terrorism.

All these and other factors have encouraged regional and global players to compete in Central Asia in the post-Cold War era. As a result, post-Soviet Central Asia is important for the geopolitical interests of the major and regional powers – Russia, the United States, China, Iran, India and other countries and major international organizations and institutions – the UN, the EU, OSCE. From a strategic perspective, the Western countries have been attaching an increased importance to Central Asia's central location at the crossroads of Eurasia[1]. Some experts note that this is the return of the Great Game of the 19th century, but with the new players. It is well known that Central Asia historically was at the center of interest of different empires and we could say that the region was more or less at the center of the Great Game at all times.[2] In the post Soviet era the newly independent Central Asian nations are confronting complex threats including international terrorism, religion extremism, illegal drug trafficking, transnational water sharing, transnational crime. Threats in Central Asia are transnational, but national and regional security is interdependent and interconnected.

In recent years among the security challenges trans-boundary water sharing is becoming more important for interstate relation in Central Asia. Historically water and its sharing were important aspects of the agriculture of the region, and significant for economic and political relation in Central Asia. During Soviet times new areas of steppe land for agriculture were assimilated and several irrigation systems were built, including a 900km one in Uzbekistan as main cotton producer of the USSR. In addition to irrigation channels, dozens of water reservoirs and hydro power stations were built, included the Charvaq reservoir (Uzbekistan), Nurek (Tajikistan), Toktogul (Kyrgyzstan) and others. In recent years among all the challenges transnational water sharing issues is becoming the most important for Central Asia nations, first of all for downstream countries – Kazakhstan, Turkmenistan and Uzbekistan. Upstream countries Kyrgyzstan and Tajikistan have attempted to build new huge hydro stations for internal use and export electricity to other countries and make economic profit. The upstream and downstream countries have different positions to this issue. Uzbekistan is requesting international expertise for the new hydro stations Rogun (Tajikistan) and Kambarta (Kyrgyzstan) for their possible effect on water sharing and the ecologic situation in Central Asia. Turkmenistan and Kazakhstan support the construction of the hydro stations. In the spring 2009, the president of World Bank Robert Zelik and Special Representative of EU to Central Asia Pier Morrell also expressed that need to be careful and invite international expertise for the new construction. Pier Morell suggested building smaller size hydro power stations. Meanwhile the government of Kyrgyzstan and Tajikistan expressed their willingness continue building Kambarta and Rogun. The problem with water sharing in Central Asia is that there is no legal framework for the status of regional rivers. It is necessary to find common approaches and acceptance within the framework of the UN and SCO legal framework for the problems. It is necessary to recognize the main regional rivers – Amudarya, Syrdradya and Zerafshan as a transnational and have dialog between Central Asian nations themselves and use international experiences in solving water sharing in different parts of the world, for instance like status of Danube in Europe.

Regional Cooperation in Central Asia: Institutional Framework

It is well known that in the post-Soviet period Central Asian republics have been co-founders of regional organizations including Central Asian Cooperation Organizations (CACO), Eurasian Economic Community (EurAsEC), Commonwealth of Independent (CIS) and Shanghai Cooperation Organization (SCO), but their effectiveness is different.

CACO-EurAsEC: From the beginning of the 1990s the Central Asia states have sought a new model of development and integration. The countries of the region have common social, economic, environmental and political problems and cooperation is necessary to solve these problems. The process of Central Asian inter-state cooperation began in 1994 when the presidents of Kazakhstan and Uzbekistan signed a treaty creating a common economic space between the two countries. Later Kyrgyzstan and Tajikistan joined them, and in 1998 this cooperation was named the Central Asia Economic Forum. In February 2002 the Central Asia Cooperation Organization was officially created at the meeting of the Presidents of Kazakhstan, Kyrgyzstan, Uzbekistan and Tajikistan.

There are many problems in the processes of the Central Asian integration, among which is the prevalence of national interests prevailing over the regional, different customs policies of Central Asian states and lack of information exchange programmes (publications, TV programmes etc). In the last two decades Central Asian republics have stopped considering themselves as political and economic partners. For instance sociological survey in Kazakhstan shows that neighboring regional countries are not among priority economic partners[3]. The same situation is prevalant in all other Central Asia countries. Interviews and sociological surveys conducted among more than 50 experts from Central Asian republics, Russia, and the UK by the author showed the main problems for regional cooperation:

1. Different national interests and economic development. (50%);
2. Rivalry between Uzbekistan and Kazakhstan for leadership (35%);
3. Fear of sub-national structures (30%).[4]

But some experts think that CACO is the first step on the way of development and there are perspectives for future development and cooperation. The majority of specialists (95%) consider the EU and ASEAN as good models for regional integration in Central Asia but with local peculiarities.

In November 2005, at the meeting of leaders of CACO in St.-Petersburg it was decided to include the CACO in Eurasian Economic Community (EurAsEC). EurAsEC was founded in 2000 to establish an economic zone comprising of Russia, Belarus, Kazakhstan, Kyrgyzstan, and Tajikistan. Moldova, Ukraine, and Armenia have an observer status in the group. In the official media the main reason for CACO joining EurAsEC and the creation of EurAsEC was that both organizations had similar purposes and joining would increase effectiveness. In January 2006 – Uzbekistan became the sixth member of the Eurasian Economic Community (EurAsEC) at a summit in St. Petersburg, but in October 2008 Uzbekistan ended its membership. Main reason is probably the attempt of other member countries to built new hydro energy stations in Central Asia, it's possible negative effect on the ecology, and most important for agriculture and downstream countries, including Uzbekistan.

CIS: Former Soviet republics also became founding members of the Commonwealth of Independent (CIS) States during the meeting held in Alma-Ata on 21 December 1991. Representatives of the CIS member states meet regularly to discuss economic, military, political and social issues of common interest. More than 2,000 agreements on various aspects of intra-CIS relations have been signed, but most of these agreements exist only on paper. But its lack of a clear purpose, and different perceptions on the part of its members, all have called into question the future viability of the CIS as a supranational entity.

SCO: In 1996 the presidents of Russia, China, Kazakhstan, Kyrgyzstan and Tajikistan established the "Shanghai Five" in order to resolve border disputes and to reduce the armed forces along their borders. The process started in 1996 and at a meeting in Shanghai on 15 June 2001 these countries founded the Shanghai Cooperation Organization (SCO) and Uzbekistan also joined the organization. During the meeting, the presidents signed a declaration establishing the SCO and the "Shanghai Convention to combat terrorism, separatism, and extremism". It is clear that SCO is mainly supported by China but for Central Asian countries, the interest in the organization is to build an alliance with Russia and China and other countries in the struggle against militant Islamists, and to maintain stability in Central Asia. At a summit in St-Petersburg in June 2002, SCO leaders decided to create a secretariat in Beijing. During the SCO summit in Tashkent in June 2004 a counter-terrorist center was officially opened in Tashkent. Expansion of the SCO's activities in economic and other spheres was declared. According to the Russian president, the main results of the Tashkent summit were the creation of an acting instrument for holding policy in Central and South Asia.[5] India, Iran, Mongolia and Pakistan received observer status at SCO. However, there are some problems in the SCO. A majority of the projects are sponsored by Chinese investment but Russia and Kazakhstan also have investment potential and could more actively participate in the SCO. It is necessary to adopt regulation of new members and develop multilateral cooperation with different regional and international organizations including UN, NATO, OSCE and others. In future, the SCO should widen its activities in economy, transport, humanitarian and other fields.

Regional cooperation in Central Asia in general has very weak institutional framework. But prospects of economic and political cooperation in Central Asia, and the speed and scale of these processes will depend on the readiness of nations to work together in regional projects, to carry out proper reforms and introduce the forms and methods of economic regulation adopted universally, as well as on the political will of the government of the member states.

Regional and International Transport Communication Strategies

Central Asia is a land-locked region and Uzbekistan, the region's most densely populated country, is one of two double land-locked countries in the world. And geographical remoteness of Central Asia from the main seaports is a serious disadvantage to the region's participation in the world trade. Central Asia republics inherited common post-Soviet system of rail, road transport communications, gas and oil pipelines. And this communication went through the European part of former Soviet Union. But in the post-Soviet era the Central Asia republics considered development of alternative regional transport communications as important for national and regional strategy and as a result it developed new transport communication to the East and South and linked it with the transport systems of neighboring countries China, Iran, Pakistan and Turkey. In particular, in May 1996 a rail link Tejen – Serakhs – Meshkhed – Bandar – Abbas was completed, which connected the railway systems of Central Asia with Iranian ports on the Persian Gulf, and passed through Turkey to Europe. Reconstruction of the Tashkent-Andizhan-Osh-Sarytash-Irkeshtam motor highway would create conditions for intensive economic exchange between the Central Asian countries and China and would promote the intensification of regional economic cooperation not only in Central Asia, but also within the framework of the SCO and Organization of Economic Cooperation.

There is also growing interest from Central Asia and outside to alternative pipelines. In December 2005 the construction of a 988 km Kazakhstan – China oil pipeline from Atasu in West Kazakhstan to the Chinese bonder town Alashankou was completed and it enable Kazakhstan to export up to 10 million barrels of oil a year.[6] In May 2006, the Indian government also officially approved its participation in the $5 billion US Turkmenistan-Afghanistan-Pakistan-India (TAPI) gas pipeline project. In the perspective Central Asian countries could also participate at different international energy projects, including EU NABUCCO project.

Stabilization and positive changes in Afghanistan grant new opportunities for Central Asian cooperation. Improvement of transport connection between Central Asia and Afghanistan would be a significant contribution toward future economic recovery and political stabilization of Afghanistan and also development of transport communications of Central Asia countries with South and East Asia.

In June 2003 Uzbekistan, Iran and Afghanistan signed agreement "On creation International Trans-Afghan corridor" and the agreement comprises the construction of a 2400 km highway road (possibly railway network in future) through Termez-Maza-e-Sharif-Heart to Iranian seaports Bandar-e Abbas and Chorbakhor. This road will allow Central Asian countries to reach the Persian Gulf and increase interlinks of Central Asia, Russia (West Siberia), and China (Hinjiang) with the Middle East, Southwest Asia and Europe. Another trans Afghan project is a transport corridor – Uzbekistan-Afghanistan and Pakistan is important for Central Asian countries trade though the Arabian Sea to the doors of South, Southwest Asia and Middle East. This will reduce the distance by 1200-1400 km.[7] The transport road project Murghab-Kulma will connect Tajikistan with the Karakorum highway in China and Pakistan, and allow Central Asian nations access to the Pakistani ports of Karachi and Gwadar. These transport projects will develop alternative transport projects and will make positive changes in the geo-strategic and geo-economic situation in Central Asia.

From 2001 there has been growing economic relations between the Central Asian republics and Afghanistan. Tajikistan and Uzbekistan are exporting electro energy to Afghanistan and also Uzbekistan built 11 new bridges in the country. Kazakhstan is exporting wheat and other goods.

The dynamics of growing Uzbek-Afghan trade can be seen in the table.[8]

In mill. USD

	2001	*2002*	*2003*	*2004*	*2005*	*2006*	*2007*	*2008*
Trade	11.4	61.7	89.9	130.4	171.5	163.7	332.4	533.1
Export from Uzb. to Afgh.	11.1	61.5	89.3	127.7	170.4	161.7	331.4	530.5
Import from Afgh to Uzb.	0.3	0.2	0.6	2.7	1.1	2.0	1.0	2.6

For more participation of Central Asia in the international communication projects it is necessary to involve investments from a wider group of investors with a view to reconstruction, modernization, and upgrading of the automobile roads and railways; to develop cooperation in the sphere of customs convention, to harmonize national legislations of the countries of region in the field of transport and customs houses. A well-developed regional transport system in

Central Asia will lead to greater potential for regional prosperity and good opportunity to develop regional and international transport network and substantial trade relations and facilitate foreign investment. The perspective planning for transport development will depend on the degree of optimum correlation of global, regional, inter-regional and national interests in realization of the projects.

Perspectives of Broader Multilateral Partnership

Russia, US and China declared their support for peace and stability in Central Asia and supported regional cooperation. These declarations were welcomed in the Central Asian countries. But, there are some contradictions between them. Russia traditionally views the Central Asia states as being within its sphere of influence and does not wish to see either China or US become deeply involved there; China expresses understanding of Russia's strong role in the region and at the same time considers US military presence in the region as endangering the safety of its own north-west region.

In the post-Soviet period there is also the growing role of other actors in Central Asia, including EU, which does not have a unified strategy toward the region and the economic and political interests of the large European states in which also differ and diverge. This is both due to the internal peculiarities of European politics and the general geopolitical situation, including the relations of the EU with the US and Russia. At the same time, the events of 2000 and 2001 show that the dominant theme in the relations between Central Asia and Europe (and more generally, the West) has become the problem of regional security as well as the struggle against terrorism and drug trade. One of the reasons is that the EU countries are the main consumers of illegal Afghan drug production.

At the EU Presidency programme 2007 Germany initiated new programme on increasing political partnership with Central Asia. It was accepted that the new EU strategy toward Central Asia in 2007-2013 was welcomed by Central Asian nations. There is also growing EU interest towards Central Asia in the energy partnership At the same time Central Asian nations also try to find alternative corridors for export of the energy resources and this could be one of the important aspects of mutual cooperation in coming years.

It well known that in the Afghanistan policy US had some institutional and geopolitical changes. US moved the Central and South Asia countries under a new bureau in the State Department.

Historically these regions had very close relations, but the present idea linking Central and South Asian regions could be successful if Afghanistan succeeded in transforming itself into a viable democratic state with a market economy.[9] From the commitments of the international community and multilateral institutions, it is clear that a massive effort to rebuild Afghanistan's transport network and economy is underway. In the Central and South Asian cooperation the role of India is very important. Slowly, but gradually India-Central Asia economic relations is growing. India's major initiative in the region has been building the North-South trade corridor. This is being built in cooperation with Russia and other countries. Although this initiative will speed the flow of goods, especially energy, from Central Asia to India via Iran, the shortest route from India to the region is through Pakistan. India also expressed interest on the energy issues. In April 2006, Indian Prime Minister visited Tashkent and seven agreements including three agreements in energy and mineral sectors were signed between India and Uzbekistan.[10] India has a positive perception of the potential of the SCO as an instrument for promoting regional economic integration, trade and ensuring energy security.[11]

It should be noted that improvements in India-Pakistan relations would be a crucial input linking South and Central Asia relations. Also India is diversifying its cooperation with Russia, US, Iran on Afghanistan and Central Asian issues. From a Central Asian perspectives it is best for US, Russia, China, the EU and international institutions to have strong dialog and cooperation in Central Asia based on bilateral and multilateral relations. Central Asian nations has strong bilateral relations with these major powers and the republics are part of different organizations – OCS, SCO, NATO (PfP programme), where interests is different. The problem of reconstruction and peace in Afghanistan is critical for US, Russia, China, the EU and also for neighboring countries including Central Asian nations. In 2008 at the summit of NATO in Bucharest Uzbekistan suggested to rebuild "6+2" platform on Afghanistan and with the addition of the NATO transform it to "6+3". Probably it is also necessary to include the EU, CSTO, SCO and India, whose economy is growing and expanding support to Afghanistan. Only in boarder cooperation and with active participation of Central Asian nations can the problem in Afghanistan be resolved. Secure and economically stable Afghanistan is very important for the future of Central Asia.

Cooperation of regional and international organizations, including the EU, NATO and partnership with Central Asia countries is important for promotion the stability and security of the Central Asia nations and to assist in their pursuit of sustainable economic development and poverty reduction. At the same time stabilization and restoration of the economy of Afghanistan is one of the key objectives. Presently NATO is leading ISAF, but the situation in Afghanistan is very complicated. The new US administration is planning to enlarge international presence in Afghanistan and these could be achieved successfully only with active participation of Central Asian nations and strong international dialog.

Conclusions

To sum up, stability and security in Central Asia is affected by the direction of integration, patterns of regional cooperation, and institution building. It is important that the Central Asia nations build strong bilateral and multilateral relations with international and regional organizations and move towards economic reform in order to attract foreign aid and direct investment. Central Asian republics – Kazakhstan, Kyrgyzstan, Tajikistan, Turkmenistan and Uzbekistan, as well as China, Iran. Pakistan, India are involved in the process of organization and harmonization of the transport arteries and communications connecting Europe and Asia, the West and the East, and providing the access to midland states, including Uzbekistan, to the World Ocean. The perspective planning for transport development will depend on the degree of optimum correlation of global, regional, inter-regional and national interests in realization of the projects. There are many problems among different actors in Central Asia and Afghanistan, including NATO, EU, OSCE and other international organizations, because they have different approaches and understanding of the situation. For greater cooperation between the Central Asia nations, major powers, international and regional organizations on Central Asian issues the following could be suggested:

1. It is necessary to develop an institutional framework of regional cooperation in Central Asia and concentrated on regional projects, including trans-boundary water sharing and other issues

2. To promote regional cooperation and integration in such way that it become a tool for better economic and trade relation and promotes stability and economic development.
3. Pakistan, India, Iran, and other neighboring countries could use different mechanisms for the partnership on Afghanistan
4. International organizations and major powers have to channel funds and external support to Afghanistan to help restore its economy and try using also technological and reconstruction potential of Central Asia republics and other neighboring countries;
5. The EU, NATO, OSCE require strong relations and joint projects on Central Asia and Afghanistan with CIS, SCO, Eurasian Economic Community, OCST;
6. It is necessary to have winder partnership between Central Asia and India on bilateral and multilateral bases;
7. International community should increase partnership with Central Asia nations in solving a wind range of security problems, including ecological one.

Challenges of the 21st century require broader partnership and cooperation. Future prospects of multilateral regional and international cooperation in Central Asia will depend on correlation of national, regional and global interests. It is necessary first of all to have strong dialogue between Central Asian republics itself. All Central Asian geopolitical, political, economic, cultural and security challenges are connected and solution should come jointly. Future regional cooperation, strong international partnership would promote more stability, economic reforms and democratization to the region and beyond.

NOTES AND REFERENCES

1. See, for example, Akiner, Sh. (ed) 2004. *The Caspian: politics, energy and security.* Central Asian forum series. SOAS, University of London. Routledge Curzon publisher. p. 405; Amineh, M.P., Houweling H. 2005. *Central Eurasia In Global Politics: Conflict, Security, And Development* (International Studies in Sociology and Social Anthropology, V. 92). Koninklijke Brill NV, Leiden, The Netherlands; Laumulin, M.T. 2005 *Sentralnaya Aziya v zarubejnoy politologii i mirovoy geopolitike. Volume 1.* Almaty: Institute of Strategic Studies; Allison R., Jonson L. (eds.),

2001 *"Central Asian security: internal and external dynamics" Central Asia security: the new international context.* Royal Institute of International affairs, London, UK; Starr, Frederick "Making Eurasia Stable", *Foreign Affairs*, vol. 75, no. 1(96).

2. For more details on Great Game of 19 century see: Martin Ewans (eds). *Britain and Russia in Central Asia 1880-1907.* Volume I-VI. Routledge, London and New York. 2008.
3. G.T. Telebaev. *Otnosheniya mejdu tyurko-musulmanskimi gosudarstvami v osenke kazahstansev.* (Relations between turk-musilmans in the avalucation of Kazakhts) \\Materiali mejdunarodnoy nauchno-teoriticheskoy konferensii "Istoricheskiy opit modernizasii tyurko-musulmanskih narodov SSSR". Aktober, Kazakhstan. 2008. S.256–257.
4. Rakhimov M, *Security issues and regional cooperation* in *Central Eurasia, Democratization and human rights*. Tashkent Uzbekistan. 2006 Number 4. pp. 64–65.
5. Interview of Vladimir Putin. http.www.Kremlin.Ru, ITAR-TASS, 17.06.2004.
6. *"Kazakhstanskaya neft-vostochniy vector",* Kazakhstanskaya Pravda, 18 April 2005.
7. Aftab Kazi, "*Transit-roue politics and Central Asia`s Indus Basin Corridor*", 4 July 2001//http://www.cacianalist.org
8. Courses. Statistic Committee of Uzbekistan. Tashkent 2008.
9. S. Frederick Starr, "A Partnership for Central Asia", *Foreign Affairs*, 84, 4 (July/August, 2005); Gulshan Sachdeva, "Rejuvenating Economic Relations between South Asia and Central Asia" *Shygys* (Almaty) 2 (2004).
10. Ramakant Dwivedi, *An Appraisal of the Indian Prime Minister's Visit to Uzbekistan* www.idsa.in/publications/stratcomments/Ramakant Dwivedi280406.htm> (July 15 2006).
11. Gulshan Sachdeva. "India's Attitude towards China's Growing Influence in Central Asia." *The China and Eurasia Forum Quarterly*. Vol. 4. No. 3, 2008, 32.

21

Problems of Regional Organisations in Countering Non-traditional Threats in Central Asian Countries and its Neighbours

Oybek N. Makhmudov

In order to effectively stabilize the region, the Central Asian countries joined several regional organisations like the OSCE, Collective Security Treaty Organisation, and Shanghai Cooperation Organisation. However these organisations could not block the penetrations of the region by religious militants groups from Afghanistan to South Kyrgyzstan and Tajikistan from 1999 to the present.Therefore the regional security structures failed to adequately prevent the threats of well organised militant groups with their tactics of guerrilla warfare. Moreover the militants effectively used the rugged, sparsely populated terrain to mask their movement into and out of Kyrgyzstan.The militants also successfully used the cover of darkness to move, while the Kyrgyz units deployed were powerless to respond in the absence of any fighting capabilities. In this context, the regional military forces proved unable to operatively manage the crisis.

In addition the regional security organisations operating in the region, have limited capacities, experiences and no unified strategies. The soldiers are not adequately trained or properly equipped to conduct effective combat operations. In response to these setbacks a battalion was speedily put together in Koi-Tash in September 1999 consisting of conscripts, volunteers, and veterans of the Soviet Afghans war. [1] It was rushed into the field without night fighting capacities, inferior air support, lack of communication, no body armour, no proper maps of the area, or essential rations, and with helmets incapable of withstanding a round from a Kalashnikov assault rifle.[2] The militants were armed with light weapons and night vision goggles, that prepared them for longer armed struggle.[3] All these were the result of the following problems:

- Absence of regional security system in Central Asia
- Lack of operational systems in regional military forces and failure at the planning and implementations stages to properly coordinate the deployment and operational activities of the armed forces between the various power ministries
- Domination of political ambitions in admitting strategies
- Absence of well-trained, mobile combat ready soldiers capable of effectively conducting operations in mountains terrain, such as in Tajikistan and Kyrgyzstan
- Lack of basic protective kit for soldiers deployed to carry out combat
- Lack of equipment and communication systems in the field
- Lack of information that made finding, fixing, targeting and then effectively engaging enemy targeting forces effective difficult. The process remains too slow and cumbersome to provide timely targeting to either air or ground assets
- Support from air assets was sporadic, inaccurate and unproductive, degrading the morale of ground forces
- Limited transnational military cooperation rendering ineffectual any efforts at pursuing fleeing insurgents difficult
- Failure to achieve a synergy of the armed forces deployed in the Batken region or gain full spectrum dominance over the militants
- Absence of common approaches in countering non-traditional security threats in region
- The large number of regional security organisations engaged in the same counter terrorist activities that only immobilises the capability to deal with terrorists in the region.

The activities of the Shanghai Cooperation Organisation and the CSTO are mostly directed to preventing threats on macro levels, in terms of conventional and regional armed conflicts. The CSTO countries cover roughly 70 per cent of the territory of the former Soviet Union.For the past three years, Russia has been proposing the desirability of limited cooperation between the CSTO and NATO in countering drug trafficking originating in Afghanistan. But NATO, at US biding, has been stalling. It has been NATO's consistent policy not to recognise the CSTO as a regional organisation, therefore it deals with the CSTO member countries on a bilateral basis. China appreciates that the contradictions and struggles between Russia and Western powers in the post cold war years are at a defining moment. Writing in the *Peoples Daily* recently, Wang Baofu, deputy director of the Institute of Strategic Studies affiliated to the elite Chinese National Defence University, said, this move of Russia indicated firstly its reluctances to make any additional unilateral compromises on the major issues of national security, secondly, its unwillingness to sit idle and remain indifferent as the US is attempting to deploy an anti-missile system in Eastern Europe in a bid to seriously affect the Russia-US strategic balance.

In this perspective it becomes necessary for the SCO to ponder seriously its relations with Iran. Without doubt, two big questions await the SCO summit; Iran's admission as a full member and the direction that the SCO partnership with Turkmenistan will assume. The double standards followed by external regional organisations in countering terrorism and the lack of the theoretical studies in new types of non-traditional threats, that even today focuses on traditional threats remains a stumbling block. This results in non-traditional actors creating critical security situations in the region that directly affects neighboured countries. In addition the Central Asian region has became a hotbed for the most ferocious religious militants groups, mostly due to geopolitical reasons as it allows neighbouring countries, Russia, China and Iran a chance to interfere.

Anti-terrorist Capabilities in Central Asia

Military reforms have been prioritised within the Central Asian militaries in the context of the growing international security interest in the region. The Antiterrorist Centre (ATC) began its work using the capabilities of the special anti-terrorist units of the law enforcement structures and security organs of the CIS nations. In view of the situation developing in the Central Asian region and the detection of tendencies of the leaders of the terrorist international to direct their attention there, the Central Asian region was a primary area of interest for the ATC. A Central Asian branch of the ATC was set up in Tashkent. Nowadays, as a new balance of power is appearing in Afghanistan, the neighbouring countries continue to believe that they have legitimate and contradictory interests to defend in that country, while the threats generated by the narcobusiness is not fully taken into account in the climate of collaboration.

Unfortunately since the terrorist attacks in 2001 in New York regional security organisations operating in Central Asia accepted the cardinal transformations in countering the new tactics of religious militants. Regional actors have their own interest and each prefer to promote their own regional organization: Russia leads the Collective Security Treaty Organisation, China – the Shanghai Cooperation Organisation, and NATO has Partnership for Peace However, all these regional organisations have their own niche. The United Sates should accept that neither SCO nor CSTO are likely to disappear soon and can be incorporated in the US security strategy in Central Asia. At the same time, for these organisations to be more effective, they should be transparent and non-exclusive. For instance, the US needs to be eventually given an observer status in the SCO.

The Shanghai Cooperation Organization mainly functions for the national interest of regional actors Russia and China. For Russia protection of the strategic south border with Afghanistan is important and for China the vital issue is providing stability for its neighbourhood in south Kyrgyzstan. For effectively countering non-traditional threats in the Central Asian region, the strength of the militants groups should also be taken into consideration. In recent times, religious militants have become a more mobile group, who also have changed their defensive strategy an offensive one. In addition non-traditional actors in the region have used the informational countermeasures against secular authorities.

The Use of New Tactics in the Region by Religious Militants

- Religion is used by the militants as "camouflages" in carrying transnational and geopolitical strategies in Central Asia.
- Militants have increased their mobility and expanded their operational theater. And as a result of widespread exodus from zones of conflicts, and through their contacts with

migrating populations, terrorists have been able to operate more extensively across borders.

Cyber tactics became an effective tool for the religious militants, essentially after the displaying of the encyclopedia of "jihad" in internet space. The main targets of cyber attacks have been directed towards damaging and disabling of the aviation and railways systems. For instance radical Uighur separatists have transformed their activity from China to Europe and hope to expand ideological programmes among Muslims in western countries. The same strategy uses the local Central Asian terrorist organizations that annually conduct councils in Europe and US for discussing incumbents of governments in the region. Also the *Hizbut Tahrir* enhances ideological activities in Central Asia that focuses on interaction both in rural and urban settings. This camouflage activity is mitigating control and attention of the Central Asia states. Since 2004 for seeking power all the radical groups have jointly begun preparations to create Caliphates in Central Asian regions and beyond.

Militants operating in Central Asia are motivated more by religious than political ends. Political terrorists have limited goals, subject in principle to negotiation. Religious terrorists are driven by hate and fanatical motivations. Accordingly, Bruce Hoffman (director Rand Corporation, US), argues that religious terrorists are motivated by morality in what they regard as a total war.[4] Religious militants see themselves not as components of a system worth preserving but as outsiders seeking fundamental change in the existing order.[5] Religious goals are always opposed to political ones. The problem is that political considerations are sometimes essential parts of a religious tradition and could affect the assumed "inability" of religious terror groups to accept restraints.[6] Also contemporary religious militant groups in the Central Asian region follow the tradition of linking themselves to their mainstream parent religions. Significant outside influences, moreover sometime combine with religious precedents and when the combination produces successful results, secular groups in turn may be inspired. "Self martyrdom" has always been a conspicuous feature of religious terrorism.[7]

Religious militants use several geopolitical strategies. Central Asian countries are situated at the center of the vital communication chain from South to North and from East to North, with neighboring regional actors like China, India, Russia and Iran. Various nontraditional actors have plans for disintegrating the Commonwealth Independent States and using the Central Asia region as buffer zones for realizing their long-term purposes. Also these activities of the militant groups are directed towards escalating ethnic conflicts between the secular and radicals within the neighboring countries. In addition the Central Asian region is located in a difficult geopolitical arena. On one side bipolar system (US and Russia), transform to multipolar with traditional and non-traditional actors, with multilevel combination of Islamic states, militant groups, influential Transnational Corporations. According to Mackinder – "Who rules heartland, controls the world".[8] The key to controlling Eurasia, says Brzezinski, is controlling the Central Asian Republics. And the key to controlling the Central Asian republics is Uzbekistan. Thus, it comes as no surprise that Uzbekistan was forcefully mentioned by President George W. Bush in his address to a joint session of Congress, just days after the attacks of September 11, as the very first place that the US military would be deployed.

In addition militant groups essentially with religious orientation are acting as ideologues for illicit youth groups. The Central Asian and South Asian regions are suitable place for foreign militant's organizations. The majority of the population is composed of Muslims (approximately 55 million plus 18 million Muslims from Xinjiang Autonomous Region of China). In addition more than three hundred million Muslims live in the South Asian region. In total this number would be an effectively tool in realizing the ideas of the "great theorist" of Al-Qaeda organization. Besides a majority of the population is composed of youths that are potential candidates for recruitment as "fighters team" of the militants. Also in Kyrgyzstan the *Hizbut Tahrir* is active. Besides in Tajikistan there are several international terrorists groups, including training camps. In Tajikistan there exists threats from emerging nuclear terrorist organizations, who have been provided uranium by international terrorists groups (as Al-Qaeda). The main purpose is in destabilizing the situation in the Central Asian countries by the penetration of radical religious ideas. With this perspective they hope to form "Eastern Turkistan" in the autonomous region of China and "Islamic Caliphate" on Central Asia territories and neighbor regions. [9] In midterm perspectives Caliphate might be the conduit for providing illicit small arms for militants activities. Ignoring these threats would mean escalating the instabilities of the political system of China that would have a direct impact on world economy.

After 2001, in Afghanistan, there has been drastic increase in the poppy cultivation, in refining of opium into heroin, and in trafficking of illicit opiates. Also the drug trade from Afghanistan to Tajikistan and Kyrgyzstan is usually controlled by religious militant groups. The criminality and violence associated with it has had and will continue to have strong interest in destructing legal systems. Therefore the drug trade threatens the very essence of political order in Tajikistan and parts of Kyrgyzstan. The trade in guns in Kyrgyzstan is also a serious threat to the local population. The illicit drug trade and small arms is usually used for financing terrorists operation. In mid term perspective the religious terrorists groups realizes the following strategies: Firstly, the activity of religious terrorists groups under the camouflage of Islam will promote the antagonistic attitude of populations and international community to the tolerant and modern religion of Islam (however adherents to these organization included fighters from various countries of Asia and Europe). The terror methods of religious terrorists groups-as "suicide terrorism" in public places (mosques, hospitals, schools) will be forming "phobias" and fears among population about the tolerant religion of Islam. Also radical ideologies of "Jihad" is directed towards globalizing the Islamic struggle and realizing the theory of "Non-territorial Islamic States" that primarily include regions from Xinjiang Autonomous region of China, Central Asia, Caucasus and Russia. In addition the ongoing conflict in Afghanistan has created a number of training camps for religious guerilla groups in Central Asia, Caucasus and the Balkans.

Besides militant groups are expanding the traffic of small arms inside and outside the region. Weapons worth billions of dollars circulate in Afghanistan and included Kalashnikov rifles, machine guns, grenades, plastics explosives and landmines that have had drastic impact on the security environments in the whole of South, Central Asia and Caucasus regions. The major exporters of small arms to Afghanistan come from Pakistan, Saudi Arabia, Iran, Russia, US. [10]. Unfortunately, these weapons are now used by non-state actors like religious terrorists and separatist movements. According to UNODCCP there is more than 500 million illegally circulated small weapons in the region. These small arms are freely available in the black markets of Afghanistan and Pakistan (Peshawar bazaars). The huge quantities of weapons accelerate the probability of military escalation between ethnic groups in the region. Therefore after

11 September 2001, the G8 countries admitted global partnerships programme against terrorists. Also the UK, France, Germany, Canada, Italy have approved huge arms supplies to Saudi Arabia despite the fact that all parties and political organizations in Saudi Arabia area illegal and thousands of political or religious detainees have been held over the years. Ongoing supply of small arms will promote regional arms race for possible diversion to armed groups, such as radical fundamentalists and terrorists groups. The massive circulation of these arms cerate the possibility for resistance against states troops by these organizations in Central Asia and the Caucasus.

In short term perspective the involvement of NATO in the region, led to deterioration of the security situation. Also the presence of religious terrorist group's based in Afghanistan led to difficulties in the construction of energy projects, for exporting of Central Asian energy resources to Indian Ocean countries. Energy is the main economic attraction factor for the Central Asian region, where estimated resources run as high 46 per cent of the world's gas reserves and 150 billion barrels of oil.[11] Actually the terrorist's organizations directed their activity in energy rich and geopolitical significant states of Central Asia. For instance Kazakhstan has been targeted by the Uighur extremists groups (with 85 % per cent of the regions proven of oil reserves, second in oil production in CIS).

Virtual Warfare – The Third Aspect of Nontraditional Threat in the Region

The virtual warfare is composed of cyberwar, netwar and informational warfare tactics. The destructive potential of cyber warfare is expected to increase exponentially with the progressive computerizations of all systems in business, social services, governance and defense. This factor should be considered while protecting local Central Asian industries (essentially auto, energy, electro, textiles) that usually work on computerized systems, because destroying this industries, would damage the economic and political potentials of the states. Unfortunately anti-terrorist strategies for controlling virtual warfare are still undeveloped and as no priority is accorded to it. Therefore cyber ware creates another critical shift in the character of new terrorist threats in the regions. The idea of the "one man army "is more completely realized in the identity of the well informed hacker than it ever has been through any other technology.

The safest mode of communication for the IMT is through the internet and use of various Islamic "chat houses". Since no one knows who is at either end of the "electronic conversation", no one knows the significance of what is being communicated. Second, the terrorist groups have become so sophisticated in encrypting their messages that even the spoken words do not communicate the real meaning of the conversation. The upside of such a means of communication is that it remains the safest way to correspond with hard-core supporters without the risk of being exposed to the security forces of Central Asia and elsewhere. The chief disadvantage of using electronic means of communication in Central Asia is that it is simply not widely available. That region of the world still remains in the information "dark ages", because of the closed nature of the governments that have little-to-no-use for electronic media.

As an affiliate of al-Qaeda, the IMU is not likely to have much trouble reaching worldwide groups of supporters. This is especially significant when one considers the latest cyberspace tactics used by al-Qaeda, whereby ad hoc websites pop up on the internet giving instructions and sending messages to its supporters for carrying out terrorist attacks and for conducting related activities. Such websites do not exist for long, to avoid being tracked down by international law enforcement agencies. The IMU is the most widespread and well-financed terrorist group. Central Asia's proximity to the "Golden Crescent" (comprising Afghanistan, Pakistan and Iran) and the "Golden Triangle" (comprising Myanmar, Laos and Thailand) makes it the most popular route of narcotics trafficking. The IMT has cleverly exploited this reality to earn hard cash. It still uses its connections with al-Qaeda, and relies heavily on narcotrafficking over a number of Central Asian routes in order to finance its activities. In order to fully comprehend the durability of the IMT's sources of financing, one has to keep in mind the role of seven factors idiosyncratic to Central Asia since the implosion of the Soviet Union.

First is the common regional language, Russian, that lowers the linguistic barriers to this trade. Second is the proximity of the Ferghana Valley to the Golden Crescent and the Golden Triangle regions. Also there exist possibilities of nuclear terrorism. Because nuclear weapons can give terrorist organizations advantage, since they can inflict large numbers of casualties and command worldwide media attention.[12] It is hard for terrorist organizations to access nuclear weapons. However militants might be able to obtain fissionable materials or nuclear weapons in a number of ways. It might purchase fissionable materials in the back market. The disintegrations of the Soviet Union, the economic crisis, and the deteriorations of control over radioactive material and nuclear bombs have encouraged black market commerce in radioactive materials.[13] Therefore the main aims of the Al-Qaeda in supporting Central Asian terrorists groups is access to uranium rich resources in Tajikistan and stocks of rockets fuels and plutonium's in Semipalatinsk, Aktay-Kazakhstan.[14] Also terrorist organizations have links with nongovernmental international organizations. For instance the militant's organizations received financial support from liberal offshore banks and NGOs (as Islamic Relief Organization), foreign law enforcement agencies, companies and wealthy individuals.

How to Counter Nontraditional Threats

For effectively mitigating nontraditional threats the following recommendations may be considered:

Firstly, there should be enhancement of educational religious broadcast programmes in Central Asian television stations. In recent times this has been limited, from insufficient resources: financial and human. In fact, the general religious educational system is deteriorating due to the lack of investment. As a result it has created vacuum in religion education, which is being filled by the Akromiya, Lashkarlar Tovba, Islamic Jihad, and Hizbut at Tahrir organizations. Also in informational warfare usually religious terrorists groups are the winner, rather than secular states. The militants strategies are focused in the media space for attracting deeds and expanding their messages to a larger audience and manage them, through psychological influences. The media has become a major forum where governments and terrorists try to legitimize themselves during and after accidents. Therefore its necessary to create an independent Mass Media center that mainly focuses on countering radical ideologies.

Therefore it is necessary to consider the following counter measures: Information about strengths and weakness of the religious group's ideologies is crucial as for instance knowledge about the use of telecommunications in their expanding radical propagandas (through internet and high digital systems). In addition the contemporary militants groups are well financed. And their ideologists and theorists are well prepared and have obtained practical experiences in carrying propaganda among populations. Also there should be attempts to prevent the manipulation of population by false religious ideas. Besides religious and cultural potentials should be used to counter terrorist ideologies in the Central Asian regions. For instance there should develop teaching the enlightenment and tolerant Halafi form of Islam in the academic institutes. Therefore there is need to launch a global educational and informational campaign, like that carried out by Hizbut Tahrir. Because in the long term perspectives, the Hizbut at Tahrir could be even more dangerous that the militants groups. The Central Asian region as the historical junction between multitudes of culture, and religion has been marked as an area of crucial geopolitical significance. In addition Samarqand and Bukhara has played a significant role in the Islamic world as civilizations with 2500 year history.

Also there should be thought on developing cooperation between Central Asia states and enhancing trust between the states. However western countries try to fragment relations between Central Asian countries and neighbors through penetrating various geopolitical programmes and projects. But for realizing effective counter terrorism tasks in regions there are several barriers. The real basis for providing regional security in region would be played by the Collective Security Organization and SCO. This would involve reforms in the collective security system. Action by Collective Security Organizations for mitigating the delivery of narcotics from the region, that financed militant activities, would be necessary to create "anti drug belt" around Afghanistan, through joint countering operations with EU, UN and Russia. But CSTO is governed by Russian interest and SCO by China and Russia, without considering national interests of Central Asian countries. That's why for effectively countering with contemporary militants tactics, there should be universal approaches: military, political, academic, educational, religious, and cultural.

Problems of Central Asian Integrations in Countering Threats

Central Asia now poses a particular set of challenges for American policy, not least because the US had no history of engagement with the region until the 1990s and thus suffers from a serious lack of expertise in government as well as in academia. In addition, although the Central Asian states occupy a single, shared geographic sphere, they cannot now, in fact, be approached as a single entity. Over the last ten years of independence, the political divisions between and among the Central Asian states have hardened. Central Asia's regional context has also become particularly complex since the collapse of the USSR. With the retreat of Russian influence, the states find themselves at the nexus of a number of interlocking regions: Russia and Eurasia, the Middle and Near East, South Asia and Asia more broadly. Central Asia is simultaneously a buffer zone and a transit area among these regions. Ethno-linguistic and religious groups are spread across the regions, with Russia, Iran, China and Afghanistan sharing groups with Central Asian states, and Turkey representing the western extension of one of Central Asia's broader cultural spheres. Thus, in looking at Central Asia's external security, economic and political environment, all the neighboring states have to be factored in as an element in the region's future. In the context of the US war on terrorism, Central Asia's linkages with Afghanistan, Iran, and Pakistan, as well as Russia, have been dramatically underscored.

Finally, the last years has also seen the economic, political and military involvement of new actors in Central Asia. Northeast Asian countries – China, Japan, Korea – have now become engaged in the region. China has put a particular priority on relations with Central Asia to foster the development and stabilization of its vast western province, Xinjiang. Beijing also sees the region as a potential market, a source of energy and other natural resources, and as a communications bridge to Iran and the Middle East. Japan has become the largest donor country to Central Asia and, like China, sees the region – if it is stabilized and developed – as a potential market, source of raw materials, and bridge to the Middle East. And Korea has a more intimate relationship thanks to the distinct Korean populations deported there under Stalin, who have now become an influential social, political and economic component in Kazakhstan and Uzbekistan. Although China, Japan, and Korea, have only begun to make their presence felt, and their impact on trade and other regional issues has not yet been so substantial, in a sense Central Asia is rapidly becoming the heartland of Asia.

In addition vital differences among the Central Asian countries merit distinguished approaches. For instance, there are different economic potentials, diverse governance issues, and distinctive foreign relations. Kazakhstan is an example of a country that has adopted a market reform and gradual democratization. It is also interested in developing regional integration and multilateral security cooperation. While Kazakhstan is interested in forging ties with Asia, it does not want to loose its European tradition and Western connection.

US Interests in Central Asian Countries after 11 September 2001

In spite of the construction in 2002 of bases in Central Asia to support the military campaign in Afghanistan, the primary US interests in Central Asia it's more geo-strategic. Central Asia's significance to the United States is as a bulwark against regional powers such as Russia, China, and Iran. Also it is strategic to protect the US commercial concerns in the exploitation of Caspian energy resources. The primary American interest is in security, in preventing the "Afghanization" of Central Asia and the spawning of more terrorist groups with transnational reach that can threaten the stability of all the interlocking regions and strike the United States. As a result, in Central Asia, America's focus is now on creating strong security ties with the states – building on military-military contacts established in the late 1990s – and on securing long-term access agreements to regional bases and military facilities, which can be used to respond to current and future security threats in Afghanistan. However, the primary goal for US policy must also be to enhance Central Asia's development not just its military role. Like Afghanistan, if they are to transform themselves from potential breeding grounds for transnational militants into viable, stable states, the Central Asian countries must liberalize economically and democratize politically.

Russian Interests in Central Asia

Central Asia has lost its former importance to Russia as a military buffer zone between the Russian and British influences, and then between the USSR and US allies in Afghanistan and Pakistan, and between the USSR and China. After the collapse of the Soviet Union Russian military troops were withdrawn from all the Central Asian states apart from Tajikistan and some token forces on the Kazakhstan and Kyrgyzstan borders with China.[15] At the present Russia's paramount concern is mainly with the security aspects. Russia's own territory has been threatened by invasions from Afghanistan through Central Asia of religious militants groups and drug trafficking.

From the beginning of his presidency in January 2000, Russia's President, Vladimir Putin, pushed the idea of a concerted campaign against terrorism with American as well as European leaders. Putin one of the first to raise the alarm about terrorist training camps in Afghanistan, and to warn of linkages between these camps and well-financed terrorist networks operating in Europe and Eurasia. Also Russia actively supported the Northern Alliance in its struggle with the Taliban in Afghanistan. In December 2000, Moscow joined Washington in supporting United Nations sanctions against the Taliban, and later appealed for additional sanctions against Pakistan for aiding the Taliban-all a precursor to cooperation with the United States in the war against terrorism after September 11.

Russia's other major interest in the region is providing energy from the region to Europe and Asia. Together, Russia, Iran, and the Central Asian states hold more than half of world gas reserves. Retaining a major role in Central Asian gas production and export is a key issue for Russia's energy industry. Energy analysts doubt that Russia can both meet its domestic demand and growing ambitions for gas exports in the coming decades without having access to and influence over the flow of Central Asian gas.

In addition, Russia has keen interest in restoration of the communications and trade infrastructure from Soviet time between Russia and Central Asia, and some capacity for increasing Russian private sector investment in the region beyond the energy sector. For realizing these projects, Russia has initiated a major project to revive and revitalize the former North-South transportation corridor from Russian Baltic ports down the Volga River, across the Caspian to Central Asia and Iran, and from there to Pakistan and India. In the Soviet period, this served as a major freight route and an alternative to the transportation of goods from Europe to Asia through the Mediterranean and Suez Canal. All of this makes for a primary focus on economic background for enhancing the military and strategic issues for Russia in the region and, therefore, increased vulnerabilities of Central Asia's security systems and development.

What are the Prospects for Cooperation between the United States and Russia in Central Asia?

The US decision to use military base in Central Asia as a point of access to Afghanistan was positive, because it promised to eliminate the militant threat from the Taliban and the IMT, who were taking refuge in Afghanistan. On the other side, the US military base in the region was seen as an excellent chance in mitigating the Russian and Chinese influence in Central Asian heartland. Although Russia's President Putin convicted the terrorist attacks on the US, the Russian leadership tried to pressure the Central Asian republics by urging them to 'act in the CIS framework, and use CIS bodies for consultations and decisions,' on issues relating to anti-terrorism, international security and Afghanistan rather than open their territories to the United States. Anyway US again have plans for military bases, including enhancing the base in Manas, and in establish new ones in Tajikistan and Kazakhstan. For obtaining control under energy resources of Central Asia, US will try involved Central Asian countries to various energy traffic projects, avoid the Russian territories.

Russia is keenly interested in restoring trade and communications, and in transforming Central Asia into a route for licit rather than illicit trade between Europe and Afghanistan and South Asia. Projects for transporting gas from Turkmenistan and the broader Caspian Basin across Afghanistan to South Asia, which were precluded by the instability in Afghanistan, could one day be revived in the context of a broader effort to restore and improve road, rail and other transportation and communication links. The future restoration of Central Asia's links with India and Pakistan, which were also ruptured during war in Afghanistan, opens up the possibility of access to Pakistani and Indian ports as well as markets for Central Asian goods. Given Moscow's ongoing interest in reviving the North-South freight transportation corridor, Russia can play a particularly important role in developing infrastructure and bringing the landlocked Central Asian countries into the global marketplace. Here, the United States could also play a role by encouraging and assisting Russia in the development of this route as a complement to the East-West transportation routes from Central Asia across the Caspian, to the Caucasus and the Black Sea. While the East-West route became a focus of early competition between America and Russia, the development of a North-South route that binds Central Asia to Europe and Asia could just as easily become a vehicle for cooperation. Without cooperation between the US and Russia, the prospects for stability in Central Asia are fairly slim. In addition the renewal of "great game" will undermine both countries efforts to ensure their national interests in the region.

However, the suicide bombings in London, Moscow, Madrid, Kabul and insurgency movements in Europe and religious conflicts in the Middle East should have an impact on the changing attitudes and short term interests of foreign actors and global organizations. Only with common efforts of both regions will threats from militants groups be mitigated. In addition Central Asian and South Asian regions posses rich geo-cultural and religious potentials that should be implement as effective countering and preventive measures to religious militant's tendencies.

NOTES

1. Kyrgyz soldiers were issued with old Soviet manpad radios, and many failed to work in the field, making it impossible to coordinate ground and air elements.
2. The militants were armed with Kalashnikov assault rifles and their rounds would not be stopped by the helmets issued to the Kyrgyz soldiers; Otorbaeva "Kyrgyz Private Relives Batken Nightmare", Military Parade, www.milparade.com/ra/content1.htm.
3. *Vecherniy Bishkek*, Bishkek, August 23, 2002.
4. See the comparative discussion of the secular and religious terrorist mindset and legitimizing measures in Bruce Hoffman, "The Contrasting Ethical Foundations of Terrorism in the 1980s", *Terrorism and Political Violence* 1 (July 1989), pp. 361–377.
5. James M. Lutz and Brenda J. Lutz, *Global Terrorism*, Routledge, London/New York 2004, p. 65
6. Bruce Hoffman, "'Holy Terror': The Implications of Terrorism Motivated by a Religious Imperative", *Studies in Conflict and Terrorism* 18 (October-December 1995), pp. 271–284 (which was also published under the same title in the RAND Paper series, number P-7834, in July 1993).
7. Murray Sayle, "Martyrdom Complex", *The New Yorker*, May 13, 1996.
8. Mackinder, Halford J. (1943), 'The Round World and the Winning of the Peace', *Foreign Affairs* 21, pp. 593–605.
9. Ahmet Davutoglu. "The Clash of Interests: An Explanation of the World (dis)order Perceptions." *Journal of International Affairs*. December 1997-February 1998 Vol. II, No. 4.
10. *Small arms Survey*, Geneva, p. 128. 2004.

11. Farringdon, Hugh (1989), *Strategic Geography*, London: Routledge, p. 8.
12. Accordingly, terrorist groups in the future may well feel driven to emulate or surpass the Tokyo incident, either in death and destruction or in the use of nonconventional WMD in order to ensure the same, if not greater, media coverage and public attention as that attack generated.
13. Graham T. Allison, *et al.*, *Avoiding Nuclear Anarchy:Containing the Threat of Loose Russian Nuclear Weapons and Fissile Material* (Cambridge, MA: The MIT Press, 1996).
14. Bismuth, cadmium, plutonium and thallium are used in electronics, nuclear power engineering and rocket making.
15. The CIS is a geopolitical sphere of influence rather than a real political entity. Therefore, the Russian military authorities declared that Russian borders start with the Afghan-Tadjik border.

REFERENCES

1. Ashrad Mohsen. *Cooperation against terrorism in the Middle East's and Africa*-International conference materials, Italy September 22–24, 2000
2. Boaz Ganor *Nuclear, chemical terrorism overviews*, Israel, 2002
3. Bruce Hoffman. *Inside Terrorism*. London, Victor Gollancz, 1998, p. 91.
4. Pierne-Chovy.arcticle. *"NARCO-Terrorism in Afghanistan"* France, 2004.
5. Weimann, Gabriel. *The Theater of terror. Mass media and International Terrorism,* New York, Longman, 1996
6. B. Raman "Terrorism in Afghanistan and Central Asia" materials from conference on Asia and Europe, November 19–20, New Delhi, 2004.
7. Julian Madsen *Strategic Insights*, Volume III, Issue 8 August 2004
8. *Reuters*: May, 4, 2001
9. Huntington. S.P., "The clash of Civilizations", *Foreign Affairs*, Summer, 1993.
10. Gurmeet Kanwal. "Nuclear Defense Shaping". *The Arsenal*, 2002.
11. Forsythu.R. *The Politics of Oil in the Caucasus and Central Asia,* London: International Institute for Strategic Studies, 1996.
12. Michael Binyon, "Taliban are Top Heroin Suppliers" *The Times,* January 7, 2000.
13. *Afghanistan, Drugs and Terrorism: Merging Wars,* Transnational Institute Brief, 13 December, 2001
14. *Oxfam*, February, 2001.
15. *Small Arms Survey,* Geneva, 2004, p. 128.
16. Amnesty International Unpublished research paper

17. Kshitij Prabha, *Terrorism an Instrument of Foreign Policy*, New Delhi, 2002.
18. Roy Allison, *Challenge for the Former Soviet Union*, 1996.
19. Walter Lacquer, "The New Terrorism: Fanaticism and the Mass Destruction," *Oxford Journal*, New York, 1999.

Contributors

Abdolmajid Eskandari is Deputy-Director, General Office of International Relations, University of Tehran, Iran.

Ajay Patnaik is Professor and former Chairperson, Centre for Russian & Central Asian Studies, School of International Studies, Jawaharlal Nehru University, New Delhi, India.

Anna Yessengaliyeva is Associate Professor, Chief of Foreign Languages Department of L.N. Gumilyev Eurasian National University , Astana, Kazakhstan.

Evgeny Vodichev is Professor of History, Russian Academy of Sciences, Siberian Branch, Novosibirsk, Russia.

Farkhod F. Tolipov is Associate Professor, The National University of Uzbekistan, Tashkent, Uzbekistan.

Jeta Sankrityayana is Professor, Department of Economics, North Bengal University, West Bengal, India.

Judith Beyer is post-doctoral researcher,Max Planck Institute for Social Anthropology, Halle/Saale, Germany.

Maria Gritsko is Researcher, Institute of Philology, Russian Academy of Sciences, Siberian Branch, Novosibirsk, Russia.

Marina N. Baldano is Head of the Department of History, Ethnology and Sociology, Institute for Mongolian, Buddhist and Tibetan Studies, Russian Academy of Sciences, Siberian Branch,Ulan Ude, Russia.

Mirzokhid Rakhimov is Head, Contemporary History and International Relations, Department of the Institute of History, Academy of Sciences, Tashkent, Uzbekistan.

Muzaffar A. Olimov is Director, Research Center SHARQ, Dushanbe, Tajikistan.

Norihiro Naganawa is Assistant Professor, Slavic Research Center, Hokkaido University, Sapporo, Japan.

Oybek N. Makhmudov is Senior Research Fellow, Department of Politology, National University of Uzbekistan, Tashkent, Uzbekistan.

P.L. Dash is Professor, Eurasian Studies, Center for Central Eurasian Studies, University of Mumbai, Mumbai, India.

Roy Allison is Reader, International Relations, London School of Economics and Political Science, London, UK.

S.A. Meiramova is Chief of Foreign Philology Department, L.N. Gumilyev Eurasian National University, Astana, Kazakhstan.

Saodat Olimova, Research Center SHARQ, Dushanbe, Tajikistan.

Sattar F. Mazhitov is Director, Ch. Ch. Valikhanov Institute of History and Ethnology, Ministry of Sciences and Education, Republic of Kazakhstan, Almaty, Kazakhstan.

Sharad K. Soni is Assistant Professor, Central Asian Studies Division, Centre for South, Central, Southeast Asian and Southwest Pacific Studies, School of International Studies, Jawaharlal Nehru University, New Delhi, India.

Sreemati Ganguli is Fellow, Maulana Abul Kalam Azad Institute of Asian Studies, Kolkata, India..

Uyama Tomohiko is Professor, Central Asian Studies, Slavic Research Center, Hokkaido University, Sapporo, Japan.

Vladimir Boyko is Director, Center for Regional Studies (Russia and the East) and Associate Professor of Asian Studies, Barnaul State Pedagogical University, Barnaul, Russia.

Russian-English translations by

Susmita Bhattacharya, Fellow, Maulana Abul Kalam Azad Institute of Asian Studies, Kolkata.

Aditi Bhaduri, Independent Researcher and Journalist, Kolkata.

Index